Francis Count Lützow

A History of Bohemian Literature

Francis Count Lützow

A History of Bohemian Literature

ISBN/EAN: 9783337204761

Printed in Europe, USA, Canada, Australia, Japan

Cover: Foto ©ninafisch / pixelio.de

More available books at **www.hansebooks.com**

A History of
BOHEMIAN LITERATURE

BY

FRANCIS, COUNT LÜTZOW

FORMERLY DEPUTY FOR BOHEMIA IN THE AUSTRIAN PARLIAMENT
CORRESPONDING MEMBER OF THE ROYAL SOCIETY OF SCIENCES IN BOHEMIA
MEMBER OF THE SPOLEČNOST MUSEA ČESKÉHO AT PRAGUE
AUTHOR OF "BOHEMIA: AN HISTORICAL SKETCH"

London
WILLIAM HEINEMANN
MDCCCXCIX

PREFACE

WITH the approval of Mr. Gosse, I have written this short History of Bohemian Literature according to a plan that differs considerably from that of certain earlier volumes in this Series. The works of Modern English, French, Italian, and even of Ancient Greek and Spanish writers, will be known to many readers of the volumes that deal with them. Bohemian literature, on the other hand, is absolutely unknown in Western Europe, and a large amount of space has therefore been devoted to translated quotations from Bohemian writers. Many of these unknown works have great interest and value.

Bohemian literature, as we possess it, is to a certain extent disappointing and unsatisfactory. In consequence of the wholesale destruction of everything written in Bohemian that continued during more than a century, countless Bohemian books, many of which are known to have been valuable, have disappeared.

Many forms of literature are scarcely represented in Bohemian. No dramatic works worthy of notice exist before the present century. Poetry also is valuable only in the earliest period and in the present century.

Bohemian literature is so closely connected with Bohemian history, that without some knowledge of the latter it is often difficult to understand the references to historical events which must necessarily be found in a history of Bohemian literature. Though I have sometimes explained such references by notes, I could not do this to any great extent without trespassing on the domain of history. Those who wish to turn their attention to the dramatic history of Bohemia will find their best guide up to the year 1526 in Palacký, whose monumental *History of Bohemia* was published in German as well as in Bohemian. Though no continuous narrative on the same plan brings Bohemian history down to the year 1620, Gindely, Tieftrunk, and Rezek have written extensively, in German as well as in Bohemian, on the last years of Bohemian independence. Professor Tomek has in his short *Geschichte Böhmens* given an outline of the history of the country from the earliest ages up to the present day. I have in my *Bohemia: an Historical Sketch*, endeavoured to give a brief account of the history of Bohemia from an early period to the year 1620, written in accordance with the requirements of non-Bohemian readers.

Bohemian writers have divided the literature of their country into three periods. The first extends from the earliest time to the days of Hus; the second from Hus to the battle of the White Mountain; the third from that battle to the present day. Chaps. I. and II. of this book deal with the first; Chaps. III., IV., V., and VI. with the second; and Chap. VII. with the third period.

Like the history, the literature also of Bohemia is, particularly in the most interesting periods, a record of incessant religious struggles. I am thoroughly conscious of the fact that an account of these struggles is a most difficult task, that the writer

"Incedit per ignes
Suppositos cineri doloso."

PREFACE

I can only express my conscientious belief that I have delineated these religious controversies in accordance with the writings of the most accredited authorities.

I have only been able to allude incidentally to some of the materials that I have used while writing this book. I have, however, principally relied on a prolonged study of the works of the Bohemian writers with whom my work deals. It is at least the privilege of a critic of so little known a literature as that of Bohemia that he is not confronted by an enormous amount of anciently accumulated criticism. In one or two cases where I felt uncertain, I have had the privilege of receiving advice from Professor Josef Kalousek, of the Bohemian University of Prague, and from Mr. Adolphus Patera, head-librarian of the Bohemian Museum in that town. I have entirely limited my remarks to the works of those Bohemian writers who have general interest, or are at least characteristic of their time. Very many names contained in the histories of Bohemian literature written in the national language have therefore been omitted.

LÜTZOW.

ZAMPACH,
New Year's Day, 1899.

CONTENTS

CHAP.		PAGE
	INTRODUCTION	xi
I.	THE EARLIEST BOHEMIAN POETRY	1
II.	EARLY PROSE WRITERS—THE PRECURSORS OF HUS	42
III.	HUS	86
IV.	THE PERIOD OF THE HUSSITE WARS	143
V.	HUMANISTS AND THEOLOGIANS	174
VI.	BOHEMIAN HISTORIANS OF THE SIXTEENTH AND SEVENTEENTH CENTURY	295
VII.	THE REVIVAL OF BOHEMIAN LITERATURE	354
	BIBLIOGRAPHY	411
	INDEX	415

INTRODUCTION

THE Slavic language, a branch of the great Aryan family of speech, was originally one. It gradually divided itself into various dialects, a certain number of which have become written languages. According to the generally accepted division, the existent Slavic languages are divided into three great classes—the North-Eastern, Southern, and Western groups. The last-named group consists of the Bohemian and Polish languages and the almost extinct dialect of the Lusatians in Prussia and Saxony.

The Bohemian language is spoken in a large and continuous part of the Austro-Hungarian Empire, comprising the greater part of Bohemia and Moravia, part of Silesia, a small portion of the Archduchy of Austria, and extensive districts in Northern Hungary. There are considerable numbers of Bohemians beyond the borders of this continuous territory, in Lower Austria (particularly in Vienna), in Prussian Silesia (where their homes adjoin those of the Bohemians in Austrian Silesia), in Russia (particularly in Volhynia), and in the United States of America.

According to the most authentic statistics, the Bohemian language is spoken by about 7,930,000 people. Of these, 7,650,000 live in the Austro-Hungarian Empire, 70,000 in Prussia, 60,000 in Russia, and 150,000 in the United States of America. Minor Bohemian colonies, such as that in London, do not require special notice : the native language also often disappears here after one or two generations.

The Slavonic inhabitants of Northern Hungary, identical with the Bohemians as regards their race, have in the present century developed a written language somewhat different from that of Bohemia. If we therefore deduct them from the total, we come to the result that the Bohemian language is spoken by about 5,750,000 people.

A HISTORY OF
BOHEMIAN LITERATURE

CHAPTER I

THE EARLIEST BOHEMIAN POETRY

IF it were possible to compare the greatest literature of the world with that of a small and little-known country, it might be said that the "Question of the Manuscripts" is the necessary beginning of every account of Bohemian literature, just as the "Homeric Question" must form the commencement of every work on the literature of Greece. The "Question of the Manuscripts" turns on the genuineness of two documents which first became known at the beginning of the present century, and were supposed to be the most ancient writings in the Bohemian language. These manuscripts have from the first attracted great notice, and they gave a great impulse to the revival of Bohemian literature in the present century. The Manuscript of Königinhof is also by no means devoid of poetical merit, and these documents will therefore always have to be mentioned, even should it be finally proved that both were forgeries.

The manuscript that was first discovered is the so-called *Rukopis Kralodvorsky* or Manuscript of Königinhof.[1] It was stated that this document had been found by Venceslas Hanka (afterwards librarian of the Bohemian Museum) in the tower of the deanery church of Königinhof, or Kralové Dvur, on September 16, 1817. It was further declared that Hanka's attention had first been attracted to the manuscript by Borč, chaplain at Königinhof, who was previously aware of its existence. The discovery at Königinhof immediately created great sensation even in countries very distant from Bohemia, a circumstance all the more worthy of note as Bohemia was then even more unknown than it now is. Goethe was greatly interested in the new discovery, to which he frequently refers in his writings, and he himself published a translation, or rather adaptation, of the *Kytice* (Nosegay), one of the lyrical poems of the Manuscript of Königinhof. Numerous translations of these poems into English,[2] German, Polish, Russian, Italian, and other languages soon appeared, and the interest was of course yet far greater in Bohemia itself, where they became the recognised models for the Bohemian writers who were then beginning to revive the national language.

Though some doubts as to the genuineness of the manuscript were expressed from the moment of its appearance, yet the majority of the Bohemian learned men, including such authorities as Palacký and Šafařik, firmly maintained its ancient origin. Within the last twenty years a change has taken place. Perhaps the majority

---

[1] Königinhof is a small town in North-Eastern Bohemia.

[2] Some of the poems of the Manuscript of Königinhof were translated into English many years ago by the late Sir John Bowring, whose knowledge of the Bohemian language was, however, very slight. The late Rev. A. H. Wratislaw published in 1852 an English translation of the Manuscripts of Königinhof and Grüneberg.

of the Bohemian philologists of the present day believe the manuscript to be a forgery, that is to say, that it was written at the beginning of the present century. Its genuineness has been attacked from the palæographic point of view; it has been attempted to prove anachronisms in the manuscript; and it has been asserted that it contains verbal formations unknown to the early Bohemian language. A chemical examination of the manuscript has, however, proved that it differs in no way from authentic Bohemian manuscripts of the fourteenth century, and it can therefore now be affirmed that the Manuscript of Königinhof cannot be attacked from the point of view of palæography.[1] The defenders of the manuscript have been less successful in their endeavours to disprove the statement that it contains anachronisms, which could not have been committed by a writer of the thirteenth or fourteenth century. The almost complete darkness which surrounds the condition of the Slavonic race in very early times renders it very difficult to form a judgment on many of the disputed points. The defenders of the manuscript also lay stress on its similarity to undoubtedly genuine collections of early Bohemian writings, such as those known as the Manuscript of Königgrätz and that of St. Vitus. It is true that the contents of these collections differ somewhat from those of the manuscript, and are mainly of a religious character.

As regards the philological test, it is certain that the manuscript contains some verbal formations of which no other example can be found in the scanty remains of

---

[1] My authority for this statement is Mr. Adolphus Patera, chief librarian of the Bohemian Museum at Prague, and one of the greatest living authorities on Bohemian palæography.

early Bohemian writings that have been preserved. On the other hand, in consequence of the very scantiness of these remains, a ʾΑπαξ Λεγομενον does not necessarily prove the falsehood of the document in which we find it. The defenders of the manuscript have shown great ingenuity in proving that many of the locutions, unknown to ancient Bohemian, may be traced to the Moravian dialect, which at all times has differed somewhat from the language of Bohemia. They therefore maintain that the poems of the manuscript originated not in Bohemia itself, but in the sister-land, Moravia.

If the falsehood of the manuscript be admitted, the question arises, Who was the falsifier? who at the beginning of the present century, when the Bohemian language was at its lowest level, had a sufficient knowledge of that language to have written these poems? Hanka, of whom it is natural to think, has left us verses of his own so vastly inferior to some of the poems contained in the manuscript, that it is almost impossible to believe him to have been its author.

Whatever may be the final result of the discussion, the Manuscript of Königinhof will always remain one of the curiosities of literature. The first part of the manuscript consists of six ballads, if we may thus describe them, five of which deal with warlike events; the first,[1] which describes a battle between the Bohemians and the Germans, has a distinctly heathen character. The sixth ballad contains a description of a tournament, and is one of those pieces in which the opponents of the genuineness of the manuscript think that they have discovered anachronisms. The second part of the manuscript con-

[1] I follow the classification of Dr. Jireček's edition (1879); recent writers have divided the contents of the manuscript somewhat differently.

sists of eight shorter songs. Some of them are by no means devoid of poetic merit, but they have a somewhat sentimental manner, which makes them appear rather modern to the reader. The adversaries of the manuscript have not been slow in noting this circumstance. I shall only translate one of the short poems of the manuscript, entitled "The Cuckoo":—

> "*In the fields there stands an oak-tree,*
> *On the oak-tree a cuckoo calls:*
> *He ever calls, he laments*
> *That spring does not last for ever.*
> *How could the wheat ripen in the fields*
> *If spring lasted for ever?*
> *How could the apples ripen in the garden*
> *If summer lasted for ever?*
> *Would not the ears of corn freeze in the stack*
> *If autumn lasted for ever?*
> *Would not the maiden be mournful*
> *If her solitude lasted for ever?*"

In view of the uncertainty concerning the authenticity of the Manuscript of Königinhof, it is obviously impossible to assign a date to it. The writers who believe in its genuine character hold that the poems were transcribed and collected in their present shape at the end of the thirteenth or the beginning of the fourteenth century, but that some of them are of far higher antiquity. The distinctly heathen character of one of these poems renders this certain, of course, if only we can dismiss the supposition of a modern falsification.

The second ancient Bohemian manuscript that was supposed to have been discovered at the beginning of the present century is that of Zelená Hora or Grüneberg, which is generally mentioned in connection with the Manuscript of Königinhof, and is printed together with it in most editions. It has now been proved that the Manuscript of Grüneberg is a falsification dating from the present century, and its genuineness is now no longer maintained by any scholars, though a natural patriotic feeling has rendered it painful to many to admit that this manuscript, which was attributed to the ninth century, and described as "the most ancient document in Bohemian, and indeed in all Slavonic literature," is nothing but a fraudulent imposture.

It is proverbially easy to be wise *post eventum*, that is, in this case, after the fact of a forgery is recognised, but it is difficult to repress very natural surprise that the mysterious manner in which the Manuscript of Grüneberg first became known did not create greater suspicion than was actually the case. The manuscript was (in 1818) sent anonymously by post to Francis Count Kolovrat-Liebsteinsky, then high burgrave (or governor) of Bohemia. That nobleman had shortly before published an appeal to the Bohemians in favour of the National or Bohemian Museum, of which he was one of the founders, and which had as principal object the preservation of the relics of Bohemian antiquity. It was not until many years later that John Kovár, steward on Count Colloredo's estate of Grüneberg, declared that he had found the manuscript in an outlying room of the castle of Grüneberg; he further stated that he had believed his master, Count Colloredo, to have been so thoroughly German in his feelings that he would have destroyed the manuscript had it been shown to him. It is difficult for others than Bohemians to realise the absurdity of such a statement. The strictly absolutist government of Austria during the first half of the present century inexorably suppressed all public demonstrations of national feeling, whether German or Slavonic. It was thus impossible that literary controversies should assume a political aspect at that period, though this has certainly happened in more recent times. It was equally absurd to suggest that Count Colloredo, a distinguished general during the Napoleonic wars, was likely to take any interest whatever in documents belonging to the early period of the Bohemian language—a language that then, and even far more recently, was almost unknown to the upper classes of Bohemian society.

The Manuscript of Grüneberg consists of two small fragments of parchment, one of which contains a few lines only, entitled "The Decree of Domestic Law." The second larger fragment is called the "Judgment of Libussa." It deals with the semi-mythical Bohemian princess who is the heroine of many ancient tales. It is curious to note that many very grave disquisitions on the early social condition and judicial institutions of the Slavonic race have been based on this apocryphal manuscript.

The "Question of the Manuscripts," at least with regard to that of Königinhof, is yet undecided. The vast literature on the subject which has gradually accumulated has incidentally thrown much light on many social and philological questions concerning ancient Bohemia and its language. The committee of the Bohemian Museum no doubt indirectly expressed its opinion when the Manuscript of Grüneberg was removed from public view, while that of Königinhof continued to be exhibited in the hall of manuscripts in the museum.

Several other Bohemian manuscripts purporting to be of very ancient origin also made their appearance at the beginning of the present century, and modern additions were made to an authentic ancient manuscript. These falsifications were soon discovered, and in some cases suspicion undoubtedly points to Hanka.

The earliest Bohemian writings, the authenticity of which is uncontested, have a distinctly Christian and religious character. One of the most ancient written documents in the Bohemian language is the hymn "Gospodi pomiluj ny" (Lord have mercy on us). The earliest version is written in a language resembling the Old Slavonic, but with many specially Bohemian locutions. The authorship of the hymn has been attributed to St. Cyrillus and to St. Methodius, or to their early disciples, but there is no evidence to prove this conjecture. The date of the hymn also cannot be fixed, but the chronicler, Comas of Prague, tells us that it was sung by the people at the installation of Bishop Dietmar of Prague in 973. The hymn is sung, in a modernised version, in the Bohemian churches up to the present day.

Another very ancient hymn that has great historical interest is that to St. Venceslas. The date of this hymn also cannot be ascertained, but there is evidence that the veneration for the murdered Prince Venceslas was already very great in the eleventh century, and the hymn is certainly very ancient. The existent version dates from the thirteenth century. The composition of the hymn, which is rhymeless, but has frequent assonances, also vouches for its antiquity. The three original strophes run thus:—

"Holy Venceslas—Duke of the Bohemian land—Our Prince—Pray for us to God—And the Holy Ghost—Kyrie Eleison.

"Beautiful is the court of heaven—Happy he who enters there—Into eternal life—And the clear light—Of the Holy Ghost—Kyrie Eleison.

"Thy help we implore—Have mercy on us—Comfort the mournful—Deliver us from all evil—Holy Venceslas —Kyrie Eleison."

Many further strophes were added to this hymn when it became famous. During the Hussite wars it was the favourite war-song of the "lords sub una" (=Catholics), while the utraquists or Hussites sang the famous "All ye warriors of God."[1]

Among the very ancient documents written in the Bohemian language are a considerable number of missals, psalm-books, and translations of portions of the Holy Scriptures, which, though of great archæological and historical interest, hardly require notice in an account of Bohemian literature.

Undeniable literary value, on the other hand, belongs to some of the many early Bohemian legends that have been preserved. Some have been known since the beginning of the revival of Bohemian literature, while others have been discovered quite recently, sometimes in parish churches or the libraries of remote monasteries. Such discoveries indeed continue up to the present day. A considerable number of these legends (with a few small writings of a more secular character) are contained in two collections, known respectively as the manuscripts of Königgrätz and of St. Vitus, the cathedral church of Prague.[2]

Many of these legends are very similar in character,

---

[1] See Chapter IV.
[2] Both manuscripts have recently been edited and published by Mr. Adolphus Patera.

and obviously adhere closely to Latin models. This, however, does not apply to all. The *Legend of Judas* differs greatly from other mediæval legends that deal with the same subject. It has a distinctly Oriental manner, and a strange similarity to the Greek tale of *Œdipus*. This is one of the few early legends the date of which can be approximately fixed. The author alludes to the murder of the last Premyslide prince (1306) as to a recent event. After referring to the death of "the hope of the Scariotic land" the author writes: "Let us on this occasion remember our country, that which has now happened in Bohemia, where there are now no kings descended from King Premysl."

One of the saints whose martyrdom the Bohemian writers have specially celebrated is St. Catherine. A long legend on this subject, which formed part of the Rosenberg Library,[1] was discovered at Stockholm, and has since been transported to Brünn. A more concise account of St. Catherine's martyrdom is preserved in the Church of St. Jacob at Brünn. Both legends have been published.

According to the longer legend, Catherine, daughter of Kost, King of Cyprus, declared that she would wed no one but Jesus Christ. She therefore refuses to marry the son of the heathen Emperor Maxentius. After fifty of the wisest masters vainly attempted to persuade her to renounce Christianity, Catherine is cruelly tortured by order of the Emperor Maxentius, and finally decapitated. The description of her martyrdom gives a curious insight into mediæval mysticism. By order of the Emperor, who is enraged at her steadfastness, "the beadles whip her with threefold whips of horse-hair," which

[1] See Chapter VI.

have "leaden knots and angles;" then her snow-white nude body appears in six colours : her body appears white, her face green; red the flowing stream of blood; black the open wounds; blue the stripes caused by the whip; golden the plaits of her hair. All these colours of course have a mystical significance. When Catherine is decapitated, milk, as symbol of her purity, flows from her body.

Less known than the legend of St. Catherine, but certainly equally valuable, is the Bohemian legend of St. Dorothy. The martyrdom of that saint has been a favourite subject for the painters and poets of many countries. In our time Mr. Swinburne has made it the subject of a beautiful poem. Several Bohemian versions of the legend have been preserved. The most interesting of them, though probably not one of the oldest, is the version contained in the manuscript of St. Vitus. It is written in short and somewhat irregular rhymes. The mediæval mystical idea of the marriage between Christ and female saints appears here even more prominently than in the legend of St. Catherine. Dorothy, who is of royal blood, refuses to marry the cruel heathen King Fabricius and to renounce the Christian faith. The poem begins with a short invocation of St. Dorothy :—

> "*Dorothy, O maiden fair,*
> *The Holy Church celebrates thy festival,*
> *For thou wast a maiden choice,*
> *One chosen by God.*
> *Thy virtues, beauty, and purity*
> *No one can describe;*
> *Adorned by these*
> *Thou wast wedded to Christ.*
> *Rejoicing now with thy husband,*
> *Help us in our misery;*
> *Lead us to eternal bliss.*"

In consequence of her refusal to renounce Christianity, Dorothy is cruelly scourged by order of King Fabricius. The description of her sufferings is very similar to that contained in the legend of St. Catherine, but we miss the curious conceit of the six colours that suddenly appear on the body of the martyr. Dorothy is finally led out to execution, and on her way meets "Theophilus, the clerk of the land," who mockingly asks her where she is going. Dorothy answers:—

> *" To a garden, a delightful one,*
> *In which manifold fruits,*
> *Apples, flowers, and roses,*
> *I shall gather."*

Theophilus replies with a sneer, "Send me some of the fruits which grow in your lord's garden." After Dorothy's death "a child beautifully dressed in purple" (that is, an angel) appears to Theophilus, carrying a basket which contains three apples and three roses. The child says, "My sister Dorothy sends you this fruit." Then, seeing this, Theophilus exclaims:—

> *" I believe in thee, O Jesus Christ,*
> *That thou art the living Son*
> *Of the True God,*
> *For whose sake the virtuous Dorothy,*
> *Guiltless, was executed to-day.*
> *I the sinner beg, O maiden,*
> *Earnestly for thy favour;*
> *Deign to intercede for me,*
> *That in the realm of thy husband*
> *I too may join thee."*

The legend of St. Prokop (which forms part of the Manuscript of Königgrätz) also deserves special notice. It incidentally throws considerable light on the condition of Bohemia at the period when Christianity was

THE LEGEND OF ST. PROKOP

introduced. There was then great antagonism between the partisans of the Greek ritual, which Cyrillus and Methodius had introduced, and the followers of the Latin Church, who from Germany had introduced their ritual into Bohemia. The monastery on the Sazava,[1] of which Prokop became abbot, was the centre of those who sympathised with the Eastern Church. Up to the time when the Slavonic monks were replaced by priests of the Latin Church (in 1096), the religious services were held there according to the Eastern ritual, and when Charles IV. again established a community of Slavonic monks at Prague, he obtained for it the Pope's permission to use the Slavonic tongue in all ecclesiastical functions and to employ the Glagolitic alphabet.[2] The legend, written in an awkward and unattractive style, has little artistic value. The author was, no doubt, a monk, since the monastery of Sazava and its records were probably his source of information. As is the case with most early Bohemian legends, it is very difficult to fix the date of that referring to St. Prokop. The existent manuscript probably belongs to the early part of the fourteenth century, though the circumstance that some rhymes have been corrupted and lines omitted has led Bohemian critics to the supposition that the legend was written a considerable time before, perhaps not long after the death of St. Prokop, who lived in the eleventh century. The legend,[3] as already

[1] See my *Bohemia, an Historical Sketch*, p. 39 and p. 93.

[2] The Glagolitic alphabet is similar, though not identical with that of St. Cyrillus. It was used by those Slavs who were in communion with the Church of Rome, but enjoyed certain privileges with regard to the use of the national language in ecclesiastical functions.

[3] It has recently been stated that this legend, as now preserved, contains modern interpolations. It is impossible at present to give a certain opinion on this subject.

stated, deals principally with the rivalry between the monks of the Eastern and those of the Roman ritual. Prokop, who had retired to the then desert region near the river Sazava, is found there by Prince Ulrick, who builds a monastery for him on the spot where they met. After Prokop's death, as well as that of Prince Ulrick, "Germans of the Latin rite" take possession of the monastery on the Sazava. The ghost of Prokop three times appears to them, and on his third apparition the Germans return terrified to Prague.

The author begins by thus addressing his readers: "Listen, old people and children—To what I wish to tell you—Of the patron of the Slavs—Of the holy Prokop—He who was born in Bohemia—Who propagated God's law in a saintly fashion—Who faithfully fulfilled the holy law—Who worked many miracles. . . . St. Prokop is of the Slav race—Born not far from Český Brod.—That village did God well bless—In which this saint was born."

The legend then proceeds to tell us of Prokop's youth and education, laying special stress on the fact that at the monastery on the Vysehrad he received instruction in the Slavonic language. Prokop obtains great favour among the monks, who wish to choose him as their provost. But Prokop flies from all worldly honours and retires to a desert district, "where is a river, and that river is called Sazava, and it still flows beneath the monastery." The meeting between the hermit and Prince Ulrick is thus described: "The Prince, named Ulrick—Called to the hunters, who were running in every direction—And speaking to them all said—'In what woods shall we hunt?'—He said, 'We must begin—Where shall we begin?'—'Let us,' he said—'try the hills near the Sazava.—Into these woods I desire to go—Let us go there; that is my counsel.'—All run after him; all obey him—But when they penetrate into the forest—They all lose the prince.—By God's will it happened—That not one of them remained with him.—To the prince a stag appears, beautiful—Large and very fleshy—Prince Ulrick is not frightened—And having his crossbow in his hand—He wished to shoot the stag —Which was running not far from him—Not fleeing hastily before him.—Just as if sense were given it—It placed itself on that rock—Where St. Prokop was working.—He was then felling an oak—And the stag sprang up behind him—Turning its antlers towards him.—Between the antlers it had a cross—Prince Ulrick well noticed this—Directly he drops his crossbow from his hand—And stops his horse—Seeing this wondrous animal—And the meek-faced monk—The prince begins to ask the monk—Having rapidly descended from his horse—'Who art thou who lives here in this solitude?— How art thou called and what art thou doing here?'— Holy Prokop directly—Answered him kindly—'I live in this solitude—As a sinner, and Prokop is my name.'" The prince then begs Prokop's forgiveness for having attempted the life of an animal evidently consecrated to Christ. He becomes yet more certain of the saintliness of the hermit when Prokop miraculously transforms into exquisite wine the water which the prince is drinking. Ulrick exclaims, "Such noble wine hast thou in this desert? I have been in many lands, but never have I drank better wine." He then tells Prokop that he will build a monastery on the spot where they are standing. Of this monastery Prokop, in spite of his hesitation, becomes abbot. The legend then gives an account of several other miracles wrought by him. Then "in the year 1054 after the birth of Christ, he was, two days before his death, informed by a divine vision of his approaching end." Before dying Prokop foretells that troubles after his death will befall the monks. Under the reign of Ulrick's successor the prophecy is fulfilled. The Slavonic monks are expelled and Germans take their places. During the first night which the Germans spend in the monastery Prokop's ghost appears to them, warning them to leave instantly; he again, equally without result, repeats his warning on the following day. Then "he shows himself to them on the third night— And shows them his power.—He begins to speak:— 'Listen, ye Germans—I have fulfilled my duty (by giving them due warning)—But you heed not my words.—Not for you did I prepare this site—But I founded it for the sons of my own country—Not for you, faithless calumniators—You are infamous Hungarians,[1] come from anywhere.—If even the prince has given you this monastery—It will to-day be taken from you.—You would not listen to good words—I will now render your dwelling on the Sazava distasteful to you.—Quick, delay not your journey—Return in haste to Prague.—After he had said this, holding a large stick in his hand—He unmercifully thrashed the Germans with it." ... The legend ends with the return of the Bohemian monks to the monastery on the Sazava.

Early Bohemian legends, as already mentioned, are very numerous. Besides those already referred to, the legends of the "tears of St. Mary," the "joys of St. Mary," the "tears of Mary Magdalene," the "legends of

---

[1] The monks were Germans, not Hungarians. The latter designation was then a term of reproach in Bohemia.

St. George and St. Anselm," are among the best. The last-named legend expresses the characteristic opinion that Judas Iscariot was probably a German! Two allegorical poems, of a religious character, entitled *The Contest of the Body and the Soul* and *Truth*, are also very ancient.

Though the chronology of early Bohemian literature is hopelessly unreliable, it can, speaking generally, be stated—leaving the manuscripts of Grüneberg and Königinhof out of consideration—that the existent Bohemian writings of a secular character are less ancient than those dealing with entirely religious subjects. Here, too, the earliest writings have the character of poetic works; for the first prose writings belonging to Bohemia were all in Latin.

Among these early works should be mentioned several poems of an epic character, which are very similar to the chivalrous poetry of other European countries. The literature of the period of the Crusades (wars in which the Bohemians took a considerable part) possessed, in many respects, an international character. Knights of many European countries met in Palestine. A brisk exchange of ideas between men whose tendencies and ideals were identical was but natural. The subjects of the songs and epics of chivalrous poetry are limited in number, and often belong to several countries when national particularities often influence the details of the narrative. Such heroes of chivalrous poetry are Alexander of Macedon, who is conceived as a Christian knight and a crusader, Tristram and Isolde, and the other heroes and heroines of the round table; Theodoric or Dietrich of Berne (Verona), and the other heroes of ancient Gothic tradition.

B

In consequence of the geographical position of Bohemia, these tales reached the country later than lands lying farther west, and often from German sources. Yet the prejudiced attempts of German writers to prove that the Bohemian remains of chivalrous poetry are adaptations and translations from the German have in many cases proved unsuccessful.

In consequence of the wholesale destruction of Bohemian literature, we are here also obliged to found conjectures on a comparatively small number of fragments.

Of only one of these epic poems has a considerable portion been preserved. This is the *Alexandreis*, of which several manuscripts of different dates are in existence. From these fragments the erudition of Bohemian scholars has, to a great extent, reconstituted the poem: we now possess more than half the poem, and can, to a certain extent, conjecture what was contained in the still missing parts. The Bohemian *Alexandreis* is undoubtedly an adaptation of the Latin poem of Philip Gaultier (Walter) de Chatillon, also known from his birthplace, Lille, as Gualterus de Insulis, who lived in the twelfth century, and died about the year 1201. Chatillon's *Alexandreis*, based on the work of Quintus Curtius, enjoyed great popularity during the Middle Ages, and was generally adopted as the classical account of the career of the great Macedonian. The author of the Bohemian *Alexandreis* is unknown, but it is possible to fix an approximative date for the poem. It was undoubtedly written during the reign of King Premysl Ottokar II. (1253–78). Ottokar, who had extended the frontiers of Bohemia from the Baltic in the north to the Adriatic in the south, was often compared to Alexander the Great, and that hero's history, therefore, had great interest for the Bohemian writers of that period. Recent critics have attempted to fix the date of the *Alexandreis* yet more accurately. In the years 1264 and 1267 Ottokar undertook crusades against the heathen Prussians and Lithuanians, and seems even to have thought of rendering parts of those districts permanently dependent on Bohemia, thus securing for the country an outlet towards the Baltic. It is conjectured that the passage in the account of Alexander's entry into Babylon, in which the author prays that "God may grant Bohemia a king who will subdue the Lithuanians, Tartars" (see later), refers to Ottokar's far-reaching plan.

Generally speaking, the author of the *Alexandreis* follows strictly in the footsteps of Chatillon, or rather of Quintus Curtius, to whom so many of the mediæval tales about Alexander can be traced. Yet the Bohemian *Alexandreis* has not only a distinctly Christian, but also a national (Bohemian) character. The Persians are heathens doomed to hell. Margraves, burgraves, and counts are found in the contending armies. The Bohemian nobles Jan, Radvan, Mladota, and Radota form part of Alexander's court. The account of the festivities on the occasion of Alexander's entry into Babylon (a portion of which I have translated) describes them as similar to those which took place at Prague on the occasion of the coronation of the Bohemian kings. For Chatillon's hexameters the author has substituted a rhymed metre, consisting of verses of eight syllables, which generally, though not always, have a cæsura after the fourth syllable. The rhymes are very rugged and often irregular.

The author's preface begins with a quaint attempt at disarming his critics. He tells us that Solomon, the wisest of men, admitted that there were three things, and even four things that he did not know;[1] "if, then, he who surpassed all others in wisdom was liable to be mistaken, then I, should any one doubt my word, need not be offended; I who compared to him am as a weary beast to a lion, a wax taper to the sun, or a shallow rivulet to the sea."

The account of the deeds of the great Macedonian conqueror strictly follows the mediæval tradition of Alexander's career. Beginning with his birth and youth, the author then gives a detailed account of his education by Aristoteles and the wise counsel given him by that philosopher. Then follows a full account of Alexander's campaigns and victories. Very interesting is the author's account of his hero's arrival at Troy. He here has an extensive digression concerning the destruction of that city, which is not contained in Chatillon's work. It is curious to meet with the world-old tale of Paris and the three goddesses in Bohemian literature. The Christian writer no doubt considered it more seemly to relate the appearance of the three goddesses in the form of a dream. He writes: "Now it happened to him (Alexander) to march—To the spot where are the bastions of Troy—Now the only traces—Are stones lying on the ground—If it does not appear idle to you[2]—I will relate to you—Why this destruction took place—Why all this happened.—Paris was the king's son at Troy—Brought up at home in honors.—His father and mother—Out of love for their child—Treated him so kindly—That they allowed him his will in all things—The prince prepared for the chace—Nothing else was on his mind.—Then it

---

[1] See Proverbs, chap. xxx. vers. 18 and 19.
[2] The author is addressing his readers.

befell—That when he was riding far away in the woods —He went astray from the other hunters—And his horse was very weary—He rode away from the path to a lonely spot—Where a fine beech-tree stood in a thicket.— Throwing his horse's bridle up to one of the branches— He fell asleep under the tree—It then befell him in this hour—That in his dream he saw three goddesses—The one who rules love—The other who rules over wisdom —And all warlike knowledge—The third who rules over (=disposes of) riches—And they had a golden apple— Which each of them desired—For on it was written:— 'To her who is the most beautiful, this shall be given.'— They chose him as judge between them—Saying: 'We give you this power—That we may dispute no longer about this—Give this apple to whichever one thou wilt —And over whatever thing each of us has power—In that will she aid you.'—Then at that moment the prince —Began to take counsel with himself—Saying: 'What is not due to me—According to my right as a prince?—I have already too great riches—Also warlike spirit have I sufficient—And sense as great as others—Why then should I require greater wisdom?—My fortune also is favorable to me—But I should wish to possess a fair woman.'—Saying this he awards the apple—To her who rules over love."

The author ends his digression with these reflections: "Oh, erring heart of man—Oh, restless designs!—For the sake of one fair woman—For indeed her beauty was great—The whole world was in arms—For ten years it strove in war—Till in the eleventh year!—How can we remember all the ills that then befell Troy!"

It is natural that in a work such as the *Alexandreis*, dealing principally with the events of war, and written for warlike knights, battle-pieces should be numerous, and indeed constitute the greatest portion of the work. The following is an extract from one of the best of these battle-pieces, the description of the battle of Arbela. Alexander has just killed "Aristomanes, prince of India." "Easy," cry the Greeks, "easy will be for us glory and praise—Now that our king has obtained such glory!—The fight was stubborn on both sides—Not few the mortal wounds—They then dealt each other—When they first met—Then the battle-axes, lances—Drew blood like water—And the Greek king rushing at the enemy—Struck at the foolish people.—Meanwhile sword, lance, and battle-axe—Aimed at him from every direction—Strike his head;—Yet his mind remains undisturbed.—Thus did he bear himself in fight—As if he had been forged out of iron—And it was easy for him to bear all blows—While fortune in everything favoured him.—Thus did death refrain from him—Though it struck down many of the best men there.—Faros was the name of one of them—The second was called Eliphas—And he was Count of Egypt—While the former was Margrave of Syria—Both were valorous men—A great loss by their deaths—Befell that heathen king. . . . But ever, as was said—Nothing availed the heathens—When they attempted to destroy the Greeks—Everywhere on the sand, on the grass—A stream flowed, rendering the earth bloody—In it lay the wretched men—Like a forest or a grove that has been felled.—On both sides hundreds were killed—The fourfold gates of hell—Then were opened wide—Such a cry was raised by the devils—As if they thought that the earth had resolved—To drive them out of hell—Then the souls flew away quickly—Like herds that scatter.—So many fell that day—That

they would have been sufficient to fill Pluto's house—
For in that battle rarely was any one spared—Until the
Greeks were tired."

Very interesting is the account of the festivities which
took place at Babylon when Alexander entered the town.
As I have already mentioned, many of the ancient Bohemian customs on the occasion of the coronation of their
kings are here accurately reproduced. The author first
describes a tournament; he writes: "Already courageously and in a manner worthy of praise—Had they fought
bravely—Striking with their heavy lances;—Many a one
on both sides, as may be believed—Had been unhorsed.
—This knightly pastime—Lasted for some time—Till
the king himself gave a sign to the people—And thus
did the time pass away.—Then all the more important
citizens—Nobles and men who held State offices—Appeared before their king—Bringing great presents—
Honouring his dignity—Goods of various sorts (they
brought)—Such as to the human eye—Give the enjoyment of pleasure—For their valuable presents—They
received much praise.—In the meantime they lead in
panthers—Lions and many great ostriches—And whatever other birds they had collected.—The beasts shaking
their cages—Began to bellow (literally neigh), not liking
their imprisonment—How could they (the people) have
had anything better?—Anything more pleasant to see:
—Many actors and jugglers—Various boxers—With
whom the streets swarmed—Gave them pleasure—And
they also enjoyed music of various sorts—The rejoicing
continued so long—That the whole night passed;—
Then only did the people go home—Never, I ween, was
there so great a rejoicing in the world.—Not even when
mighty Rome—Chose her king—Was there so great joy.

—Nor did they (the Romans)—With such overwhelming honours—Receive their emperor—As were then awarded to him (Alexander)—And rightly were they given to him,—The honours which he then received.—For starting with but a small force—And after enduring many troubles—He had struggled so vigorously for his cause —That the whole world bowed down before him—May God deign to listen to his Christian people and ordain this,— That there be such a king in Bohemia!— I warrant that then in a short time—Lithuania and the Tartars—Men of whatever name—The Besermans and the Prussians—Also the unconformed (not yet baptized) Russians—Would be in such a state of terror—That they would accept baptism—And renounce their idols— And this could happen—Were but one obstacle removed —That is, that the Germans, who are strangers here—Wish and hope—That on the bridge of Prague—[May God avert this]—No Bohemian be seen any longer[1]—And it may perhaps soon happen—That we shall see none of them (the Germans) any more—Admire your king, O city of Babylon—For, know it, he is worthy of wonder —He the conqueror of the whole world—The terror of all other kings!"

It has already been stated that the author of the *Alexandreis* is unknown. There is, however, no doubt that the book is the work of a Bohemian noble. The whole current of thought, the descriptions of battles and the pomps of chivalry, the author's pedantic accuracy with regard to the different grades of the nobility, his dislike of the German townsmen (up to

---

[1] This appears to have been a proverbial expression. In *Dalimil's Chronicle* (see later) King Ottokar is made to say that soon no Bohemian will any longer be seen on the bridge of Prague.

the time of Hus the Bohemian cities were mainly inhabited by Germans)—these and other circumstances tend to prove that this supposition is correct.

Portions of other epic poems belonging to chivalrous literature have also been preserved; among them are some belonging to the circle of legends of which Theodoric was the centre; such are *The Garden of Roses*, *Laurin*, and others. They are evidently adaptations from the German, and possess little originality and less interest. Other fragments deal with the tale of the Round Table. Among these *Tristram* and *Tandarius and Floribella* may be mentioned. The former poem, as the late Mr. Wratislaw has remarked, is strikingly similar to parts of the *Morte d'Arthur*. This specially applies to one of the fragments which contains a description of the combat between Tristram and the "noble from Ireland whose name was Morolt." *Tandarius and Floribella* also differs little from many other poems of chivalry. The heroine is imprisoned and eventually rescued by Tandarius. Numerous descriptions of tournaments and single combats fill up the greatest part of the book.

Closely connected with the chivalrous poetry of an epic character are some early lyric poems that have been preserved. They, however, all belong to a period considerably later than the *Alexandreis*, and Bohemian critics have no doubt correctly attributed them to the reign of King John. Here, too, the songs that have been preserved are not numerous. A favourite form of these early Bohemian lyrics were the so-called *Songs at Daybreak* (in Bohemian *Svitanicka*), which have a great affinity to the French *aubades* and to the *albes* of the Provençal minstrels. The motive of these songs, several of which have been preserved, varies but slightly.

They tell of the parting of two lovers, caused by the approach of dawn, and of the fears which they express with regard to the "false gossips," rivals, or inquisitive people who may be watching them. A translation of the best of these songs may be of interest.

> *" Dear clear day, how have you surprised me,*
> *You that have awakened the false gossip;*
> *The day rises there*
> *Where two lovers live together.*
> *Almighty Lord God,*
> *Deign Thou to guard these two.*
>
> *From the east a breeze arises,*
> *Trembling over hill and vale;*
> *The moaning of the woods, their noise and crashing ceases;*
> *The game flees, the birds scream;*
> *Everything tells us, everything shows*
> *That the night has vanished.*
>
> *Above us the morning star has disappeared,*
> *For into the distance it has vanished,*
> *Hastily retiring behind the hills.*
> *It does not stop,*
> *It wishes to rise higher.*
> *It is time for us, my beloved, to take leave.*
>
> *The heart of my beloved was aggrieved*
> *When, rising, she perceived the daybreak;*
> *Then spake my beloved:*
> *' Why have we two slept so long?*
> *Hasten, my beloved,*
> *Lest disgrace may overtake us.'*
>
> *Clear daylight is here, I know;*
> *The sky appears light blue,*
> *The splendour of the sun is rising,*
> *Therefore my heart is in fear.*
> *Almighty Lord God,*
> *Deign Thou to guard us two.*

Oh, my beloved, listen to my advice:
When you are with your lover, hope in your heart
That thy pleasure and mine may not be changed to grief
Because of the malice of the evil gossip,
For no one knows what his intentions are;
Therefore it befits us to be on our guard.

The gossip is fair to all in his speech,
But his heart is full of evil, false craft.
I should wish that maidens and matrons
Would always hate the gossip.
And that man shall be my comrade
Who will never be at peace with such a one (as the gossip).

For in this world there is nothing more difficult
Than to beware of gossips;
For he is friendly with you to your face,
But, like a snake, he bites you from the back;
His speech is sweet as honey
And his heart is as cruel poison.

Dear God, do not grant success
To him who troubles the comfort of lovers,
As his heart is endeavouring (to find)
Where the two lovers live together.
Almighty Lord God,
Deign Thou to guard these two."

It will be noticed that the refrain "Almighty Lord God," &c. (slightly varying in the middle of the poem), recurs three times. It has been conjectured that these *Songs at Daybreak*, which were discovered in the archives of Bohemian castles, were the works of knights or nobles, men somewhat similar to the "Minnesänger" of Germany. By the song which I have translated it will be seen that these songs are tainted with the peculiar views concerning conjugal fidelity which characterise so large a part of chivalrous literature, where Tristram is so often the hero and King Mark so often the knave.

A few ancient love-songs which have not the character of the *Svitanicka* have also been preserved. Of these, the so-called *Cantio Zavisonis*, written in Bohemian in spite of its Latin name, deserves notice. It was formerly falsely attributed to Zavis of Falkenstein, the lover of Queen Kunegund, and one of the most celebrated Bohemian nobles of his time. The fact that Falkenstein wrote verses in prison shortly before his death (as the historians tell us) led to this supposition, which is contradicted by the manner of the poem. Nothing except the name "Zavis" is known of the author of this strange love-song, one of the best of early Bohemian literature. I have translated a few of the best lines:—

> "*Now all joy has left me,*
> *Now for me all comfort has ceased,*
> *My heart swims in wistful blood,*
> *All this because of the beloved one for whom I long.*
> *By the glance of her eye*
> *She has sharply struck my heart.*
> *I live in flaming yearning,*
> *My life sickens with love,*
> *All for the sake of her dear beauty.*
>
> . . . . . .
>
> *My longing cannot decrease;*
> *Pity me, oh air! pity me, all creation!*
> *Carbuncles, sapphires, and all precious stones,*
> *Rays of the sun and everything on the earth,*
> *Pity me, lilies! pity me, most precious roses!*
> *My beloved wishes to take my little life*[1] *from me*
> *If she will not have compassion on me.*"

Neither the mysterious Zavis nor the author of the Song at Daybreak which I quoted before were devoid of poetical talent. But they, as well as other writers whom

---

[1] *Životek*, the diminutive of *život* = life.

I have not specially noticed, were greatly deficient in the technique of versification; nor did they adhere with sufficient care to the Western metres and forms of song which they endeavoured to adopt. These verses, therefore, lose little by translation. Bohemian writers have attributed the absence of polish and finish which we find in these early writings to the fact that, while in France, Provençe, and Germany the different courts were the centres of knights' poetry, the Bohemian court at all periods had a distinctly German character, and favoured poetry in the national language but little.

The poems of a chivalrous character which I have noticed above have little distinctly national except occasional invectives against the Germans. That poetry was indeed, as noticed before, international in its very essence. With the decline of this manner of poetry (which in Bohemia took place about the middle of the fourteenth century) a different style of poetry arose, which dealt mainly with national subjects from a national point of view. It was attempted to acquaint the Bohemians with the earliest legends and traditions of their race; the satirical verses which now become numerous have a distinctly local flavour and deal principally with the faults and shortcomings of the Bohemian people.

The most important writer of this period is the author of the so-called *Dalimil*, a rhymed chronicle of the events of Bohemian history, which, beginning with the deluge, ends with the close of the reign of Henry of Carinthia (1310). The book was mostly written during the reign of John of Luxemburg, Henry's successor. In no prince was the cosmopolitan element inherent in chivalry so thoroughly developed as in King John. The conduct of a prince who considered that Paris was the most chivalrous city in the world, and who (anticipating the modern American) declared that he did not care to live anywhere except there, who visited Bohemia but rarely, and then only for the purpose of levying taxes, and who expressed open contempt for the national language, was bound to produce a strong national reaction in Bohemia. The beginning of the great national movement which culminated in the Hussite wars can undoubtedly be traced as far back as to the reign of King John.

The author of the so-called *Chronicle of Dalimil* is unknown; the researches of recent Bohemian scholars, however, prove that he was a Bohemian noble, probably belonging to the northern districts of the country. From the contents of the book, which is plentifully supplied with dates, it can be gathered that the author began writing in 1308 and finished his work in 1316; of the events from 1279 downward he writes as an eye-witness.

Dalimil's Chronicle is one of the most important works of Bohemian literature and the first historical work written in the Bohemian language. Its popularity, to which the pronounced Bohemian-nationalist views of the author no doubt largely contributed, was very great. In proof of this it may be mentioned that, in spite of the wholesale destruction of Bohemian writings, nine complete manuscript copies of the Chronicle are in existence; the oldest of them, curiously, is to be found in the library of Trinity College, Cambridge. The work was first printed in 1620, during the brief reign of Frederick of the Palatinate, but this edition was from political motives destroyed after the occupation of Prague by the Austrian troops in the autumn of the same year. The book has been several times printed and published in the present century.

The author has availed himself largely of the *Chronicon Bœmorum*[1] of Cosmas, particularly when dealing with the most ancient records of Bohemia. He indeed in his preface refers to Cosmas as his principal authority, while stating that he also had access to the records of various monasteries, which he enumerates. The intense patriotic feeling that animated the writer shows very clearly in his preface. He writes: "Many search for historical tales—But they heed not those of their own country—Acting thus unwisely and strangely—Treating their own nation unfavourably—For had some one but sought glory there—Books about his own country he would have found—By which he could have known what is our race—Learnt from whence we came.—I have long searched for such books—Ever have I desired—That some learned man should undertake—To connect (in one work) all the deeds of the Bohemians;—Up to now have I desired this—Till I truly ascertained—That no one will undertake (to do) this—Therefore I must myself undertake (this task)."

Then follows the passage already referred to, in which the author declares his indebtedness to Cosmas as well as to the chronicles of Prague, Breznov, Opatovic, and Vysehrad. The preface ends thus: "Vain words I will as far as possible avoid—But yet set down my whole meaning clearly—That every one may thus learn more willingly—And have more regard for his nation.—Hearing my speech, the wise man will become yet wiser—The sad man will be freed from sadness.—I have written this down plainly—And I beg that a better man—May for the glory of our country—And because of the craft of our enemies—Improve my words by fair rhymes—And

[1] See Chapter II.

embellish the subject with brilliant speech—But he should not jeer at me—Saying, he meddles with what he does not understand—Of one thing I am full certain —That I have my nation much at heart—That has encouraged me in this work—That has aroused my energy."

The first part of the book narrates the well-known tales of the making of Bohemia ; the appearance of Čech and his companions in the land ; their settlement near the mountain Rip ; the adventures of Krok, Premysl, and Libussa ; and the deeds of the early Premyslide princes. All these semi-mythical tales are related in very much the same manner in which Cosmas had told them two centuries before, and Hayek was to tell them two centuries later.

Among the most interesting episodes in the Chronicle are the descriptions of the murder of Prince Venceslas by his treacherous younger brother Boleslav, and of the first meeting of Prince Ulrick and the peasant-maiden Bozena, whom he afterwards wedded. The peculiar national prejudice of many Bohemian nobles, founded not on pride of birth, but on intense racial antipathy, appears very clearly in *Dalimil's* account of Prince Ulrick's marriage. When the nobles reproached him for his unequal alliance, he answers: " We all descend from one father—And he ranks as a noble—Whose father had much silver—And as nobility and peasantry are thus intermingled—Bozena shall be my wife— Rather would I entrust myself to a Bohemian peasant-girl—Than that I should take a German queen as my wife—Every heart clings to its nation—Therefore a German woman would less favour my language ;—A German woman will have German servants—German will she teach my children—Then there will be division of languages—And thereby certain ruin to the state."

Of interest also is the author's account of the reign of the great King Ottokar II. He writes as a violent enemy of that king, and attributes the disastrous close of his reign to the fact that he neglected his Slavonic countrymen and showed too great favour to the Germans.

The geographical position of Bohemia, which is the outpost of the Slavonic race that advances farthest westward, has been the cause why that country has always been the scene of racial feuds. National animosities were as violent at the beginning of the fourteenth as they unfortunately are at the end of the nineteenth century. Ottokar's part in this struggle belongs to the political history of Bohemia; but it may be incidentally remarked that, as regards the accusation of having unduly favoured the Germans to the detriment of his own countrymen, the greatest of Bohemia's kings has found an eloquent defender in Palacky, the greatest Bohemian historian. The so-called *Dalimil* thus describes the close of King Ottokar's reign: "Then the king began to heed no longer his own (countrymen)—Towns and villages he began to give to the Germans—The Germans appeared to surround him—Against the nobles he used violence—His officials he instigated against the lords of Vitkovic—Against other nobles also he began to use violence.—Therefore many nobles became angry—They appealed to Rudolph, king of the empire (*i.e.* of the Germans), against him—Saying, 'It is better that the land should be a desert—Rather than that by the king's order the Germans should hold it.'—Rudolph arrives in Austria—On the advice of the Germans the king goes to meet him—Then the king makes over all his lands to Rudolph

—Rudolph, keeping the others, makes over Bohemia and Moravia to the king. . . . Alas for the noble king —That he did not remain true to his own nation— Thus would he have obtained great fame — And also great riches—With the help of which he could have made yet further conquests—And defeated all his foes. —But the king continued to revile his countrymen— To injure them whenever he could."

A lengthy account of the grievances of various great Bohemian nobles against King Ottokar follows. The writer closes the chapter dealing with that king by these words: "When, therefore, the king had need of the Bohemians—He did not receive willing aid from them— They left him when he required them.—When the king saw that he could not rely on them in the hour of need —As they would not forget their sufferings and the evil (which they had endured)—The king said: 'When I return from the wars—I will inflict much evil on the Bohemians—I will thus stain the Petrin)[1] with their blood—That no Bohemian will any longer be seen on the bridge of Prague.—Truly he could no longer wish to live.'—When he spake such words publicly.—Few Bohemians did he take with him—He marched with Germans, made them his own—Zavis[2] and his brother were with Rudolph—This was very harmful to the Bohemian king —For he (Zavis) knew the strength of his forces—And had friends in his army—When at daybreak they were preparing for battle—Zavis sent a message to the king, saying—That if he were gracious to him—He would be

---

[1] A hill near Prague (known in German as the Laurenz Berg), where the executions then took place.

[2] The head of the family (or rather clan) of Vitkovic, whom Ottokar had exiled.

willing to render him service.—The king would not hear of the proposal and advanced—Saying, 'Rather than that I did this, I would let myself be killed.'—Then the king with his Germans rushed into battle against Rudolph—And alas! he fell there—This misfortune occurred on the day of St. Rufus, a Friday—(That holy martyr's day is a great festival)—It was in the year since the birth of the Son of God—One Thousand Two Hundred and Seventy-eight." Dalimil's chronicle, as already noted, enjoyed great popularity in Bohemia for many years, in fact, up to the sixteenth century, when Hajek's chronicle took its place. In consequence of this popularity the chronicle found continuators, and several of the manuscripts contain additions that are obviously by a different writer. Shorter tales relating warlike events in a manner and metre similar to *Dalimil* also vouch for the popularity of the chronicle. Such are the tales of *William of Zajïc*, *Ottokar and Zavis*, and *The Death of King John*, the most interesting one to English readers.

To the early literature of Bohemia a considerable amount of didactic and satirical poetry also belongs. The most important of the writers of such verses is Smil Flaška, lord of Pardubic, the earliest Bohemian writer whose name and personality are well known. He is the author of the *Father's Advice to his Son*, of the *New Council*, one of the many beast-epics of the Middle Ages, and of a collection of proverbs. Other satirical writings, such as the *Contest of Water and Wine* and the *Groom and the Scholar*, were formerly, though incorrectly, attributed to Smil. All these satirical and didactic poems have little poetical value, but are of great interest for the student of the social condition of Bohemia in the fourteenth century. They contain, however, a vast amount of allusions of a local or national character, which render it very difficult to give an account of them or quote from them without entering into disquisitions and explanations which would have little interest for English readers.

Smil Flaska, lord of Pardubic, played an important part in the history of his times. He was born about the middle of the fourteenth century. From his father, William, a brother of Ernest of Pardubic, the first Archbishop of Prague, he inherited very considerable estates in the districts of Bohemia that are near Pardubic. During the prolonged struggle between King Venceslas IV. and the Bohemian nobles, Smil was among those who opposed the king. He was killed (in 1403) in a skirmish near Kutná-Hora (Kuttenberg) while leading the forces of the "League of the Lords" against the citizens of Kuttenberg, who were on the side of King Venceslas.

Smil's *Advice of a Father to his Son* is a work of great interest, as it clearly shows what were then considered to be the duties of a young Bohemian noble,—what was required to make him a perfect gentleman, as a recent Bohemian writer on Smil has expressed it. Smil begins by telling his readers that an old nobleman, addressing his son, who has just attained maturity, and to whom he presents sword and lance, advises him as to his conduct in life. The various counsels are then enumerated. Piety is first mentioned. The father says: "This is my first advice, O son—Have God at every hour—In your heart with all your might—Humbly both by day and night—Remember, too, His dear Mother—Her sacred sufferings bear in your mind—This you should always have before your eyes—Remember this, my son."

Smil is by no means devoid of worldly wisdom; witness the following passage: "Be liberal as far as is seemly—Do not by shabbiness injure your soul—Neither must you come to ruin by too great liberality—Dignified measure (moderation) is honourable in all things.—To your poor friends be amiable—And take special heed to be generous to them—Visit them in their distress—These are honourable and knightly debts (duties).—Reward those who serve you faithfully—Who heartily strive for your glory—Who wish to raise you higher—Than your own power (alone) could reach;—To these your hand should not be niggardly.—To be too haughty, O my son—To impose your will on the people—That I by no means advise.—For he who is too proud—Haughty more than is well—He cannot be beloved of the people. —Even if by his bravery in battle he could penetrate victoriously through all ramparts—Yet by his haughtiness he vexes—Every one in every way—Too great haughtiness, therefore, does not become a great lord. . . ."

In the last part of the counsel the father advises his son with regard to his duties towards ladies, repeatedly inculcating chivalrous devotion to them. He writes: "Dear son, nearly all have I said—(To my best knowledge)—That is truly necessary for your fame—But carefully will I give you—Yet one more token of knightly honour.—You should honour all good ladies—Defending with true faith their fair name—Should any one by evil speech against women attempt to curry favour—You should declare—That evil speech ever remains evil —And that honest words should contradict it.—According to honour and wise advice—You should everywhere spread their (*i.e.* the ladies') glory—You should ever obey their will—Be constantly in their service—And be grateful for their favours. . . . Therefore, my son, reflect on this—Consider the favour of ladies as gold—And indeed as worth more than precious stones—Compared to this there is—No thing as precious in the whole world."

Very different from the *Counsel of the Father* is Smil's other important work, *The New Council*, written in 1394 or 1395, somewhat later than the book referred to before. As I have already mentioned, it is one of those beast-epics in which mediæval writers put their social and political ideas into the mouths of various animals, while certain animals generally became the representatives of persons or of classes of the people. Smil's work, one of the most noteworthy of these writings, is an elaborate and very striking satire on the condition of Bohemia at this period. The young lion who, on his accession to the throne, assembles all animals around him in council, is undoubtedly King Venceslas IV. of Bohemia; and the eagle, who is the first to appear before the king, represents Moravia, the land that for many centuries was suzerain to Bohemia. To most of the other animals who (forty-four in number)—a quadruped always alternating with a bird—successively appear before the king, an allegorical significance can be attributed. The leopard, who follows the eagle, is the representative of the Bohemian nobility; and, true to his character, he says to the king: "Allow no foreigners in your council; put not your trust in the peasant; rather consult your high-born and noble lords on the welfare of the land." The wolf here, as in many other beast-epics, represents the monks; the fox, who tells the king that "he has need of us, the lower ones," is the representative of the citizens, who were always opposed to the nobility, and therefore favoured the increase of the royal power. The starling is the representative of the ordinary court-poets; while the nightingale personifies Smil himself and those poets who were enthusiastic for the Bohemian nation. The praise of poetry which Smil puts into the mouth of the nightingale is considered the finest part of his work; and I shall translate a passage from it. The last "counsel," that of the swan, is couched in deeply religious language. Smil has indeed in this passage closely imitated the celebrated hymn, "Dies Iræ." Of this "counsel," also, it may be well to translate a small portion.

Smil in his first verses expounds the motive of his tale; he writes: "King Lion once upon a time—Sent many messengers—To his princes, to his lords—To all counties, in every direction—He sent for the large beasts and the small ones—Saying that they should all appear before him—This also he decided, that the eagle should receive notice—That, taking all the other birds with him—He should appear before the throne of the king."

The praise of poetry which Smil puts into the nightingale's mouth is worth quoting; he writes: "Listen gladly to sweet sounds—As it is natural to you—And is a wholesome pastime.—Singers, musicians, on whatever instrument they play—By these shall thy mind be strengthened.—Great is the pleasure afforded to you—By the sound of sweet songs—Particularly at springtime — When all plants begin to revive — When all creatures are merry—When May already with manifold flowers—Preciously refreshes the whole world.—The air everywhere is mild—Everywhere sweet sounds are heard—At day, at night-time, and at dawn—The soft song of birds—(Is heard) in the woods, in the groves, in the fields.—In such things, O king, seek comfort."

The swan's song, the last "counsel" in the book, is also one of the most interesting parts of Smil's work. He here strongly exhorts the young king to lead a virtuous life, and vividly describes the terrors of the day of judgment; he writes: "On that day of wrath, that day of darkness—That day of anguish and of rage—Of misery, of evil, and of pain—That sudden day of wrath and woe—The day of the awful trumpet and its roar—Fearful will be the fate of a sinner."

The "counsel" of the swan, and with it the whole poem, ends with these lines: "Therefore let every one seek salvation—For this is not our lasting dwelling-place—Let us here with our whole might—Strive for our future happiness—By doing deeds of mercy, remaining constant to the true faith.—Aid us in this, dear Jesus Christ—May we be saved from eternal misery—And rather live in happiness eternally with Thee.—Who faithfully strives for this—Him help, O Lord God—Grant him your grace and eternal life—Which is always certain for those who are with Thee. Amen."

Besides the two works mentioned, a collection of proverbs which goes by Smil's name is undoubtedly a genuine work of the author. This is not the case with two satirical poems that were up to recently attributed to Smil. One of these is the *Groom and the Scholar*, a satirical dialogue, which dates from the reign of King Venceslas IV. The two characters of the dialogue meet at a tavern, and interchange ideas as to the happiness of their respective states. The scholar, of course, is one of the mendicant students so frequent in the Middle Ages, and the groom taunts him bitterly with his poverty and misery, and his constant liability to the rod. The student, on the other hand, reminds the groom of the hard and lowly work he is obliged to do, and the scanty wages which he receives. The discussion—not unnaturally, the reader of the dialogue will think—finally degenerates into a free fight!

The contest of water and wine, also formerly attributed to Smil, is a curious satirical dialogue between water and wine regarding their superiority. They are finally reconciled, and it is stated that "Water is a necessity for the world, but we require wine also." Among many other satirical poems, the *Satires on Trades* should be mentioned, which give a curious insight into low life in early Bohemia. They, however, teem with local allusions and far-fetched puns, and are more interesting to Bohemians than to other readers. A satirical poem in dramatic form is the *Mastičkář* (= quacksalver). Of didactic poems, *Cato*, an adaptation from the Latin, may be mentioned. The curious little work contains a collection of moral precepts which are put into the mouth of Cato.

CHAPTER II

EARLY PROSE WRITERS—THE PRECURSORS OF HUS

IN Bohemia, as in most countries, we find the national language employed in poetry long before an attempt is made to use it in prose. Latin was the language exclusively used by the writers on history, legal matters, and theology. The writers indeed were generally ecclesiastics, to whom the Latin language was necessarily familiar. Even as late as the second half of the fourteenth century Thomas of Stitný was blamed for using the Bohemian language in his theological and philosophical works.

A few very early Latin prayers and lives of saints originated in Bohemia, but the earliest prose work which possesses general interest is the Latin *Chronicon Boemorum* of Cosmas, commonly called Cosmas Pragensis. Cosmas, "the father of Bohemian history," has always enjoyed a great and well-deserved reputation, and has often been called "the Bohemian Herodotus" by his countrymen.

We are better informed as to the life of Cosmas than is the case with regard to most early Bohemian writers. Writing in 1125, he calls himself an octogenarian, and it may therefore be considered as certain that he was born about the year 1045. He was probably of noble descent, and early in life adopted the ecclesiastical career. He became canon and afterwards dean of the chapter of Prague, and accompanied the bishops of Prague—whose position then gave them considerable political importance in Bohemia—on several missions. The last chapter of Cosmas' book, dealing with matters of which he had some personal knowledge, has therefore far greater value than the rest of the work. The regulations concerning the celibacy of the clergy were not at that period, nor indeed far later, observed by the Bohemian priests, and his ecclesiastical dignities did not prevent Cosmas from marrying, at the age of forty-one, Božetecha, to whom he was sincerely attached, and to whom he refers in his chronicle as "rerum cunctarum comes indimota mearum."

It was only after Božetecha's death in 1117 that Cosmas — perhaps to solace his sorrow by study — began his great historical work. The writer was then a man of over seventy years, and traces of senile garrulity can be found in his book. Still Cosmas appears to us as a man of great learning and perspicacity, sharpened, no doubt, by some knowledge of the practical politics of his day. With regard to the critical faculty, he was undoubtedly superior to the contemporary chroniclers of other countries. In his writings he almost always distinguishes between popular traditions, "senum fabulosæ narrationes," for which he could find no authority, and records which he believed to be founded on truth. The classical reading of Cosmas was very extensive for his times. His writings show a thorough knowledge of the works of Sallust, Ovid, Virgil, Terence, Lucan, and Horace. Of these, the last-named, if we may judge by Cosmas' frequent quotations, appears to have been a special favourite. The Latinity of Cosmas, if we may venture to employ that word when dealing with a writer of the twelfth century, contrasts favourably with that of most of his contemporaries, and in his works we sometimes meet with slight but charming reminiscences of the style of more classic periods.

Cosmas' work consists of three books, which were written at different periods and at first appeared separately, each book in the earliest MSS. containing a separate dedication. Cosmas afterwards published his work as a whole, dedicating it to his friend Severus, provost of Mélnik. The work is written in the chronological manner universally adopted at that time. In the earlier part of the first book, which, beginning with the deluge, deals with the establishment of the Čechs in Bohemia and the reigns of their early princes, Cosmas wisely abstains from giving any dates. From the deluge Cosmas proceeds rapidly to the establishment of Čechus and his companions in Bohemia. It is interesting from the historical point of view to note that all recollection of the earlier inhabitants of the country, both of the Celtic and of the Teutonic race, had already faded out of the memories of the people. Obviously guided by recollections of his classical readings, Cosmas describes the time of the first establishment of the Bohemians in their new homes as if it had been a golden age. "Most happy," he tells us, "was that age, content with moderate expenditure, not inflated by restless pride. The gifts of Ceres and Bacchus were unknown, and indeed did not exist; their evening meal consisted of acorns and the flesh of wild beasts; uncorrupted watersprings afforded them wholesome drink. As the splendour of the sun and the moisture of the water, the fields and pastures, and even marriage was common to them all. ... The use of wool and linen, and indeed of all clothing, was unknown to them. In winter only they used the skins of wild beasts and of sheep as clothing. No one could say of anything, 'It is mine,' but, as is usual in monastic communities, they said with their mouths, their hearts, and their deeds, 'Everything we own is ours (in common).' Their stables had no bolts, and they did not close their doors on the poor, for there were neither robbers nor poor. ... No arms were to be seen except arrows, and these they only used against wild beasts."

In Bohemia, as elsewhere, the "golden age" was of short duration. Cosmas, continuing his narrative, tells us the tales of Crocus and Libussa, of Premysl, the ploughman-prince, and of the foundation of Prague, which we afterwards find in an enlarged form in the works of the so-called Dalimil and of Hajek. Many of these tales, such as that of the ploughman-prince, are common property of most Slav countries; but the strange tale of the "war of the maidens," *divči válka*, which is said to have occurred after Libussa's death, evidently founded on the ancient traditions concerning the Amazons, is found in the records of no other Slav country. Bohemian scholars have recently attempted, with great ingenuity, to trace the manner in which this Eastern tale found its way to Bohemia.

From the year 894, the date which Cosmas fixes as that of the conversion of the Bohemian prince Bořivoj, he adopts the chronological system. Cosmas, however, very frankly admits that many of his statements are founded on slight and doubtful authority. For the second and third books of his work, on the other hand, Cosmas claims perfect accuracy. As he writes at the end of the first book: "Henceforth, with the aid of God and of St. Adalbert, we intend to narrate those events which we have either seen ourselves or truthfully gathered from those who saw them." This statement is not absolutely true, for Palacký, who critically examined the writings of the early Bohemian historians, has discovered numerous errors, particularly in the chronology of the second book. The third book, which begins with the year 1092, and was continued by Cosmas up to the year of his death in 1125, is the most valuable and also the most interesting part of the work. As already stated, Cosmas often accompanied the bishops of Prague on their travels through Germany, Lorraine, Italy, and Hungary, and this part of his work gives many interesting details referring to the social and political conditions of his times.

The work of Cosmas immediately obtained great and deserved success, and its popularity continued for a very considerable period. This is proved by the very numerous MSS. of the *Chronicon Boemorum* that are still in existence. It is therefore not surprising that Cosmas found many imitators and continuators. They belonged, as he had, to the ecclesiastical calling, and, like him, wrote in Latin. The works of these writers are of interest only to students of Bohemian history; it will therefore here be sufficient to mention a few of the most important chronicles. The earliest of these chroniclers is the writer known to us as the "Canon of Vyšehrad;"[1] his chronicle continues the work of

---

[1] The Vyšehrad hill, now part of the city of Prague, was the site of one of the oldest Bohemian monasteries.

THE CHRONICLERS 47

Cosmas from the year 1125, and ends with the year 1142. Another also anonymous chronicler is the "Monk of Sazava." He has incorporated the whole of Cosmas' chronicle with his work, but has added many interesting facts, some of which refer to his own monastery. The monastery on the Savaza had, since the year 1096, been in the hands of friars who used the Latin ritual, but our author relates the foundation of his abbey by St. Prokop, and the subsequent disputes between the German and Bohemian monks (so vividly described in the *Legend of St. Prokop*[1]) with an impartiality that deserves the highest praise. From the end of the year 1125, with which Cosmas' chronicle ends, to the year 1162, the last of which his own work treats, the monk of Sazava of course writes more independently. His work is on the whole trustworthy, and he often writes of contemporary events as an eye-witness. It is, however, to be regretted that the annals of the last years, when the monk no longer had Cosmas for a guide, are written in a briefer, more succinct manner than the earlier parts of the book, for the writer is here dealing with some of the most obscure years of Bohemian history. Several minor chronicles, also written in Latin, and probably by ecclesiastics, are also to be counted among the continuations of Cosmas' work. Such chronicles are that of Vincent, canon of Prague, dealing with the years 1140 to 1167, and that of Gerlach or Jarloch, abbot of Muhlhausen. Jarloch's chronicle begins with the year 1167, and the existent portion ends with the year 1198. It is, however, probable that he continued his work to a far later date, perhaps nearly up to the time of his death, which only occurred in 1228. After the year 1198 we

[1] See Chapter I.

have no knowledge of Bohemia from the writings of native authors during a considerable number of years. Somewhat later we find the chroniclers Peter of Zittau, abbot of Königraal, and Francis, provost of Prague; the work of the former writer deals with the annals of Bohemia from 1253 to 1338, while the work of Francis, beginning with the year 1333, carries on the history of Bohemia up to the year 1362.

More interesting than any of these chronicles are the works of several writers who flourished during the reign of Charles IV. (1346-1378). Though Charles only acquired the Bohemian language when already grown up, and always used Latin in his own writings, yet his interest in the language of his favourite country was very great. It is during his reign, and probably through his influence, that we find Bohemian translations of Latin historical works appearing almost simultaneously with the Latin originals. Charles IV. himself ranks among the Bohemian historians. His *Commentarius de Vita Caroli Bohemiæ Regis et postea Imperatoris ab ipso Carolo conscriptus* is of the greatest interest, and gives an insight into the true nature of the great sovereign which we scarcely find elsewhere. The book very clearly shows us Charles's attachment to his country, his piety, and his strong tendency to mysticism, the latter a characteristic of the king of which perhaps only Bohemian historians have taken sufficient account. If it were not contrary to the plan of this book to give lengthy quotations from works not written in the Bohemian language, the *Commentarius* would certainly deserve a more extensive notice. The book has unfortunately reached us in a very incomplete state. It appears probable that the writer intended to conclude his work with his election as King of the Romans; but the part which is undoubtedly the work of Charles does not go beyond the year 1340. Additions by a very inferior writer continue the work up to the year 1346, when the electors at Rhense chose Charles as King of the Romans. It appears, however, that Charles had collected notes in view of continuing his historical work, and that he made over these notes to Canon Benes of Weitmil, who afterwards incorporated them with his own chronicle. The *Vita Caroli* was translated into Bohemian very shortly after its appearance, probably by the so-called "Pulkava." The personality of "Přibik, son of Dluhý of Radenin, surnamed Pulkava," was formerly very obscure, and his chronicle was attributed to a person of the name of "Pulkava of Tradenin." Recent researches of Bohemian scholars have afforded us some information as to the career of a man who enjoyed high favour with Charles IV., and held what may be called the position of court-historian. Přibik was a layman, rector of the collegiate school of St. Giles at Prague. He took orders later in life and became rector of the parish of Chudenic, but probably carried on the duties of his office by means of a substitute. It was by the direct order of his sovereign that he composed his Bohemian chronicle, which, beginning, as was then usual, with the dispersion of the human race, narrates the history of Bohemia up to the year 1330. The book first appeared in Latin, but was almost immediately translated into Bohemian. Charles took great interest in this work and furnished the writer with numerous documents, so that he can almost be considered as his collaborator. Recent Bohemian writers have gone further, and have suggested—though without bringing forward sufficient evidence—that Charles was himself the author of the Latin chronicle, and that "Pulkava" only wrote the Bohemian translation, or rather adaptation, for the contents of the two books are by no means identical. This is one of the many questions concerning ancient Bohemian literature that is still obscure. Pulkava's work is written in the same fashion as the work of Cosmas, whom, indeed, all early Bohemian historians imitated, whether they expressly called themselves continuators of his work or not. Published under the auspices of Charles, Pulkava's chronicle enjoyed great popularity and is preserved in numerous MSS., from one of which the Bohemian version was printed in 1786. The work has, however, little historical value, and the style of the Latin version is inferior to Cosmas.

Of the many other writers of history who flourished during the reign of Charles, it will be sufficient to mention Benes (Benessius) of Weitmil, a canon of the chapter of Prague. Charles IV., as already mentioned, furnished the author with many notes, that were incorporated with his work. The chronicle of Benes, written in Latin, deals with the history of Bohemia from the year 1283 to the year 1374, about which time the author appears to have died. The part of the work which describes King John's last campaign and his death at Crécy has great interest, not only for Bohemian readers. Laurence of Breznov, who is generally mentioned in connection with the writers referred to above, belongs rather to the period of the Hussite wars.

While Bohemian was at this period, at first only in the form of translations, taking its place beside Latin as a language adapted to historic writing, it was already extensively used for writings on matters of law. Such works hardly belong to a history of literature; yet the *Kniha starého pána z Rožmberka*, the book of the old Lord of Rosenberg, deserves mention. It contains an enumeration of the laws and customs of Bohemia as they existed in the author's time. It is the oldest prose work in the Bohemian language, and dates either from the beginning of the fourteenth or from the last years of the thirteenth century. Another early legal work is the *Výklad na pravo zemske*, exposition of the law of the land, which is attributed to Andrew of Duba. Several other very early Bohemian writings on legal matters have been preserved.

One of the earliest and most curious prose works in the Bohemian language is the singular dialogue known as *Tkadleček the Weaver*. The book was one of the first that were printed when the revival of the Bohemian literature in the present century began. It was published by Wenceslas Hanka[1] in 1824, and was greatly admired. Recently the value of the book has, I think, been unduly depreciated. It certainly abounds with affectations and conceits such as were usual in the literature of most countries at the time—about 1407—when the book appeared; yet the complaints of the lover sometimes reveal a touch of real passion, and the style is generally fluent and lively. The monotony and the repetitions for which the lovers' long speeches are blamed are no peculiarity of the *Weaver*, but rather are ever inherent to the speech of the discarded and distressful lover. Far inferior to the speeches of the lover are the

[1] See Chapter VII.

answers of the personified Misfortune to whom he addresses his complaint.

Of the author of this very interesting work little is known. His Christian name was Ludvik, and he represents himself as being himself the discarded lover who addresses his complaint to Misfortune. He adopted the name of the Weaver, being, as he writes, "a weaver of learned lines." He was, according to recent research, not a nobleman of the Bohemian court, as had been formerly supposed, but a literary man who was in the service of the Dowager-Queen Elizabeth at Königgrätz, employed as a "writer" in some not clearly defined position. While it thus appears that the Weaver was a man of comparatively humble position, a more thorough study of the book has also proved that the fair Adlička, who had forsaken him to marry another, was not, as has been written, "one of the beauties of the Bohemian court," but that she was (as her lover indeed himself tells us) employed at that court as a "topička" (literally, lighter of fires), a word that we must reluctantly translate by "housemaid." Ludvik is, therefore, yet another instance of the facility with which a literary man idealises his mistress. It has been proved in recent years that the *Weaver* in many respects resembles a somewhat earlier German book entitled *Der Ackermann aus Beheim*, which dates from the year 1399. Without entering into the controversy that has arisen on this subject, it will be sufficient to state that the *Weaver* is not an adaptation, far less a translation of the German work, though there are certainly many resemblances between the two books. It may be interesting to quote part of one of the laments which the Weaver addresses to Misfortune. He thus expresses his grief: "After a loss a man often incurs mockery; the sorrow of others is to many an object of ridicule, such as thou hast bestowed on me, O unfortunate Misfortune! Through thee this has happened to me, the unhappy and thrice unhappy weaver. This all know and feel, this they fully understand. For already have all said and loudly affirmed it, that my most delightful, most excellent serving-maid[1] has been endowed with diverse gifts, happy and most choice; greater were her gifts than any that Nature has allowed any one to have; for all these gifts that she had from fortune, she had them not from fortune only; she obtained them also from the supreme Creator. Not only was she endowed with goodly customs, but a shapely form, a beautiful figure, and noble birth also God gave her, who had chosen her for her virtues and (who gave her also) much that was very good, sweet, and honourable; hardly ever has God given to one person so many remarkable, good, and prosperous gifts. And yet you mockingly tell me that my most excellent serving-maid, my most beloved maiden, is not different from others. And not only this (do you say), but also that I could find many other matrons and maids such as she, did I but cast glances around me. . . . I wonder at this: what devil has sent you to me? what devil gave you power over me? what devil or what demon,[2] or what fiend[2] has roused you and instigated you against me? I wonder indeed at the meaning of

[1] I have always thus translated the Bohemian word *topička* referred to above.
[2] The Bohemian words are *veleš* and *zmek*, names of heathen Bohemian divinities, which, after the acceptation of Christianity, acquired the signification of evil spirits.

this. I trust in my Creator for this, that He has not given you this power, and that you have not from Him this authority, and that this is by no means just. But you tell me that God has instructed you—chosen you for this! but I know not this; rather do I know that I have been deprived of all my comfort, of all my pleasure, of all good merriment; to me is bequeathed poverty and eternal grief; my name is marked out and written down in the doleful register of the longing and anxious ones until I die. Now indeed there is truly discord between me and the beloved and adored one; now indeed there is a quarrel worse than all other quarrels and discords. This indeed may be called truly discord and anger, which never again will change to peace. Oh, that I should ever have known what wrath between two lovers is. Alas and again alas, and woe to you, wicked, infamous Misfortune! Oh, wicked Misfortune, now, indeed, through your evil anger all my happiness, and with it my youth, is at an end. Why then am I still alive? what can I rejoice over? in what can I find pleasure? where can I seek refuge in this my great need? What shall I now love, what can I love now that everything is lost to me. In what shall I now find pleasure, what shall render me merry and happy, when I no longer love her through whom everything appeared lovable to me. Little now will be my joy, for little mercy shall I find. . . . And for what purpose have you endeavoured to do this, shameful, wicked, false Misfortune? Alas, alas! Woe, ever woe to thee. Gone is all my grace, gone are all my many qualities. O Misfortune, to whom shall I now go for counsel in this my hateful adversity? to whom shall I complain of my loss in this my depression and sorrow? I have no one to whom to complain of my misfortunes, of whatever nature they may be, except you, evil, disagreeable, and displeasing Misfortune, from whom I expect no relief.

"Alas, alas, and again alas! What yearnings have besieged me, what woe has bound me, what orphanage (*i.e.* bereavement) has subdued me! What longings and more than longings have overwhelmed me, and still overwhelm me from day to day, from hour to hour, so that I know of them neither beginning, nor middle, nor end. I am like a child that has been separated from its mother before the time, like a kitten which, though not yet grown up, is deprived of milk. As the colt of an ass that has not yet acquired strength is driven and forced to work before the time, thus I, evil Misfortune, am subject to you and given over to you before the time and in my youthful years; and still I do not know in what manner and wherefore and by whose orders. Alas, alas, O Misfortune! were it but possible that you, instead of Lot's wife, could be changed into that statue of salt, then at last your end would be certain. For it is you, O Misfortune, evil and shameful, and yet again evil Misfortune, who hast made of me more than a widower, more than an orphan, more than a man in whom all hope is dead. Every widower, when he is deprived of her who comforts him and loses her—knowing that it cannot be otherwise, and that his wife cannot return to him—gets over it, and so to speak forgets her, if not for ever, yet occasionally. But how should I forget my dearest, my most excellent and most beloved serving-maid? for she is yet alive, she is yet in good health, she is full of strength; she is as the pastime for another, not for me. And yet greater therefore is my bitterness, my sorrow, my anguish."

A short extract from one of Misfortune's replies to the Weaver will be sufficient. I shall here quote from Mr. Wratislaw's translation: "How much more fortunate then dost thou desire to be that I may honour thee more than the Emperor Julius or the King Alexander, or the excellent, truly excellent Emperor Charles, at this time king of Bohemia? who, powerful as they were, could not at times escape my power and my contrariety. Prithee, imagine how many of my misadventures have happened to those only whom thou knowest, and of whom thou hast heard in thine own days, whether of higher or lower rank; and neither thou nor any one else will be able to express in writing or words how many times this has happened to them. . . . If thou wilt, as thou canst, recollect thine own adversities only in thine own mind, how many of them hast thou also had from me? For it would have been more proper to cry out against me about them, or to argue with me about that which once threatened thy life, thy property, thy honour, and all the good that thou hadst, and it would have been convenient to speak of that rather than of that damsel of thine. Therefore, Weaver, hold thy peace, speak no more with me of thy darling."

Other early Bohemian prose-writings are the *Tale of Alexander the Great*, founded on the writings attributed to Callisthenes, but probably a translation from the Latin. It has little in common with the rhymed Bohemian *Alexandreis*. The *Chronicle of Troy*, also one of the earliest existent works in Bohemian prose, is also probably a translation from the Latin. The chronicle

THE PRECURSORS OF HUS 57

is remarkable as being the first Bohemian work that was printed (at Pilsen in 1468). These and other translations which require no special mention prove that the development of the Bohemian language was proceeding rapidly at this period.

I shall now refer to a group of writers and thinkers who are generally known as the precursors of Hus. This designation is still correct, though more extensive study of the works of Hus has recently proved it to be so to a lesser extent than was formerly supposed. It will be mentioned, when treating of the writings of Hus, that they show very little trace of the study of the works to which I shall now refer, while the influence of Wycliffe, from whom Hus quotes extensively, is constantly perceptible in his works, particularly in those written in Latin. Some ideas common to Wycliffe and Hus can also be traced far farther back; still many thoughts which we frequently meet with in the writings of Hus, his indignation against the immorality and avarice of the clergy, his endeavours to encourage the study of the Bible and to extend the use of the national language in the religious services, are clearly to be found in the writings of his Bohemian precursors. Štitný, in particular, was also a precursor of Hus in that sense that he greatly developed and perfectioned the Bohemian language, endowing it with a phraseology such as was necessary for the proper rendering of difficult theological and philosophical definitions.

By employing his native language for subjects which had hitherto only been dealt with in Latin, Štitný set an example that was afterwards followed by Hus.

The great prosperity which the wise rule of Charles IV.

had assured to his country had produced a great change in the hitherto simple fashion of living of the Bohemians, and of the citizens of Prague in particular. A more sumptuous mode of life now prevailed, and the contemporary writers are eloquent in their references to the luxurious fashion of dress, the extreme devotion to the pleasures of the table, and the general immorality of the citizens of Prague. The clergy, with a few honourable exceptions, gave by no means a good example to the laymen. Simony, and immorality—according to the Catholic creed a far greater offence on the part of a priest than of a layman—were almost general, both among the monks and the members of the secular clergy.

This deplorable condition of his beloved Bohemia did not escape the notice of Charles IV., whom his countrymen in his lifetime already described as " Otec Vlastí " (= Pater Patriæ). Hoping to improve the moral condition of the country by calling in foreign priests, Charles in 1358 invited the Austrian monk Conrad Waldhauser to Bohemia. Conrad, a native of Upper Austria, had lately attracted great attention by the eloquent sermons he had preached at Vienna. A German by nationality, Conrad was ignorant of the Bohemian language, but though he was thus unable to make himself understood by the mass of the people, the impression produced by his sermons was none the less very great. The educated citizens of Prague were then, as now, almost as familiar with the German as with their own language. Graphic accounts of his eloquent denunciations of the corruption and luxuriousness of his age have been preserved ; they sometimes read like a modern account of a revival meeting. The Teyn Church, where Conrad preached, soon became too limited for his audience; people assembled in squares and public places to listen to his sermons. The ladies of Prague discarded their jewellery and sumptuous clothing, while many men publicly confessed their sins. Though Conrad's preaching was in the strictest conformity with the teaching of the Church of Rome, he yet incurred the hostility of the monks, particularly the Dominicans and the Augustines. The protection of Charles, however, ensured his safety, and Conrad's death, in 1369, put a stop to the controversy which his sermons had caused. Waldhauser has left a considerable number of Latin works; of these, the *Postilla Studentium Sanctæ Universitatis Pragensis super evangelia dominica* and the *Apologia*, which contains his defence against the attacks of the monks, are the most important.

Among those on whom the preaching of Conrad Waldhauser produced a strong and permanent impression was the Moravian MILIČ of Kremsier, who, after Conrad's death, became his successor as rector of the Teyn Church at Prague. We find a considerable amount of information concerning Milič in his biography, contained in the *Miscellanea* of the learned Jesuit Balbinus. This biography, which dates from the second half of the seventeenth century, written, if not by Balbinus himself, by a member of his order, is noticeable for its conscientious impartiality. It is the foundation of all the more recent notices of Milič. The date of the birth of Milič is unknown; we only learn that he was of humble origin, and was probably born in the town of Kremsier in Moravia. He took orders early in life, probably in the year 1350. From the year 1360 downward he seems to have held an important official position in the chancery of Charles IV.; somewhat earlier he had already become archdeacon and canon of the cathedral of St. Vitus at Prague.

The ever-increasing reaction against the corruption of the times, which had already found expression in Waldhauser's sermons, caused Milič in 1363 to renounce all these dignities. In spite of the remonstrances of his Archbishop, Ernest of Pardubic, he decided to devote himself entirely to the preaching of the word of God. He first preached for a short time in the small town of Bischof-Teinitz, and then in several churches at Prague. The sermons of Milič vigorously inveigh against the immorality and corruption of the times, and do not spare the secular clergy and the monks. As Milič preached in Bohemian, his teaching was accessible to the great mass of the people, whom Conrad's German sermons had not reached.

The constant contemplation of the evils of his time, of poverty and vice as he saw them in the streets of Prague on the rare occasions when he left his studies for a few moments, produced a remarkable, though not at that period exceptional, effect on the imaginative mind of Milič. It seemed to him that all the preliminary symptoms described in the Revelation of St. John had already occurred. He therefore came to the conclusion that Antichrist was about to appear—he is said to have fixed on the years 1365 to 1367 as the date of his arrival —and sometimes even that he had already come. In a sermon preached before Charles IV., Milič openly denounced that sovereign as the "greatest Antichrist." Though he was imprisoned in consequence of this sermon, Milič remained but a short time in prison. The magnanimous prince condoned the offence against his

person in consideration of the great benefits which
Milič had conferred on Bohemia, both by his eloquent
preaching and by the example of his own spotless and
ascetic life. In 1367 Milič proceeded on a journey to
Rome, where Pope Urban V. was then expected from
Avignon; he wished to inform the Pope of his conviction of the impending end of the world and arrival
of Antichrist. Milič arrived in Rome before the Pope,
and, as he himself tells us in his *Libellus de Antichristo*, he caused a placard to be published on the
doors of St. Peter's Church announcing that he would
shortly preach a sermon declaring that Antichrist had
come. Milič was immediately arrested in consequence
of this act, and imprisoned in a monastery of the
Minorite Friars. The errors in doctrine which he was
accused of were probably a mere pretext for proceeding against a man whose eloquent sermons against the
avarice and immorality of the clergy had rendered him
obnoxious to many monks. As the biographer of Milič
tells us, " The friars of the mendicant orders were greatly
incensed against him (Milič) because of his sermons on
the admission of simoniacs to religious orders, and on
the possession of worldly goods by clerical persons, both
men and women. He was therefore thrown into heavy
bonds, together with Theodoric the hermit, a priest of
saintly memory, who had accompanied him."

Eventually Milič and his companion were released by
order of Pope Urban, who had meanwhile arrived in
Rome. They returned to Prague towards the end of the
year 1368, and were received with great enthusiasm by
the people. The citizens of Prague rejoiced all the more
on the return of their beloved preacher because during
his absence they had often heard the mendicant friars

announce from the pulpit, " Beloved brethren, very soon Milič will be burnt!" After his return to his native land, Milič, who in 1369 succeeded Waldhauser as rector of the Teyn Church at Prague, continued to devote his life to preaching and to good works. He devoted much energy to rescue work, and reclaimed a very great number of fallen women, for whom, aided by gifts from pious citizens of Prague, he founded a refuge, to which the name of Jerusalem was given. The ascetic and saintly life of Milič did not, however, disarm his constant enemies, the mendicant friars. In 1374 a new accusation against him, consisting of twelve "articles," was brought forward, and Milič travelled to Avignon to defend himself before the Papal See. Evidence as to the result of the trial is very uncertain, but on the whole it appears that the views of Milič were favourably received at Avignon; but the time was now near when he would be beyond the reach of all earthly jurisdiction. Milič died at Avignon, probably in June 1374.

Of the literary works of Milič we unfortunately possess very scanty remains. It is certain that copies of his Bohemian sermons were circulated for a considerable time after his death, but all trace of them has disappeared long since. If we consider the great eloquence which all contemporary writers attribute to Milič, this cannot be sufficiently regretted. The Bohemian book entitled *Of the Great Torments of the Holy Church*, which has often been attributed to Milič, is really a work of Magister John of Příbram. Of the numerous Latin writings of Milič, only a few, of which the *Libellus de Antichristo* and the *Postilla* are the most important, have been preserved. The biographer of Milič has stated very frankly the reason why so many of his works are lost. He writes: "Milič wrote much, and because he, perhaps too audaciously, attacked the vices of the clergy, and those of the mendicant friars in particular, the Hussites (as it is the custom of heretics) praised him as if he had been a friend of their sect, and used his statements as arguments for their own doctrines. Therefore Archbishop Zbynek of Hasenburg caused the writings of Milič to be publicly burnt on a pile, together with those of other heretics.

It is certainly principally through the example of Milič that the better known THOMAS OF ŠTITNÝ received the first impulse towards writing his now celebrated works. Štitný, indeed, himself writes: "Had it not been for the priest Milič, perhaps all these books which I have written would not have existed."

Thomas of Štitný was born in 1330 or 1331 at Stitný, a small castle or "tower," to use the Bohemian designation, in Southern Bohemia, which appears to have been in the possession of his family for some time. At a very early age, probably shortly after its foundation in 1348, Štitný visited the University of Prague, where he remained for some years devoting his time to the study of theology and philosophy. He did not, however, seek academic honours, and thus incurred the enmity of the "magisters" of the University, who considered him as an intruder on their domain. Their indignation was increased by the circumstance that Štitný wrote in Bohemian at a time when Latin only was considered to be the fitting language for those who treated the subjects on which Štitný wrote.

His theological and philosophical studies did not, however, so completely engross the interest of Stitný that he did not listen attentively to the sermons of the famous preachers whose eloquence was then attracting the attention of the citizens and students of Prague. He indeed tells us, in the preface to his book *Of General Christian Matters*, that this (his first original) work contained "what he heard at sermons and from learned men, as well as what he had conceived in his own mind." In his *Discourses for Sundays and Feast-days*, Štitný refers more precisely to the sermons which he had heard at Prague. Alluding to the attacks which had been made against his own works, he writes: "Thus within my own recollection the devil incited many against Conrad, that noble preacher of God's truth, because he showed up the craftiness of a false priesthood, and because he taught God's truth. Thus also have they acted towards the good Milič, and evil people still speak evil of him, but (they speak) injustice."

At a time which cannot be exactly ascertained, but which was probably somewhat later than the generally accepted date, 1360, Štitný left Prague and returned to his home. After the death of his parents he administered the little family estate, and continued living there for some time with his three sisters. He married about this date, but in 1370 was already a widower. He had several children, for whose benefit he first began writing, though the later editions of his works are evidently written for a wider circle of readers. Stitný outlived all his children except his favourite daughter Anne (Anežka), who was his faithful companion during the last years of his life. In 1381 Štitný returned to Prague, and now devoted his time entirely to his studies. After his death, in the year 1401, his daughter Anežka occupied part of a house next to the Bethlehem Chapel, where Hus was to begin preaching in the following year. It is known that several pious ladies lived in community in a house near Hus's chapel, and a letter addressed to them by him has been preserved. If, as is probable, Anežka of Štitný was one of these pious ladies, the fact forms an interesting link between Thomas and his greater successor.

Štitný did not begin writing early in life. His earliest works, translations from St. Augustine, St. Bonaventura, and other writers, date from about the year 1370. His first original work, the books *Of General Christian Matters*, one of the two on which his reputation as a Bohemian writer mainly depends, appeared in 1376. It is, however, certain that he had in 1374 already published several smaller tracts or pamphlets that were incorporated with his larger work. The books *Of General Christian Matters* are therefore rather a collection of minor writings, some of which had already appeared, than a work written from the first on a settled plan and with a continuous range of thought. It was a peculiarity of Štitný that he constantly re-wrote his books, changing their contents very considerably. Of his first book we possess four different MSS., differing considerably. The last, published under the new name of the *Books of Christian Instruction*, appeared only in 1400, a year before the author's death. In 1852 Erben edited and published the books *Of General Christian Matters*, following the readings of the best MSS. His work includes a biography of Štitný, which, though recent research has proved that it contains a few minor errors, is still of the greatest value.

The books *Of General Christian Matters* possess in Erben's edition two prefaces: the first is addressed to

Štitný's children, the second to the larger circle of readers for whom the later editions of his works were intended. In the first preface Štitný gives us a general account of the contents of his work, informing us that it will consist of six books.

The first, "Of faith and of hope and of love."

The second, "Of virgins and of widows and of married people."

The third, "Of the master of a family, of the mistress, and of the household."

The fourth, "How the nine orders of people bear the similitude of the nine choirs of angels."

The fifth, "How the devil tempts us."

The sixth, "How we purify ourselves from our sins."

In his second preface Štitný defends his resolution to use the Bohemian language in his writings. "Those who blame Bohemian books," he writes, "perhaps wishing alone to appear learned, will do well to fear God's vengeance, and to remember how guilty those are who would stop letters and needful messages contained therein; thus preventing the Lord God, the Eternal Bridegroom, from instructing His bride in His will, and comforting her in her distress." Štitný's views on this subject will remind English readers of those of his contemporary Wycliffe. The second preface also contains a passage showing the great importance which Štitný attached to the reading of the Scriptures; Štitný's teaching, as indeed that of all the Bohemian reformers, differs greatly from that of the Church of Rome on this important point. He writes: "This also mark carefully, beloved brethren, that the Holy Scriptures are, as it were, letters sent to us from our home; for our home is heaven, and our friends are the patriarchs and prophets, apostles and martyrs, and our fellow-citizens are the angels with whom we ought to be, and our King is Christ."

The first and last books of Štitný's work are of a purely theological character, differing thus from Books II. and III., which contain much shrewd advice of a more worldly character, though always founded on a distinctly theological basis. Štitný had not, when writing this book, reached the height of scholastic learning which he afterwards attained in his *Besedni Reči*. The beginning of the first chapter of the books *Of General Christian Matters* is a good specimen of Štitný's earlier manner of writing on theological subjects. He writes: "Scripture tells us, 'Without faith it is impossible to please God,' just as it is impossible to build a house without a foundation. Therefore, he who would have a firm house must first put up a firm foundation. And if we would have fruit, it must first originate from the root. And although the root in itself is not beautiful, yet all the beauty of stem and fruit originate from it. Thus, if there were no faith, all things would be useless for our salvation; without faith, indeed, other good things could not exist. For faith is the foundation and root of everything that is good, though its beauty is not in itself so evident, yet could there be neither hope nor love without faith. And how can I hope for anything if I do not first believe that it exists. Therefore it is necessary that whoever wishes to be saved should hold the common faith of Christianity."

The second book *Of General Christian Matters*, as already mentioned, differs considerably from the first. Štitný begins by telling us that "after having finished the first book, which deals with the three general matters that are necessary to all, of whatever condition they may be, and without which no one can be saved, I have written for you this second book. It deals with purity, and how it should be preserved by those who wish to dwell with God in His kingdom, in whichever of the three conditions[1] they may belong. For that heavenly city, the godly, holy, New Jerusalem is thus ruled, and is so very pure that, since the beginning of ages, nothing impure has entered it, as indeed the holy St. John had declared in the Book of Secret Revelation."

Štitný's book, *Of Virgins, of Widows, and of Married People*, is written from a highly moral and wise point of view, but he deals with his subject in a somewhat outspoken manner, and caution is often necessary when quoting from it. It is interesting to find in the writings of a moralist of the fourteenth century views as to the relative position of the sexes similar to some that have quite recently given rise to considerable controversy. In the chapter entitled, "What those who wish to get married should beware of," Štitný writes: "To those maidens who seek a husband, and to bachelors also, will I give this advice, that every young man should preserve himself for his bride free from all impurity as completely as she does so for him; for it is God's law that no man should outside of the bonds of matrimony commit any offence with any woman. For as a young man would be displeased should the maiden whom he wishes to marry quit the state of virginity, in the same manner he also should preserve his innocence. A man indeed is stronger than a woman, and as it is shameful for a virgin to leave her state except through matrimony, thus before

---

[1] *i.e.* virgins, widows, and married people. See p. 66.

God it is no lighter sin for a man. And thus it is beseeming for both man and woman to preserve themselves pure till the time of their marriage, and to prepare themselves for it by penitence, for marriage is a sacrament."

Very quaint is the part of the second book which deals with inequality between married people. Štitný writes: "It is necessary that those who wish to marry should all seek their equals, so that inequality may not cause discord and displeasure. If you are young, beware of old people, and one of noble birth should seek his equal, for often evil is caused by that discord (which arises) when those who are very unequal marry. If an old man marries some one younger, he ever fears that the younger one may not love him, and being therefore anxious about this, he does not feel complete love for his partner, for where there is suspicion there cannot be complete love. Also the humours of the young do not please the old, nor those of the old the young. Some one indeed said, and he spoke the truth, 'When I was young the old people did not please me, and now that I am old, the young people do not please me.' And even if an old man does not displease a young wife, and even if she is good, yet will she not be free from the lies of evil people. They will indeed give her evil advice, saying, with mischievous intent, 'What an old husband you have!...' And then evil people will in the fields sing songs about them, the devil instigating them to do so, for he wishes to corrupt a good woman, to bring before her mind what she had not thought of, so that she may be seized by longing. And it will be precisely the same thing with a young man who has an old wife. Jesting with them, people will say to him, 'There is your beauty!

why, it is your mother!'" In this book Štitný constantly praises the state of celibacy, strictly in accordance with the doctrine of the Church of Rome.

The third book, which, as already stated, treats "of the master of a family, the mistress, and the household," contains much wise and homely advice, and incidentally throws considerable light on the family life of a Bohemian country gentleman in the fourteenth century. The position of the head of the family is thus defined: "Every landowner is the master of his servants, and should restrain them from everything that is evil: he should first attempt to do this by kindness; if he cannot at once put a stop to evil habits, he should endeavour to do so gradually, but in no case allow any new evil habit to spring up. If kindness does not succeed with them (the servants), then show your right to rule (over them). Remember always that that priest Eli in the Old Testament was indeed good himself, but his sons did evil. He, it is true, said to them, 'You do evil,' but he did not manfully punish them for their misdeeds. He thus incurred God's wrath, and was given as an example to all fathers and heads of families who do not heed what the members of their households do. But a master of a household must beware of sudden, useless anger. If he cannot entirely get rid of anger, let him at least be softened, and he should be cruel neither to his servants nor to his wife, remembering that God is your only Lord and theirs also. On this, too, should every one reflect, that it is improbable that any one be without faults; and it often happens that when you will not pass by a single fault, perhaps not a serious one, you either spoil (the servant) yet more, or you are obliged later to overlook more serious faults in another (servant whom you take in the place of the former one). Thus the tilter must in tournaments overlook some faults in his charger, if but he is on the whole serviceable."

Štitný's work, like those of all moralists of all periods, contains many reflections on the vanity of the female sex. He writes: " St. John Chrysostom tells us that if a man has a dissipated wife, he should not forbid her everything at a time, lest she become refractory, but from those things that are, as it were, most serious, from those let him first try to dissuade her. If she paints herself, then remark before her what a shameful thing it is to grease yourself in a nasty manner, or to cram the hair of others on your head; (also remark to her), often one thus acquires shame while wishing to receive honours. If wise men remark these things on her, they will take her for a mad woman, and other women, who perhaps have some grudge against her, will, even though they praise her, betray her and make fun of her, and often her own servants will be obliged to hide themselves from shame of this (their mistress's appearance). In fact, while wishing to appear young, she becomes aged in consequence of this painting."

The leading idea of the fourth book *Of General Christian Matters* is one which we meet with very often in Štitný's works, but which he has perhaps developed here more clearly than elsewhere. It is the mystic idea of the analogy which, according to Štitný, exists between the different conditions of men and the various choirs of angels. He writes: "It is my duty—as indeed I promised in the preface to these books—to explain in this my fourth book in what manner the conditions of men in this world are similar to the various choirs of the angels; but let no man attack me, as if I had said that such or such people of this or that condition will be in the same choir, as angels of any particular class. It will be well for them if they obtain heaven; but whether a man of this or that condition will be in this choir or that, that is a matter which I cannot judge. Yet in this world certain conditions of men are more similar to particular choirs of angels than others. And indeed it often happens that some common little peasant[1] or small tradesman has greater love for God than some monk. Yet both will be with God, but I do not know in which choir each of them will be." Štitný then proceeds to address admonitions to the divers classes of men. The first class mentioned are the priests and monks, whom he compares to the cherubims. The somewhat lengthy discourse about the monks is very interesting, and I shall quote a portion of it in Mr. Wratislaw's translation. Štitný writes: "And thus they have fallen away in love; they have not the peace of God in their minds; they do not rejoice with God in devotion, but quarrel, hate each other, condemn each other, priding themselves against each other; for love has sunk low in them on account of avarice, because they have forsaken God for money, breaking His holy laws and the oath of their own promise. And besides this (which is the most dreadful wickedness), they are irritated, they are annoyed at every good preacher or every good man who understands their error; they would gladly make him out a heretic that they may have greater freedom for their cunning."

The fifth and sixth books *Of General Christian Mat-*

---

[1] *Sedláček*, the diminutive of *sedlák* = peasant. The diminutive is used very frequently in Bohemian.

THE "REČI BESEDNI" 73

ters again deal, like the first one, with purely theological subjects. It will be unnecessary to deal with them in detail, as Štitný's later work gives us a clearer insight into his theological views. It is easily noticeable that Štitný's studies gradually become more profound, and there is a marked difference between the simple and homely manner in which the books *Of General Christian Matters* are written and the more learned and more brilliant style of the *Reči Besedni*.

The *Reči Besedni*, which we may translate into English by "Learned Entertainments," also known as *Rozmluvy nábožné*, "Religious Conversations," is the second great work of Štitný, and according to most Bohemian critics his masterpiece. A considerable number of MSS. containing the "Religious Conversations," both separately and together with the other works of Štitný, have been preserved, and we have two versions that differ considerably, the author having re-written his work as he did the books *Of General Christian Matters* also. Extracts from the book were printed some years ago, but it was only in 1897 that Professor Hattala published a complete edition of the *Reči Besedni*. The work is, like all the writings of Štitný, mainly a theological treatise, but philosophy, then of course the handmaiden of theology, has a considerable share in this book. The study of Aristotle and of numerous scholastic writers is very evident, but, speaking generally, Stitný must be classed among the realists in distinction from the nominalists. He has, however, incorporated with his book such numerous quotations, or rather extracts, from other writers, that his system appears somewhat eclectic.

The general purpose of the book is an attempt to

define the personality of God and His attributes according to the system of mediæval scholasticism. Faith (Víra) here, as in all Štitný's works, is assumed as existent, and only incidentally is an attempt made to reconcile religion with science. The science of course is that of the fourteenth century, which scarcely knew the words with

> "*Greek endings, each the little passing bell*
> *That signifies some faith's about to die.*"

Štitný's book, treating of abstract matters such as had never before been dealt with in Bohemian, is yet written in a clear, lucid, and forcible manner, and it is perhaps doubtful whether any other modern language had at that period arrived at a sufficient degree of development to produce a similar work on subjects which mediæval custom reserved to the Latin language. In this respect Stitný was a true precursor of Hus, and Palacký has rightly said that a nation which produced and understood such a writer as Štitný could not henceforth be called rude and uncultivated. The portion of this work which has principally attracted the attention of Bohemian scholars is that dealing with Krása (beauty), or rather, as Štitný words it, "the wisdom of God, as it is shown to us in the beauty and splendour of creation." It is impossible to quote detached passages from this treatise, as it may be called, which is contained in chapters ix. to xii. of Štitný's book, nor are these chapters perhaps specially characteristic of the general purpose of Štitný's work. Some of the ideas expressed in these chapters are considerably in advance of the times, and his theories sometimes recall the views of modern German writers on æsthetics.

THE "REČI BESEDNI" 75

The *Reči Besedni*, in Professor Hattala's edition, contains two prefaces. The first, by an unknown writer, gives a few interesting details concerning the author of the *Reči Besedni;* it tells us "that during the reign of Wenceslas of Bohemia, the fourth of that name, there lived a renowned knight, Thomas of Štitný, a good man of letters, honourable in his times and irreproachable in his noble life up to his death. Leading a pious and peaceful life, he composed these books in the Bohemian language. . . . Possessing a sharp intellect, he produced beautiful, enchanting works, in which he used the writings of the Old and of the New Testament, and of the holy fathers."

The second preface, by Štitný himself, explains his reason for writing his work in the form of a dialogue between father and son. "Thinking then and remembering," he tells us, "how pleasant it was to me in my youth to listen to my father or mother when they talked on Christian matters, and how it was through them that I acquired some knowledge of Scripture, I devised these books, (written) as if children questioned their father and he answered them."

A quotation from the first chapter of the *Religious Conversations* will be interesting as showing the manner in which Štitný opens up the discussion of his difficult subject. The chapter entitled, "How the children now begin to question their father as to what God is and how He can be known to us," begins with the following question: "Dear father,[1] we would be glad to ask you, and to understand, what God is?" The father answers thus: "O children, you have asked a short,

---

[1] Literally "little father," *tatíku*. The frequent diminutives of the Bohemian language are very difficult to render in English.

but far-reaching and very sublime question. Our intellect cannot err in believing that God exists. All creation proclaims that God is (its) creator; for no thing has made itself. Therefore all men, heathens, Jews, Christians, heretics, and philosophers, hold (= consider) something as (being) God. But what God is, that the mind of men does not fathom! Therefore it can be said that God is the ineffable Supreme Being, than whom nothing better, nothing more blissful, nothing more majestic can be imagined, nor indeed anything as good, as blissful, as majestic. For herein He (God) rises above all comprehension, above all minds of men and angels; He is always more excellent than any one can express or imagine. Thus will you ascertain what God is not, but you cannot attain to the knowledge of what He is. For whatever may be the highest majesty a man can imagine, yet He (God) is above this. If a man attains to as high a heart as he can, yet God will be raised above that. Thus many heathen errors and heresies arose, because men having in their minds imagined God in this or that fashion, they then said, 'This is God.' This indeed is true sense, to know our folly and ignorance, (wherefore) it is impossible for us to gaze on the brightness of solemn divinity, and, as it were, on the spiritual splendour of inward light, in which resides God, to whom we cannot accede. Rather let us in meekness, holding the strong and true Christian faith, merit that we may once contemplate our God, through our Lord Christ, when in that eternal kingdom of His our eyes shall be entirely and truly cleared. Let not sin so entirely blind us that we—God forbid it!—for some reason or other forget God, not loving Him in true faith above everything else. For the Scripture sayeth, 'If you do not believe, you will not understand.' Therefore, children, it beseems you to think and speak of so sublime a subject with awe and dread and discretion, and to listen with attentive ears and a pious heart, with love and not from frowardness."

Chapter xxii. of the *Reči Besedni* strongly brings out the acumen and lucidity with which Štitný elaborated his often difficult theological definitions. The comparisons by which he endeavours to render clearer the dogma of the Trinity are very striking. The chapter begins as usual with a question: "How then did it happen that only the Son of God accepted human nature in the unity of His person?" The father answers: "The Father or the Holy Ghost could have done so, as well as the Son. But the Lord God wished thus to accomplish this; thus in the council of all the persons of the glorious Godhead, the Holy Trinity, was it decreed —That the wisdom of the Son of God should, as was fitting, overcome the cunning of the devil; that the devil should truly lose his dominion over men when the Divine Wisdom was led to death in the human personality of one who was not obliged to die; and that the same person who in the Holy Trinity is eternally the Son should become the Son of Man.

"And that you may in a manner understand this also, how the Son of God Himself in His own personality received the human nature, and not the Father nor the Holy Ghost—though the whole Trinity is one God, and at the same time each person is a complete divinity— let us consider the similar case of the sun. Not that it is the same with it as with the Creator, but I say there is a resemblance.

"The sun has also its Trinity—that is, the body of the

sun, the light which proceeds from it, and also the heat of the sun; but when the sun comes to us it gives us its light and its heat. But the light alone takes (on itself) that colour of the glass or the membrane or the cloud through which it appears to us; but the sun itself and the heat will not have this colour.

"Oh, wondrous power! oh, unfathomable wisdom! oh, most delightful goodness, how charming it is to gaze on you that have deigned to open our eyes! And does it not beseem us to admire this: how in Christ in this Unity are gathered together—and how properly and how usefully for us—three things in their nature most dissimilar, as it appears to our minds. But what is impossible to God? Oh, there is something new, greater, and eternal joined together in this Unity. The spirit is new; that was created when the Son of God accepted to become a man. The body is greater than it was when long ago it was created for Adam; for from that body the bodies of all men proceeded, and afterwards the body of Christ, which He took from the pure virginal blood of her whom He chose for Himself as a mother. The Word of God, then, the Son of God the Father, that is eternal. And all this met in the one person of our Lord Christ. And in this strange act of the entire Holy Trinity the threefold power of God was shown. Firstly, because out of nothing He created something. Secondly, because He made something new out of something greater. Thirdly, because out of something mortal He made something eternal, or, as I should rather say, because out of something dead He made something eternal."

Štitný's two works—his books *Of General Christian Matters* and his *Religious Conversations*—give us all that is really valuable in his teaching, and the other works are comparatively of slight interest. Stitný's literary activity was, however, very great during his whole life. It has already been mentioned that he re-wrote the books *Of General Christian Matters* four times, and the *Religious Conversations* twice. A third work of considerable size, not yet printed, appeared in 1392, entitled *Speeches for Sundays and Fast-days;* and to his death Štitný continued to publish smaller writings, partly original, partly translated from other writers. In the last years of his life the mysticism, almost always latent in the mind of a Bohemian, obtained preponderating influence on the views of Štitný. His latest work is a translation of the visions of St. Bridget, a Swedish saint belonging to the early part of the thirteenth century. As a recent Bohemian critic has justly remarked, the visions of St. Bridget exercised on Stitný's mind, in his last years, an influence similar to that of the " prophetess," Christina Ponatovská, on Komenský.

Waldhauser, Milič, Štitný, and many minor writers on theology, who do not require special notice, energetically attacked the avarice and immorality of the clergy, and loudly demanded Church reform. Yet they were careful to avoid all attacks on the dogmas of the Roman Church, and, indeed, looked to the Pope, as the head of that Church, as to the person who would initiate Church reform. Different from these views were those of MATTHEW OF JANOV, the last of the precursors of Hus whom I shall mention. Matthew obviously writes under the strong impression produced by the great schism in the Western Church, which began in 1378, four years after the death of Milič. Štitný, indeed, lived on for many years later, but age appears to have weakened his energy and his enthusiasm, and he has indeed, in the last editions of his writings, considerably attenuated many remarks contained in the earlier ones.

Great, on the other hand, was the influence of the schism on the writings of Matthew of Janov. The idea of his master, Milič, that the Pope should himself become the originator of Church reform, appeared an absurdity at a moment when two rival pontiffs were preparing to organise, by the sale of indulgences, so-called "crusades" against their opponents, whom they already attacked with the ecclesiastic arm of excommunication and the foulest personal abuse. The only remedy that appeared possible to Matthew of Janov—undoubtedly one of the profoundest thinkers of his age—was a reform of the Church in which the individual churchman was to take the initiative, and such a reform, he thought, could only consist in a return to the ways of the primitive Church, as described to us in the Scriptures.

Matthew's life was lived and lives for us in his books. Very few words will suffice to tell all that is known of the circumstances of his outer life. The year of his birth is uncertain, but we know that his father was Wenceslas of Janov, a poor Bohemian knight, and that when very young he proceeded to Prague to pursue his studies at the university there. He here fell under the spell of the eloquence of Milič of Kremsier, for whom he expresses unlimited admiration, and whom in one of his writings he describes as "the son and semblance of our Lord Jesus Christ, possessing a distinct and visible resemblance to His apostles." Matthew left Prague some time before the death of Milič, and pursued his studies at Paris for six years, obtaining there the degree of "Magister." He thence became known as "Magister Parisiensis," by which name he is generally described by contemporary writers. After spending some time at Rome and Nüremberg he returned to Prague, and in 1381 became a canon of the Cathedral of St. Vitus on the Hradain at Prague.

In distinction from both Waldhauser and Milič, Matthew obtained no special reputation as a preacher, but principally devoted his time to the composition of theological works. Some of these works attracted the attention of his superiors, and were condemned in 1388 by a Synod of the Archdiocese of Prague. Matthew was obliged to sign a document, which has been preserved to us by Palacký, in which he withdrew a considerable number of opinions contained in his works. In this recantation Matthew withdraws his former statements concerning images of Christ and the saints, which, indeed, he promises henceforth to "adore and venerate." He further affirms "that the saints in heaven, and their bodies and bones, and also other sanctified things, such as the garments of Christ, of the blessed Virgin, and of the saints, ought to be venerated here on earth." In the last paragraph of the recantation Matthew admits that people, specially laymen, should not be advised to receive communion daily. It is curious that Matthew's far-reaching theories concerning the return to primitive Christianity are not even alluded to in this recantation. As the chronology of the works of Janov—of which no single complete MS. has been preserved—is very uncertain, it is impossible to decide whether he had not then expressed these views, or whether it was thought advisable to leave them unnoticed.

Matthew's sentence, no doubt in consequence of his recantation, was a very mild one; he was suspended from exercising his functions as a priest, except in his own parish church, during half a year. Janov died in the prime of his life in 1393, and retained his canonry up to that time.

There is sufficient proof that Matthew of Janov was a very voluminous writer, but his works have reached us in a very incomplete state, and they were entirely unknown before the present century. It is not difficult to account for the almost complete oblivion into which these important works had fallen. Though the teaching of Matthew was on many points similar to that of the Hussites, yet no reverence for his person and his memory was felt by them. They could not refrain from contrasting his recantation with the very different behaviour of Hus under similar circumstances. If some of his works have been preserved through the agency of the party that favoured Church reform, this was because such writings were attributed to Wycliffe or Hus. The adherents of the Church of Rome were, of course, anxious that, after his recantation, the former heretic theories of Matthew should, as far as possible, be buried in oblivion. They, not without reason, regarded some of the opinions of Matthew as most dangerous for their Church. The celebrated Protestant divine Neander, who perhaps has studied the works of Janov with more care than any one else, declares that a thorough study of Janov's works proves that, independently of Wycliffe, there existed in Bohemia at the end of the fourteenth century a strong reaction against the Roman hierarchy, founded on principles somewhat similar to those of the later German reformers. In his *Kirchengeschichte*, also, Neander has expressed the opinion that the views of Hus not only did not go farther than those of Matthew of Janov, but that they indeed remained somewhat behind those of the earlier divine.

It is certain that some of Janov's writings were in Bohemian, as a decree of the archiepiscopal vicariat (dating from the year 1392) has been preserved in which Matthew was ordered to submit for inspection two Bohemian books which he had just written. All trace of both these books has long been lost. There is, however, no doubt that the majority of Janov's books were written in Latin. Those that have been preserved consist of a large number of religious pamphlets, written at different periods. Towards the end of his life Matthew collected these writings and published them in a large book entitled *Regulæ Veteris et Novi Testamenti*. The work is divided into three books consisting of chapters, some of which retain the designation under which they had formerly appeared as separate pamphlets. No complete MS. of the *Regulæ Veteris et Novi Testamenti* is in existence, but it would be quite possible to reconstruct the work from the different MSS. and publish it; there seems, however, to be at present little probability that any one will undertake this task.

No work of Matthew of Janov has up to now been printed except the pamphlet *De abominatione in loco sacro*, which forms the last chapter of the third book of the *Regulæ*. This treatise was formerly attributed both to Wycliffe and to Hus, and it is printed in the large edition of the works of the latter writer that was published at Nüremberg in the sixteenth century. Palacký has conjectured that several smaller pamphlets included in this large edition of the works of Hus really belong to Matthew of Janov. It is indeed only recently that Palacký, Dr. Lechler, and Mr. Wratislaw have attracted attention to the work of Janov, and have quoted extensively from the MS. copies. I shall attempt to give some idea of his most characteristic theories by quoting a few short passages from his works. Matthew's special love and veneration for the Bible appears very clearly in a passage contained in the introduction to the *Regulæ*. "I have in these my writings," he tells us, "principally used the Bible, and but little the sayings of the learned doctors; both because the Bible occurs to me promptly and copiously, whatever matter I may be considering or writing on, also because through it and through its divine truths, which are clear and manifest in themselves, all opinions are more solidly confirmed, more stably founded, and meditated on more usefully; then also because it is the Bible that I have loved since my youth, and called my friend and bride—truly the mother of beauteous affection and knowledge and fear and holy hope.... And here I confess that the Bible has never been severed from me, from youth to age, and even to decline, neither on the road nor in my house, nor when I was busy, nor when I enjoyed leisure."

A short quotation referring to the schism, which then attracted the entire interest of all lands belonging to the Western Church, clearly shows Matthew's views on this subject. He writes: "This schism has not arisen because they loved Jesus Christ and His Church, but rather because they (*i.e.* the priests) loved themselves and this world." Of the reform of the Church Matthew writes: "It therefore appears to me that it is necessary, for the purpose of re-establishing peace and union in the Christian community, to eradicate all weeds, to condense the Word of God on earth again, and bring back Jesus Christ's Church to its original, salutary, and condensed condition, retaining but few regulations, and those only that date from the time of the Apostles." Later on, writing on the same subject, Matthew says: "All the (above-mentioned) works of men, ceremonies and traditions shall be totally destroyed and will cease, while our Lord Jesus shall alone be exalted, and His Word alone shall remain in all eternity; and the time is near when these things shall be abolished."

CHAPTER III

HUS

THE life and death of Hus and the principal events of his career form perhaps the one incident in the annals of Bohemia that is familiar to most English readers. I therefore give but a summary account of the career of the great Bohemian, for here, as everywhere, the need of compression confronts me. I feel the more justified in omitting many interesting incidents, as English literature in the late Mr. Wratislaw's *John Hus* possesses a short but trustworthy biography of Hus founded on lately-discovered documents. The work is superior to any other on the same subject. Even in Bohemian literature no equally trustworthy biography of Hus has as yet appeared. The sympathies of Mr. Wratislaw are indeed very evident, but he has never attempted to slur over or to attenuate the arguments of the adversaries of Hus.

The study of the life and of the writings of Hus has until recently been greatly neglected in Bohemia, and even now no complete modern edition of his works exists. A recent editor of a selection from Hus's letters scarcely exaggerates when he writes: " Two wrongs have been committed on Magister John Hus—one was committed when at Constance long ago his life was violently brought to an end; the other consists in the neglect with which his works are treated at present by the national (*i.e.* Bohemian) public."

John of Husinec, or JOHN HUS as he is usually called, was, according to ancient tradition, born on 6th July 1369; neither day nor year of his birth are, however, absolutely certain. Many tales told of the early days of Hus are taken from the records of the Bohemian brethren, written many years after his death. From the year 1400 onward authentic accounts of the events of the life of the Bohemian reformer exist, and from the year 1409 to the time of his death we have a continuous and detailed record of his life.

At a very early age Hus proceeded to Prague to pursue at the university there the studies required for the purpose of entering the Church. With his usual candour and simplicity Hus himself tells us that he originally decided to adopt the ecclesiastical career rather for the purpose of gaining a living than through any special vocation. It is, however, certain that during his years of study he already led a pious and studious life. He has indeed confessed[1] that before he was ordained "he had been fond of playing chess, thus wasting time and causing irritation" (to his partners). Such a confession, written while he was preparing for his fatal journey to Constance, proves indeed how little he had to confess, and is a touching instance both of his extremely sensitive conscience and of the profound humility so characteristic of Hus.

In September 1393 Hus took the degree of bachelor of arts, in the following year that of bachelor in divinity,

---

[1] Letter to the "disciple Martin," dated October 10th, 1414, printed in *Documenta Mag. Joannis Hus Vitam Doctrinam, Causam Illustrantia.* I have based this summary account of the career of Hus mainly on this important collection of documents, published by Palacký in 1869.

and in 1396 that of master of arts. His reputation for great learning seems to have spread very rapidly at the university, for in 1401 we already find him dean of the Faculty of Arts, and in the following year he became, for the first time and at an unusually early age, rector of the university of Prague. He seems soon to have attracted attention by his great learning, and by the acumen which he displayed in the learned disputations that formed so large a part of the routine of mediæval universities. His learning was at that period noticed rather than any special religious fervour. His lectures, as Dr. Lechler has conjectured, were probably founded on Wycliffe's philosophical works, which became known to the Bohemians earlier than the theological works of the English divine.

A change appears to have come over the mind of Hus about the beginning of the fifteenth century. He has himself told us that after his ordination as a priest (probably in 1400) he led a yet simpler and more ascetic life. The principal cause of the enthusiasm, both religious and national, that henceforth distinguishes Hus was, however, undoubtedly his appointment in 1402 as rector and preacher at the Bethlehem Chapel in Prague. The foundation of the Bethlehem Chapel, which took place in 1391, and was the work of Kříž, a tradesman of Prague, and John of Milheim, one of the courtiers of King Wenceslas, is an important manifestation of the desire to reform the Roman Church and to enlarge the sphere of the native language, which was then gaining ground in Bohemia. In their deed of endowment the founders stated that their object was the encouragement of the preaching of biblical doctrines in the Bohemian language. No special provision for the reading of masses was made, and no doubt many Bohemians, after hearing mass in other churches where German sermons were still preached, then proceeded to the Bethlehem Chapel. The stress laid on the preaching of the Gospel, one of the points to which the partisans of Church reform attached great importance, proves that the founders, or at least Milheim, sympathised with this movement. The increased use of the Bohemian language for preaching and its general development greatly irritated the Germans in Bohemia, who believed their preponderant position in the town and University of Prague to be menaced. The Germans in Bohemia were therefore thoroughgoing partisans of the Church of Rome, rather from antagonism to their fellow-citizens of Slav nationality than from any sympathy for the abuses then prevailing in the Roman Church. This division by nationalities, according to which the Bohemians favoured Church reform, while the Germans defended the authority of Rome, continued during the whole period of the Hussite wars, and indeed far later. It was only with the appearance of Luther that this distinction entirely ceased.

The sermons of Hus at the Bethlehem Chapel immediately attracted general attention. His great eloquence is evident in the few sermons of Hus that have been preserved, as well as in the fragments of them which he undoubtedly afterwards introduced into his *Postilla*. He seems to have preached on a wide range of subjects, and by no means to have eschewed the topics of the day. In one of Hus's earliest sermons[1] he refers

[1] This sermon was probably not preached at "Bethlehem," but at the Church of St. Michael at Prague; for the events referred to occurred in 1401, while Hus was only appointed preacher at "Bethlehem" in 1402. He may, however, have preached there occasionally before that date.

to the invasion of Bohemia by the troops of the Margrave of Meissen, the ally of Rupert, Elector-Palatine, whom the enemies of King Wenceslas had elected King of the Romans. It is easy to imagine the strong impression which Hus's fiery words produced on his Bohemian audience, which, though thoroughly aware of the many faults of King Wenceslas, yet supported him against his German rival. "The Bohemians," Hus said, "are more wretched than dogs or snakes, for a dog defends the couch on which he lies, and if another dog tries to drive him away, he fights with him; and a snake does the same. But us the Germans oppress, seizing all the offices of state while we are silent. Bohemians in the kingdom of Bohemia, according to all laws, indeed also according to the law of God, and according to the natural order of things, should be foremost in all the offices of the Bohemian kingdom; thus the French are so in the French kingdom, and the Germans in the German lands. Therefore should a Bohemian rule his own subordinates, and a German German (subordinates). But of what use would it be that a Bohemian, not knowing German, should become a priest or a bishop in Germany? He certainly would be as useful as a dumb dog who cannot bark is to a herd! And equally useless to us Bohemians is a German; and knowing that this is against God's law and the regulations, I declare it to be illegal!" Though the date of this sermon is certain, and its immediate motive consisted no doubt in the cruelties that German troops were then committing in Bohemia, yet it is evident that Hus already had in view the preponderating influence which the Germans exercised in the university and city of Prague.

It is noteworthy that Hus was during the early days

of his priesthood on good terms with his ecclesiastical superiors at Prague. This continued to be the case even after discussions on the teaching of Wycliffe had in 1403 begun to disturb the peace of the university. At a meeting of the magisters which took place in May of that year, and over which Walter Harasser, then rector of the university, presided, the twenty-four articles from Wycliffe's writings which the London Synod had already declared either heretical or erroneous, were laid before the assembly by John Kbel and Wenceslas of Bechin, canons of the chapter of Prague, the archiepiscopal seat then being vacant. Besides these twenty-four articles, the representatives of the archbishopric brought twenty-one other articles to the notice of the magisters, which a German member of the university, one John Hübner, had selected from Wycliffe's writings, and submitted to the ecclesiastical authorities. The articles of Hübner, as Hus truthfully declared, contained various statements that cannot be found in Wycliffe's works. "After these articles had been read out, and Magister Walter Harasser, the rector, had carefully noted down the votes of each and all the magisters present as representatives of the university of Prague, it was decided by a majority of the votes of the members of the university that no one should dogmatise, preach, or assert, publicly or privately, the articles which had been presented to the lord rector by John, official of the archbishopric, and Wenceslas, the archdeacon, under penalty of violating his oath."[1] A renewed discussion on the teaching of Wycliffe took place somewhat later; this time, however, the matter was only brought before the Bohemian "nation," one of the four sections into which the univer-

[1] Palacký, *Documenta*, &c.

sity of Prague was then divided. The condemnation of the articles taken from Wycliffe's works was renewed with a restriction—suggested by Hus—which stated that no master or scholar of the Bohemian "nation" should defend these articles in their false, erroneous, or heretical sense.

Shortly after the first deliberation on Wycliffe's articles, Zbyněk Zajic of Hasenburg was elected Archbishop of Prague. A member of one of the most ancient Bohemian families, Zbyněk had—though long ordained a priest and for some time provost of the town of Melnik—devoted himself mainly to political and military matters, as was then so frequently the case with ecclesiastics of high descent. Though his ignorance has been exaggerated, he certainly possessed no profound knowledge of theology. He brought, however, to his new office a strong feeling of indignation against the immorality and dishonesty of the clergy of his archdiocese, and had, at least at first, a firm determination to remedy these evils by establishing a system of severer discipline among his subordinates. It is a striking proof of the great respect in which Hus was then held, both because of his pure and honourable life and because of his great learning, that the Archbishop's attention was immediately directed to him. "At the commencement of his rule," the Archbishop, as Hus afterwards recalled to his memory, "ordered him, whenever he noticed any irregularity contrary to the rules of the Church, to bring such irregularity to his (the Archbishop's) knowledge, either in person, or, in case of absence, by means of a letter."[1] The Archbishop gave a further proof of his confidence in Hus

[1] Palacký, *Documenta*.

when he appointed him one of the preachers before the synod of the diocese. These assemblies were held by Archbishop Zbyněk more frequently than by his predecessors; he no doubt thought that they would contribute to the reformation of his clergy, which he had so much at heart. Of the sermons preached before the synod by Hus, only few have been preserved, but they are sufficient to prove how mercilessly he censured the immorality, avarice, and haughtiness of the Bohemian clergy. These accusations, which were unfortunately but too well founded, caused many to become enemies of Hus, those in particular to whom Hus's words were specially applicable.

The amicable relations that at first existed between Hus and his Archbishop did not continue long. In 1408 the clergy of the city of Prague and of the archdiocese forwarded to the Archbishop a written statement complaining of Hus's preaching in the Bethlehem chapel. In this document—printed by Palacký—it was stated that Hus had, "in opposition to the decisions of the Holy Church and to the opinions of the holy fathers, and to the injury, shame, detriment, and scandal of the whole clergy and the people generally," declared heretics all those priests who received remuneration for the administration of the sacraments or for other ecclesiastical functions, whether such payment took place before or after the ceremony. Hus was further accused of having spoken strongly against the ecclesiastics who held numerous benefices. Hus indeed wrote an eloquent defence of his preaching, and certainly succeeded in proving that Archbishop Ernest of Prague had, when issuing an enactment against the avarice of the clergy in 1364, used language almost identical with his own. Hus was none the less deprived of his office of preacher before the synod.

It is important to note that this denunciation of Hus in no way accused him of having preached anything contrary to the dogmas of the Roman Catholic Church; up to the year 1409, indeed, no such charge was ever brought forward against him. For the present, the priests of the diocese only stated that Hus had shown extreme and imprudent zeal in his endeavours to reform the clergy; such endeavours necessarily met with the approbation of the worthier priests; the others could not, at any rate, openly oppose them.

Relations with the Archbishop were yet further embittered by a letter which Hus addressed to him in July 1408 in defence of Nicholas (or Abraham) Velenovic, a priest who had been accused of preaching Wycliffe's doctrine with regard to communion. As a Protestant divine, Dr. Lechler has truly remarked, this letter reaches the extreme limit of what is permissible to a priest when writing to his ecclesiastical superiors. At the end of his letter Hus addresses the Archbishop in these words: "Therefore, most reverend father, open your eyes inwardly and within, love the good, observe those who are evil, do not let the ostentatious and avaricious flatter you; rather let the humble and the friends of poverty find favour with you; oblige the indolent to work; do not hinder those who work steadfastly at the harvest of the Lord."[1] It was inevitable that the form, if not the contents, of this letter should cause offence. It is indeed a characteristic of Hus, that while always speaking of himself with extreme humility and almost exaggerating his petty failings, he yet uses authoritative,

[1] Palacký, *Documenta*.

not to say provocatory, language when he considers himself as defining "God's law."

The definitive rupture between Hus and the Roman Catholic Church, "the principal beginning of accusations and grievances against me," as Hus himself wrote, was brought on by events which had vast importance for the whole Christian world. The schism in the Western Church still continued, in spite of many efforts to effect a reconciliation between the two rival groups of cardinals and their respective leaders. France therefore decided no longer to recognise as legitimate either of the two claimants to the papal throne, Benedict XIII. and Gregory XII., and to remain neutral up to the time that a general meeting of the cardinals of both parties should have chosen a new pontiff. Bohemia was one of the countries that had hitherto recognised the "Roman Pope," Gregory XII., but King Wenceslas, no doubt honestly wishing to re-establish the unity of the Church, decided to follow the example of the King of France. He therefore brought the matter before Archbishop Zbyněk, and also consulted the university of Prague. The Archbishop immediately answered that he would never forsake the allegiance of Pope Gregory. At the university opinions differed. The Bohemian "nation," of which Hus was now the recognised leader, was strongly in favour of the king's proposition. The Bavarian and Saxon "nations," as well as the Polish one—which then consisted principally of Germans from Silesia—took the opposite view. At a general meeting held under the presidency of Henry of Baltenhagen, a German who was then rector, it was decided that the university should continue to recognise Gregory XII. as the legitimate Pope. Hus energetically defended the proposal that the university should declare to remain neutral up to the time that a new and legitimate Pope should have been chosen, and he thus incurred the particular enmity of the Archbishop. At the end of the year 1408 a decree was placarded in Bohemian and Latin on the doors of the churches of Prague, stating that Hus, "as a disobedient son of the holy mother, the Church," was forbidden to exercise any ecclesiastical functions. Hus addressed an eloquent letter to the Archbishop defending his conduct, but it made no impression on the mind of that ecclesiastic.

An important indirect result of the decision of the university was that a fundamental change in its organisation now took place. After the vote by which it had been decided to ignore the king's wishes, and to refuse to accept neutrality in the struggle between the two Popes, both parties at the university sent deputations to Kutna Hora (Kuttenberg), where Wenceslas and his court were then residing. The representatives of the Bohemian party, who were headed by Hus, no doubt hoped for a favourable reception, as they alone had maintained the views of the king with regard to the papal schism. They were, however, mistaken. The king received them very ungraciously, and even accused Hus and other Bohemian magisters of being the cause that Bohemia had acquired the evil reputation of being a heretical country. On the other hand, the king was most gracious to the German magisters, who had probably come to apologise for their opposition to the royal will, and he assured them that he would maintain all their privileges.

A complete change in the views of the ever-vacillating king took place in the following month. At that moment

Nicholas of Lobkovic, a man of learning, and, it is said, a friend of Hus, had obtained considerable influence over Wenceslas. As "supreme notary," or director of the Bohemian mines, Lobkovic resided at Kutna Hora, then an important mining centre, and he was thus thrown into constant contact with the king at this time. Under his influence, Wenceslas, in January 1409, published the "Decrees of Kutna Hora," which entirely changed the constitution of the university of Prague. As has already been mentioned, the university was divided into four nations, three of which—perhaps contrary to the intentions of Charles IV., the founder of the university —always voted together, and were jointly known as the German nation. The Bohemians were thus in their own country permanently in a minority. A complete change was effected by the decrees of Kutna Hora. The king stated that, "whereas the German nation, possessing no rights of citizenship in the kingdom of Bohemia, has hitherto held three votes" (at the university), "while the Bohemian nation, the lawful heiress of that kingdom, possessed and enjoyed but one, we consider it unjust and most improper that foreigners should enjoy in abundance the profits" (*i.e.* benefices, foundations, &c.) "of the natives, who consider themselves aggrieved by this deprivation, and we declare that the Bohemian nation shall, . . . according to the regulations existing in favour of the French at the university of Paris, and according to similar rules which exist in Lombardy and Italy, possess in future three votes at all councils, judgments, examinations, and other acts and dispositions of the university."[1] Four days later a decree of the king forbade all persons in Bohemia, both

[1] Palacký, *Documenta*.

ecclesiastics and laymen, to continue their allegiance to Pope Gregory.

All resistance to the king's will now ceased at the university. In the year of the publication of the decrees of Kutna Hora, all German professors and students, that is to say, all those members of the university who supported Pope Gregory, and were opposed to Church reform, left Prague. The university now became a stronghold of that party which was favourable to Church reform, as well as to the national aspirations of the Bohemian people. It was but natural that the reconstituted university should choose John Hus, the leader in the struggle, as its rector, though he had already held that office a few years before.

The position of Hus was now more assured and more prominent than at any previous period. His popularity with the Bohemian people, who attributed to him the change in the regulations of the university so favourable to their nationality, was greater than ever, and they flocked to his sermons in the Bethlehem chapel in even greater numbers than before. King Wenceslas was grateful to Hus for his aid in obtaining the neutrality of the university during the schism in the Church, and his consort, Queen Sophia, made no secret of her veneration for the great preacher whose sermons at Bethlehem she often attended. Archbishop Zbyněk, indeed, continued inimical to Hus, but circumstances rendered it for the moment difficult for him to harm the preacher at Bethlehem. The Council of Pisa had deposed both claimants to the papal throne, and had elected a new pontiff, who took the name of Alexander V., and who was recognised by the greatest part of Europe. The two previously elected Popes did not renounce their claims, and still found followers. The Archbishop of Prague, who still recognised Gregory, was therefore naturally without influence on Pope Alexander. It was thus for the moment fruitless that the Archbishop appointed an "inquisitor" who was to inquire into the complaints raised against Hus and his followers, and specially into the right of Hus to continue preaching at the Bethlehem chapel. Hus entirely ignored these proceedings, and some of his followers even brought before Pope Alexander a complaint against the conduct of the Archbishop, stating that he had raised false accusations against them. The matter went so far that Zbyněk was summoned to appear before the new pontiff.

On September 2, 1409, Archbishop Zbyněk—inconsistently, as Hus maintained—renounced the allegiance of Pope Gregory, and recognised Alexander as the legitimate pontiff. The reconciliation between the generally recognised Pope and the Archbishop of Prague had a marked influence on the destiny of Hus. The united strength of the Roman Church is now directed against him, and matters proceed much more rapidly. As early as December 20, 1409, a decree of Pope Alexander stated that, "through the action of the enemy of the human race, recently in the city of Prague, the kingdom of Bohemia, the marquisate of Moravia, and other provinces, the false opinions—savouring of heresy and division of the Church—once brought forward by the condemned heresiarch, John Wycliffe, have been fully circulated, particularly with regard to the sacrament of the altar."[1] The letter continues to declare that in future no sermons shall be preached except in "cathe-

---

[1] Palacký, *Documenta*.

drals, collegiate churches, parish churches, and churches belonging to monasteries." This was directly aimed at Hus, whose Bethlehem chapel fell under none of the categories mentioned above. The letter or decree ended by instructing the Archbishop to appoint four doctors of theology and two doctors of canon law, under whose advice he was to proceed against those who spread the heretical tenets referred to. The Archbishop was to oblige all such persons to recant their erroneous opinions, and to deliver up for destruction all MSS. of the works of Wycliffe which they might possess. Should they refuse to do this the Archbishop was not only to deprive them of all benefices that might be in their hands, but he was also to invoke the aid of the "secular arm" against them.

The papal decree, for reasons that are not known, only reached Prague in March of the following year, and was made public on the 18th of that month. Hus appealed to Pope Alexander, and again somewhat later to his successor, John XXIII., but both appeals remained without result. While awaiting the papal decision, Hus had, in company with some of his adherents, delivered up about two hundred volumes containing writings of Wycliffe; they declared that if it were proved that these writings contained matter contrary to the doctrine of the Church, they were prepared publicly to recant such errors.

Archbishop Zbyněk had, meanwhile, after consulting the doctors of theology and canon law, issued a decree forbidding all preaching except in the places specified by the papal command; at the same time he ordered that all the copies of Wycliffe's works that had been made over to the ecclesiastical authorities should be immediately burnt. It is probable that the decision of the Archbishop, which he published at a meeting of the synod of the archdiocese on June 16, was known before that day. On the same day, the 16th of June, the members of the university already protested against the intended burning of Wycliffe's works. They maintained that sufficient time had not elapsed since the writings of Wycliffe had been delivered over, and that it was impossible that a thorough examination of the theological tenets contained in them should already have taken place. They also stated that many of these writings had no connection with questions of dogma, but dealt with logic, philosophy, natural history, and similar matters. However, neither Hus's appeal to the Pope nor the declaration of the university, nor the appeal to King Wenceslas, in which that learned body begged that the burning of the books be at least deferred, was of any avail. On July 16 two hundred books containing writings of Wycliffe, some—as the contemporary chronicler tells us—beautifully bound, were solemnly burnt in the courtyard of the archiepiscopal palace, in the presence of the Archbishop, the members of the chapter, and many other priests. This measure was followed two days later by the solemn sentence of excommunication pronounced by the Archbishop against Hus and his adherents.

The burning of Wycliffe's works met with almost general disapproval in Prague. A chronicler, writing probably shortly after these events, tells us : "Instantly a great sedition and discord began. Some said that many other books besides those of Wycliffe had been burnt ; therefore the people began to riot; the courtiers of the king were incensed against the canons and priests;

many opprobrious songs against the Archbishop were sung in the streets."[1]

The rioting in Prague became so serious, that Wenceslas, who had been absent, returned hastily to his capital, and while ordering that the owners of the books of Wycliffe that had been burnt should be compensated, he forbade, under penalty of death, the singing of opprobrious songs, which had been one of the causes of the riots. Hus and his adherents were still confident that the Pope would, in consequence of their appeal, cancel the decree of the Archbishop. In the meantime they determined to defend publicly the orthodoxy of some of Wycliffe's works which the Archbishop had condemned. In the then usual manner a meeting of the university was convoked, before which Hus, on July 28, defended the orthodoxy of Wycliffe's treatise, *De increata, benedicta et venerabili Trinitate*. On the following days some of his adherents, before the same forum, defended other works of Wycliffe.[2] Hus also continued, in spite of the Archbishop's prohibition, to preach at the Bethlehem chapel, and his services were more crowded than ever. When Hus read to his audience a letter he had received from Richard Wyche,[3] an English adherent of Wycliffe, and in the name of the Church of Christ in Bohemia saluted the Church of Christ in England, more than ten thousand people are stated to have been present at the sermon.

The papal see had meanwhile entirely identified itself with Archbishop Zbyněk. Without entering into details regarding the character of John XXIII.—it cannot be

[1] *Staŕr Letopisove Ceští* (Ancient Bohemian Chronicles). See Chapter IV.
[2] Palacký, *Documenta*, gives the names of the speakers and the list of the works they defended.   [3] See later, page 131.

condemned more severely than was afterwards done by the Council of Constance—it is not surprising that the declared enemy of simony and of the corruption of the clergy found little sympathy with him. Cardinal Colonna, whom Pope John had authorised to give judgment on the Bohemian affairs, rejected the appeal of Hus and his followers to the papal court. That court at the same time expressed its entire approval of the conduct of the Archbishop, and enjoined on him to take immediate proceedings against Hus with the aid of the "secular arm." At the same time sentence of excommunication was passed on Hus, and the city of Prague was declared to be under interdict.

Though such attempts were obviously hopeless, endeavours were still made to mitigate the irritation of the papal court against Hus. King Wenceslas and his consort, as well as several of the most prominent Bohemian nobles, addressed strong remonstrances to Pope John and the Roman court, complaining of what they considered his exaggerated severity against Hus. Queen Sophia's letters were couched in very energetic language. She wrote: "An order contrary to Scripture, agitating the people and disturbing the order of our kingdom, has been published on the suggestion of those who are opposed to the preaching of the gospel. In consequence of this the preaching of the gospel has, except in monasteries and parish churches, been prohibited by the Archbishop of Prague, even in chapels that have been sanctioned by the apostolic see, under penalty of excommunication. Your Holiness well knows that the preaching of the Word of God should not be confined to certain places, but that, on the contrary, it should be allowed in hamlets, streets, houses—in fact everywhere according to the requirements of the people." The queen proceeds to request the Pope to withdraw his prohibition, and ends by stating : "We will not endure that the preaching of the Word of the Lord in our castles and cities should suffer such hindrance."[1] This interesting letter was undoubtedly written specially in the interest of the Bethlehem chapel, at which the queen was one of the most assiduous worshippers. These letters remained without result, and negotiations which took place on the initiative of King Wenceslas were also fruitless, though the Archbishop in the last months of his life seems to have been himself in favour of a compromise. A court of arbitration, composed principally of Bohemian nobles, met by wish of the king, but the desired reconciliation between Hus and the Archbishop was soon found to be impossible.

Archbishop Zbyněk died in September 1411, and was in the following month succeeded by Albert of Uničov, a Moravian who had formerly been court physician to King Wenceslas. Uničov is described to us as a man of conciliatory character, and this appears all the more probable from the fact that he was in great favour with King Wenceslas. The king had always wished that the Bohemians should settle their differences among themselves, and as far as possible without foreign intervention. This had indeed been the basis on which the recent negotiations had been conducted.

But neither the Archbishop nor any one else could at this moment have arrested the march of events that were rapidly approaching a crisis. A comparatively un-

[1] Palacký, *Documenta*.

HUS AND INDULGENCES

important event dispelled the last hopes of those who still hoped for an agreement.

King Ladislas of Naples still recognised Gregory XII. as Pope, and had therefore incurred the bitter enmity of Pope John XXIII. The latter decided on undertaking a crusade against the King of Naples, and caused a decree to be read in all churches promising all those who should contribute to the expenses of the intended expedition the same remission of sins that had been formerly granted to those who fought against the infidels in Palestine.

In May 1412, Wenceslas Tiem, Dean of Passau, arrived at Prague, and immediately began to collect money for the intended crusade. This caused great irritation among the population of Prague, then almost entirely favourable to Hus and his doctrines. Hus and his followers had already previously frequently denounced the system of indulgences, and they now renewed their attacks with increased vigour. A very stormy meeting of the members of the university took place on June 7, though the theological faculty had forbidden all bachelors of theology to attack the papal decree. Hus in an eloquent speech sharply attacked the practice of granting indulgences in the manner then usual at Rome. Of the contents of this speech we can form a certain judgment from a pamphlet on the same subject which Hus published about this time and which has been preserved. He emphatically maintained that priests had the right of remitting sins to those only who showed signs of repentance and penitence, but not merely on receipt of a sum of money. Hus's teaching was here very similar to that of Wycliffe, and his opposition to the crusade against the King of Naples recalls that of Wycliffe against the Flemish crusade of Henry Spencer, Bishop of Norwich.

Meanwhile the Theological Faculty of Prague again condemned as heretical the forty-five articles drawn from Wycliffe's works, now adding six more which were attributed to Hus; it was stated that they had been extracted from his speech against indulgences (on June 7) and from his pamphlet on the same subject. About the same time a considerable portion of the clergy of Prague forwarded to Pope John a written complaint against Hus. The author was a German, one Michael of Deutschbrod, also known as Michael de Causis, one of the most steadfast opponents of Hus and of Church reform. In this document Hus was accused of railing (*oblatrare*) against the clergy and against the papal indulgences, and also of having "by means of his writings spread his pestilential opinions through various districts of the kingdom of Bohemia, Poland, Hungary, and the marquisate of Moravia."[1] The consequence of these denunciations was a papal decree pronouncing the "aggravation" of the excommunication of Hus which had already been proclaimed by Cardinal Colonna in the previous year. Several of the former adherents of Hus, such as Stanislas of Znaym and Stephen Paleč, now abandoned his cause, and the latter afterwards became one of his most dangerous opponents at the Council of Constance.

The greatest part of the population of Prague, however, continued to be devoted to Hus, and the continued preaching in favour of indulgences caused disturbances in the city, particularly after three young men who had interrupted these sermons had been decapitated. Further rioting seemed certain, and it was probably the fear that

[1] Palacký, *Documenta*.

his person might be made a pretext for disorders that induced Hus willingly to accept King Wenceslas' suggestion that he should leave Prague for a short time. The king promised, during his absence, to endeavour to reconcile him with the ecclesiastical authorities. After publishing an "Appeal from the sentence of the Roman pontiff to the supreme judge Jesus Christ,"[1] Hus left Prague at the end of the year 1412. He first retired to Kozí Hrádek, a castle belonging to one of his adherents, John of Austi, situated near the spot where the town of Tabor was soon to arise. Afterwards Hus spent some time at the castle of Krakovec, which belonged to Lord Henry of Lažan, one of the courtiers of King Wenceslas, and a zealous adherent of Hus. In contradiction to the papal prohibition, Hus continued to preach, and large crowds assembled to listen to his sermons, which he often preached in the fields. He also remained in constant communication with his congregation at Prague, to whom he paid two short visits during his exile. He addressed to them several letters, which, next to those written while in prison at Constance, are the most valuable of all the letters of Hus that have been preserved. He did not limit his literary activity to these letters. Some of his most important works indeed now appeared in rapid succession. His most important Latin work, the treatise *De Ecclesia*, the principal cause of his condemnation at Constance, was written about this time. Of his Bohemian works the *Výklad* (Expositions) had been finished in November 1412, before he left Prague; but other important Bohemian works, such as the one entitled *The Daughter (Dcerka), or of the Knowledge of True Salvation*, and the treatise on "the

---

[1] Printed in Palacký, *Documenta*.

traffic in holy things" (*Svatokupectoi*), date from this period of exile.

Wenceslas had meanwhile attempted to redeem his promise to Hus. On the king's suggestion, a diocesan synod met at Prague in 1413, which attempted to reestablish unity among the Bohemian clergy. On this attempt failing, Wenceslas appointed a committee consisting of four ecclesiastics, who were to hear the views both of Hus's representatives and of his opponents. This attempt also failed, as was indeed inevitable, in consequence of the total divergence of the opinions of the disputants. Two of the opponents of Hus, Paleč and Stanislas of Znaym, even refused to appear before the committee after its second meeting, and were therefore banished from Bohemia by the indignant king, who still entertained the hope of restoring religious unity in his country.

It was, however, before a far larger forum that the case between the enemies and the partisans of Church reform was now to be brought. In consequence of the intolerable condition of the Western Church, which, since the Council of Pisa, possessed three rival pontiffs, the demand was raised on all sides that a General Council be summoned for the purpose of ending the schism. The influence of Sigismund, king of the Romans and king of Hungary, brother of Wenceslas of Bohemia, finally induced the reluctant Pope, John XXIII., to consent to the meeting of the Council; and it was decided that its members should assemble at Constance on November 1, 1414. The assembly was, as already mentioned, convoked for the purpose of ending the schism, but the fact that the discord in the Church of Bohemia had now become widely known in Europe naturally drew the attention of the Council also to the views of Hus and his adherents. King Sigismund suggested that Hus should attend the Council, and there develop his views, and at the same time vindicate the orthodoxy of the Bohemian nation, on which he as well as his brother Wenceslas laid great stress. Before Hus set out on his journey, King Sigismund offered him a letter of safe-conduct, which allowed him, according to the words of Professor Tomek, "to come unmolested to Constance, there have free audience, and return unharmed, should he not submit to the authority of the Council." It is not necessary to discuss here the various opinions as to the exact meaning of the letter of safe-conduct; the statement of Dr. Tomek, the greatest living authority with regard to Hus, may be considered as decisive. That the letter was not merely a guarantee that Hus should reach Constance in safety, is proved by the fact that he only received it after he had arrived there; still less can the remarks of Hus himself, who in his letters before leaving Bohemia expressed forebodings of coming doom, be used as an argument to prove that the letter of safe-conduct had little value. Hus was well aware that no official injunctions could ensure him against possible violence on the part of such fanatical enemies as Michael de Causis; nor could the possibility that the thesis "that no faith should be kept with heretics" might be used against him escape the sagacity of Hus.

Such apprehensions did not induce Hus to waver even for an instant in his decision to attend the Council; he felt assured that, whatever might subsequently be his fate, he would be allowed freely to expound his views before the assembled Council. After having addressed a letter of farewell to his pupil Martin, and another—one of the most precious that has been preserved—to his Bohemian friends, Hus, on October 11, 1414, started from the castle of Krakovec directly for Constance. In his company were the Bohemian noblemen Wenceslas of Duba, John of Chlum, and Henry of Lacenbok, who were instructed to assure his safety during his journey. Among Hus's companions also was Peter of Mladenovič, private secretary to Lord John of Chlum, who left a valuable record of Hus's last journey, his trial and death. Hus and his companions arrived at Constance on November 3, and he at first occupied lodgings in the house of a widow named Fida; the house, situated in the street now known as the Husgasse, near the Schnetzthor, is still shown to travellers. Hus confined himself to his room to avoid publicity, and also to prepare the speech he intended to deliver before the Council.

He was not, however, allowed to remain at liberty long. On the 28th of November he was arrested by order of Pope John XXIII., and at first confined for a few days under strict guard in the house of a canon of Constance. Thence he was conducted to a monastery of Dominican friars situated on an island in the Rhine, and confined in a dark and gloomy dungeon in immediate vicinity to a sewer. He remained here from December 6 to March 24, 1415. Endeavours were made to justify the arrestation of Hus by the totally unfounded assertion that he had attempted to escape from Constance in disguise. Even the writers most hostile to Hus now admit that there was no truth in this rumour.

As might have been expected from the nature of his prison, Hus became seriously ill, and was for some time in danger of his life. His Bohemian friends had meanwhile protested energetically against his imprisonment, but their attempts to rescue him from his dungeon remained without result. It was hoped that Sigismund, who arrived at Constance on Christmas Day (1414), would interfere in favour of Hus, but though he at first expressed some indignation, this led to no consequences. From the beginning of January of the following year, Sigismund granted the Council full liberty of decision with regard to Hus's fate. It is, indeed, more than probable that during the last months of Hus's trial the king was in favour of his execution, hoping that this event would intimidate the Bohemians.

The Pope had meanwhile appointed a committee, consisting of three bishops, for the purpose of undertaking a preliminary examination of the teaching of Hus. The commissioners examined numerous witnesses, all of whom were ordered to take their oaths in the presence of Hus. Thus, on one of the days when his illness was at its worst, fifteen witnesses were consecutively introduced into his prison. Hus demanded that a legal adviser should be allowed him, but this was refused him on the plea that it was illegal that any one should afford aid to a heretic. It may be noted that the condemnation of Hus had been decided on long before his three days' trial in June 1415, perhaps even, as some writers have conjectured, as early as in the previous November, when he was arrested. As soon as Hus had somewhat recovered, the act of accusation—mainly the work of Paleč and Michael de Causis—was brought to his knowledge. The accusation, consisting of forty-two articles, was principally founded on statements contained in the Latin treatise *De Ecclesia;* the last articles only dealt with statements extracted from other works of Hus. According to Mladenovič, the authors of the accusation "had chosen their quotations from the treatise (*De Ecclesia*), falsely and unfairly abbreviating some in the beginning, some in the middle, and some at the end, and inventing matter that was not contained in the book." Hus immediately published his defence, proving that he had taken many of the passages in his works that were attacked from the writings of Augustine, Gregory the Great, Bishop Grossetête of Lincoln, and other writers of unimpeached orthodoxy; he also complained that the quotations from his book were incorrect.

New material for accusations against Hus had been meanwhile brought forward. After his departure from Prague, one of his pupils (Magister Jacobellus of Mies[1]) had defended the necessity of communion in the two kinds, afterwards the distinctive doctrine of the Hussites. The followers of Hus at Prague appealed to him, but he confined himself to declaring in his letters that communion in the two kinds was permissible. When, however, the Council of Constance had, on June 15—after the last day of Hus's trial and a few days before his death—entirely forbidden communion in the two kinds to laymen, Hus went somewhat farther. He declared the prohibition of communion in the two kinds to be in direct contradiction to the Gospel,[2] and advised those among his friends who were uncertain with regard to the new teaching of Jacobellus, no longer to oppose it, as unity among the Bohemians was necessary in view of the dangers that, as Hus foresaw, would shortly menace the country.

---

[1] See Chapter IV.

[2] The passage which Hus had in view is in the Gospel of St. Matthew, chap. xxvi. vers. 26-28.

The Council of Constance had in March 1415 deposed Pope John XXIII., and the authority of the commissioners whom he had appointed to judge Hus ceased, while the decree of imprisonment issued by the Pope also became invalid. Sigismund, to whom the guardians of Hus applied for orders, contented himself with handing the prisoner over to the custody of the Bishop of Constance, by whose order he was now imprisoned in the castle of Gottlieben, not far from Constance. He remained there from March 24 to June 5, and was held in yet severer custody than in the Dominican convent. His feet were fettered with chains, and at night his hands were also fastened to the wall by a chain. All intercourse with his friends was forbidden, and we have therefore no letters from Hus written at Gottlieben, while he had been allowed to write when in confinement in the Dominican monastery.

Having passed judgment on the Pope, the Council now devoted its attention to questions of dogma. On May 5 the forty-five articles of Wycliffe, that have been so often mentioned, were again condemned at a plenary meeting of the Council. This may be said to have decided the fate of Hus, for the identity of many opinions advanced in his treatise *De Ecclesia* with Wycliffe's views was known to all. No agreement whatever was, indeed, possible between Hus and the members of the Council; for while Hus maintained that he had been summoned to the Council for the purpose of freely expounding his views, the Council now held even more decidedly than at first that their mission as far as Hus was concerned was limited to hearing his recantation of all the opinions that had rightly or wrongly been attributed to him, and then deciding what punishment he should receive.

H

It is probably mainly due to the energetic remonstrances of the Bohemian nobles who were present at the Council that Hus was at least allowed to appear before that assembly. His prison was again changed, and he was now conducted to a Franciscan monastery at Constance, where he spent the last weeks of his life. On June 5 he appeared for the first time before the Council. "When Hus attempted to speak he was interrupted, and when he was silent the cry arose, 'He has admitted his guilt.'"[1] As Hus afterwards wrote: "They almost all screamed at me, as did the Jews against Christ. . . . Many exclaimed, 'He must be burnt;' among them I heard the voice of Michael de Causis."

This meeting of the Council did not last long. The more moderate prelates, no doubt, realised how injurious to their own cause such violence was. At the second and third hearing of Hus (on June 7 and 8) the proceedings of the Council had a more orderly character. The questions with regard to the heretical opinions contained in the treatise *De Ecclesia* and to Hus's views on communion—on which subject an English prelate declared his doctrine was in conformity with that of the Church—were again thoroughly discussed. The whole proceedings can, however, scarcely be termed a trial, and the conviction of the Bohemian reformer was a foregone conclusion.

Four weeks, however, contrary to the expectations of Hus, passed from the date of his last trial to the day of his execution. Repeated attempts were made to induce him to recant, and several members of the Council visited him in prison for this purpose. On one occasion, as Hus writes, "Michael de Causis, poor man, accompanied

---

[1] Mladenovič in Palacký, *Documenta*.

the representatives of the Council, and while I was with them, said to my guardians, 'By the grace of God we shall soon burn this heretic, and I have spent many florins for this purpose.' Be it known to you that in writing this I do not desire vengeance of him; that I leave to God. Indeed, I pray earnestly for him."

All attempts to obtain a recantation from Hus having failed, there was now no reason for further delay. On July 6, Hus was brought for the last time before the Council. The various accusations against him, some founded entirely on falsehoods, were then read out to him, and he was informed of his sentence. It was decreed that his books, both Latin and Bohemian, should be destroyed, and Hus, as "a manifest heretic," delivered to the secular authorities for punishment. After the ignominious ceremonies of degradation and deconsecration had been performed, Hus was immediately handed over to the authorities of the free town of Constance to receive the customary punishment of heresy. The horrible form of death applied by Nero to the early Christians, when his Palatine gardens were lighted with live torches, had unhappily in the Christian world been adopted as the recognised punishment of those whose religious views differed from those held by the majority of the community to which they belonged. Hus was therefore immediately led forth to the stake by the soldiers of the municipality of Constance.

The execution of Hus is an event of such world-wide importance that it is not surprising that legends concerning his last moment, founded on no contemporary evidence, soon sprang up. Such are the words, "O sancta simplicitas," attributed to Hus when he saw an old woman collecting fagots for his stake, and his pretended prophecy of the advent of a successor (Luther).

A short extract from the work of Mladenovič, which contains a minute description of the last moments and the death of Hus, may be of interest. Mladenovič writes: "When he (Hus) had arrived at the place of torture, he began on bent knees, with his arms extended and his eyes lifted to heaven, to recite psalms with great fervour, particularly 'Have mercy upon me, O God,' and 'In Thee, O Lord, do I put my trust.' He repeated the verse 'Into Thine hand I commit my spirit,' and it was noticed by those standing near that he prayed joyfully and with a beautiful countenance. The place of torture was among gardens in a certain field on the road which leads from Constance to the castle of Gottlieben. Some of the laymen who were present said, 'We do not know what he has formerly said or done, but we now see and hear that he prays and speaks holy words.' ... Rising from his prayers by order of the lictor (*i.e.* soldier or town official), he said with a loud and intelligible voice, so that he could be heard by his (followers), 'Lord Jesus Christ, I will bear patiently and humbly this horrible, shameful, and cruel death for the sake of Thy Gospel and of the preaching of Thy Word.' ... When a rusty chain was placed round his neck, he said, smiling to the lictors, 'Our Lord Jesus Christ, my Redeemer, was bound with a harder and heavier chain, and I, a poor wretch, do not fear to be bound with this chain for His sake.' ... When the lictors lighted the pile, the magister first sang with a loud voice, 'Christ, Son of the living God, have mercy on me,' and then again, 'Christ, Son of the living God, have mercy on me.' When he began again, now singing,

'Who art born from the Virgin Mary,' the wind blew the flames in his face, and still silently praying and moving his lips and head he expired in the Lord. The space of time when he had become silent, but still moved before dying, was that required to recite rapidly two or at the utmost three Paternosters."

The works of Hus, both Latin and Bohemian, are very numerous, and in recent times they have again attracted considerable notice. Still a complete modern edition of the works of Hus has not yet appeared, and the bibliography of the existent writings of the Bohemian reformer—for many of his works have entirely perished —is still very deficient. A complete edition of the existing Latin works of Hus was published in Nuremberg in 1558, but it omits several works that Hus is known to have written, and includes works by Matthew of Janov and others. The various Bohemian works were also frequently printed both at Nuremberg and in Bohemia itself up to the beginning of the seventeenth century. I shall first mention the Latin works of Hus, but devote greater space to his Bohemian writings. This is not only in accordance with the general plan of this book, but also justified by the fact that the Latin writings of Hus have less interest, and particularly less originality, than those written in his own language. This applies even to the great treatise *De Ecclesia*, which, however, cannot be passed over, as it had so decisive an influence on the fate of Hus.

The earliest Latin works of Hus are in complete conformity with the teaching of the Roman Church. Such a work is the treatise *De omni Sanguine Christi Glorificata*, written during the time when Hus enjoyed the favour of the Archbishop, and probably by his order. Hus had been sent with two other priests to investigate so-called miracles which, as was stated, had been performed by a relic containing the blood of Christ, which was exhibited at Wilsnack, a small town on the Elbe. In his treatise Hus asserted that it was impossible that the blood of Jesus Christ should be materially contained in any one spot. It was, he said, only to be found in Holy Communion.

Somewhat later—about the year 1410—the tone of Hus's writings changes. He no longer writes as an unconditional adherent of the Church of Rome, and the influence of Wycliffe's ideas gradually becomes evident. Hus's writings, still mainly Latin, are numerous at this period; they deal with then current theological controversies, and it would be of little interest to enumerate their titles. One of these treatises, addressed to a countryman of Wycliffe, entitled *De Libris Hæreticorum Legendis; Replica contra Anglicum Joannem Stokes*, deals almost entirely with Wycliffe's doctrine. John Stokes, a licentiate of law, was a member of an English embassy which was sent to Bohemia by King Henry IV. It was rumoured at Prague that Stokes had during his stay there stated that Wycliffe was in England considered a heretic. Hus immediately challenged the Englishman to a public disputation before the university in the then customary manner. On the refusal of Stokes to attend the meeting, Hus yet delivered his speech in defence of Wycliffe before the university, and afterwards founded his pamphlet principally on the contents of the speech. Many of the minor Latin writings of Hus are indeed based on speeches delivered before the university, and even in his larger Bohemian writings he has often introduced large portions of his sermons.

THE TREATISE "DE ECCLESIA"

Of Hus's Latin works, as already mentioned, the treatise *De Ecclesia* requires particular notice. The work, written when Hus was exiled from Prague, and probably finished in the year 1413, is to a great extent a transcript of Wycliffe's work on the same subject, and has therefore little literary interest. But neither the events of the life of Hus nor the ideas expounded in his Bohemian works are intelligible without some knowledge of the treatise *De Ecclesia*. The Roman Catholic hierarchy, far more powerful and far less dependent on public opinion in the fifteenth century than in the present day, could not but see that—independently of all dogmatic differences of opinion—the acceptation of views such as those contained in the treatise *De Ecclesia* must necessarily produce a fundamental change in the organisation of the Church.

The keynote of the treatise *De Ecclesia*[1] is Hus's peculiar doctrine with regard to predestination. He divides all men into two classes, those who are—either conditionally or unconditionally—predestined (*predestinati*) to eternal bliss, and those who are "foreknown" (*presciti*) to damnation. The mass of the *predestinati* form the true Holy Catholic Church,[2] but the Church as at present constituted includes the *presciti* as well as the *predestinati*. Of the true Church, Christ is the only Head. As man He is "Head of the Church within it" (*caput intrinsecum*), as God He is "its Head without it" (*caput extrinsecum*). Christ is the true Roman Pontiff, the High Priest, and the Bishop of Souls. The Apostles did not call themselves "Holy

---

[1] I have borrowed this summary of the contents of the treatise *De Ecclesia* from my *Bohemia: an Historical Sketch*.

[2] See later, page 125.

Father" or "Head of the Church," but servant of God and servant of the Church. A change came with the "donation of Constantine" (that singular fiction which played so large a part in the theological controversies of the Middle Ages). Since that time the Pope has considered himself as head (*capitaneus*) of the Church and Christ's vicar upon earth. It is, however, according to Hus, not certain that the Pope is Christ's successor in this world. He is then only Christ's representative and the successor of St. Peter, and the cardinals are only then the successors of the Apostles when they follow the examples of faith, modesty, and love which the former gave. Many Popes and cardinals have not done this, and, indeed, many saintly men who never were Popes were truer successors of the Apostles than, for instance, the present Pope (John XXIII.). St. Augustine did more for the welfare of the Church than many Popes, and studied its doctrines more profoundly than any cardinal from the first to the last. If Pope and cardinals give their attention to worldly affairs, if they scandalise the faithful by their ambition and avarice, then they are successors not of Christ, not of Peter, not of the Apostles, but of Satan, of Antichrist, of Judas Iscariot. Returning to his former point, it is not certain, Hus continues, that the Pope is really the head of the Church; he cannot even be sure that he is not *prescitus*, and therefore no member of the true Church at all. St. Peter erred even after he had been called by Christ. Pope Leo was a heretic, and Pope Gregory was but recently condemned by the Council of Pisa. It is a popular fallacy to imagine that a Pope is necessary to rule the Church. We must be thankful to God that He gave us His only Son to rule over the Church, and He would be able to direct it even if there were no temporal Pope, or if a woman occupied the papal throne.¹ As with the Pope and the cardinals, so with the prelates and the clergy generally. There is a double clergy, that of Christ and that of Antichrist. The former live according to the law of God, the latter seek only worldly advantage. Not every priest is a saint, but every saint is a priest. Faithful Christians are therefore great in the Church of God, but worldly prelates are among its lowest members, and may indeed, should they be *presciti*, not be members of the Church at all.

The Latin letters of Hus will be mentioned later in connection with those written in Bohemian.

Of greater literary interest than the Latin works of Hus are those written in his own language. The latter are written in a more independent and popular manner, and it is on them that his value as a writer depends. That Hus was a strong Bohemian patriot is, I hope, evident even from this short sketch of his life. Almost his first sermon referred to the oppression of his countrymen by the Germans, and no one more energetically aided the Bohemians in their endeavours to secure the control over the national university. Yet Hus was by no means a national fanatic or a hater of Germans, as has been so often stated. It is sufficient to refer to his often-quoted words: "If I knew a foreigner of any country who loved God more and strove for the good more than my own brother, I would love him more than my brother. Therefore good English priests are dearer to me than faint-hearted Bohemian ones, and a good German is dearer to me than a bad brother."²

---

¹ An allusion to the story of Pope Joan.
² *Výklad*, *i.e.* "Exposition of the Ten Commandments," chap. xliii.

Hus, like all Bohemian patriots, entertained a warm affection for the national language. One of his earliest writings deals with the correct spelling of the Bohemian language, and the diacritical signs still used in Bohemian are mainly an invention of Hus. He was also strongly opposed to the introduction of foreign words into the language, and refers to this subject frequently in his "Exposition of the Ten Commandments." In that work he sharply attacks the citizens of Prague who interspersed their Bohemian speech with numerous German words, and compares them to the "Jews who had married wives of Ashdod, and whose children spoke half in the speech of Ashdod."

Hus's merits as regards the development of his language are also very great. That language had indeed already, principally by Štitný, been raised to a level that rendered it available for the exposition of theological and philosophical matters. But the style of Hus contrasts favourably with that of his predecessors by its greater facility and simplicity. This may partly be attributed to the fact that Hus, particularly during the time of his exile from Prague, associated much with the humbler classes of the people, who, knowing no language but their own, naturally spoke it very purely and without interpolations from other languages. This spoken language was adopted by Hus for his writings. He indeed himself writes at the end of the *Postilla*, "That he who will read (my writings) may understand my Bohemian, let him know that I have written as I usually speak."

As already stated, the bibliography of Hus is as yet very uncertain, and it is not easy to fix the exact dates of his works. It may, however, be generally stated that his earliest Bohemian writings were composed in the years from 1406 to 1410, that his most important works in that language date from the last years of his life (1412–1415), and that the period of his exile from Prague was that of his greatest literary activity.

The earliest important Bohemian works of Hus are a series of Expositions (*Vÿklad*) dealing consecutively of Faith, the Ten Commandments, and the Lord's Prayer. Each Exposition is followed by a shorter, more condensed treatise dealing with the same subject as the longer one that precedes. Of these Expositions the first one, dealing of Faith, has most interest. It consists of a continuous comment on the different articles of the Apostle's creed. Hus writes: " We believe that the twelve Apostles, immediately after Christ's ascension to heaven, composed this creed. And as there were then twelve Apostles, besides Paul and Barnabas, who were called after the ascension of Jesus, thus, according to general opinion, each article was expounded by one particular Apostle. But be it known to you, that the learned do not agree as to what particular article each Apostle expounded." Hus then proceeds to attribute to each Apostle the exposition and defence of one of the articles, obviously following the method then usual at the theological disputations at universities in which he so frequently took part. In Chapter XVIII. the defence of the tenth article, which refers to the Holy Catholic Church, is attributed to St. Simon. It is interesting as containing some of the very distinctive ideas of Hus. He writes: " Every Christian must believe in the Holy Catholic Church. The reason is, that every Christian must love Christ, who is the husband of that Church, and that Church is Christ's spouse. . . . And as no one will honour his mother if he has no knowledge of her, therefore it is very necessary to know the Holy Church through faith, for ignorance of the Church causes many errors among the people. Therefore be it known to you that the first Bohemian who translated the Greek word *ecclesia* misunderstood that word; therefore he foolishly rendered it by the word 'church' or 'chapel,' as if he believed that the bride of Christ was a church made of stone or a chapel made of wood. But had he translated the word *ecclesia* by 'congregation,' then so many would not have erred. Others, again, err, saying that the Pope is the Holy Church; others, that it is the Cardinals with the Pope; while others, again, say all priests together, and yet others (say) all Christians together, constitute the Church.

"Therefore be it known to you that all men from Adam to the last man form one congregation, which God has divided into two; one division has been chosen (for salvation) from eternity, the other from eternity has been rejected, and it is known to God only which (division) each man belongs to. The first division is the universal community of saints, the second is the universal community of the damned. There can be no higher Church, according to God's will, than the first-named (community). It contains all the good, and the other all the evil, and yet these two (divisions) constitute one community, one assembly, just as sheep and goats form one herd, although the sheep are always in a way divided from the goats, and these from them. Therefore though *ecclesia* sometimes signifies a church of wood or stone, sometimes the Pope with the Cardinals, sometimes the priesthood generally, sometimes the whole community of Christians—as the Church of Prague may signify all Bohemians or a community only of good

Christians—yet the Holy Catholic Church is the community of all those who have been chosen; that Church is called the bride of Christ, of whom it is written in the verses of Solomon, 'I am His bride, He has adorned me with a crown.'"

The other Expositions are inferior to the one just mentioned, both as regards their interest and the style in which they are written. The Exposition of the Ten Commandments is in its teaching generally in conformity with the Roman Church; only in occasional passages are the opinions peculiar to Hus evident. After dealing generally of the commandment "Thou shalt not kill," Hus discusses in a separate chapter its application to members of the clergy. It must be remembered that Hus's time was an age of warlike pontiffs and of bishops who commanded armies. Incidentally this chapter throws strong light on Hus's very elevated and ideal view of the duties of the priestly order. It is to this, no doubt, that his strong animadversions on the behaviour of some members of that order (for which he has been severely censured by hostile writers) should be largely attributed. The Chapter (XLVIII.) begins thus: "As in our times bishops and priests wage war, it is good for us to know whether it is fit that they should go to war and thus kill their fellow-creatures. It appears fit to some, firstly, from this reason, that the priests of the old law fought bravely according to God's commandment; why then should not the priests of the new law fight, who have to defend their faith as the others did, and a much higher one? Secondly (you say), the Pope goes to war, and gives the other bishops power to go to war, and to speak against this is heresy; and who speaks thus will become a heretic if he obstinately persists in it.

Thirdly, St. Peter the Apostle fought bodily, when on Maundy Tuesday, being already a priest, he cut off the ear of Malchus. The fourth reason is that the priests, and specially the Pope, have two swords, the spiritual and the temporal one; so also had the Apostles when they said to Christ, 'Lord, behold here are two swords. And He said unto them, It is enough.'[1] The fifth reason is this: many priests are strong, and that strength were given them in vain, could they not use it for fighting; why, therefore, should they not fight? The sixth reason is: if bishops did not fight with temporal arms, the Church would be in an evil state; for laymen would lay hands on priests, rob them and beat them; who would then wish to be a priest?

"But our Saviour Jesus, King and Bishop at the same time, is the best mirror in which we should seek for wisdom; for every action of His is a lesson for us, as St. Augustine has said."

Hus then proceeds to refute the arguments enumerated above, depending mainly on the example of Christ. The passage, written with singular lucidity and penetration, is unfortunately too long for quotation. Here, as in many places, Hus speaks strongly of the pride and arrogance of the clergy.

At the end of the chapter Hus addresses a warning to the clergy. Should they persist in their pride, "you will," he writes, "be judged and condemned, and your prayer will be as a sin. Your days will be short, and another will take your place. O priest, give up your pride, be meek like Jesus, and you will be glorified like He (was)! Suffer insult, robbery, abuse, blows. Be

[1] St. Luke xxii. 38.

ready to die for Christ, and give up warfare, which is a very uncertain path to salvation."

The treatise entitled *Dcerka* (Daughter), also known as the treatise "on the true road to salvation," dates from about the same time as the Expositions. It was addressed to some pious ladies who lived in common in a house near the Bethlehem chapel, and to whom Hus also wrote a letter, which has been preserved. The treatise has been called the Daughter, from the fact that each of the ten chapters begins with the words, "Listen, daughter, and see, and incline thine ear." In a short preface Hus very clearly explains the purpose of the book. He writes: "Listen, daughter, who hast promised Christ (to retain) virginity. Listen, daughter, and incline your ear, and know that I wish you to know yourself, knowing in whose similitude you were created; secondly (I wish) you to know your conscience; thirdly, the wretchedness of this world; fourthly, the temptations of our earthly existence; fifthly, the three enemies (the body, the world, and the devil); the sixth point on which I insist is that you should truly do penance; the seventh, that you should value the dignity of your soul; the eighth, that you should assiduously look to the coming judgment; the ninth, that you should value the eternal life; the tenth, that you should love our Lord God more than anything." Hus then deals with each of these points in one of the ten chapters of the book.

Somewhat later than the Expositions, and the Daughter, Hus published his celebrated treatise, *O Savtokupectví*, on "traffic in holy things," or simony, which he completed on September 2, 1413. This valuable book is written in a manner similar to that of the works mentioned above, but the polemical tendency is here yet more evident, for Hus is here treating of the great plague-spot of his time. The constant note of just indignation renders the book very striking, and it would —as Mr. Wratislaw has truly remarked—well bear translation as a whole. I shall, from want of space, be unable to give more than one quotation. In Chapter IV. Hus deals with the question, Can a Pope be guilty of simony? He writes: "Let us see if it is possible for a Pope to be a simoniac. Some say it is impossible, for he is the lord of the whole world, who is entitled to take what he wishes and do what he wishes. Therefore is he the most holy father whom sin cannot touch? Now, you must know that many Popes were heretics, and generally bad, and they were deprived of the papal dignity. Therefore be not in doubt that the Pope can be a simoniac. And if some one maintain that he cannot commit simony or any deadly sin, then he must desire to raise him higher than St. Peter or the other Apostles. And to the argument that he (the Pope) is the lord of the whole world, who may take what he will and do what he will, I will answer that there is but one Lord of the whole world who cannot sin, and whose right it is to rule and do as He will, and that Lord is the Almighty God. And further, if, according to the argument, it is said that the Pope is the most holy father, whom sin cannot touch, I deny this; for one only is our most Holy Father, the Lord God, whom sin cannot touch."

After maintaining that it is possible for a Pope to be a simoniac, Hus continues thus: "Let us see in what manner he (the Pope) can be a simoniac. He can be so, firstly, if he desires the papal dignity for the sake of riches and of worldly advantage. No rank in Christendom, indeed, is nearer to a fall. For if he (the Pope) does not follow Christ and Peter in his way of life more than others (do), then he should be called not a successor, but an adversary of the Apostles. Therefore every one who strives for this dignity for the advantage of his person or for worldly honours is infected with simony. The second manner of committing simony consists in the various regulations which he (the Pope) issues for his bodily advantage and contrary to God's law, perhaps not openly, but they are regulations that may lead to something contrary to God's law. And is it not contrary to God's regulations that the Pope should decree that his cooks, porters, equerries, footmen, should have first claim on the most important benefices, even in lands of which they do not know the language? And again, that no one can announce anything (in church) if he has not paid down money, and whatever similar arrangements may be made. The third manner in which a Pope can commit simony consists in appointing bishops or rectors for the sake of money; and that case has been made quite clear to us recently, when many thousands of florins were paid down for the Archbishopric of Prague."[1]

At the end of the same chapter Hus refers to the question of indulgences, which from his time to that of Martin Luther was ever before the Christian world. He writes: "With regard to the giving indulgences for money, St. Peter has sufficiently shown that they are worthless when he refused to give for money to Simon

---

[1] This refers to the allegation that Albík of Uničov, the successor of Archbishop Zbyněk, had paid a large sum for his investiture with the Archbishopric of Prague.

the power to lay his hands on people, so that they might receive the gift of the Holy Ghost; no, the Apostles laid their hands on the people, not for money, but gratuitously for their salvation; obeying the words of their Saviour, who said, 'Freely ye have received, freely give.' And thus they worthily received the Holy Ghost, for the Apostles were worthy bishops, and the people who truly believed truly repented their sins."

The last of the great works of Hus, and also the last one which I shall mention, is the *Postilla*, which Hus finished about the month of September 1413. It may be considered more popular in manner than his other Bohemian works, and, written so shortly before his death, it was long revered as the testament, or the "last will," of the great Bohemian divine. The book consists of expositions, or, as perhaps they should rather be called, sermons, explaining the evangel of each Sunday in the year. The Bible being then very scarce in Bohemia, the text from the Bible which is referred to precedes in every case the exposition or reading (Čtenie), as Hus himself worded it. The indignation against the corruption of the Roman Church, which becomes more accentuated in each successive work of Hus, finds here its strongest expression. "The evil priests," he writes, "do not tell the people that Christ said, 'If you do not repent your sins you will all perish.' They have so obscured the truth, which is Christ, that preachers mention the Pope more than Christ, and they praise and defend the institution of papacy more than the law of our Lord Jesus Christ. Therefore are His faithful sons oppressed in the lands; for in Bohemia, in Moravia, in Meissen, in England, and elsewhere there is much suffering, as I know. They murder, torture, and curse faithful priests, and it is useless to appeal to Rome; there indeed is the summit of the wickedness of Antichrist, that is, pride, lewdness, avarice, and simony; thus has simony and avarice poured from Rome into Bohemia."

Of more general interest than any other work of Hus are the collections of his Latin and Bohemian letters, and they are perhaps his only writings that will appeal strongly to modern readers. They also, more clearly than any other work, bring out the real individuality of the great Bohemian reformer. His sincere and unostentatious piety, his sometimes almost childlike simplicity, his very touching humility, the warm friendship of which he assures his friends, the unconditional forgiveness which he extends to his enemies, all these appear very clearly in these letters, in which Hus never writes *ex cathedra*. I nowhere more regret that limited space will oblige me to restrict my quotations. The letters of Hus that have been preserved extend from July 1408 to within a few days of his death. Those written while in exile from Prague and those from prison at Constance have the greatest value. Of the earlier letters a Latin one, addressed to "Master Richard the Englishman," dating from the year 1410, deserves notice. Though it is usually stated that the family name of Hus's correspondent was "Fitz," it appears very probable that the person addressed was Richard Wyche, a chaplain who was about this time accused of being a Lollard, and who was—according to Foxe—burnt for the same cause in 1439. Richard Wyche had sent a letter to Hus and the Bohemians, admonishing them to remain steadfast in the faith. In his answer Hus writes: "Preaching before nearly ten thousand people, I said, 'See, beloved brethren, what interest in your salvation faithful preachers in foreign countries take, they who are ready to shed out their whole heart, if only they can preserve us in the law of Christ,' and I added, 'Our most beloved brother Richard, the associate of Master John Wycliffe in his evangelical work, has written you such a comforting letter, that even had I no other written assurance, I should be ready to risk my life for Christ's Gospel, and I will do so with the help of our Lord Jesus Christ!' The faithful of Christ were so inflamed by this letter that they begged me to translate it into the language of our country.

"I do not know what further I should write to your reverence. I am not able to instruct those who are far more learned than I; by what words can one who is weaker comfort those who are stronger soldiers of Christ? What, then, shall I say? You have taken all words of Christian instruction from my mouth. It only remains for me to beg of you help by means of prayer, and to render thanks for all the good which, through your labours and by the help of Jesus Christ, Bohemia has received from blessed (*benedicta*) England."

Hus's letters from exile, as already mentioned, were very numerous. During his absence the adherents of the papal party endeavoured to suppress the religious services in the Bethlehem Chapel, and some Germans had even made an attempt to destroy the chapel. In a Bohemian letter addressed to the citizens of Prague Hus refers to this matter: "God be with you, dear sirs and masters," he writes. "I beg of you firstly to consider this matter before God, to whom great wrong is done; for they wish to suppress His holy word, to destroy a chapel that is useful for [the teaching of] the word of God, and thus to frustrate the salvation of the people; secondly, consider the insult to your land, your nation, or race. In the third place, only consider the shame and wrong which undeservedly is done to yourselves. Fourthly, consider and endure cheerfully that the devil rages against you and Antichrist snarls at you, for he will not harm you if you are lovers of God's truth. Indeed he has raged against me for many years, and yet I trust to God he has not harmed a hair on my head; rather has my happiness and content increased." The letter ends with these words: "Therefore, considering these things, and placing truth and the praise of God foremost and living worthily in charity, let us resist the lie of Antichrist to the end; for we have with us as a helper our Almighty Saviour, whom no one can vanquish, and who will not desert us as long as we do not desert Him; He will then give us the eternal reward. . . . I have written this down for you, as I cannot well come to you, so that the priests who endeavour to stop the religious services may not harm your minds."

Many letters written by Hus at Constance have been preserved; some date from the time when he was still at liberty, others from the period when he was imprisoned in the Dominican monastery, and afterwards in that of the Franciscans. During his stay at Gottlieben he was, as already mentioned, entirely prohibited from writing. In the first of the letters written from the dungeon in the Dominican monastery addressed to the citizens of Prague, and dated January 19, 1415, Hus refers to the severe illness which had befallen him in consequence of the unhealthy condition of his prison. The letter, which is written in Bohemian, begins thus: "May the Lord God be with you that you may persevere in your resistance to evil, to the devil, to the world, and to the flesh.

"Beloved brethren, I write to you while sitting in prison, but I am not ashamed, for I suffer hopefully for the sake of the Lord God who has graciously visited me with a severe illness and has again restored me to health, and who has permitted that those should become my bitter enemies to whom I have done much good and whom I have sincerely loved.[1] I beg of you to pray for me to the Lord God, that He may deign to be with me; for it is on Him and on your prayers that I rely to remain unto death in His grace. If the Lord deigns now to call me to Him, may His holy will be fulfilled; and if He deigns to return me to you, then also be His holy will fulfilled! Verily I am now much in want of help; but I know that God will submit me to no misfortune or temptation except such as are for my own and for your benefit, so that having been tried and found steadfast we may obtain a great reward. . . . I have no one to advise me except our merciful Lord Jesus, who said to His faithful: I will give you a mouth and wisdom, which all your adversaries shall not be able to resist. Dearly beloved, remember that I have worked with you with great devotion, and that I am anxious for your salvation even now when I am in prison and suffering grievous persecution.

Want of space obliges me to quote but from one other letter of Hus, written in prison, though they all well

[1] This refers to Stephen Paleč and other former adherents of Hus who had deserted the cause of Church reform.

deserve to be better known. This is the letter written on June 10th, two days after his trial before the Council had ended. Hus was then in expectation of immediate death, though, as already stated, attempts were still made to obtain his recantation, and his execution only took place on July 6th. The letter, also written in Bohemian, is addressed "To the whole Bohemian nation." Hus writes: "Faithful in God, men and women, rich and poor, I beg and entreat you to love the Lord God, praise His word, hear it gladly, and live according to it. Cling, I beg you, to the divine truth, which I have preached to you according to God's law. I also beg that if any one has heard either in my sermons or privately anything contrary to God's truth, or if I have written anything such—which, I trust to God, is not the case—he should not retain it. I further beg, then, if any one has seen levity in me in word or deed he should not retain it; but let him pray to God for me that God may forgive me. I beg you to love, praise, and honour those priests who lead a moral life, those in particular who strive for God's word. I beg you to beware of crafty people, particularly of unworthy priests, of whom our Saviour has said they are clothed like sheep, but are invariably greedy wolves. I beg the nobles to treat the poor people kindly and rule them justly. I beg the burghers to conduct their business honestly. I beg the artisans to perform their labours conscientiously. I beg the servants to serve their master and mistress faithfully. I beg the teachers to live honestly, to instruct their pupils carefully, to love God above all; for the sake of His glory and the good of the community, not from avarice and worldly ambition should they teach. I beg the students and other scholars to obey and follow their masters in everything that is good, and to study diligently for the praise of God, for their own salvation, and for that of others."

Hus then mentions by name the Bohemian and Polish noblemen present at the Council who had afforded him aid, and expresses his thanks to them. He then refers to his sovereign, King Wenceslas, and more particularly to Queen Sophia, who had always aided the cause of Hus, as far as it had been in her power. He then continues: "I write this while in fetters, expecting my sentence of death to-morrow, full of hope in God, resolved not to recede from the divine truth nor to recant errors which false witnesses have invented and attributed to me. How God has acted towards me, how He is with me during all my troubles, that you will only know when, by the grace of God, we shall meet again in heaven." It is touching to notice that the imminent vicinity of death by no means lessened Hus's interest in his beloved Bethlehem Chapel. Towards the end of the letter from which I have already quoted he writes: "I beg all of you, particularly you men of Prague, to be careful of Bethlehem as long as the Lord God will permit that God's word be preached there. The devil has been much incensed against that spot, and he has stirred up parsons and canons against it, well knowing that that spot is hostile to his kingdom. I trust in God that he will graciously deign to preserve that spot, and that he will obtain there greater advantages by means of others than was possible through so feeble a person as I am."

From the time of Hus to the present day it has constantly been attempted to define his doctrine, and to trace the origin of the opinions that are peculiar to him. According to one theory, the teaching of Hus did not aim at a reform of the Church in the manner of the later Church reformers, but was rather an endeavour to return to the Eastern Church, from which Bohemia first received the Christian doctrine. In the seventeenth century Paul Stransky[1] wrote that even after the Latin rites had been generally accepted in Bohemia, "humble people and the populace, contented with the former religious institutions of their land, tenaciously adhered to the rites of the Greek Church." The same theory has in the present century been maintained by Eugene Novikov, Hilferding, and other Russian writers. The patient and thorough investigation of this matter by modern Bohemian historians, particularly by Palacký, Dr. Kalousek, and Dr. Goll, has, however, proved to a certainty that all reminiscences of the Eastern Church had in Bohemia died out before the time of Hus.

It would be natural to attribute Hus's peculiar views principally to the influence of the writers of his own country who immediately preceded him and who have been noticed in the last chapter. It is therefore surprising to note that Milič, Stitný, and Matthew of Janov are scarcely noticed in the works of Hus that have been preserved. It has, however, been conjectured that further references to them may have been contained in the lost works of Hus. In sharp contrast with this independence of the writings of his countrymen is the strong influence of Wycliffe on the ideas and writings of Hus, which the recent publication of many of Wycliffe's works has rendered yet more evident. It is certain that the works of Hus, specially those written in Latin, contain lengthy extracts from Wycliffe's writings, and that many of the

[1] See Chapter VI.

leading ideas of Hus can be traced to the same source. This fact has been strongly brought forward by Professor Loserth, who has quoted in parallel columns passages from Hus's treatise, *De Ecclesia*, and passages from Wycliffe's treatise of the same name, which are identical. In a lesser degree Loserth has found this dependence on Wycliffe also in other works of Hus. The German professor, however, deals principally with the Latin works of Hus, whereas his Bohemian writings—though the influence of Wycliffe can here also be traced—are far more independent and original. It must also be remembered that in the fifteenth and even the sixteenth century the modern ideas with regard to literary property were unknown. Many writers, particularly on theology, incorporated with their works whole pages from the writings of their predecessors, and this without any acknowledgment. It would also be incorrect to imagine that Hus followed Wycliffe blindly. He indeed writes: "I hold those true doctrines which Master John Wycliffe, professor of holy theology, held, not because he said these things, but because the Holy Scripture says them." On the important question of transubstantiation Hus, differing herein from Wycliffe, upheld the teaching of the Church of Rome. It must further be considered that in many cases ideas common to Hus and to the English reformer can be traced far farther back. This matter has been fully expounded by the recent foreign and Bohemian writers on Hus. It will here be sufficient briefly to state that the disapproval of the enormous riches, of the arrogance and avarice of the higher members of the Roman clergy—so constantly expressed by Hus—can be traced back as far as to the German

Emperor Frederick II. After Pope Innocent IV. had pronounced the Emperor's deposition in 1245 at the Council of Lyon, Frederick in a circular addressed to all princes declared "that it had always been his intention to reduce the ecclesiastics, particularly those of highest rank, to that state and condition in which they had been at the time of the primitive Church, that is, leading an apostolical life and imitating the humility of Christ."

In the following century Marsiglio of Padua in his celebrated work, *Defensor Fidei*, wrote strongly against the interference of the clergy in temporal matters. He already maintained that the Church consisted of the whole community of Christian men, be they ecclesiastics or laymen. The Pope, according to Marsiglio, can claim no right of supreme judgment in temporal matters, even over the clergy, and the "power of the keys" does not entitle him to place a man under civil disabilities by means of excommunication. Somewhat later, in his *Dialogues*, William of Ockham expressed similar opinions, though he did not go as far as Marsiglio.

If we endeavour briefly to define the ideas of Hus as far as they differ from the tenets of the Church of Rome —for on most points he was entirely in accord with that Church—we may state that his two leading ideas, closely connected with one another, are his theory of "Christ's law" and his conception of the "true Church." According to Hus the law of Christ, or "God's law"— an expression that afterwards became a watchword of the Hussites—is contained in the writings of the Old and New Testament, which contain all God's commands to man. The second fundamental principle of Hus is his conception of the true Church, which, according to him, consists of the totality of the elect. It is doubtful whether this theory was in direct opposition to the doctrine of the Church of Rome, in the development which it had reached in the fifteenth century. Long before his rupture with the Church, Hus, speaking before the archiepiscopal synod, had defined the "Ecclesia" as "Prædestinatorum Universitas." The head of this Church, according to Hus, is Christ, not the Pope, whose predecessors held no higher rank than other bishops.

It remains to cast a glance on the individuality and character of Hus. He has always been judged in a most opposite manner, according to the religious opinions of those who wrote about him. As Schiller has said of another very different, great Bohemian, it can be said of Hus too:—

"*Von der Parteien Gunst und Hass verwirrt
Schwankt sein Characterbild in der Geschichte.*"

I must rely on what I have already written, but principally on my extracts from the works of Hus, to bear witness for the sincere piety, the enthusiasm for the law of God, the patriotism, the humility and the sincerity of Hus. That he was faultless, I do not attempt to prove, and no one would have resented such an attempt more than the great Bohemian, who, in one of his last letters, begged those who might have heard that he had committed some offence against God's law, not to follow his example, but to pray God to forgive him. It is certain that Hus was imprudent when, by high-coloured descriptions of the misdeeds of their priests, he incensed the ignorant and excitable population of Prague. Neither can it be denied that—no doubt influenced by his firm belief that he was speaking in the name of Christ, not in his own—Hus sometimes showed traces of the self-willed obstinacy which the enemies of Bohemia have ever declared to be characteristic of its inhabitants.

Such slight blemishes, visible indeed to the modern writer, were not unnaturally ignored by the enthusiastic followers of Hus. To them he was "The Martyr," and the National Church of Bohemia, up to the time of its suppression in the seventeenth century, continued to celebrate the 6th of July, the anniversary of the death of Hus.

If, neglecting for a moment the minutiæ of mediæval theological controversy, we consider as a martyr that man who willingly sacrifices his individual life for what he firmly believes to be the good of humanity at large, who "takes the world's life on him and his own lays down," then assuredly there is no truer martyr in the world's annals than John of Husinec.

The name of Jerome of Prague was, particularly among older writers, so closely connected with that of Hus, that it would appear incorrect altogether to omit mentioning his name. He had by no means the great influence on the development of Hussitism in Bohemia —in which country he appeared but occasionally and for short periods—which was attributed to him before the studies of the present century had rendered the past history of Bohemia clearer. What influence he obtained was through his eloquence, not through his pen, so that his place in a history of Bohemian literature is a very modest one. One letter still preserved has been, on doubtful evidence, attributed to Jerome. It is more pleasing, at any rate, to doubt its authenticity. It is supposed to have been written after he had recanted his former opinions. In this letter (dated August 12, 1415), addressed to Lord Lacek of Kravář, Jerome states that "the dead man (*i.e.* Hus) wrote many false and hurtful things."

CHAPTER IV

THE PERIOD OF THE HUSSITE WARS

THE death, or, as his adherents considered it, the murder of Hus was followed by prolonged bloody wars, during which Bohemia, for a time, successfully repelled the forces of a large part of Europe. Such a period was naturally not fruitful of literary production. The writers deal almost exclusively with theology, and are, with a few very noteworthy exceptions, of secondary importance. This applies specially to the very numerous theological tracts or pamphlets, the names of which Jungmann has, in his great History of Bohemian Literature, rescued from oblivion.

The adherents of Hus divided into two parties very shortly after the death of their great leader. The more moderate party, which always endeavoured to obtain a reconciliation with Rome, and some of the members of which only differed from that Church in their views as to the ceremony of communion, became known as the Calixtines, or as the "Praguers," from the fact that the town, and specially the university of Prague, was their centre. The more advanced Hussites received the name of Taborites, as the town of that name soon became their stronghold. There were minor differences of opinion in both camps. Some of the Calixtines or Utraquists, as they were also called, were prepared to accept the entire teaching of Rome if only the right of receiving communion in the two kinds were granted to them. Other Utraquists, who maintained that they alone had preserved the teaching of Hus in its purity, differed from the Church of Rome on other points also, as had been the case with Hus himself.

Among the Taborites also a more moderate party, led by Zižka, and known after his death as the "Orphans," disagreed with yet more advanced Church reformers. Finally, it should be mentioned that the intense religious excitement, and the widely spread belief in the approaching millennium, led to the formation of yet more advanced religious sects, against some of which even the Taborites had no hesitation in employing the "secular arm."

All these parties found exponents of their views, but it will here be possible to mention only very few of the very many theological controversialists of this time. The principal champion of the moderate Utraquists was Magister John of Přibram, who is stated to have been a pupil of Matthew of Janov. His polemical works are all directed against the Taborites, and even against the more advanced members of his own party. His constant adversary was the English Hussite, Peter Payne, known to the Bohemians as "Magister Engliš." Přibram endeavoured, not very successfully, to prove that the teaching of Hus was quite independent of that of "the foreigner Wycliffe," and availed himself of the national prejudices of the Bohemians for the purpose of alienating them from the teaching of the English reformer and his pupil, Peter Payne. The most important work of Přibram bears the name *Of the great Torment of the Holy Church*, and was long attributed to Milič of Kremsier. One of his most noteworthy books also is his *Lives of the*

Priests of Tabor, written, like the first-mentioned book, in Bohemian. Přibram here violently attacks Nicolas of Pelhřimov, the "false and monstrous bishop of the Taborites," as he calls him. Other minor Bohemian works of Přibram, as well as some written in Latin, have been preserved. He died in 1448.

To the moderate faction of the Calixtine party belonged also Peter of Mladenovič, who has already been mentioned as one of the companions of Hus on his fatal journey to Constance. He wrote a Latin work entitled *Relatio de Magistri Joannis Hus causa*, which has been edited by Palacký, and contains a full account of Hus's journey to Constance, his imprisonment, and his death. This work—from which I have quoted in the last chapter—was very precious to the Hussites. Up to the time of the suppression of the National Church of Bohemia in the seventeenth century, it was customary in the Utraquist Church services to read a portion of the narrative of Mladenovič instead of the evangel on July 6, the anniversary of the "martyrdom" of Hus. Mladenovič also wrote a shorter Bohemian account of the sufferings of Hus. He died in 1451 as administrator of the consistory of the Utraquist Church.

Of the more advanced writers of the Calixtine or Utraquist Church, Magister Jacobellus of Mies (or Stříbro) is the most prominent. He became, immediately after the death of Hus, the leader of that party which adhered most closely to his teaching. He had already, during the captivity of his master, maintained the necessity of communion in two kinds, a doctrine which Hus had sanctioned in one of his letters.[1] Like most Bohemian divines of his time, Jacobellus wrote a

[1] See Chapter III. p. 112.

K

Latin *Postilla*, as well as numerous other polemical treatises, both Latin and Bohemian. Some Bohemian hymns written by him have also been preserved. Jacobellus is, however, most worthy of notice as being the principal author of the celebrated *Articles of Prague*, that played so important a part in Bohemian history. After this event we find little mention of Jacobellus, and he died in retirement in 1429. Closely connected with Jacobellus is his friend the Englishman, Peter Payne,[1] whose name has already been mentioned. I have here no space to sketch out his adventurous career. He was obliged to fly from England, no doubt as being an adherent of Wycliffe, and settled in Bohemia, obtaining, in 1417, the degree of Master of Arts at the University of Prague. He belonged, like Jacobellus, to the more advanced Utraquists; and when the ideas of Přibram gained ground in that Church, even joined the Taborites. Peter Payne was also one of the Bohemian envoys at the Council of Basel, where he was occasionally in violent conflict with his countrymen, the English bishops. Though living so long in Bohemia, Magister Engliš appears never to have thoroughly mastered the language of the country. It is at least certain that when challenged by Magister Přibram to a public theological disputation in that language, Peter was obliged to decline. Some religious treatises, written in Latin, in which Payne defends the teaching of Wycliffe, have been preserved. He appears toward the end of his life to have cast his lot entirely with the men of Tabor, and was still living in that town in 1452.

Among the members of the advanced Calixtine party,

---

[1] Mr. James Baker has written an interesting monograph on Peter Payne, entitled, *A Forgotten Great Englishman*.

which was led by Jacobellus, and afterwards by Archbishop Rokycan, we must mention Vavřinec (Laurence) of Březov, who, though principally known as a historian, was as devoted to theological studies as almost all his contemporaries. His *Chronicon*, written in Latin, is perhaps the most valuable contemporary record of the Hussite wars. The book unfortunately ends abruptly with the year 1421, perhaps in consequence of the death of the author, of whom, however, little is known. The Bohemian writings of Březov are inferior in interest to his Latin work. He wrote in his own language a "book expounding dreams," at the request of King Wenceslas IV., at whose court he probably held an appointment, and a *Chronicle of the World*. He is also the author of a Bohemian translation of the *Travels of Sir John Mandeville*.

The leader of the more advanced Utraquists, after the death of Jacobellus, was Magister John of Rokycan, the first and last Calixtine Archbishop of Prague. The long and eventful life of Rokycan—born in 1397, he died in 1471—belongs to Bohemian history. It will here be sufficient to mention his writings. Rokycan was undoubtedly a very voluminous writer, though probably the great majority of his works have been destroyed. Those still in existence are principally theological writings of a controversial character. His most important work is his *Postilla*, written in Bohemian, which strongly recalls Hus's work of the same name, though, both as regards profundity of thought and style, Rokycan's work is far inferior to that of his master.

The priests and other members of the Taborite community were probably not inferior in literary activity to the adherents of the Utraquist Church. Unfortunately, after the battle of Lipan (in 1434), and the capture of the city of Tabor by King Georg (in 1452), almost all these works were destroyed. The customs and constitution of that strange military-religious community, that in many ways recalls the later Puritans, will therefore probably never be exactly known. We gather indeed some information from the writings of the enemies of the Taborites, such as Æneas Sylvius. His account of his visit to the city of Tabor is very interesting. It appears particularly to have surprised the Italian humanist how general in the town the knowledge of the Bible was. "The Italian priests," he writes, "should be ashamed, they of whom it is doubtful whether they have even once read the New Testament; among the Taborites you would hardly find a poor woman who could not answer any question referring to the Old or to the New Testament." With regard to the doctrines of the Taborites, we are also obliged to rely mainly on the statements of their enemies, particularly of Magister Přibram, who has already been mentioned.

The leader of the Taborite party was Nicholas of Pelhřimov (Pilgram), surnamed "Biskupec," the only bishop of the short-lived community of Tabor. Little is known both of his life and of his writings. He was, like most Bohemian divines of his time, engaged in incessant theological controversies. Chelčicky's *Reply to Nicholas* has been preserved, but the letter of Nicholas in answer to which it was written is no longer in existence; a polemical work of Nicholas addressed to Rokycan has also been lost. The principal work of Biskupec, however, his Latin *Chronicon Continens causam sacerdotum Taboriensium*, has been preserved, and was edited and published by Professor Höfler in the present century. It is interesting as being the only existent definition of the doctrines of the Taborites written by a member of the community.

I follow the example of Jungmann and Jireček, as well as of the most recent writers on Bohemian literature, in including among the writers of the Taborite party the celebrated Bohemian warrior John Žižka of Trocnov, born about the year 1378. It has already been mentioned that Žižka was the head of the more moderate division of the Taborists, which after his death assumed the name of the "Orphans." Žižka's writings consist indeed only of the curious work entitled *The Regulations of War* (Řád vojenský), four letters, and a war-song or hymn, but they are among the most precious relics in the Bohemian language. They give a thorough insight into the real nature and character of the hero of the Hussite wars, who has so often been compared to Oliver Cromwell. The *Řád vojenský* is no mere collection of military regulations; besides establishing the rule of an iron discipline, it also enforces religious practices, and repeatedly proclaims—in a manner very unusual in the fifteenth century—the absolute equality of the different classes of men who composed the Hussite armies. It is perhaps only after reading these regulations that the victories of the Hussites over immensely superior forces become intelligible.

Of Žižka's letters, the most noteworthy is the celebrated *Letter to the Allies of Domažlice*. The citizens of Domažlice (Tauss) had been attacked by the Germans, and applied to their Hussite comrades for aid. Žižka wrote to them: "Dear Brothers in God!—I beg you for the sake of the Lord God to remain in the fear of God as His most beloved sons, and not to complain if He chastises you. Remembering the founder of our faith, our Lord Jesus Christ, you will defend yourselves bravely against the wrongs which these Germans endeavour to inflict on you. You will thus follow the example of the ancient Bohemians, who, valiantly using their lances, defended both God's cause and their own. And we, dear brethren, seeking the law of God and the good of the commonwealth, will do everything possible, that every one of our men who is able to wield a club or even to hurl a stone should march to your aid. And therefore, dear brethren, be it known to you that we are collecting our men from all parts of the country against these enemies of God and devastators of the Bohemian land. Therefore instruct your priests, that they may when preaching rouse the people against the armies of Antichrist. Let it also be proclaimed in the marketplace that all able men, young or old, must be ready at any moment. And we, God willing, shall be shortly with you. Have bread, beer, fodder for the horses ready, as well as all weapons of war. For indeed it is time (to march), not only against the internal enemies, but also against the foreigners. Remember your first campaign, when you fought bravely, humble men against the great, few against many, unclothed against men in armour. For the arm of God has not been shortened! Therefore trust in God and be ready. May the Lord God grant you strength!"

Very similar to the *Regulations of War* and to the letters of Zižka are the sentiments contained in the well-known Taborite war-song, *All ye Warriors of God*, which has often been called the Bohemian *Marseillaise* of the fifteenth century. Want of space obliges me to quote only some of the first and the last lines of this spirited song, which, according to the most recent researches, is undoubtedly a work of Zižka:—

> *"All ye warriors of God,*
> *Fighters for His law,*
> *Pray to God for help,*
> *And trust in Him,*
> *With Him victory ever will be yours.*
>
> *Fear not those, the Lord hath said,*
> *Who would your body harm.*
> *For love of your fellow-creatures*
> *He has ordered you to die;*
> *Therefore strengthen manfully your hearts.*
>
> *Christ will recompense your sorrows,*
> *Hundredfold repay you,*
> *Who for Him doth lose his life*
> *Will win eternal bliss;*
> *Happy he who dies for the truth.*
>
> . . . . . .
>
> *Therefore manfully cry out:*
> *'At them! rush at them!'*
> *Wield bravely your arms;*
> *Pray to your Lord God;*
> *Strike and kill! spare none!"*

The eventful life of Zižka belongs to Bohemian history, but it may yet not be out of place to mention here that his life and career have constantly been systematically misrepresented by writers hostile to his faith; and particularly outside of Bohemia scarcely any other writings referring to Zižka were known. He thus passed down from one generation of writers to another as a ferocious and bloodthirsty robber and fanatic. The real Zižka was, as repeatedly mentioned, the leader of the moderate Taborites, and the contemporary writers mention several cases when Zižka reproved the barbarity of his soldiers. It is none the less impossible to acquit him altogether from the accusation of cruelty, but it is certain that his conduct in this respect was far more humane than that of his adversaries, the so-called crusaders, who several times invaded Bohemia and openly proclaimed their intention "to let no heretic live." The account of the death of Zižka, according to which he died blaspheming, and ordered that his body should be flayed, his skin used as a drum, and his body thrown to the wild beasts—first mentioned by Æneas Sylvius, and since repeated by countless writers—is also totally devoid of truth. It may be of interest to quote the account of Zižka's death given by one of the contemporary chroniclers.[1] It runs thus: "Here (at Přibislav) brother Zižka was seized by a deadly attack of the plague. He gave his last charge to his faithful Bohemians, (saying,) that, fearing their beloved God, they should firmly and faithfully defend God's law in view of His reward in eternity. And then brother Zižka recommended his soul to God, and died on the Wednesday before the day of St. Gallus" (October 11, 1424). Even had we no historical evidence to the point, this tranquil death would appear a fitting end for the great Bohemian general. He who had so often fought what he firmly considered God's battle, assuredly did not dread entering into God's peace.

It has already been stated that besides the two great divisions of the Hussites, minor religious sects sprung up in Bohemia in consequence of the general religious exaltation which prevailed in the country, particularly in the earlier part of the fifteenth century. These sects

[1] *Stari Letopisove Česti* ("Ancient Bohemian Chronicles"); see later.

went far beyond the teaching of the Calixtines, and even of the Taborites. They were frequently influenced by chiliastic ideas, which not unnaturally lead to socialism. Of such fanatics the one who attracted most attention was the priest Martin Huska, also known under the name of "Loquis." He obtained a considerable following among the people of Bohemia, who called him "the Lion of Daniel" and "the Angel of God's Legion." His influence soon became prejudicial to the strict military discipline which Žižka maintained at Tabor. He was arrested by order of that general, and, after he had repeatedly broken his promise to discontinue his preaching, was burnt on August 21, 1421. It is stated that Huska was the author of numerous theological treatises, but none of them have been preserved. The little we know of his opinions is derived from the writings of Přibram, who frequently quotes his works.

I shall next refer to one of the most independent and original of Bohemian writers, PETER CHELČICKY. Though only recently well known in Bohemia, and still almost unknown elsewhere, Chelčicky is well worthy of a far more extensive study than limited space will here permit me to devote to him. Though a contemporary of the theologians whom I have mentioned in this chapter, and on terms of acquaintance with some of them, Chelčicky everywhere impresses us as an independent thinker. As Professor Jagič has recently written in his Russian preface to the Petersburg edition of the *Net of Faith*, it is difficult to calculate how great would have been the influence of Chelčicky's works had they been written in English, German, or French instead of in Bohemian. Chelčicky may be described as a socialist, but his socialism was rather that of the primitive Church or of Count

Tolstoy—to whom Chelčicky has often been compared—than that of the modern disturbers of public order. Horror of bloodshed and of all violence is indeed one of the distinctive tenets of Chelčicky, and absolute obedience to all, even the most unjust authorities, is enjoined by him. Chelčicky's ideal is the communism of the primitive Church such as he imagined it. The source of all evil is the "donation of Constantine."[1] When the Church was then for the first time enriched, an angel, Chelčicky tells us, spoke the words: "To-day has poison been infused into the Church of Christ." This mystical conception of the primitive Church is the foundation of most of Chelčicky's tenets. As the primitive Christians had no part in the government of the Roman empire, therefore no true Christian can hold any office of state. He may, indeed must obey, but he should not command. In the primitive Church, according to Chelčicky, all were equal. Therefore the "bands," that is, the temporal and ecclesiastical grades and ranks among men, are hateful "to the meek and poor Lord Jesus." In his intense hatred of all temporal and spiritual authority, Chelčicky sometimes appears to expound very modern ideas, but we must always remember that we are reading the words of a writer of the fifteenth century and of a fervent Christian.

Very characteristic of Chelčicky is his hatred of bloodshed. While the magisters of the Calixtine Church had, after a prolonged discussion, decided that war in self-

[1] The fable of the "donation of Constantine" and its fatal consequences is met with constantly in mediæval literature. Dante alludes to it in the *Inferno* (Canto xix. v. 115-118)—

"Ahi Constantin di quanto mal fu matre
Non la tua conversion ma quella dote
Che da te prese il primo ricco patre."

defence was permissible, and even a duty for those who held the true doctrine, Chelčicky maintained the absolute sinfulness of war under whatever circumstances. In his *Reply to Rokycan* he writes: "Has Christ repealed His command—'Thou shalt not kill'? If Christ has not revoked that order, then it must still be obeyed both at Prague and at Tabor." Chelčicky was, therefore, entirely out of sympathy with his countrymen during the momentous period (from 1420 to 1434) when their great victories attracted the attention of all Europe. It is a natural consequence that even at a period of general national enthusiasm, Chelčicky—similar in this respect to the socialists of all times—shows an almost complete absence of pride in his distinctive nationality.

A result of Chelčicky's intense hatred of all social privileges and distinctions was his repeated quaint jibes against the nobility and the clergy, and his pronounced affection for the humble life of the peasantry, another of the many traits in Chelčicky in which he appears similar to Tolstoy. Though the uncontested fact that he was able to spend a considerable time at Prague at his own expense proves that Chelčicky was not entirely without means, and it is probable that he was a small landowner, yet he always speaks of himself as a peasant. Thus, in his *Reply to Rokycan* he writes: "If, therefore, I, the peasant, strike out blindly with my club, your reverence must not be scandalised."

Chelčicky has nowhere attempted to expound his views on the constitution of Church and State systematically. In the *Sít Víry* ("Net of Faith"), undoubtedly his masterpiece, we find the nearest approach to such an attempt. The sum of his teaching—as I have written elsewhere—constitutes an attempt to establish a theory of religious nihilism, substituting for all secular and ecclesiastical authority the ill-defined "will of God."

The details of the life of Chelčicky are still obscure, though the recent researches of Bohemian writers, specially of Professor Goll—to whose Bohemian and German works I wish here to acknowledge my indebtedness—have established a certain number of facts as certain. It would perhaps be unnecessary again to mention that the foolish tale that Chelčicky was a cobbler is devoid of truth, had not this statement found its way into an English work dealing with Bohemia that has appeared within the last few years. Peter Chelčicky was born at Chelčic near Vodnan, in Southern Bohemia, towards the end of the fourteenth century, probably as the son of a small landowner. He proceeded to Prague early in life, and remained there for a considerable time occupied with studies principally of a theological character. It is, however, certain that he never took orders, as was formerly supposed, and that he did not pursue his studies at the university. He was indeed debarred from doing so by insufficient knowledge of the Latin language. As he has himself told us, he acquired but a very slight knowledge of that language during his stay at Prague. He had, however, read portions of the works of Wycliffe, to whom he refers frequently, and who is probably the "Magister Protiva" who is often quoted by Chelčicky.

He, however, as he himself tells us, acquired most of his knowledge of the opinions of Wycliffe and other theologians from his frequent conversations with numerous Bohemian priests. It is specially recorded that he had frequent intercourse with the priests of the

THE WRITINGS OF CHELČICKY

Bethlehem Chapel, that stronghold of the Bohemian Church reformers. Neither the date of Chelčicky's arrival at Prague nor that of his departure is certain. It is very probable that he was in that city during the last years of the life of Hus, and a passage in one of his writings renders it probable that he was personally acquainted with the great Bohemian reformer. Chelčicky was in Prague during the stormy years 1419 and 1420, and the terrible scenes that he then witnessed no doubt intensified his horror of bloodshed. He probably left Prague not long after the bloody battle of the Vyšehrad (November 1, 1420), and spent the rest of his life on his farm at Chelčic. Though living in retirement, Chelčicky continued to take part in the numerous theological controversies of his time, and it also appears that towards the end of his life some of his followers formed a small community known as the "Brothers of Chelčic," of which he became the head. Chelčicky died about the year 1460.

There is sufficient contemporary evidence to prove that Chelčicky was a voluminous writer, but many of his works have been lost, and up to the beginning of the present century they had all fallen into almost complete oblivion. The strongly democratic character of these writings, and the bitter invectives against the aristocracy and clergy which they contain, rendered them specially obnoxious during the period of reaction that followed the battle of the White Mountain. It is indeed only within the last ten or twelve years that some of Chelčicky's works have been edited, and much further work is required before we can thoroughly appreciate his position in Bohemian literature.

We possess four larger works of Chelčicky, the *Reply to*

Nicholas of Pelhřimov, the *Postilla*, the *Net of Faith*, and the *Reply to Rokycan*, which, according to Dr. Goll, than whom there can be no higher authority on this subject, were probably written in the order in which I have enumerated them. Many minor works of Chelčicky are also still in existence, and may be considered as connected with one of the larger works, some part of which is in them treated in a more detailed manner. The *Net of Faith* (*Sít Víry*) is superior both as regards style and lucidity to the rest of Chelčicky's works, and I will therefore devote to it more space than to the author's other writings.

The *Reply to Nicholas* (of Pelhřimov), bishop of the Taborites, who has already been mentioned in this work, is probably the first important writing of Chelčicky, and dates from about the year 1424. Peter has himself told us how it came to be written. When Bishop Nicholas was passing through Vodnan, he sent a messenger to the neighbouring village of Chelčic inviting the peasant-theologian to meet him. When Peter arrived, he found the bishop sitting on the dyke of a fishpond, and Nicholas asked him what the people thought of their (*i.e.* the Taborites) doctrine with regard to the sacrament of communion. Chelčicky replied that some approved of it, but others blamed it. The bishop then said that their teaching was in accordance with that of the Bible. This meeting was followed by several others, and a correspondence between Chelčicky and Nicholas sprung up. Chelčicky, in one of his letters which has not been preserved, appears to have written very sharply to the bishop, as in the existent *Reply to Nicholas* he refers to the fact that he had offended his correspondent. The subject of the *Reply*, as probably of the whole correspondence, is the one that then absorbed all public interest in Bohemia: the correct definition of the real presence of Christ in the sacrament of communion. Chelčicky maintains the real presence of Christ in the sacrament, and lays stress on the fact that Wycliffe, whose immense influence on the religious views of the Bohemians is everywhere noticeable, held the same doctrine. He sharply attacks the view of the Taborite priests, which was similar to that afterwards adopted by the Calvinists.

Though all dates concerning Chelčicky are very uncertain, it is probable that he ceased writing for some time after the appearance of his first treatise. He felt, as already stated, no joy in the victories of his countrymen, and therefore probably remained silent till comparative quiet returned to Bohemia. When this result was obtained in consequence of the battle of Lipan and the agreement between the Bohemians and the Council of Basel known as the "compact," Chelčicky again began writing. His first considerable work after the *Reply to Nicholas* is his *Postilla*, written probably between 1434 and 1436. The *Postilla*, though the largest, is far from being the most interesting work of Chelčicky. The *Postilla*, a commentary on the gospel of each Sunday in the year, was a very favourite form of literary expression among the Bohemian theologians. Besides the Latin *Postilla* of Waldhauser, those of Hus and Rokycan — both written in Bohemian — have already been mentioned, and many others, the work of minor writers, are still in existence. The leading ideas of Chelčicky, his absolute objection to bloodshed, his detestation of all distinctions of rank and class, his contempt for the luxury of the rich, and love of a lowly life, these and other similar views are repeatedly —Chelčicky was indeed ever prone to repetition—expounded in this as in his other works.

It will, however, give a far truer insight into the ideas of Chelčicky if we dwell more lengthily on his masterpiece, the *Sít Víry*, or "Net of Faith," where these views are far more clearly expounded, than elsewhere. This book, which has only recently become widely known, is one of the most valuable that have been written in the Bohemian language. The democratic character of the Slav race is noticeable in almost every line of this book, and Chelčicky's very scanty knowledge of Latin, often disadvantageous to him when he attempted theological definitions, here is the cause of the independence and originality which characterise his work. Chelčicky's descriptions of the habits and manners of the different classes of Bohemians in his time, though sometimes coarse, are often quaint, and occasionally very witty. The practice acquired by his earlier writings had also greatly improved his style, and he writes here with a facility that we do not find in his other works. The subject of the *Net of Faith* is a passage from the Bible[1]—which the author quotes at the beginning of his work—which tells us how Simon, by order of Jesus, cast out his net and the net broke. As Simon Peter's net then broke in consequence of the multitude of fishes, thus since the donation of Constantine, "damned persons, heretics and offenders," have entered the net of faith, which has been pierced by "the two whales," the Pope and the Emperor, the embodiments of spiritual and secular authority. The *Net of Faith* consists of two parts, the contents of which are thus described by the

[1] Gospel of St. Luke, chap. iv. ver. 4–6.

author of the preface to the first printed edition [1521]:—
"The first part," he writes, "explains whence and how such fearful corruption entered the Holy Church, and also states that he who would dig out its true ground and foundation, which is Jesus, must first remove much rubbish, which has been brought into the Church by man; and then only will you find its true foundation."

"The second part of the book explains how 'bands'[1] addicted to various and manifold learning and unchristian religious practices sprung up and mightily increased; and all these bands form a great obstacle to the true knowledge of the creed of our Lord Jesus, for they have clothed themselves with the spirit of haughtiness, and are thus as adverse as possible to the humble and poor Lord Jesus."

The first part of the work, as stated above, deals with the corruption into which Christianity had fallen, and at the same time formulates Chelčicky's ideal Christianity more clearly than the writer has done elsewhere. In chapter xi. Chelčicky writes of the primitive Church: "Therefore, if we consider these early Christians, we will see that they were sufficiently guided in their faith by the Apostles according to the law of Christ; for that law in itself is useful for the purpose of directing God's people to salvation; for only by means of the direction given by that law can God's people be led to that true innocence which God loves in them; they should in-

---

[1] The Bohemian word *rota* is not easy to interpret. It can be translated by "bands" or "classes," but it has an invidious signification which the English word "classes" does not render. The word is frequently used by Chelčicky with reference to the aristocracy and higher clergy. Chelčicky wrote a separate treatise, *O rotách Ceských*, but it has not been preserved.

fallibly seek Him with their whole heart, and preserve truth and affection towards all people, friends or enemies; they should wish or do evil to no one; and if such things are done to them, they should suffer without revenge, returning evil for evil neither to the good nor to the evil; for such and similar matters does the law of Christ enjoin. And those who will not be bound by such injunctions cannot be justified before God. Therefore is it impossible that worldly people, who love the world and wish to live for the world, should submit themselves to this law, for they would have to give up the world if they wished to fulfil this law. Thus, indeed, the first godly assemblies progressed in Christ's law: abandoning totally the errors of the heathens, the incredulity of the Jews, and all the vanities of this world, they . . . rapidly progressed without any of the rights of citizens, and without the rule of a high priest, guided only by the law of Christ."

"But later, when these twofold laws, those of the State and those of the Pope, were established, then immediately the state of Christianity was diminished and it declined. And those who write chronicles reflect on this, and we see it with our eyes that these two laws produce the most harmful disturbances and death of faith and of God's law. . . . I therefore ask, Is the law of God sufficient without worldly laws to guide and direct us in the path of truly Christian religion? Then, though with trembling, I say, It is so, for Christ's law was sufficient to guide Christ's manhood (*i.e.* Christ as a man), as well as all His disciples, without the interference of any worldly institutions."

The subversive character of these theories, which lead to the assertion that the necessity of secular authority is only founded on the wickedness of humanity, and that the ideal state should be ruled by Christ alone, did not escape Chelčicky. In the last chapter of the first part of the "Net" he writes: "From these things (*i.e.* statements) some one might say that I insult the (worldly) power. Let him say nothing of the sort, though he may wish (to do so); for I do not insult it (*i.e.* power), but honour it, as is seemly, and I say that it is good when God uses it well, and through it carries out what He considers good. But the evil which men do and wish to carry out through it (worldly power), that I blame before the people. . . . God is Lord of the world, and could rule and restrain it without that power if He wished to do so; therefore if we maintain that He wishes to rule the world by means of temporal authority, and that those men rule the world as officials of the Lord God, then those who have power over the world can restrain and command it easily if they ordain that which they see is good for the world." It is evident that this passage is evasive, and contains no answer to the questions to which the former quotation naturally gives rise.

The second part of the *Net of Faith* has as a second heading the words, "Of the bands, and of each of them separately;" but it must not be confused with Chelčicky's lost work, *Of the Bands in Bohemia*. Chelčicky deals first, and deals very severely, with the "band" of the nobles. His animosity against those who bear arms is sometimes very quaintly expressed. He writes: "All the value of noble birth is founded on an unjust invention of the heathens, who obtained coats of arms from emperors or kings in reward of some deed of prowess. And some buy these coats of arms for the sake of their vanity, such as a gate,[1] a head of a wolf or of a dog, a ladder, or half a horse, or a trumpet, or a knife, or a pork sausage, or something of that sort. In such coats of arms lies the value and dignity of noble birth. And this nobility has the same glory as the arms from which they derive the value of their nobility. But if money did not fall to them as well as noble birth, hunger would soon make them ready to abandon their coats of arms and seize the plough! . . . Therefore he who can prove that he is well born, and has (in his arms) a ladder or half a horse, receives letters (*i.e.* patents of nobility) declaring that he is better born than Abel, the second son of Adam, and he obtains such consideration that he is always considered as being good; should he even commit the worst actions, his coat of arms does not permit that he should be bad."

These attacks on the nobility continue during three chapters. The following passage contains a curious description of the dress worn by the nobles of Bohemia in the fifteenth century. Chelčicky writes: "The men wear copes reaching to the ground, or they wear a short round jacket and a hood which reaches down to the saddle of their horse, and with it a monk's cowl and a neckerchief, or a short cloak, and with it long hair reaching down to their shoulders, and on it a small rough hat like a cone; they look out from under it as from a dovecot, for verily they do not know what monsters they make of themselves. The abominable women also deck themselves out with so many petticoats that they can hardly drag themselves along in them, and

---

[1] Some of the objects enumerated above really formed part of the coats of arms of Bohemian noble families.

with fanciful toilets and graces that are not graceful. Their head-dress is broad and high, and ends in a horn. Thus do they walk about like the celebrated courtesans of the Pope, to the surprise and offence of the whole world. And all this is in consequence of their noble birth, which reeks of injustice. Therefore can the true faith never be insulted by heathens or by Jews as it is by this race (the nobles), who found their claims on their coats of arms, and who have unjustly entered into the realm of the faithful. And they are odious in particular to the crucified Jesus; for their proud ways are contrary to the shame which He endured on the cross; they who, acting in everything in a manner contrary to Him for the purpose of worldly glory, yet wish to sit at table with Him and share the gain of His suffering. Therefore from all these causes they are displeasing to God, and harmful and burdensome to men. For the toiling community bears a heavy burden in the nobles; for they devour the poor, and everything good that is found in the land, that they grasp and devour, and greatly do they harm the whole people."

It must not be thought that Chelčicky's democratic views were opposed to the privileges of the nobility only. The special rights enjoyed by the citizens of some Bohemian towns, the privileged position of the clergy, even the intellectual superiority of the masters of the university, all were equally odious to the fanatical leveller Chelčicky. Of the citizens he writes thus: "I shall now speak of the knavery of the citizens, who are the strength of Antichrist, adverse to Christ, an evil rabble, who are full of boldness in committing bad actions, and help one another in vigorously combating truth and in cunningly suppressing it by means of hypocrisy; they speak well·

of it (= truth) yet they are guests at the assemblies of evil people, and of the shameless knaves who follow the path of Judas. Therefore have these knavish townsmen too grievously torn the net of faith when they resisted the faith; they with their special town-privileges, which are similar to the government of the heathens and founded on the same principle; they are similar to the bands who have coronets and crests, and in many matters they draw at the yoke (that is, act) together. Too much, indeed, has the knavery of the townsmen increased, too strong are the worldly institutions, and too great is the power of Antichrist; for through them (the townsmen) he is prosperous in his war against Christ. Therefore faith, like a net, could not contain these many knaveries and remain intact; they have torn it open by their opposition to Christ's truth; only the lying and dead phantom of faith have they left, and the false name of Christianity."

Somewhat later Chelčicky develops his views on the foundation of cities. It has been conjectured that he derived these views from the Waldenses; but the influence of the Waldenses on the Hussite movement, and on Chelčicky and the Bohemian Brethren in particular, is a question on which the principal Bohemian authorities disagree. A similar theory as to the origin of cities can also be traced to Wycliffe, who is perhaps the "Magister Protiva" whom Chelčicky quotes. In any case, the theory of an original communism, which was destroyed by the murderer Cain, is very characteristic of Chelčicky. He writes: "Magister Protiva, dealing with the foundation of cities, spoke thus: Cain, after the murder of his brother, built a town, the foundation of which was the cause that he acquired goods by means of robbery and violence. Thus was he enabled to enjoy the fruits of his thievery, and by the invention of landmarks he changed the former simplicity of men's lives, of their weights and measures, into craftiness or cunning, and he introduced corruption. He first laid down landmarks, and he first fortified towns with walls; and being afraid of those whom he and his band had offended and robbed, he assembled his followers in his towns."

Chelčicky then deals with the clergy. He is particularly severe on the mendicant friars, of whom he writes thus: "It is thus as regards the poverty of the monks: If it were true poverty it would be blessed, but their poverty is insatiable and endures no want; therefore has it only the name of poverty. Although they may not have many good treasures, yet they can gather together so much that they can live in abundance just as he who possesses treasures. Thus (such a monk) is called poor though he is free from all the privations which poverty causes. Many citizens indeed would accept this sort of poverty if they could—relying on the regulations that permit constant begging—gather together so much money that they could have a more abundant fare than their neighbours, even should the latter earn much money by usury. And if a poor monk obtains such abundance for his dinner-table that he disdains beef and delicious peas with fat bacon, but wags his tail when he sees game, birds or other delicacies that are better than peas, then he has got himself a good livelihood by his begging; and he and his companions the other monks have made a better business out of begging than some squire who has a plough and two fields, or even a large farm. Far indeed is such a mendicant friar from poverty; as he is always begging, he would not scorn it should some one offer him gold; the covetous monk would stick it into his bag, buy himself value (that is, an annuity), give up the obligation of begging and rather become a lord, winning from God with a trump."

After passing judgment on the priesthood, Chelčicky proceeds to criticise the men of learning, or rather the theologians, for in his time, particularly in Bohemia, scarcely any other learning was known. He writes: "As regards the bands of masters of colleges, they are among Christians, those of whom, one would think, that they were as a light of the world, and that the faith of Christ had in them its strongest pledge; (this) in consequence of their sure faculty of judgment and of their virtues, and also (would one hope) that in time of persecution the faithful people would find support among them. When, in time of persecution, the frivolous run away, they who are stronger in faith should take the weight on themselves; for one would think that they only studied science so zealously—and gave it to be understood that they do so for the sake of faith—because they wished to defend the faith against heretics, and against the other enemies of the Christian truth. But these their speeches which they boastfully deliver are not true, and they have given no proof (of their zeal) during the present time of persecution. I know of no one whom, with all their learning, they have assisted. That is a living proof. As to Hus, he had the faith in himself. Had he not been granted special strength by God, the learning of the colleges, all of them that there are in the Romish Church, would have stifled the faith in him; for all these colleges flocked together to Constance against him. But dear God gave him so much holy learning, that the Antichristian spirit of all those ravens did not possess sufficient learning to extinguish in him the true faith. . . . What the principal Antichrist's popes, cardinals, bishops, abbots, the bands of monks and parsons, could not obtain for their own advantage, and for the benefit of their dishonest cause, adverse to Christ, that the masters of colleges have succeeded in obtaining. Thus these college-men, as if they grieved for their father Antichrist, and for the shame that befell him when truth was proclaimed, have employed all their learning at two councils, which lasted several years, one at Constance and the other at Basel, for the purpose of skilfully laying snares against the truth ; and for this have they sought the aid of worldly power, that they might carry through that which their learning had discovered, and on which they had deliberated, and thus prove the truth of their teaching, and they had already won over to their side [1] the entire might of the empire, so that having pronounced the truth heretical and condemned it, they might destroy it by means of the imperial power. But God, who observes the thoughts and counsels of the wicked, did not allow them to obtain that which in their deliberations they had aimed at, and for which they had employed their learning."

I will give a last quotation from the *Net of Faith*, illustrating Chelčicky's views as to the manner in which the Church first became possessed of worldly goods. It will be noticed how naïvely he here refers to the grievances of the Bohemian peasants of his time, and without

---

[1] In this passage Chelčicky's style, as is frequently the case, is rather involved. His meaning is that, in distinction from all other ecclesiastics, the doctors of theology had been successful in obtaining the aid of the temporal power for the purpose of suppressing the views which they had declared heretical.

hesitation speaks of them as existing at the time of Constantine. "The emperor," Chelčicky writes, "having made a lord of the Pope by means of the gift of a royal estate, and having given him the honour of royal glory, ordered that everywhere in his dominions churches should be built, and fields with ploughs attached to them. Then the apostles of Antichrist, having settled down in these churches, and being clever and thrifty men, amply enlarged the gift of Constantine; besides their (church) farms, they obtained lordly donations, woods, fishponds, taxes on the people, rich tithes; they taxed all religious functions and their services, and for the purpose of obtaining money they introduced the ringing of bells, and in all the land near their church they sell (religious rites) at the burial of the dead."

I have dealt somewhat more fully with the *Net of Faith*, as being Chelčicky's most valuable and most characteristic work. It will therefore be sufficient to notice but briefly his remaining writings, particularly as there is a marked decline in the interest of what he composed after the year 1340, when the *Net of Faith* appeared. Of the four books which—following Dr. Goll—I have called Chelčicky's principal works, it only remains to notice his *Reply to Rokycan*, which is generally considered the most important of his polemical writings. While Rokycan, the Utraquist archbishop, was in exile from Prague, he met Chelčicky, and a conversation between them began concerning "the men who are called priests, and the slight advantage they have conferred on men." The conversation was followed by a correspondence of which only this treatise has been preserved. It is a lengthy diatribe against the "band" of the ecclesiastics, and attacks not only the Roman clergy, but also the priests of the Bohemian National (Utraquist) Church, whom Rokycan, now returned from exile, was endeavouring to organise hierarchically.

As already mentioned, many minor works of Chelčicky have become known, some quite recently. Of these, the most important are the *Exposition of the Passion according to St. John* and the treatise *On the Beast and its Image.* They are commentaries, the former on the last chapter of the Gospel, the latter on the Revelation of St. John, a saint whose particular influence on Chelčicky is often noticeable. Of other minor works, the treatise *On the Body of Christ* and that *On the Foundation of Worldly Laws* are most worthy of notice.

Though he cannot be considered its founder, Chelčicky's influence contributed greatly to the formation of the society of the "Bohemian Brethren." I have, however, preferred to deal with the "Unity," as it was called, in the next chapter, when I shall consecutively deal with its theological writers from the founders of the association down to Komensky.

In other than theological works the period of the Hussite wars is very poor. Of historians, Lawrence of Březov and Mladenovič have already been mentioned. It remains to notice a series of chroniclers, whose writings I have already quoted, and who are known as the Staři Letopisove Cešti, or "ancient Bohemian chroniclers." These writings, the work of different authors, many of whom were probably eye-witnesses of the events which they describe, form a chronological account, written in the national language, of the occurrences in Bohemia from 1378 to 1526. The most interesting part of these chronicles refers to the period of the Hussite wars, and to Žižka's campaigns in particular. A considerable portion of the graphic account of Žižka's campaign in Hungary and his retreat from that country has been translated into French by Professor Léger in his *Nouvelles Etudes Slaves*. "Written by a Xenophon," the learned Professor truly says, "in good Greek of Athens, it would no doubt have become classic." The account of the campaign is unfortunately not adapted to quotation on a small scale. One legal work also belongs to this period, *The Book of Law* of Ctibor Cimburg of Tovačov, generally known as *Kniha Tovačovská*, or the Book of Tovačov. The same writer has left an allegorical dialogue entitled *Truth's Quarrel with Falsehood*.

The period of the Hussite wars produced but few poetical works, and these, with the exception of Žižka's beautiful war-song, have little value. They consist mainly of coarse invectives exchanged between the Romanists and the Utraquists. Far more songs written by the friends of Rome than by their adversaries have been preserved. This is, however, probably a consequence of the fact that for a long period every Bohemian work written in a sense hostile to Rome was sought out and destroyed. A curious Romanist song is the one that has the words, "Woe to you, Hus," as a refrain. I will quote the last strophe, in which the writer thus addresses the Hussites:—

> "*You are wanton like bulls,*
> *Cows, mice, Moors;*
> *Murder, robbery, unchristian craft,*
> *These form your religion:*
> *Woe to you, Hus!*"

A curious satire on two monks who had fled from their

monastery to join the Hussites, entitled *The Painted Monks*, is also written from the Roman standpoint. A few ballads describing warlike events of the period have also been preserved. The best is that which describes the battle of Aussig (Usti) in 1426. It is evidently the work of an enthusiastic Hussite.

CHAPTER V

HUMANISTS AND THEOLOGIANS

THE comparative tranquillity in Bohemia which was the consequence of the battle of Lipan (1434), and of the agreement between the Bohemians and the Church of Rome which is known as the "compact," naturally had a favourable influence on the intellectual development of the country. The period which, beginning with the last years of the fifteenth century, ends with the downfall of Bohemia in 1620, is the one in which the Bohemian language obtained its greatest extension. I shall again refer to this point at the beginning of Chapter VI.

Two events of the greatest importance to the development of Bohemian literature occurred in the latter half of the fifteenth century. The one is the growth of the humanist movement in Bohemia; the other is the foundation of the sect of the "Bohemian Brethren." Utterly opposed to one another as the views of the humanists and the Bohemian Brethren were, the two currents of thought were not quite without reciprocal influence. Some of the best writers of the "Unity," as the association of the Bohemian Brethren was generally called, such as Blahoslav and the translators of the Bible of Kralice, show proof of thorough study of the Bohemian writings of the humanists. On the other hand, even such an extreme "ultramontane" as the humanist Bohnslav of Lobkovic does not display such absolute and abject submission to the Church of Rome as we find in Southern Europe. Lobkovic admits, to a certain extent, the corruption of the Church of Rome, on which his countrymen laid so great stress, and his language when referring to Pope Alexander VI. is very outspoken.

Though, in consequence of the Hussite wars, the humanist movement was late in reaching Bohemia, it had there a considerable influence, though of a rather indirect nature. No great original work can be attributed to the Bohemian humanists, and when they used their native language it was generally for the purpose of translations, by which, it is true, they greatly enriched and developed it.

In no country had the humanist great sympathy with the national language. In Bohemia the early humanists, whose representative man is Bohuslav of Lobkovic, positively detested it. Lobkovic's often-quoted epigram on Gregory Gelenius,[1] who had translated some of his Latin verses into Bohemian, clearly expresses his feeling on the matter. He wrote: "Into the national language has some one translated my verses. Now the people read them, the lords and nobles. But I am indignant at this work of the two-legged donkey,[2] and I commend his wit and his muse to perdition."

If the early humanists had little sympathy for Bohemia, the national or Utraquist party felt the strongest distrust of the "new learning." A movement that originated in Italy, the site of the Papal power, to which Bohemia refused allegiance, and reached the country through Germany, the ever-hostile neighbour-land, could not appeal to the Bohemians. It must, however, be re-

---

[1] See later. [2] "Irascor facto bipedis vehementer aselli."

marked that the undoubted feeling of antipathy which existed between Lobkovic, Slechta, and other early humanists on one, and the mass of the Bohemian people on the other side, did not include many well-known humanists who adhered to the then predominant Utraquist Church of Bohemia, and did much, at least by means of translations, to improve the language of their country.

Among the early strictly "ultramontane" Bohemian humanists, the most prominent personage is BOHUSLAV HASIŠTEIN OF LOBKOVIC. Born about the year 1460, he was educated in the doctrine of the Utraquist Church, to which his father, a firm adherent of King Georg, had belonged. It is not quite certain when he was formally received into the Roman Church, but this no doubt happened during his stay in Italy. At a very early age he proceeded to the University of Bologna, where he pursued his studies for some time, and no doubt also became acquainted with the teachers of the humanist learning, of which Bologna was then a stronghold. Henceforth Bohnslav is for his whole lifetime a humanist, with all the qualities and defects which belonged to that state of life.

Towards the end of the year 1482, Bohuslav returned to Bohemia, and here, at an exceptionally early age, obtained the dignity of provost of the Vyšehrad at Prague. Humanism had by this time spread in Bohemia, and he became the centre of a small society which devoted itself entirely to the study of the classic languages. Of this small group the shining light, of course after Bohuslav himself, was Victorin Cornelius ze Všehrd, the friend and afterwards the detested enemy of Bohuslav. One of the minor lights of this *cénacle* has described the position of the two leading Bohemian humanists in the following Latin verses :—

> " *Primus Boleslaus, Cornelius altera Lux est*
> *Sidera nos alii, sed sine luce sumus.*"

In the year 1490 Lobkovic undertook an extensive voyage to Palestine and Egypt. On his return to Europe, Lobkovic, who, as his correspondence very clearly proves, was by no means devoid of political ambition, attempted to play a more important part in the affairs of his country. For this purpose mainly Lobkovic aspired to the important bishopric of Olmütz in Moravia, and he was unanimously chosen by the chapter, which, according to very ancient regulations, had the right of election. Unfortunately about this time Alexander VI. was chosen as Pope, and he immediately appointed to the see of Olmütz the Cardinal of Monreale, a relation of the Borgia family. Even the strongest partisans of the papal cause were incensed at this decision, which intrusted the bishopric of Olmütz to an Italian, ignorant of the Bohemian, and even of the better-known German language, at a moment when the influence of the Bohemian Brethren was very strong in Moravia. A letter of remonstrance was, in the name of the principal Moravian nobles, addressed to Pope Alexander. This remonstrance, couched in rather strong language, was probably the work of Lobkovic, and has been printed by Professor Joseph Truhlař in his recently published collection of the Latin letters of Bohuslav of Lobkovic. This letter had no result, and Lobkovic appears never to have forgiven Pope Alexander. We possess several Latin epigrams written by him on that pontiff, in which Lobkovic has followed Juvenal and Martial so faithfully that I must refrain from quotation. Even after the death of Alexander, Lobkovic in his *Farragines* published an epigram stating that even the guardian of hell had declined to admit Pope Borgia, as he might corrupt the other inmates of the infernal regions!

That Lobkovic, however, remained a stanch adherent of the Church of Rome is proved by an occurrence that took place somewhat later, and caused great excitement among the small group of Bohemian humanists. It is very characteristic of the times. Some citizens of Prague, who belonged to the most moderate faction of the Utraquist party, had, in 1493, presented an address to the Roman pontiff. With little political foresight, Lobkovic, thoroughly believing that the separation of Bohemia from the Roman Church had now at least come to an end, wrote an enthusiastic letter to John of Domoslav, a writer in the law-courts of Prague, and one of his very numerous correspondents. In this letter, written in his best Latinity, Lobkovic rejoiced over the final suppression of heresy, and enclosed a prayer in verse in which he invoked the aid of Providence for the purpose of the restoration of Bohemia to Catholicism. What followed is not very clear, but it seems that Domoslav showed Lobkovic's poem to Victorin Cornelius ze Všehrd, who had that year been appointed to high office in the law-courts of Prague, and was his official superior. Všehrd, a fervent Utraquist, was indignant at the suggestion of a reunion with Rome, and, as a true humanist, he also immediately composed a Latin poem, parodying that of Lobkovic The poem ended with the words:—

"*Boemicus sanguis si quid tibi restat aviti*
Roboris, indigno subtrahe colla jugo!
Qui domini tanto servasti jussa superni
Tempore, papalibus contaminari cave!"

This parody Všehrd communicated to Domoslav, who —it is difficult to understand from what motive, unless it was sheer love of mischief-making—immediately forwarded it to Lobkovic.

The indignation of Lobkovic was very great, and he expressed it in a lengthy very Ciceronian letter to Domoslav, which is contained in Professor Truhlař's collection of the letters of Lobkovic. He regrets that Domoslav should have sent to him "the blasphemies of one who, with sacrilegious mouth, raves against the Church of Christ."[1] Lobkovic then proceeds to compare his former friend to Dathan and Abiram, Wycliffe, Arius, and the Emperor Julian. After a long and tedious polemical discourse, Lobkovic very characteristically ends his letter by stating that the heretic, besides his other misdeeds, had "placed a tribrachys in the fifth place of his first verse;" a lengthy list of similar errors follows, and concludes with the remark that Všehrd had, at the end of the last line of his poem, used the second syllable of the word "papalibus"—in the passage I have quoted —as long, contrary to what he had done in an earlier passage of the poem.

In his later years Lobkovic spent most of his time at his castle of Hassištein, and does not seem to have continued his attempt to obtain political influence. He collected a large library at his castle, and devoted his time to study and to the company of the humanist friends who visited him at Hassištein. He died there in 1512.

As Lobkovic wrote only in Latin, a writer on Bohemian literature can deal with his works very briefly. The fact that a Bohemian noble of high rank wrote in a

[1] "Blasphemias cuiusdam in ecclesiam Dei ore sacrilego debacchantis."

sense favourable to Rome at a time when almost the whole of his country was opposed to that Church, has caused Lobkovic to receive much exaggerated praise from writers whose literary judgment was guided by their political and religious sympathies. His works, both in prose and in poetry, are numerous, but have little value. Even in the best of his elegies he is far inferior to his contemporary Sannazaro. The Latinity of his letters is certainly very good, and he ranks very high among the humanists in this respect; but the elaborate style hardly dissimulates poverty of thought and narrow-minded prejudice. His letter or harangue to King Vladislav, written 1497, is in itself sufficient to convict Lobkovic of incapacity as a politician. The purpose of the letter was to entreat the king to re-establish the Roman Catholic archbishopric of Prague, but Lobkovic proceeds to beg the king to extirpate heresy in Bohemia entirely. He quotes, as examples for the king, Charles the Great, who forcibly converted the heathen Saxons, and Ferdinand of Arragon, "who alone among kings emulates you in virtue," by whose agency Baetica, the noblest province of Spain, was restored to our Christian fold. It is, of course, a matter of opinion whether the forcible reconversion of Bohemia to the Roman Church, such as actually took place in the seventeenth century, was desirable or not; but it requires but a very slight knowledge of Bohemian history to realise that such an attempt at the time of the reign of Vladislav was doomed to most certain failure. It is, however, possible that the letter was intended merely to be a rhetorical exercise.

The influence of Lobkovic on the development of Bohemian literature was undoubtedly harmful. The outspoken contempt for the national language expressed by so renowned a humanist could not but discourage its cultivation by others. Lobkovic, in his strange identification of Bohemian writings with what he considered heretical opinions, is an undoubted forerunner of the Jesuit book-destroyers of the seventeenth century. A recent critic writes : " These Latin works of Bohemian humanists appear as a vast sepulchre, bearing the epitaph: 'Here, under an elaborate Latin monument, true Slav hearts lie buried.'"

Though he can scarcely be considered as a humanist, John of Lobkovic should be mentioned in connection with his brother Bohnslav. Differing in most things from his brother, with whom, in consequence of questions of succession, he was for some time on bad terms, he used the Bohemian language for his two works which we possess. He wrote a curious work entitled *Knowledge and Instruction for my son Jaroslav, as to what he should do and what omit.* The book, written in 1504, was afterwards printed under the less unwieldy title of the *True Bohemian Mentor.* It enjoyed great popularity in Bohemia, and a copy of this book was a frequent gift of fathers to their sons.

As a proof of the noble spirit in which the book is written, I shall quote a portion of the chapter entitled "On subject people (*i.e.* serfs), and how you should behave towards them." John of Lobkovic writes : " Be gracious to your subjects, if you wish that the Lord God should be gracious to you. For if you forgive them their offences, then will the Lord God forgive you your offences. For we say in the Lord's Prayer, ' Forgive us our trespasses, as we forgive them that trespass against us.' Thus we ourselves, when we sing the Lord's prayer, submit to this, saying, 'Forgive us as we forgive.' And thus if we do not forgive their offences to those who have offended us, our own sins will not be forgiven to us by God.

"Hear cheerfully every one, rich or poor, on his request, and either help him to justice or order those whose business it is to do so. By this you will obtain the love of the people and their prayers to God for your long life and happiness in everything.

"If some poor man of yours (subject or serf) has committed some not very great offence against you, forgive him once and twice; even if he offends a third time, be merciful. Only if it is a serious matter, justly meriting the penalty of death, then act towards him as is fit. . . . Give just judgment on your subjects and every one on whom you sit in judgment, for that is God's command.

"When sitting in judgment, pay no regard to the person if he be rich or poor, or to favour or disfavour, or to presents, which blind the judge and disgrace justice. Deliver judgment impartially to every one, this one or that."

Lobkovic's advice as to the treatment of serfs is very interesting, as having been written only a few years after the Diet of Bohemia had in 1487 established serfdom, which was contrary to the original customs of Bohemia. It is certain that the rule of the Bohemian nobles over the peasantry belonging to the same race was very mild, and that the condition of the peasantry became far worse when, after the battle of the White Mountain, the landowner was almost always a foreigner, generally a German. John of Lobkovic is also to be mentioned as a traveller. In 1493 he undertook a journey to Palestine by way of

VICTORIN CORNELIUS ZE VŠEHRD 183

Venice, Dalmatia, and Greece, of which he has left us a description entitled *A Pilgrimage to the Grave of God.*

Of Bohemian humanists the most important one next to Bohnslav of Lobkovic is VICTORIN CORNELIUS ZE VŠEHRD, born at Chrudim in 1460. His friendship with Bohnslav of Lobkovic, which was ended by a bitter religious dispute, has already been mentioned. Všehrd for some time held an important office at the law-courts of Prague, which he lost in 1497, it is said through the influence of Bohnslav of Lobkovic. Všehrd was one of the most learned lawyers of his time, and he has left us a legal work in Bohemian entitled *Ten Books on the Rights of the Bohemian Land*, which has great historical value. After his rupture with Bohnslav Lobkovic, Všehrd seems to have abandoned his exclusive devotion to Latin. Belonging to the National Utraquist Church, he was devoid of the dislike to the national language which up to the beginning of the seventeenth century was general among the adherents of the Roman Church. He, however, attempted no original work, but endeavoured to aid the development of the Bohemian language by enriching it with translations from foreign authors. He has himself explained his purpose in the preface to his translation of St. John Chrysostom's work *On the Amendment of the Fallen.* He writes: "I have gladly translated (this book) for this reason also, that I hope thus to extend, to ennoble, to increase our language; for it is not so narrow and unpolished as it seems to some. Its abundance and richness can be seen by this, that whatever can be expressed in Greek or in Latin can be so in Bohemian also. . . . May others compose new books written in Latin and—pouring water into the sea—extend the use of the Roman language. I wish, by translating the books and works of really good men into Bohemian, rather to enrichen the poor than that, flattering the rich with bad and unwelcome presents, I should be despised and insulted. I could indeed write Latin as well as others who are my equals; but knowing that I am a Bohemian, I will indeed learn Latin, but write and speak in Bohemian." Besides the above-mentioned translation, Všehrd also translated into Bohemian several works of St. Cyprian. It must be mentioned that when translating from the Greek, Všehrd used Latin versions. With the exception of Pisecký, the knowledge of Greek which the Bohemian humanists possessed was not very extensive. Všehrd did not confine himself to humanistic studies, but continued to practise as a lawyer up to his death in 1520.

Among other Bohemian humanists, Gregory Hrubý z Jeleni and his son Sigismund—both are better known under the Latinised name of "Gelenius"—deserve special notice. Gregory Gelenius, born about the year 1450, was one of the most industrious translators of classical works into the Bohemian language, and as such has deserved well of the language of his country. The works of Cicero particularly appealed to him, and he not only translated several of them into Bohemian, but also published an *Admonition to the Citizens of Prague*, which is an adaptation of Cicero's speech *Pro Lege Manilia*. Gelenius did not limit his translations to the classical writers. He translated several of the Latin works of Petrarch, the *Encomium Moriæ* of Erasmus, whose fame in Bohemia was very great, and some of the Latin poems of Bohuslav of Lobkovic. I have already alluded to the indignation with which Bohuslav received this attempt to translate his verses

THE GELENIUSES

into his national language, which he so greatly despised. Gregory Gelenius died in 1514.

Gregory's son, SIGISMUND GELENIUS, was perhaps the most learned of the Bohemian humanists. Born in 1497, he travelled in Italy when very young, and during a stay at Venice acquired a thorough knowledge of Greek. He also seems to have been acquainted with the Semitic languages. Sigismund endeavoured, but unsuccessfully, to obtain a professorship of Greek at the University of Prague. Disappointed by his failure, he left Bohemia, and, on the suggestion of Erasmus, proceeded to Basel, where he was employed by the publisher John Frobenius, who was then preparing a series of editions of classical authors. Sigismund Gelenius is one of the greatest philologians of the sixteenth century, and obtained special notice as editor and annotator of the works of Ammianus Marcellinus, Pliny, and Livy. He spent his whole life at Basel, and refused repeated invitations to return to his country. The celebrated Bohemian Brother, Blahoslav, who visited him at Basel in 1550, has recorded that he still "spoke Bohemian very well." Sigismund Gelenius died at Basel in 1554.

In connection with the two Geleniuses I shall mention Wenceslas Hladič, or PISECKÝ, as he called himself, from the town Pisek, where he was born in 1482. He studied at the University of Prague, and there took his degrees as Bachelor and as Master of Arts. He afterwards travelled in Italy, having been chosen by Gregory Gelenius as tutor or companion to his son Sigismund, who was to pursue his studies there. Pisecký and his pupil proceeded to Padua, and from there to Bologna. Bologna was then a centre for the numerous Greek refugees who had after the fall of Constantinople left their country.

As a true Bohemian of his time, Pisecký, while in Italy, engaged in a theological controversy with a monk at Bologna on the subject of communion in two kinds. The Latin treatise which he published on this subject was afterwards translated into Bohemian by Gregory Gelenius. Wenceslas Pisecký was indeed not influenced in his religious opinions by his stay in Italy, and always remained faithful to the Utraquist Church. In one of his letters he complains that his country is little known in foreign lands—a complaint that a Bohemian of the present is unfortunately still entitled to echo—and writes bitterly of Æneas Sylvius, whose book on Bohemia was then and long afterwards considered the standard authority on the subject. He writes: "Æneas Sylvius, who was ignorant of the laws of historical writing as they have been transmitted to us by the Greek writers, deals in the manner of a gladiator (gladiatorio prorsus animo) with the Bohemians."

The most important result of Pisecký's Greek studies was a Bohemian translation of Isocrates's oration to Demonikos, which his protector, Gregory Gelenius, published in 1512, a year after the premature death of Pisecký, who died suddenly at Venice from the plague, or, according to other accounts, from poison. Pisecký's version, in which for the first time a Greek work was translated directly into Bohemian, still has great value, and has by a recent critic been described as a model of Bohemian diction. As a proof of the importance that was attached to the translation, we may quote the very simple Bohemian "Epitaph" which Gregory Gelenius prefixed to the work of Pisecký. It runs as follows:—

"*The town of Pisek was my birthplace;
The University of Prague gave me learning;*

The Italian land taught me Greek.
Therefore have I left a memorial behind me,
Isocrates translated into Bohemian speech.
More work I cannot undertake, for I am dead.
Good Bohemian, be thankful that I accomplished this,
Now that my earthly life is ended."

Another very distinguished Bohemian humanist was JOHN ŠLECHTA, who was afterwards ennobled and received the title "ze Všehrd." He must not, however, be confused with Viktorin Cornelius ze Všehrd, who has already been mentioned. Born in 1446, Šlechta was like Bohnslav of Lobkovic, with whom he was on terms of friendship, and many of the early Bohemian humanists, a fervent adherent of the Church of Rome. Like Lobkovic, also, he had a strong dislike to the language and to the religion of his country. Like most humanists, he was a great letter-writer, and many of his letters, some of which are in his own language, have been preserved.

A curious proof of the intense dislike which some, though by no means all, Bohemian humanists felt for the peculiar religious views which attracted the attention of foreigners to their country can be found in the correspondence of Šlechta with Erasmus of Rotterdam. Šlechta, in a letter referring to the "Bohemian Brethren," informed his correspondent that "an emissary of 'Pikardus'[1] had infected first Žižka's army and then all Bohemia with pestiferous doctrines of sin; thence the 'Bohemian Brethren' proceeded to recognise communion in the two kinds, and to choose as bishops and priests

---

[1] This imaginary personage was supposed to have been the founder of the sect of Pickhards or Beghards, a vague designation which was applied to many mediæval heretics, but more particularly to the Waldenses.

rude laymen who had no culture, were married, and had children."

The answer of Erasmus is very characteristic; he regrets that the Bohemians do not conform to the universal custom as regards communion, but he openly states that he does not understand why Christ's original regulations on this subject have been changed. As to the choosing of their own bishops and priests, this does not, to Erasmus, appear contrary to the early regulations (consuetudo veterum).

The most ambitious work of Šlechta was, no doubt, his *Microcosmus*. The book, which was written in Latin, has been lost, and we can therefore only judge of it from the preface that is still existent, and from the numerous references to it that can be found in the correspondence of Šlechta and his friends. Šlechta appears to have forwarded copies of his book to many of his friends, wishing to obtain their opinion as to its contents. In his preface Šlechta declares that he intended dealing with the relations of the body to the soul according to Plato's works, of which, by means of a Latin translation, he appears to have had some knowledge.

Another Bohemian humanist who, by means of translations into his native language, has deserved well of his country, is Nicolas Konáč, or Finitor, according to the Latinised version of his name. Bohemian writers on the literature of their country devote much space to notices of the numerous translations made by Finitor, but it will here be sufficient to mention that the most important of these Bohemian translations was that of Æneas Sylvius's work on Bohemia. Late in life Finitor wrote, in Bohemian, an allegorical work of mystic tendency that enjoyed great celebrity in its time. The work, that only appeared after the death of Konáč in 1546, is entitled *The Book of Lamentation and Complaint of Justice, the Queen and Mistress of all Virtues.*

It would be easy to continue this enumeration of Bohemian humanists. Though these translators devoted themselves rather too much to the works of the fathers of the Church and to contemporary writers such as Erasmus and Sebastian Brand, and too little to the real classics, yet their work greatly contributed to the improvement and development of the Bohemian language. The study of ancient literature, which was undoubtedly furthered by their work, had a refining and elevating influence on some of the men who, in the last years of Bohemian independence, played a prominent part in the politics of their country. I shall return to this point in the next chapter.

Writing for readers who are not Bohemians, it will be sufficient to mention but two other Bohemian humanists, the two Veleslavins. They enjoyed great celebrity, and it became customary to call the period in which they flourished—the last years of the sixteenth and the first of the seventeenth century—"the age of Veleslavin."

Adam Daniel Veleslavin, born in 1545, studied at the University of Prague, and took his degrees there. He afterwards for some time lectured on history at that university, but after his marriage in 1576 to the daughter of the celebrated printer and publisher, George Melantrich, he became a partner in the business of his father-in-law. In this capacity he greatly furthered the development of Bohemian literature, and it is due to him that many books in that language were printed. Thoroughly acquainted with the art of writing his own language, he thoroughly supervised all the books that issued from his press, and, as Dr. Jireček writes, there is not one of them that doesn't show traces of having been corrected by him. He was occupied with lexicographic works in his own language, and with translations from other languages. Of his many works we may mention his *Politia Historica*, a translation, or rather adaptation, of the vast German work of Lauterbeck, which is entitled *Das Regentenbuch*, and his translation of the work of Æneas Sylvius on Bohemia, which, in spite of its hostility to their country, greatly interested the Bohemians. The preface to this edition, Veleslavin's own work, contains an interesting account of the early historians of Bohemia.

Of his mainly philological works, Veleslavin's *Silva Quadrilinguis* and his *Nomenclator Quadrilinguis* are the most important; both contain alphabetic vocabularies of the Bohemian, Latin, Greek, and German languages. The works issued from the Veleslavin press are so numerous that it seems certain that he had many collaborators in his critical work. Bernard of Hodijov and William Ostrovecký are specially mentioned as having acted as "sub-editors" to the works published by Veleslavin. Though he appears to have by no means been a man of genius, the influence of Veleslavin on Bohemian literature was very great, and it was an undoubted loss to the country that he died prematurely in 1599.

The son of Adam Daniel, ADAM SAMUEL VELESLAVIN was born in 1592, only seven years before the death of his father. In his youth he was involved in the domestic quarrels and civil war which troubled Bohemia in the years 1618 to 1620. He was an enthusiastic adherent of the "Nationalist" party, to use a modern expression, and was obliged to fly from Bohemia after the fatal battle of the White Mountain. We have no record of him from the time that his exile began. His fortune was confiscated by the triumphant Catholics, and his printing-presses, which he had inherited from his father, were made over to the Jesuits. He had up to the downfall of Bohemian independence continued the editorial labours of his father, and had completed the publishing of several works begun by him. He also published in 1613 an edition of the Bible dedicated to the "defenders," that is, the leaders of the Protestant movement.

In connection with the humanists, who also wrote much Latin verse, we now turn to the Bohemian poetry of this period. But even the "golden age" of Bohemian literature, as the sixteenth and the first years of the seventeenth century have often been called, produced little valuable poetry. It is indeed only in the earliest times and again in the present century that Bohemia has been distinguished through its poetry. The sixteenth and seventeenth century produced indeed a certain amount of satirical poetry, but it requires no further notice.

The only writer of this period who composed a large amount of Bohemian poetry was SIMON LOMNICKÝ of Budeč, born in 1552, who was much praised as a poet by his contemporaries. Though most of his poetical writings, particularly his more ambitious efforts, are devoid of true poetic feeling, yet, as being the one poet of that time who wrote in the national language, his place is marked in an account of Bohemian literature. He enjoyed, as already mentioned, great celebrity, and was often described as "the poet of the Bohemian land," "Poeta Cechicus," or the "founder of Bohemian song." More interesting than his larger works are his shorter songs, *vers d'occasion* as they may be called, which he sent to his patrons, the Bohemian nobles. In Bohemia, as in Italy and in other countries, it was then the fashion that important domestic events, such as marriages or deaths, which occurred in noble families should be celebrated in verse, and many poets, of whom Lomnický was one, obtained rich gifts from their patrons in remuneration of verses of this description.

Lomnický is also interesting as being the type of a very numerous class of Bohemians—particularly of the middle class—during the last years of independence. Many Bohemians shared Lomnický's sensual and material view of life, and his inability to feel any genuine political or religious enthusiasms. This fact indeed convicts as utter idealists, and therefore unpractical politicians, men such as Harrant and Budova, who believed that their countrymen were prepared to sacrifice their lives for a Church similar to that of Geneva, and for a constitution similar to that of Venice. Though perhaps only Lomnický welcomed in 1619 Frederick of the Palatinate, and celebrated in 1621 the "just punishment" of his adherents, yet the feeling of indifference to everything beyond personal, mainly material, advantages which Lomnický so cynically displayed, was shared by many Bohemians at the moment when they were confronted with the most decisive crisis in their history.

Lomnický is a voluminous writer, and, as already mentioned, found it advantageous to be so. Besides the numerous gifts which he received from the noble patrons to whom he dedicated his works, he was also ennobled by Rudolph II. in recognition of his poetical works. Of his larger works, one of the earliest is his *Advice to a Young Landowner* (or farmer), which has always been the most popular of Lomnický's writings, and has in recent times, since the revival of Bohemian literature, been twice reprinted. The book is devoid of poetic merit, but is curious as a study of the social life of Bohemia. In the preface Lomnický has explained the purpose of the book, which is personified, and thus addresses the reader : "God be with you, gentle reader— And you in particular, young farmer.—I am again sent out to you—If you will take me to yourself—We will converse together—Rhyme together in Bohemian.—You will, I am sure, say that I am right—And occasionally even smile at my remarks—Through me you will learn— What is beseeming for your household—You will not require much patience—For I have but little to say— For only to a moderate extent—And having regard to brevity—Will I teach you husbandry—You may imagine what I leave unsaid." The reader of this singular book will sometimes regret that Lomnický did not leave more things unsaid.

Lomnický begins his book by moralising on the inequalities of fortune. He writes in the first chapter of his book : " It is a well-known thing in the world—Both in winter and in summer—Both when buying and when selling—That no one always possesses happiness—With one man everything succeeds—With another everything goes amiss—In every sort of trade—One has gain, the other loss. . . . Thus too with agriculture—As with every other description of work—One is successful in everything—With another everything is failure—One man has a virtuous wife—Faithful, bashful, loving— Another marries so slatternly a drab—That all food becomes nauseous to him—One has obedient servants— Requiring but little correction—Another may scold as much as he likes—Nothing will be better—His house will be hell—They (=the servants) will take no notice of him—Perhaps even laugh at him.—In your own children too—You can see how different they are—Some give pleasure—Others cause but grief." This quotation is sufficient to prove that Lomnický extended his reflections far beyond the domain of agriculture. His book contains chapters "on wisdom," "on enemies," "on ill-conducted old women," "on female servants and their punishment," "on conjugal fidelity," "on dress," and on many other matters as little connected with his subject.

Somewhat later Lomnický published his *Cupid's Arrow* (*Kupidova Střela*), a poem which contributed greatly to his fame among his contemporaries. Though the book was not, as has been frequently stated, dedicated to Rudolph II., but to Lord William of Rosenberg, it found great favour with the King of Bohemia, and probably induced that prince to confer on Lomnický the rank of a noble, which he had long desired. In this book also Lomnický poses as a moralist, and inveighs against the vices of his age. Bohemian authors, perhaps the only ones who have seriously criticised Lomnický's writings, have generally, and perhaps rightly, doubted whether his virtuous indignation was sincere. Lomnický, indeed, in this very book, confesses that he was a "lover of sweet Venus," and all his works—not even the *Advice to a Landowner* excepted—show a predilection for *risqué* subjects and situations. Similar in tendency to the *Arrow* is Lomnický's book entitled *Dance, a short treatise on dancing, considered as an exaggerated exertion of the luxurious body*, which was dedicated to his most prominent patron, Lord Peter of Rosenberg. A considerable number of religious poems from the pen of Lomnický have also been preserved, mostly in MS. only. They are written from the Roman Catholic standpoint, which the author generally recognised, though he seems at the time of the coronation of Frederick of the Palatinate to have developed a sudden zeal for communion in the two kinds.

I have already mentioned that in my opinion the minor works of Lomnický possess far greater value than his more extensive works. Of such poems the song in celebration of the marriage of Joachim Ulrick, Lord of Hradec, and the recently printed *Epithalamium* on the marriage of William, Lord Stavata of Chlum, to the noble Lady Lucy of Hradec, have great interest. The last-named song contains a good deal of coarse wit, and offensive allusions to members of the Bohemian nobility who were present at the wedding. The recent editor of this curious poem remarks, that on this occasion the only remuneration which Lomnický deserved from his noble patrons was a sound thrashing! It must not, however, be forgotten that Lomnický held somewhat the position of a licensed buffoon in the houses of the great Bohemian nobles.

Very different from this and similar writings of Lomnický is the burial-song which he wrote on the occasion of the death of his principal patron, Lord Peter Vok of Rosenberg,[1] in 1611, and which, it is said, he recited when walking in the funeral procession. It is characteristic of the enigmatic nature of Rosenberg that, though perhaps not generally popular, he should yet have inspired with a sincere feeling of affection not only men such as Březan, but even so thoroughly egotistical and un-

[1] See Chapter VI.

principled a time-server as Lomnický. Yet no one who reads this poem in its entirety can doubt that here, at least, Lomnický is thoroughly sincere. The poem loses greatly by quotation; yet I shall translate a few lines from a song that undoubtedly shows us Lomnický at his best. It begins thus:—

" *There was once in this Bohemian land a noble lord well known to all the people,*
Whose glory was great, whose name, Peter Vok of Rosenberg, was everywhere celebrated. . . .
He was as a shining light to this country, for which the race of Rosenberg will no longer shine.[1]
The father of the fatherland is dead! No more, Bohemians, will you be able to lay on him the burden of power.
Already is he buried in the monastery of Vyssi Brod, which his ancestors erected and founded.
At that monastery many noble lords assembled; much grief had they at this funeral.
On Candlemas Day was he sorrowfully buried;
Let every one record the day
When death deprived us of this glorious lord; a great loss have we felt, a great grief has God inflicted on us.
When seventy-two years of age he finished his earthly course, left this world.
Born at Krumlov, he died at Trebon; suddenly struck by illness, he saw the day of death.
In worthy old age he left this world; departed from earthly misery to eternal fame."

Somewhat later, Lomnický, addressing the other mourners, writes:—

" *I, the founder of song, lament for him together with you, for my love drives me (to do so),*
Saying: 'My benefactor, too deeply for me do you sleep; but thou, the friend of the poor, knowest thy (heavenly) reward.'
That I may yet serve his memory, I have written this short simple song.

[1] Lord Peter was the last of the illustrious family of Rosenberg.

Weeping has moistened my pen, more tears have I shed than any one who before me sang and wailed.
Bend your heads downward, dear friends; sprinkle with your tears the much-beloved rose.[1]
Pray faithfully for it to the Heavenly God, that it may blossom and grow for ever in His paradise."

At the end of his poem Lomnický reflects on the shortness of human life, and alludes to the curious tradition, that appears then to have been prevalent in Bohemia, that the extinction of the house of Rosenberg would be the prelude to great troubles and changes in Bohemia. Lomnický writes :—

"*Our lifetime here becomes shorter; it perishes like a flower; we must betake ourselves hence into that other world.*
Little time will pass till they carry us from our house; like a little leaf we fall from the tree.
But you, O Bohemian land, be careful of your fate, for all the words of Christ will be fulfilled;
Many wonders happen; the people murder one another; foul pestilences arise everywhere.
Frequently very noble lords leave us; the able and leading men disappear.
Thus this noble who lies on the bier, let him be an example to us; for we must remember
That there is a prophecy that when this family is extinct there will be no peace in the Bohemian kingdom;
Indeed, that after the departure of this most glorious rose, things will go from bad to worse.[2]
Let no one be surprised that I dare to write thus, for this disorderly world cannot exist long.
We also must all die, must go to the distant land, taste death.
Nothing remains but to prepare for it; however much a man may cry he must pay his penalty.

[1] The red rose was the device of the lords of Rosenberg.
[2] Rosenberg died in 1611. The Bohemian uprising against the House of Habsburg began in 1618, and the battle of the White Mountain—the term of Bohemian independence—was fought in 1620.

Let us then do penance, lead a virtuous life, if we wish to be with God.
Death and misery cannot harm us, for it (i.e. death) brings us from death to (eternal) life.
O Jesu Christ! Thou who art our highest Lord, when we die deign to be with us;
Receive our spirit in Thy most holy hand. Deliver us from Satan; do not let us go to torment;
Rather deign to allow us to behold Thee with our eyes, and to meet Lord Peter again in heaven."

I have already alluded to Lomnický's political rhymes, which deserve some notice, though their poetic merit is slight. Lomnický's rhythms have at least the merit that they lose little by translation. When Frederick of the Palatinate arrived in Bohemia in 1619, Lomnický, with his usual facility, immediately began singing the praise of the new sovereign. His verses for a time obtained great popularity at Prague, and—what was probably of greater importance to the needy poet—he received a considerable remuneration from the treasury of the king. Some of these verses have been preserved in the vast historical work of Skála ze Zhoře.[1] On the arrival of Frederick, Lomnický welcomed him with these words: "O King Frederick—We entreat thee with all our might—Drive the enemies from our land—Do not let them rob us any more.—May God give you His blessing—And grant you a happy reign—And also a glorious victory—Over those who are our enemies—Then may we have true freedom.—Receive in the two kinds—The body and the blood of our Lord Jesus.—Do thou effect this O King Frederick!—Confound the rebellious ones (*i.e.* the Austrian party)—Then ever more and more—Shall we praise you according to God—Celebrate your dignity."

[1] See Chapter VI.

Several other poems in the same sense, and dating from about the same time—the end of the year 1619—have been preserved. The battle of the White Mountain, in the following year, produced an immediate change in the views of the unscrupulous time-server Lomnický. He celebrated the executions at Prague on June 21st, 1621, in a ballad, of which I shall quote a few lines. The song begins thus :—

> "*An evil beginning almost always has an evil end:*
> *He that writes this song knows that this is no lie.*
> *Ill began the Calvinists, ill ended the Estates,*
> *Rebels all.*
> *Yes, they roused up the whole world from vain pride, from wickedness;*
> *They conspired together against his Highness* (i.e. *Ferdinand*).
> *Having a king, their lord, already lawfully chosen*
> *And crowned,*
> *They yet chose another for themselves, one of their band,*[1]
> *Who was of the Calvinist faith, of that blind community;*
> *They wanted to have superiority in everything, to be lords and freemen,*
> *To insult the others.*"

After this not very veracious account of the origin of the Bohemian troubles, Lomnický refers to the details of the executions. He writes :—

> "*Every one received punishment according to his offence.*
> *He also did not remain without torment who had sinned with his tongue,*[2]
> *And, as the right demands, who had committed greater offence*
> *Had severer punishment.*

[1] In Bohemian *rota* (see note, p. 161).

[2] Probably an allusion to the celebrated Doctor Jessenius, rector of the University of Prague, whom the Bohemians employed in their negotiations with Hungary, and who was famed for his eloquence. His tongue was cut out before he was decapitated, and his body was quartered after death.

Some were exiled for ever from the country;
Others in prison still hope for mercy;
Others, again, have been whipped: it is the fault of the rebels
That this happens.
O most mournful spectacle! many were amazed,
Many a heart fainted, many shook from horror,
For there is no record that there ever occurred before
So great woe.
Twelve heads were placed on the bridge-gate,
That it might be proclaimed to every corner of the world
Who were the rebels, the wretched " directors," [1]
The cause of all evil.
The remains of those who were quartered were placed at the cross-
   ways in the streets;
The hands of some were chopped off, having those fingers
Which had sworn falsely, which had been raised
To promise faith."

The song ends thus:—

" *O Jesus, we pray to Thee, listen to our voices.*
   Grant to us that we may shortly behold our beloved sovereign
      (*Ferdinand II.*),
   And, rejoicing with him, together praise and honour you,
   Glorify you for ever.
   This story will be the wonder of the whole world,
   And wherever the news reaches it will displease the evil-minded,
   For no one before ever heard or read in the chronicles
   That the devil's pride was so greatly humiliated.
   Many, many people then perished in a short time;
   Their day was ended, they came to the term of their life.
   O God! from a similar evil end
   Deign to preserve us all."

Though severely reprimanded, Lomnický himself escaped punishment, perhaps in consequence of his speedy recantation. The quaint tale that Lomnický was summoned to the presence of Ferdinand, reminded of the

[1] This was the name given to the members of the Provisional Government formed at Prague in 1618 after the Defenestration.

benefits that he had received from Rudolph, the sovereign's ancestor, that he had returned an impertinent answer, and that Ferdinand had then ordered him to be immediately whipped in his presence, has no historical foundation. Lomnický's last years were spent in great poverty. His former patrons, the great Bohemian nobles, were either dead or were penniless exiles in distant countries. The new Austrian authorities, whom he now pestered with demands for pecuniary aid, took little notice of Lomnický. The year of his death is uncertain, but was probably not later than the year 1623.

The foundation of the community—or "Unity," as it was generally called—of the Bohemian Brethren is of the greatest importance for Bohemian literature as well as for Bohemian history. It can be generally stated that, with a few exceptions, all the men who, during the last years of Bohemian independence, were most prominent in literature and in politics belonged to the "Unity." It is true that this is partly due to the fact that the community soon mitigated its original extreme severity, abandoned the views, derived from Chelčicky, that all participation in public life and all "worldly wisdom" is forbidden to the true Christian. It thus became possible that great nobles, politicians, and men of learning should join the community. The foundation of the Bohemian Unity, the consecration of the earliest priests, and the exact tenets of the first members of the community, are still very obscure, and even Dr. Goll, the recognised authority on this subject, declares that many points are doubtful.

The foundation of the Unity was undoubtedly an outcome of the great religious convulsion in Bohemia that was caused by the death of Hus. The intellectual originators, though not the actual founders, of the Unity were Chelčicky and Rokycan. It is difficult to do full justice to Rokycan. His energy and courage were indefatigable, and had it been possible to found in Bohemia a Church agreeing mainly with the doctrine of Rome, but not recognising the papal authority and retaining its independence with regard to certain points of ritual, Rokycan alone could perhaps have achieved this object. It was a necessary consequence of Rokycan's difficult position—he was Archbishop-elect of Prague, but never recognised by the Papal See—that his teaching somewhat differed at times in accordance with the state of public affairs. When an agreement with Rome seemed possible, his eloquent sermons dwelt rather on the points in which the Utraquists agreed with Rome. When, as always happened when the negotiations with Rome had lasted some time, the Papal See declared itself resolutely opposed to all the demands of Bohemia, Rokycan preached strongly against the tenets of Rome, and particularly against the avarice and immorality of the Roman clergy. It is a peculiarity of the Bohemian Church reformers that, from the days of Hus to the time of the complete suppression of religious liberty, they always laid great stress on this point.

During the reign of King Ladislas Posthumus (1439–1457), who, in consequence of his early education, was hostile to the Utraquist creed, then professed by the great majority of the Bohemians, the preaching of Rokycan, whom the king viewed with marked disfavour, was of a very advanced character. Following directly in the footsteps of Hus, Rokycan in his sermons strongly denounced the corruption of the times and laid particular stress upon the worthlessness of the Roman clergy. Many of his remarks on this subject have been recorded by the writers of the Unity. "A stag with golden antlers on the bridge of Prague," he declared, "was not so great a rarity as a good priest." These sermons made a great impression on the vast audiences to whom they were delivered; for the almost exclusive interest in religious matters was then characteristic of most educated Bohemians. Among the listeners who were most impressed by Rokycan's fiery eloquence was a young man known to us by the name of "Brother Gregory," who was destined to become the founder of the Unity. Even after the careful researches of recent years, Gregory's life is still surrounded by mystery. It is stated that he was a nephew of Archbishop Rokycan, and also —what renders that statement at least improbable—that he belonged to a noble though poor family. His family name, according to some accounts, was Krejči, which in Bohemian signifies "tailor." It is, however, more probable that he received that name because, after the foundation of the Unity, he sometimes practised the trade of a tailor. The strict rules established by Gregory himself obliged the priests of the Unity to live in poverty and by the work of their hands. In his earlier years Gregory appears to have lived at a Utraquist monastery at Prague, that had been founded by Magister Přibram. It is, however, certain that he had not been ordained as a priest.

Gregory, accompanied by some friends, visited the Archbishop, and sought his advice on religious matters, and specially on the subject of unworthy priests. To understand the importance of this constantly-recurring subject, it must be remembered that Hus, Chelčicky, and other Bohemian reformers denied all ecclesiastical powers to unworthy priests, whom they considered as "not the clergy of Christ, but of Antichrist." The Archbishop's answer appears surprising, even if we consider that the ever-varying relations between the Pope and the Church of Bohemia were then at their worst. He advised his visitors to study the works of Chelčicky and to visit him. Gregory followed this advice, and travelled to Chelčic, where he visited Chelčicky shortly before his death. There is no doubt that the aged theologian's opinions greatly influenced Gregory, and some of Chelčicky's adherents were no doubt among the first members of the Unity.

The relations between Gregory and Rokycan did not long continue friendly. After the death of King Ladislas, George of Podebrad was elected King of Bohemia. The new king endeavoured, at the beginning of his reign, to obtain a reconciliation with Rome. He was ready to conform to the Roman doctrine if that Church recognised Rokycan as Archbishop of Prague, permitted communion in the two kinds, and accepted that part of the "Articles of Prague" which enjoined poverty on the Bohemian clergy and opposed their notorious immorality. While these negotiations were proceeding, Rokycan advised Gregory and his friends to leave Prague and to retire to a more secluded spot. He had obtained permission from King George, who owned the estates of Litic and Senftenberg in Eastern Bohemia, to allow Gregory and his friends to settle in the secluded village of Kunwald, near the small town of Senftenberg. It has been stated by many historians, including Palacký, that Rokycan had suggested this emigration to Gregory, wishing to be rid of allies who had now become unwelcome. Dr. Goll has recently expressed his doubts as to this conjecture. It is certain that no immediate and complete rupture between Gregory and Rokycan took place. Gregory arrived at Kunwald towards the end of the year 1457, and was soon joined by many enthusiasts, who desired to lead a simple life, according to the customs of the primitive Christians. Among the early disciples of Gregory was Michael, the parish priest of Senftenberg, and another priest named Matthew. After the death of Chelčicky, some of the "Brothers of Chelčic"[1] also joined the community of Kunwald, as did some of the remaining Taborites, and probably, though this point is doubtful, some Austrian Waldenses also.

The new community soon became obnoxious to the Government of King George, and the "first persecution," as it is termed in the writings of the Unity, began in 1460. Some of the fanatics, known at that period all over Europe as the "Pickharts" or "Beghards," had about that time joined the community of Kunwald, and drew on it the indignation of the Bohemian authorities. In 1461 Gregory returned for a short time to Prague. It has been suggested that he did this in opposition to a promise made to Rokycan; but of this there is no sufficient proof. At Prague Gregory held secret meetings of his adherents, among whom were a considerable number of students of the university. Gregory received notice—perhaps from Rokycan himself—that these gatherings were being watched. He therefore, at a meeting on March 15th, begged all present to disperse immediately. Some did so, but others declared that they were doing no wrong; and when Gregory drew their attention to the fact that they were risking imprisonment, and even tor-

[1] See Chapter IV. p. 157.

ture, they answered, "Well, we will have torture for breakfast, and the funeral pile for dinner." The Government officials shortly afterwards arrested the remaining members of the assembly, and several underwent the torture of the rack. Not all displayed fortitude; several, as a member of the Unity, writing shortly after these events took place, quaintly expresses it, "having breakfasted, did not wait for dinner." Those who dreaded further punishment were obliged to pronounce a solemn recantation in the presence of Rokycan.

Whether Gregory himself underwent torture is uncertain, though most of the writers of the Unity, from Brother Lucas to Brother Jaffet, state it is a fact. Brother Jaffet[1] tells us that Gregory "was tied to a post, placed on the rack, and burnt. Weakened by long fasting, he then fainted, and no longer felt pain; only when he had been released he felt his side, and understood what had been done to him." Rokycan visited Gregory in prison, and, to use Brother Jaffet's words, condoled with him with the "compassion of a crocodile." Seeing the traces of his sufferings, he exclaimed, "Dear Gregory, how I pity you. Remember that I always told you if you pursued your endeavours you would suffer and it would fare badly with you."

Dr. Goll has recently expressed doubts whether torture was inflicted on Brother Gregory, though he admits that his followers were tortured. There is, however, no doubt that the tradition of the sufferings of Brother Gregory, the founder of the Unity, can be traced back to the earliest records of the community. It is, therefore, difficult to believe that the traditional account is a mere

---

[1] *Historie o puvodu Jednoty* ("History of the Origin of the Unity"), quoted by Jireček.

fiction. Of modern writers Palacký and Jireček maintain the truth of the ancient record of the Unity. What is, however, certain is that Rokycan's part in these events has been misrepresented. Political reasons at that moment rendered it advisable for King George to appear as the enemy of the extreme antagonists of Rome. Rokycan's influence on the king was then very slight, but such as it was, it induced George after a time to liberate Brother Gregory from prison.

Difficulties had meanwhile arisen in the small community, of which first Kunwald and then the neighbouring small town of Reichenau (Rychnov) on the Kněžna was the centre. Gregory was indeed the intellectual leader as well as the founder of the community, but the priests Michael and Martin seem, probably in consequence of their having been ordained as priests, to have claimed a certain superiority over the other brethren. To obviate these difficulties, Gregory resorted to what must then have appeared a most venturesome step. He decided that his followers should, in accordance with the example of the Apostles, elect priests from among their number. The doctrine of the necessity of the apostolic derivation of the clergy was then held even by sects that were strongly opposed to Rome. This is no doubt the reason why, according to most accounts, the new priests were subsequently consecrated by a Waldensian priest or bishop. It must be added that the part played by the Waldensian in the first ordination of the clergy of the Unity becomes much more prominent in the works of later writers than it was in those of contemporaries. Dr. Lechler has recently expressed doubts as to whether the intervention of a Waldensian at the first ordination that took place in the Unity is a historical fact. Such an intervention appears to him to be in contradiction with the previous decision of the brethren to elect priests on the strength of divine inspiration. It must, however, be noticed that in Brother Gregory's account of the ceremony, written in Bohemian, and therefore perhaps unknown to Dr. Lechler, who was a German, the Waldensian priest is already mentioned. The point, like many others connected with the origin of the Unity, will perhaps never be settled. It has given rise to an extensive controversial literature.[1]

A meeting of the brethren of the Unity took place at Lhotka, a small village near Reichenau, in 1467. I will quote a portion of Gregory's account of the proceedings to which I have just referred. Gregory's Bohemian is very rugged and lends itself but little to translation. Following the example of Dr. Goll, who has translated a large part of the account contained in Gregory's *Fourth Letter to Rokycan* into German, I give a nearly literal translation. It would be easy to smooth down Gregory's style, but at the risk of not conveying the exact meaning. He writes: " Among us some doubt and irresolution sprung up. We therefore conformed in everything to the Acts of the Apostles and the example of the first saints, wishing to act in everything in the name of God both in word and deed. Therefore, trusting to His promises contained in the words, 'Whatsoever you will ask of the Father in My

---

[1] Of English works on this subject, I may mention the "Extract of the Letter of the late Bishop Jablonsky to his Excellency C. Zinzendorf: As touching the succession of Episcopal Consecration; the Bohemian Brethren have got their Ordination from the Waldenses about the year 1467, and have kept the same carefully and without interruption." Printed in *Acta Fratrum Unitatis in Anglia*, 1749, as Appendix VII.

name, He will grant you,' and again, 'Whenever two or three are gathered together,' and so forth, we deliberated as to whether God wished that we should separate entirely from the jurisdiction of the Pope and of his priesthood, and secondly, whether God wished that we should establish a separate organisation on the model of the Primitive Church. We further deliberated as to what persons should arbitrate in disputes and have such authority that all should maintain peace and submit to their verdict. And further, who should serve and who obtain the first places and possess the power of office, according to the words, 'To you I give the keys,' and again, 'Whom you forgive their sins.'

"And we, many of us from Bohemia and other lands, decided to pray to God, should He then wish it (*i.e.* that they should establish a separate organisation), that He might give us a sign, according to the example of the Apostles when they chose a twelfth. And we ordered all brothers in the different districts to pray and fast in view of this. Then we assembled in numbers and prayed to the Lord God that He might give us a sign whether He then wished this or not. And it so happened that He did wish it, and we had the faith that it was God's will that it should happen thus. . . . And when the day came, many of us again assembled from Bohemia and Moravia, and we prayed to God with the same confidence as before, and we chose nine men, of whom three, or two, or one were to be it (*i.e.* the head of the new Church). But if God had not wished it that year, then no one would have been chosen. We should have remained without priests till God, in consequence of our prayers and of our faith, had shown us that He wished it, and also what persons should be chosen. But as we had abandoned the priests who derive their power from the papal office, firmly believing that God did not desire that we should heed them in regard to our obedience (=obey them), therefore we firmly believed that God would grant us what we prayed for. And the Lord did so, because of our faith and our prayers, and ordained that it (the choice) should fall on all three.[1] And God thus manifested His wisdom and power to us in such a manner that we all felt clearly that God had visited us, and had done great things to confirm us in the faith. More than sixty brethren were assembled, and with full confidence and joy we received the Holy Ghost, and thanked God that He had visited us at the end of days and done His work.

"We then conversed together on the confirmation of their priestly office (*i.e.* that of the three who had been chosen as priests), how it could be done in the most seemly manner and without offence to the people; though we believed without doubt that they were already ordained and confirmed by our Lord Christ, as God had shown us. But we wished to appear righteous, not only before God, but also as far as possible before all men. Therefore we sought it (*i.e.* confirmation) from one (priest) whom we had received from the Romans, and from another who belonged to the Waldenses, who spring from the primitive Church, a man of whom we were confident that he was in the state of grace. And

---

[1] That the choice was made by the drawing of lots, which is here only hinted at, is more fully explained in the later accounts of Brother Jaffet and Komensky; they tell us that the brethren chose nine of their number, and then intrusted a boy who was unaware of their intentions with twelve slips of paper; of these, nine were blank and three contained the word "Jest." The nine chosen men then drew the slips of paper, and all those containing the word "Jest" were drawn; this was considered as signifying that God wished the Unity to have three spiritual chiefs.

we took these two for the ordination of the three. If God wishes it so, we said, let Him show it. And we prayed to God that He might, should He desire this confirmation by the Waldensian, give such grace to that elder that he might do it from love and in true faith.

"And God gave it (grace) to him, that he did it in true faith; and, encouraging us, he spoke good words and praised God, saying, 'God has done this for the benefit of our salvation.' And then he confirmed these three in their priestly office by laying his hands on them and by prayers, according to the example of the primitive Church and the instructions of the Apostles. And as regards Jesus's having from on high pointed out the three that were chosen, and the one of them who was to have highest rank, he to whom it had been disclosed (perhaps Gregory himself) said, 'Believe firmly that this is so.'"

Though the later members of the Unity studied the art of literary composition, and indeed attained mastership in it, this was not the case with Brother Gregory. His writing shows that he was entirely absorbed in his endeavour to place his religious views before his former friend and present antagonist, Rokycan, to whom the letter is addressed. It has been very difficult to render Gregory's words clearly without entirely altering his manner of writing. The passage quoted above, and indeed the whole *Fourth Letter to Rokycan*, is, however, worthy of notice. It is the only account by an eye-witness of the meeting at Lhotka, which marks the beginning of the Unity, and was written by Brother Gregory in 1468, only a year after the assembly.

The consequence of the meeting at Lhotka was a renewed persecution of the members of the Unity.

Rokycan published a very severe edict against them, for their attempt to establish an independent clergy was as obnoxious to the Utraquist as to the Roman priests. Brother Gregory lived for seven years after the assembly at Lhotka, and as he is stated to have been over fifty when the community of Kunwald was founded in 1457, he must have attained a considerable age. His entire energy and activity were to the last devoted to the Unity. Its constitution, which conferred the principal power on the so-called smaller[1] council, at whose head was a president ("ordinator"), often, though not in the fifteenth century, called "bishop," is the work of Gregory. Though in every respect the leading spirit of the Unity, Gregory never aspired to be the recognised leader of his Church. That rank was from the time of the meeting of Lhotka assumed by the priest Matthew, who at the time of that meeting was a young man of the age of twenty-five. Whether the fact that Matthew had been ordained as a priest by the Church of Rome was not one of the causes of his election, cannot perhaps now be ascertained. The remarks of Gregory, quoted above, seem to be in opposition to this view. Matthew was on terms of friendship with Brother Gregory, and accepted his guidance on all matters of doctrine and discipline. He is described as a man of weak character, and the discord that broke out among the brethren after the death of Gregory seems to confirm this view.

The small town of Brandeis on the Adler,[2] situated in the picturesque valley of the Orlice or Adler, was one of the early centres of the community of the brethren, and it was here that Brother Gregory spent the greater part

---

[1] In Bohemian *úzky*, literally "narrow."
[2] In Eastern Bohemia, between the towns of Wildenschwert and Pardubic.

of his last years. He continued, however, to the end of his life to pay frequent visits to other communities of the brethren. Brother Gregory died at Brandeis on August 12, 1474, and was buried, "like the prophets of the Old Testament, in a rock-grave near the bank of the Orlice, that is, opposite the castle." Gregory, the patriarch of the Unity, as he called himself in his later years, was certainly one of its greatest men. He combined the most fervent religious enthusiasm with the talents of a clear-headed and indefatigable organiser; and though changes took place in the institutions of the Unity after his death, yet on the whole the structure erected by Gregory continued to exist till the time when the battle of the White Mountain destroyed all communities that were opposed to Rome.

Dr. Goll, who has given a masterly sketch of the career of Gregory, thus describes him:[1] "Gregory had created for himself the ideal image of a true Christian, an abstemious, kindly, patient, gracious, merciful, economical, pure, humble-minded, peaceful, worthy, zealous, yielding, compliant man, qualified and ready to do all good works. But this model was not for Gregory a model only. He believed that Christians can come near to the model, nay, even attain it. 'We believe this,' he writes in the *Fourth Letter to Rokycan*, 'that he who has God's true and living faith has the power also to mortify the evil in himself and to act righteously; his faith by means of love will induce him to do what is pleasing to God, good actions and such as are useful to his fellow-creatures. . . . Though by nature hasty and irritable, a true Christian must be abstemious, meek, and silent. A model for this model is

In the Journal of the Bohemian Museum (*Časopis Musea Královstí Českeho*) for 1886.

found in our Saviour Himself. He suffered for us and gave us an example in His acts, accomplishing the work that His Father had laid upon Him. A true Christian must take on himself those burdens which were Christ's also; he must endure adverse things and injuries affecting his estate, his honour, and his life quietly, considering that it must be thus.'"

After reading Dr. Goll's definition of the doctrine of Brother Gregory it is scarcely necessary to state that theological controversy plays a very small part in Gregory's writings. The imitation of Christ was the purpose of his life and is the leading motive of his writings. Readers of the portions of the *Fourth Letter to Rokycan* which I have already quoted will have noticed how little importance Gregory himself appears to attach to the confirmation of the priests; it was sufficient for him firmly to believe that the choice had been made in accordance with God's own command.

The literary remains of Gregory, all written in Bohemian, are considerable. There are seven so-called *Letters to Rokycan*, which, though they were all undoubtedly sent to the Archbishop, were yet intended for a wider circle of readers. Two of these letters, the fourth, from which I have quoted extensively, and the sixth, were afterwards republished by Gregory in an enlarged form, the former under the title of *The Sufferings of the Brethren under King George*, the latter under that of *The Answer of the Ancient Brethren*. We have letters also addressed to other people. The form of a letter was then a very favourite one for expounding theological views. Other writings of Gregory are *The Book on Good and Evil Priests, On the Holy Church*, and *On the Narrow Path*. A treatise, evidently dating from the first days of the Unity, and entitled *How*

People should Behave with regard to the Roman Church, is also generally attributed to Gregory. Recent research renders it probable that it is not his work.

It is, of course, out of place to give here an historical account of the development of the Unity, though such a work would have great interest. The brethren were, however, such indefatigable writers that it is necessary frequently to refer to the history of the community.

Discord broke out among the brethren, who had already become numerous, shortly after the death of Gregory, probably about the year 1480. Matthew, who had been the nominal head of the community during Gregory's lifetime, appears to have been a well-meaning man of weak character, who became helpless after the loss of his sagacious adviser. Several different causes of discord are mentioned as appearing at about the same time. A theological controversy as to the means of salvation was indeed settled by means of a compromise proposed at one of the numerous meetings of the brethren by Brother Prokop, noticeable also as one of the theological writers of the Unity. Shortly afterwards, however, discussions as to "worldly power" led to a rupture. Gregory had, on the whole, held the opinions of Chelčicky,[1] according to which no true Christian should take part in the government of the State, nor should he take oaths or possess worldly goods. Gregory also shared Chelčicky's dislike to towns, "the foundations of Cain." These views had been strictly carried out during the first years of the Unity. The new members had, on joining the community, been obliged to despoil themselves of all worldly possessions and con-

[1] See Chapter IV.

form to the other doctrines of Chelčicky mentioned above.

In the last years of the fifteenth century men of higher rank, townsmen and nobles, of whom Kostka of Postupic was the first, began to join the community. It now became more difficult to maintain the early regulations in their entire severity. Some of the brethren complained that they incurred persecution on the part of their fellow-citizens because they had refused to hold municipal offices or to appear as witnesses in the law-courts. Two parties soon formed themselves in the Unity. One, known as the "large party," was in favour of somewhat relaxing the rigour of the original regulations; this was evidently necessary if the community was to expand and to acquire the protection of some of the nobles, without which it could hardly have continued to exist long in Bohemia. The other party, known as the "small party," adhered strictly to the original regulations. Many attempts at a reconciliation were made, and frequent meetings of the elders of the Unity took place for this purpose, generally at Reichenau on the Knĕžna, or at Brandeis on the Orlice. A last effort of reconciliation was made in 1496, when numerous members of both parties met at Chlumec. Here, as at the previous conferences, both parties maintained their previous views, and the discussion only proved that the standpoints were entirely different and an agreement impossible. Though even after this attempts at mediation were made, the "small party," led by Brother Amos, now seceded from the main body of the community, and after a few years it entirely disappears. The "large party," on the other hand, freed from the original exaggerated regulations, obtained great and deserved fame in

Bohemia; it became the cradle of almost all those who, in the last century of Bohemian independence, were prominent as statesmen or authors.

Among the early writers of the "large party," PROKOP OF NEUHAUS or Jindřichuv Hradec deserves mention, though his fame has been obscured by the greater name of his successor, Brother Lucas, who finally secured the victory of the "large party." Prokop appears to have been one of the original members of the community of Kunwald. When the controversy as to the means of salvation sprung up among the brethren, Prokop, as already mentioned, succeeded in inducing the contending parties to accept a compromise. When the discussion whether the brethren were entitled to possess worldly property and to hold state offices began, Prokop expressed views which, though they were not quite in accordance with either party, really prove him an adherent of the "large party." It was on this subject that Prokop wrote his *Explanation of the Fifth Chapter of St. Matthew*. He here writes that, "though difficult, it is admissible that nobles and mighty men should be received into the Unity and be considered members of it, if they avoid deadly sins, for which poor men also go to hell, and if in all important matters they conform to Christianity and lead a Christian life." Prokop continues to state "that, speaking generally, the brethren may exercise the duties of town-councillors and of other offices, and that they may appeal to the temporal power for aid; for this is for the general good."

It will be seen by this quotation that Prokop generally agreed with the views of the "large party," though he sometimes differed from Brother Lucas, with whom he was indeed several times engaged in controversies. Prokop was the principal orator of the "large party" at the meetings at Reichenau in 1494 and at Chlumec in 1496. He was then, as Blahoslav tells us, "the foremost man of the Unity." Prokop spent the greatest part of his life at Brandeis, and died there in 1507. He has left a considerable number of works, all written in Bohemian. Besides the *Explanation of the Fifth Chapter of St. Matthew*, which has already been mentioned, he wrote *Five Letters to Brother Lucas on his* (*Lucas's*) *work entitled 'The Bark,'* and the *Book against Antichrist*.

Better known than Prokop is Brother Lucas, the foremost representative of the "large party" during its struggle; he is yet more noteworthy as the man who after its victory reorganised the Unity, and, to a certain extent, altered its institutions in a more enlightened and liberal manner. The works of Lucas, all written in Bohemian, are numerous; he is indeed, next to Komenský, the most voluminous writer of the Unity. Lucas, generally known as LUCAS OF PRAGUE, was born about the year 1460. He was greatly impressed by the writings of the early members of the Unity, and, together with his friend the young nobleman Lawrence of Krasonický, he joined the community about the year 1482. He soon attained a prominent position among the brethren, and in 1490 was already a member of the "smaller council." When the differences of the Unity between the "large" and the "small" party arose, Lucas declared himself energetically in favour of the former, and was indeed one of its representatives at several assemblies. The discord among the brethren, and the religious uncertainty which was one of its results, seems to have rendered yet stronger the desire for a return to the primitive Church, which, sometimes more obvious, sometimes scarcely perceptible, can yet be traced in the writings of all Bohemian reformers. Some of the brethren maintained that in distant Eastern lands Christians yet existed who had retained the purity of the primitive Church, both as regards doctrine and the conduct of life. The Unity decided to send out several brethren, who were to discover these communities which entirely conformed with the primitive Church. Lucas, with two companions, started for this purpose for Constantinople, where they separated. Lucas himself appears to have visited Mount Athos and the communities of the Bulgarians, and of the Bohomils in Bosnia. Fertile writer though he was, Lucas has unfortunately left us no account of his travels, for which we could well have spared one or two of his sixty-eight theological works. The first of these works, entitled *The Bark*, was written shortly after his return from his journey. As already mentioned, it involved him in a controversy with Brother Prokop.

After the assembly of Chlumec and the final victory of the more enlightened party among the brethren, it was resolved to reorganise the community, and to model their institutions to a certain extent on those of the Waldenses. The exact relations between the two communities will perhaps never be known, particularly as the history of the Waldenses or Vaudois is itself very obscure. It is, however, certain that the brethren were fully conscious of an affinity between themselves and the older community. Lucas was intrusted with the mission of visiting the Waldensian communities, and started for Italy and Savoy accompanied by Brother Tuma of Landskron, known as "Němec" (or the German). Among the places they visited was Florence, where they were present at the death of Savonarola (May 23, 1498). Of this journey also Lucas has left us no account. On his return to Bohemia, Brother Lucas obtained a yet more important position in his community. After the death of Matthew an assembly of the brethren which met at Reichenau in 1500 decided to elect several bishops. Lucas was one of those chosen, and appears to have exercised greater influence than his colleagues. The Roman Catholic monk Wolfgang, with whom Lucas engaged in one of his many theological controversies, indeed describes him as "the anti-pope."

During the persecution which again befell the Unity at the beginning of the sixteenth century Lucas displayed admirable courage and energy. Rightly believing that ignorance was the cause of many of the attacks on the brethren, he was indefatigable in expounding their real teaching. He wrote an appeal to the king and a letter to the people of Bohemia, protesting against the judgment of those who had declared that the brethren were "worse than Jews and heathens, indeed equal to devils." Lucas also appealed to Erasmus of Rotterdam against the ignorant misjudgment which resulted in so much suffering for the brethren. He despatched two members of the community to Erasmus as bearers of a written "confession" or "apology" of the Unity. Erasmus, with characteristic prudence, declined to be entangled in the controversy.

About the year 1514 the attitude of the Bohemian officials became less hostile to the Unity. Contemporary records give no reason for this change; but Blahoslav's statement that "the king investigated the doctrine of the Unity and decided in its favour" is most improbable. The influence of some powerful noblemen who had joined the brethren probably secured for the Unity what was really only the tacit toleration of its existence. The fiction that only the Utraquist Church, which was the "State Church," and the Roman creed were recognised in Bohemia was maintained up to a far later date. The last years of the eventful life of Lucas were influenced by the appearance of Luther. Luther's teaching soon became known in Bohemia, and was welcomed by the people of that country. They felt as if their isolation, which had long weighed on them, was ended when even the Germans, the mortal enemies of Utraquism, communicated in the two kinds. The more advanced Utraquists specially sympathised with German Protestantism, and it did not for a moment seem impossible that Bohemia should adopt the teaching of Luther. The brethren, and Brother Lucas in particular, however, declared that they should always maintain their own community distinct from both the German Protestants and the Bohemian Utraquists. They have often been praised for this, but it is very probable that by joining the German Protestants the Bohemians would have obtained powerful allies when, at the beginning of the seventeenth century, the Jesuit reaction attacked their country. The isolation in which the Bohemian brethren, and to a lesser extent the Bohemian Utraquists, continued, alone accounts for the incredible apathy with which the German Protestants viewed the suppression of Protestantism in Bohemia. At the negotiations which preceded the Treaty of Westphalia, the

Swedish envoys alone made an ineffective appeal in favour of the Unity and the other non-Roman inhabitants of Bohemia.

In a treatise published in 1522 Lucas attacked Luther's teaching on several points, but on receiving a conciliatory answer from the great German reformer he decided on entering into negotiations with him. He sent a member of the Unity, Brother Roh[1] or Horn, to Wittenberg with copies of several of his works. Luther does not seem to have had a very clear idea of the identity of the community which wished to enter into relations with him, for he addressed his answer to "his dear nobles and friends the brethren called Waldenses living in Bohemia and Moravia." The contents of the letter appear to have displeased Lucas, who wrote several treatises for the purpose of "strengthening" the brethren against the teaching of Luther. Lucas, indeed, somewhat later sent a second messenger to Wittenberg, but the disagreement continued, and subsequently a complete rupture took place. To the end of his life Lucas continued to labour at the reorganisation of the Unity. One of his latest and most important works was his *Zpráva Knĕžka* ("Instruction for the Clergy of the Unity"), published in 1526; he died two years later.

It has already been mentioned that Brother Lucas was a voluminous writer. Dr. Jireček in his biography published in 1875 enumerates sixty-eight works of Lucas, some of which, it is true, are known only by repute and have not been preserved. Since the appearance of Dr. Jireček's book, Dr. Goll has discovered works of Lucas that are not included in his list. Among the works of

---

[1] The Bohemian word *roh* signifies "horn" in German and English.

Brother Lucas known now only by name but enumerated in Dr. Jireček's list is an "Answer to the ten articles of Master Jerome Dungesham[1] of Oxford, (written) against the apology of the Brethren published in 1514." The first work of Lucas, was as already mentioned, his *Barka* or "Bark." This work too was believed to be lost, but within the last years Dr. Goll has discovered a MS. which contains this once celebrated work of Lucas. The allegorical name of the book is thus explained by the author. He tells us that in the first part of his work the bark signifies the Unity, and that it is his purpose to explain out of what planks it is constructed, what are its requirements, who is its captain and guide, and what is the destination of its course. In this first part of the work the captain is Jesus Christ. The second division of the book deals with "The Bark of Antichrist," with the foolish and misguided people who occupy it, and with the weighty reasons for flying from that bark, the course of which leads to perdition. Like so many Bohemian works of this period, the "Bark" treats mainly of Antichrist. It is interesting as being very similar, and in parts identical, with one of the ancient books of the Waldenses. It undoubtedly throws some light on the obscure question of the relations between the Bohemian brethren and the older community.

Of the many other works of Lucas I shall be able to notice even briefly but very few. The two *Professions of the Faith of the Unity*, addressed to King Vladislav, and similar documents addressed to Erasmus and Luther, have been already mentioned. Very curious is Lucas's work entitled *The Revival of the Holy Church, and the reasons which render it certain that such a revival has*

---

[1] I quote the name as given by Dr. Jireček.

taken place in the shape of the Unity. Lucas draws a curious mystic parallel between the life of Christ and the development of the Unity. He also refers to the simplicity of the primitive Church, and to the gradual increase of the power of the Bishops of Rome. In distinction from his predecessors, Lucas no longer believes in the " donation of Constantine." He only tells us that Constantine placed the Bishop of Rome before all other bishops. "Constantine," Lucas tells us, "seated Sylvester on a white horse. This appeared wonderful to the people, and in their Latin or Italian speech they exclaimed, ' Pape ! Pape !'[1] that is, 'What a great, great wonder !'" Only Charles the Great, Lucas tells us, added temporal power to the ecclesiastical supremacy. It is particularly noticeable that in this book also Lucas does not allude to his travels, though on several occasions it would have been natural to do so. It is almost certain that this silence is intentional. Dr. Goll has, with great sagacity, suggested its cause. The brethren now believed that the true primitive Church had been revived in their own community, and did not wish to recall the fact that they had formerly sought for it elsewhere.

The polemical works of Lucas are very numerous, and are directed indifferently against all those who did not accept the doctrine of the Unity as expounded by him. His controversies with Luther have already been mentioned. A work of Lucas's is directed against Zwingli, whose teaching had also penetrated into Bohemia. He also engaged in a theological controversy with "Wolfgang, the barefooted friar." Wolfgang, one of the earlier champions of the Church of Rome, played a

[1] This passage recalls Dante's "Pape Satan ! Pape Satan Aleppe !" (*Inferno*, Canto VII.).

curious part in the great theological controversy that absorbed almost the whole intellectual activity of Bohemia during two centuries. I shall again refer to him. Another controversial book of Lucas's directed against Brother Kaleņec, a member of the "small party" in the Unity, is interesting as containing the author's opinion on Chelčicky, whose memory was naturally very popular with the smaller and more retrograde fraction of the Unity. Lucas writes: "You take refuge with Peter of Chelčic, and recommend to others his books, such as the *Net of Faith*. I, who have read and copied out many of his books before I joined the brethren, will say that in many matters he thought wrongly, and in a manner contrary to Scripture, and that he wrote obscurely and without moderation. I have also heard from those brethren that were with him much that was not praiseworthy, particularly that he was very irritable and vindictive. Thus, having fallen out with a priest, he would not forgive him till his death; so that priest himself told me. And he (Chelčicky) unjustly defamed the Taborite priests, particularly as regards their teaching on the sacrament."

A year before his death, Brother Lucas again returned to his favourite subject, the identification of the Unity with the primitive Church, in his treatise *On the Origin of the Unity*. Dealing with the manner in which the consciousness of the corruption of the Church reached Bohemia, Lucas writes: "The movement began through the Waldenses in England, where Wycliffe was the king's chaplain, but only read mass. And a Waldensian with whom he was acquainted said to him that he only fulfilled half the duty of his office, because he did not preach; and he proved this from Scripture. . . . Then of those who at that time (in England) suffered much adversity and martyrdom, some went to other countries, and particularly to Dresden, and thence some of them afterwards proceeded to Bohemia." Though unhistorical, this account is curious as containing what was probably a very old tradition. Lucas here, as was frequently the case with Bohemian writers of his time, describes as "Waldenses" all early opponents of the Church of Rome.

Brother Lucas was certainly one of the greatest men of the Unity, probably the greatest theologian whom the community produced. It was principally through the reorganisation of the community, that is his work, that the brethren were able to play a considerable part in Bohemian history. It is, however, an exaggeration to consider Lucas as a "second founder" of the Unity. The main lines of Brother Gregory's great structure remained. Of Lucas as an author, Brother Blahoslav[1] writes as follows: "Brother Lucas wrote a great many books, but he was not a very good Bohemian (writer); he imitated Latin more than is befitting, and his knowledge of German was also harmful to him, for his family came from a place where much German was spoken. 'In summe Latinismos et Germanismos plurrimos admittere solebat.'[2] Therefore, and also for another reason,[3] his works appeared to many not clear and displeasing."

In connection with Lucas I shall briefly refer to his associate Krasonický. Krasonický was, like Lucas, an adherent of the "large party." He appears to have

[1] See later.

[2] The Latin passage is written in that language in Blahoslav's (Bohemian) work, which I quote. The Latin spelling is also that of Blahoslav.

[3] This, no doubt, refers to some theological difference between Lucas and Blahoslav.

been a fertile writer, but many of his works are known only by name. Among those that have been preserved is a treatise addressed to Brother Amos, the leader of the "small party." Another work of Krasonický, recently discovered by Dr. Goll in the town-library of Görlitz, is addressed to Cahera, then administrator of the Utraquist consistory. Its subject is the sacrament, a question on which so large a part of the theological controversy of the period revolved. Krasonický's treatise, however, goes far beyond the immediate limits of his subject. Of the foundation of the Unity he gives an account that is far more detailed than that of Brother Gregory, from which I have quoted, though it does not contain many facts that are found in the writings of yet later writers. Krasonický also refers to the then all-important question of apostolic succession, the existence of which he altogether denies. Even should it yet exist, he writes, it certainly cannot be found within the Church of Rome. Like Brother Lucas, Krasonický maintains that St. Peter never visited Rome. When referring to those who had borne witness to the corruption of the Roman Church, he mentions "Dr. Jerome Savonarola." He writes of him: "The works that he composed, his letters to the emperor and others, prove what his opinions were. Half the city mourned over him when the Pope first caused him to be tortured, then publicly proclaimed what torture had forced him to confess, and at last caused him on the public square of Florence to be first hanged on a cross with two companions, and then to be burnt." Dr. Goll is, no doubt, right in conjecturing that this accurate account of the death of Savonarola is derived from Brother Lucas, who was an eye-witness of that event. Other existent theological works of this period are ascribed both to Krasonický and to Prokop, who has already been mentioned. Blahoslav describes Krasonický as "a sensible and learned man, a friend of ancient simplicity." Even in Blahoslav's days many of Krasonický's works had already been lost.

Of the writers of the "small party" it will be sufficient to mention Brother Amos, its first leader. He is known to have written three theological treatises, one of which has been partly preserved in a work of Brother Lucas, written for the purpose of refuting it. Amos, like Krasonický and the majority of the writers of the Unity, wrote only in Bohemian.

The life of Bishop AUGUSTA (born 1500, died 1572) belongs, like that of Archbishop Rokycan, rather to the political history of Bohemia than to literature. Though his fame as a preacher is far greater than as a writer, he was the author of a large number of theological works. Born in humble circumstances—his father was a hatter—and not having received a very extensive education, Augusta's talents, and yet more his indomitable energy and determination, soon brought him to the fore. Born a member of the Utraquist Church, he joined the Unity at the age of twenty-four. He was prepared for his clerical duties by Brother Lucas, and in 1532 became one of the elders—or bishops, as they were often called—to whom the entire government of the Unity was intrusted. His influence soon became predominant among the brethren. While Brother Lucas and Augusta's younger contemporary, Blahoslav, wished above all to preserve the separate character of the Unity, Augusta was in favour of a close alliance, if not of a union, with Luther and the German Protestants. Augusta, for this purpose, twice visited the great German reformer at Wittenberg, and also had, in 1546, an interview with the Protestant Elector of Saxony. In the following year war broke out in Germany between the Emperor Charles V. and the German Protestants, whose leaders were the Elector of Saxony and the Landgrave of Hesse.[1] After the defeat of the Protestants at the battle of Mühlberg, Charles's brother, Ferdinand, King of Bohemia, dealt severely with their Bohemian sympathisers. Augusta was arrested and imprisoned for a long time in the castle of Pürglitz or Křivoklat. His companion, the young priest Bílek, has left us a very interesting account of Augusta's prison life.[2]

During the whole term of his imprisonment, which only ended in 1564, Augusta maintained his claim to the leadership of the Unity. When the only other bishop died, the brethren, who had established secret communications with him, asked if they should elect new bishops, but Augusta refused his consent. After his liberation he resumed his rule over the community, residing first at Brandeis-on-the-Adler, afterwards at Jungbunzlau. The obstinacy and tenacity, not to say narrow-mindedness, which is ever characteristic of Augusta, involved him in incessant controversies during the last years of his life. It is perhaps to his opponents that should be traced the rather unfavourable account of his last years, according to which he "found great pleasure in expensive clothes and furs, as well as in select dishes, handsome carriages, and generally in an ostentatious manner of living."

Like so many members of the Unity, Augusta was a voluminous writer, but some of his works have been lost, and many of the others have remained in MS. Of

---

[1] See Chapter VI.   [2] See Chapter VI.

one of them, the *Sumovnik* (Summary), Blahoslav, who had seen the MS., writes: "As that book, the *Summary*, has already come into the hands of many pious and sensible people, it will, if it sees the light, cause the members of the Unity and others also to jump up from terror. The book is indeed remarkable, great, and no doubt for many of great value; and I do not doubt that this manner of writing Bohemian and the style of writing will also please many. And some of the young, no doubt, will be found whom not only these many unheard-of things, but also the new words and phrases will please, and they will with pleasure wish to use them. But as I write my judgment on this book, also *non ut theologus sed ut grammaticus*,[1] that is to say, (I write) not of the contents of the book, *quod non est hujus loci*,[1] but only of the form of language *de genere sermonis de verbis et phrasibus.*"[1] The continuation of Blahoslav's commentary on the "*Sumovnik*" is rather disappointing. It consists merely of critical remarks on the diction and style of Augusta. With the exception of the remark that heretics who love impious speeches generally also write in a monstrous style, we are told nothing of the "unheard-of things" contained in the book. It must, however, be remembered that Bohemian theologians of the sixteenth century—to whom every one who differed from their opinions was "Antichrist"—were very much given to expressions of horror and terror in their writings. Of Augusta's other works, his *Profession of creed sent in the name of the whole Unity to his Majesty at Augsburg*, his

---

[1] The passages quoted in Latin are in that language in Blahoslav's Bohemian book. I shall continue quoting Blahoslav's writings as he published them, without further mention of the fact. The constant use of Latin words and phrases is a particularity of Blahoslav.

Dispute of Brother Augusta with the Calixtine (Utraquist) Clergy, and more particularly his collection of hymns, enjoyed for a time great popularity. The hymns of Augusta, in particular, were widely used by the brethren up to the time of the dissolution of the Unity. Blahoslav, the only literary critic of this period, gives his opinion of Augusta in these words: " Brother John Augusta," he writes, " was a remarkable and great man, who wrote many books as well as hymns. All that he wrote before he was imprisoned was written in good Bohemian; phrases *excultæ, verba selecta; delectabatur admodum archaismis, tamen decenter. In summa totum genus dicendi fuit floridum atque excultum. Valebat ingenio et memoria, ac diligenter legebat bonos authores* in our Bohemian language. *Fluebat igitur sua vis copiosius et exultans,* though he sometimes wished to be too *lepidus et asiaticus....* In his sermons he seemed somewhat coarse though fervent. *Ardebant omnia,* words, pronunciation, and gesticulation. *Referrebat zelo illo magna ex parte Lutherum.* When, twenty-six years ago, I heard Augusta, and shortly afterwards Luther, it appeared to me that I had never heard two such enthusiastic preachers, nor two who in every way so greatly resembled one another."

A somewhat younger contemporary of Augusta was Brother Blahoslav, whom I have just quoted, and who, like him, also became one of the bishops of the Unity. His writings differ somewhat from those of the brethren I have mentioned above. The influence of humanism, absent from their works, is distinctly noticeable in Blahoslav. He also wrote on theology—what Bohemian writer of that period did not?—but it is evident that other studies were far more to his taste. He tells us, indeed, in the last chapter of his *Grammar*, that, in consequence of the state of his health, " writing on more serious, and ever on theological matters, was beyond his strength ;" but there is no doubt that this statement should be considered as apologetic. Many of the brethren probably thought that their bishops should devote themselves exclusively to theological studies. From the same reason, also, Blahoslav mentions, in justification of his philological studies, that the Unity had intrusted him with the task of translating the New Testament into Bohemian.

BLAHOSLAV was born at Přerov (Prerau) in Moravia, then one of the centres of the Unity, in 1523. In early youth he studied at the school which the brethren had established there. He then travelled to complete his studies; visited Wittenberg—where he heard Luther preach—Königsberg, and Basel. On his return to his country, he was first employed as teacher at the school which the brethren had established at Prostějov. He here had as a pupil John of Žerotin, member of a family that always supported the Unity, the father of Charles of Žerotin,[1] who was famous during the last years of Bohemian independence. The authorities of the Unity afterwards sent Blahoslav to Jung Bunzlau (or Mladá Boleslav) in Bohemia, where he was employed in arranging the archives of the community. He here began the composition of the great historical work that was in his own time his principal claim to literary fame, but which has perhaps irreparably been lost.

In the year 1557 Blahoslav became an elder or member of the smaller council of the Unity, and somewhat later on he was chosen as one of the bishops, when

[1] See Chapter VI.

Eibenschütz (Ivančice) in Moravia became his habitual residence. Like all the bishops of the brethren, he, however, spent much of his time in travel, visiting the scattered communities. He soon became one of the foremost members of the Unity, and in consequence of his enlightened and conciliatory nature was often employed as a negotiator. In 1555 and on several subsequent occasions he visited Vienna, where Archduke Maximilian, afterwards the Emperor Maximilian II., who had by the Estates already been recognised as heir to the Bohemian throne, then resided. The mediator between Blahoslav and the Archduke was the Lutheran preacher Pfauser,[1] who for a time had great influence over Maximilian. The ability of Blahoslav on several occasions protected the Unity from the dangers to which, as a community not recognised by Bohemian law, it always was exposed. When Augusta returned from prison, differences of opinion between the two bishops arose, of which we have no exact account. It is, however, certain that Blahoslav disapproved of Augusta's sympathy with the German Protestants, particularly Luther and Melanchthon. Blahoslav's intense devotion to his own language no doubt rendered him hostile to everything that tended to increase German influence in Bohemia. Augusta, to win over to his side some of the oldest among the brethren, in whom Chalčicky's hatred for the "band of masters of colleges" was yet not quite extinct, expressed in his sermons great contempt for learning and culture. In answer Blahoslav wrote his *Filipika proti Misomusum* (the enemies of the Muses), which I shall presently notice. Blahoslav, whose health had long been failing, died at Krumau in 1571, a year before Bishop Augusta.

[1] See my *Bohemia, an Historical Sketch*, p. 270.

According to Dr. Jireček, the total sum of the works of Blahoslav amounts to twenty-eight; many of them, however, including his most important work, have been lost. His controversial writings on theology, as was then usual, mostly took the form of letters. Such writings are the letters to Brother Zachary, to Martin of Žatec (Saaz), to the Lord Marshal Berthold of Lípa, &c. Like Augusta, Blahoslav was a great writer of hymns, many of which are preserved in the *Kancionali* or hymn-books of the Unity. The composition of these hymns no doubt induced Blahoslav to write the curious treatise entitled *Music*, or, to give the full name as prefixed to the second edition of Blahoslav's book, " Music, that is, a small book containing the information necessary for singers. Written in the Bohemian language on the wish of several good friends, and first printed in the year of the Lord 1558 at Olmütz; now carefully corrected and reprinted; rules and instructions necessary to chanters and composers of hymns are added." In the preface to this quaint work Blahoslav writes: "A branch of pride, and not the least one, consists in the desire to be known to many, to be considered witty and sensible, and to be esteemed in consequence. The desire to obtain distinction by one's virtues and other similar things is indeed praiseworthy. Yet it is senseless to undertake too difficult a work and strive with much effort for an object as vain as the steam of smoke. There are many, too, who might be compared to that Herostratus, who, wishing to obtain great fame, burnt down the great Temple of Diana at the risk of his life. . . . Those only will I mention who, in our days, publish books in the Bohemian language, wishing thus to obtain great fame for themselves; some who wish to help their neighbours as much as they can, from sincere love and in a beseeming manner, I do not allude to; on the contrary, I praise their pious undertakings and holy labour; but many are guided and incited by that branch of pride which I have mentioned above, which drives them to attempt that also which is beyond their power. Thus they do what they are unfit to do, thinking it sufficient that they have done it. But how? that they don't think of or care. Many out of good Latin or German books make bad Bohemian ones, serving no other purpose than that the noble Bohemian language, already somewhat spoilt, should become yet more corrupted. This will perhaps bring matters to that point that the Bohemians will become unable to speak Bohemian correctly and rightly to understand their language and its peculiarities. Thus did it happen to the Italians, who had so amended their language that when the old Italians—that is, the Latinists, Cicero and the others—came to them, they could not understand them. And what happens with regard to translations from other languages, that happens also with regard to the composition and publication of various little songs, particularly when those who undertake this task do so not for the purpose of stirring up others to piety and godliness; often indeed they (the writers of verses), on the contrary, seek and desire by means of their useless, mischievous, and even obscene verses, which pre-occupy men's minds, either to obtain the praise of men and worldly advantage, or even to insult and injure their guiltless fellow-creatures. Who can doubt that such men should be classed with the senseless Herostratus, and that they deserve derision and contempt rather than flattering praise?

"For such godless people I should not wish to work; nor do they require it. Nature itself entices a man to frivolities, the world gives sufficient evil example, and Satan himself drills them and whispers in their ears what they are to do and when. Thus that Naso, an excellent master of the devil's works, wrote well when he said:—

> '*Est deus in nobis, agitante calescimus illo
> Impetus hic sacræ semina mentis habet.*'

Satan excited him (Ovid), and sharpened his wits to enable him to write those insidious and penetrating *carmina* on matters of love, by means of which he then caught young men, just as a bird-catcher catches titmice on a sticky lime-twig. Why, even among those of our own language (*i.e.* nation) there were similar verses, before the devil induced the people of our corner of the world to give way entirely to gluttony and drunkenness. Such worldly songs, written down in musical notes or in words in a masterly manner, we remember to have heard in our childhood, and we wondered at them. Such people (the writers of worldly songs) then I do not endeavour to instruct. They have their own good teacher who incites them."

Blahoslav's views expressed in his preface are infinitely more interesting than the contents of the little book itself. Blahoslav deals in separate chapters with the subjects of songs, the words, the rhythm, the "clauses," and the syllables.

The *Replika proti Misomusům* — written, like all the existent works of Blahoslav, with the exception of a small Latin historical treatise, in the national language— has already been mentioned. Bishop Augusta had, in his sermons and elsewhere, spoken contemptuously of learning, and it was believed among the brethren that he had Blahoslav particularly in view. The latter repelled these attacks in the treatise which I have just named. "It is, and has been for years," he writes, "the custom of some somewhat prominent men to quote, for the purpose of disparaging the ancient teachers (*i.e.* the fathers of the Church), a saying of Brother Lucas, according to which he had written nothing which he had not found within the Unity. And they explained it thus: that Brother Lucas had taken nothing from the ancient teachers, but that he had learnt what the Unity possessed when he joined it, and then wrote, &c. I also a year ago heard Brother Augusta state this. Most certainly those who thus expound Brother Lucas did not understand, and do not understand his words. Could but Brother Lucas hear them, what evil thanks would he render them! Where is that saintly man, Brother Lawrence Krasonický, that he could by word of mouth vividly explain this to them. What he has written in his books they will not read, because of the weakness of their intellects, and because their minds are full of vanity.

"But as those men who could have treated this subject usefully are no longer with us, I will write down briefly what is now on my mind.

"In the days of Brother Lucas the Unity had many enemies against whom he had to write by order of the elders. He had to write in a fashion that did not stir up enemies nor open the gates of the Unity to the foe, but rather reduced to silence, and even to assent, one opponent by this, another by that argument. That he continued obnoxious to some in spite of his labours is known. There were also some who feared that he would lead them back to Rome, the doctors (*i.e.* the ecclesiastics of the Church of Rome), &c. And because of these foolish and false ideas about him he had to make such speeches as should close the mouths of some. Real truth did Brother Lucas speak when he said that he wrote nothing that he did not find in the Unity. He found in it truth as the essence (of doctrine) as to service (ritual), &c. This truth he wrote, he adorned, he spread, explaining its various branches wisely and to many. . . . Some one will perhaps say that I praise learning and the learned. Yes, it is true that I praise both learning or knowledge and cultivated people. But I do not praise those who use their learning or knowledge for evil purposes. I will say, as an example, 'We praise wine, and we praise also drinking or the use of wine, but drunkenness and drunken people we do not praise.' Generally we do not praise the evil use of God's good gifts. 'Abusus non tollit rem.' The sword is good, but it can serve one to good, another to evil purposes.

"Others again may say: 'You attach too much importance to learning and the learned.' Indeed some good men say that through learning discord has entered into Churches, and that this might happen to the Unity also. He would indeed attribute too much importance to learning and knowledge who should fancy that without the 'seven arts' God's truth, that is, the Gospel, cannot be preached, or that our salvation is founded on this learning or knowledge. But he who would say this must indeed be very silly."

"I, on my part, hold that those who work for the word of God require for that purpose a special gift of God which is called eloquence, which enables them to declaim, to teach, to admonish, to warn. The Lord at first gave eloquence to His servants as a gift in so miraculous a manner, that it was not necessary that they should learn. But then wonders and miracles ceased. Henceforth, as the Spirit of God recognised that eloquence is necessary to the Church, it is not harmful to teach eloquence whenever and to whatever person it is possible (to do so). Surely a man cannot wait till God miraculously throws down eloquence to him from heaven! That would indeed be as if a peasant neither sowed nor ploughed, but waited till manna rained down on him from heaven."

"Do not our young men, I say, when they are taught to preach, learn besides piety and knowledge of God's word, eloquence as well? It is obvious to all that many of these young men, though they do not know Latin, are more learned in their speech, and more eloquent than some fairly learned Latinists. Still it is certain that if, besides their other studies, they also learnt Latin and were acquainted with dialectics and rhetoric, they would be much more intelligent, more capable, readier for all work, and more useful."

Blahoslav here expresses the views of the more cultivated members of the Unity, men to whom to so great an extent the literary development of Bohemia is due. That it was necessary that Blahoslav should write such a treatise proves, on the other hand, that the ideas of Chelčicky and the "small party" still found adherents among the brethren.

Another work of Blahoslav that has been fortunately preserved is his *Grammatika Česká*. Only one MS. of this work is known, and that was only discovered by Mr. Hradil in 1857 in the library of the Theresian College in Vienna. This book is indeed an example of the obscurity which still covers ancient Bohemian literature, and of the possibility that, of the many other ancient books that are known to have existed but have been lost, some may be yet recovered. The condition of Bohemian literature in this respect recalls rather that of ancient literatures than that of other modern European countries. Blahoslav's *Grammar* has great interest in spite of its rather unattractive name, which is not indeed quite correct. Besides a full account of the construction of the Bohemian language based on Latin grammar, with which Blahoslav was thoroughly acquainted, the book contains a series of short but very pertinent critical notes on some earlier Bohemian writers, beginning with Hus. I have already quoted Blahoslav's criticisms on Lucas, Krasonický, and Augusta. It may be interesting here to quote his self-criticism also. Under the heading of "The Works of Blahoslav" he writes: "It seems to me, if some think that my opinion on this subject is just, that no good Bohemian can blame my manner of writing Bohemian, as shown in my version of the New Testament, which has been twice published and printed at Ivančice. Also of the little book called *Additions to* (*i.e.* notes on) *Music*, or simply *Music*. I think that, particularly in its last edition, it contains good and also graceful Bohemian writing. Of other similar works of mine I am silent; let the result show the truth. 'Decere nam mihi videtur ut de metipso quam modestissime loquor, cum mihi sim bene conscius, quam et mihi sit curta suppellex.' We know that we are all imperfect, but yet to a different degree, some more and some less."

Posterity has on the whole confirmed Blahoslav's judgment. His works, particularly his translation of the New Testament, are still considered models of Bohemian writing. One cannot, however, help regretting that he, who was so severe on "Latinisms," should have interspersed his writings with Latin words, and sometimes with Latin sentences, that are most disturbing and irritating to the reader. Blahoslav seems to have inserted these patches of Latin as evidence of his learning, in the same manner as English novelists some time ago were given to introducing into their writings fragments of French as evidence of their knowledge of the ways of society.

Of later writers of the Unity I may mention Brother Jaffet. He entered the ecclesiastical service of the Unity in 1576, and afterwards became a member of the "small council." He also was a voluminous author, but many of his works have been lost and the others remain in MS. His most important works were the *Voice of the Watchman*, which appeared about the year 1600, and a work which he published in the year 1607 under the somewhat long-winded title of *The Sword of Goliath for the defence of God's people against their enemies, that is, the Description of the ... constant succession ... of true and genuine bishops and priests within the Unity of the Brethren*. In the preface to this work Jaffet declares that his purpose is to prove that the brethren have always preserved the apostolic succession which they received from the Waldenses. As a proof of this assertion, Jaffet published a list of the ordinations which took place within the Unity from its beginning. This list Dr. Gindely, who had thoroughly studied the history of the Unity, declared to be spurious. Brother Jaffet died at Horaždovic in 1614. He was one of those enemies of Rome on whom vengeance was wrought after their death. When his burial-place, the former Minorite monastery of Horaždovic, was in 1621 returned to the monks of that order, the remains of Brother Jaffet and of three other Bohemian brethren were disinterred and burnt in the churchyard.

It would be very easy to continue this account of the theologians of the Unity. All their writings still have an intense interest for Bohemians. Writing for other readers, I shall limit myself to the authors already mentioned, who are indeed the most prominent and representative members of the Unity.

It would, however, be impossible to pass in silence the name of WENCESLAS BUDOVEC OF BUDOVA. He was a prominent leader of the Brethren, a very striking figure in Bohemian political life, and belongs to literature also, as the author of several Bohemian works, mostly of a theological character. He was born in 1547 as a member of a noble but not opulent family, and was educated in accordance with the doctrine of the Unity. When eighteen years of age, Budova, as was then customary for young Bohemian nobles, undertook extensive travels, visiting Germany, the Netherlands, England, France, and Italy; that he visited Rome also is specially recorded by his biographers. Shortly after his return to Bohemia in 1577, he was attached to the embassy which Rudolph II., German emperor and King of Bohemia, despatched to Constantinople. A man of studious nature, and, like most Bohemians of his time, intensely interested in theological research, Budova employed his spare time—always granted amply to an able man who is member of an embassy but not the ambassador—in endeavouring to obtain information on the Mohammedan religion. The result of these studies was his celebrated *Anti-Alkoran,* which I shall again refer to. It may here be mentioned incidentally, as a proof of the bitterness of religious animosity in Bohemia at the beginning of the seventeenth century, that Budova was afterwards accused by the Romanists of having written a book in praise of Mohammedanism; whereas the mere name of the book should have been sufficient to disprove so absurd an assertion. After spending about seven years in Turkey, Budova returned to Bohemia, and took an important part in the political events that led to the granting of the "Letter of Majesty" to the Bohemian Protestants[1] by Rudolph II. in 1609. He acted, indeed, not only as leader of the brethren, but of all those who were opposed to the increasing pretensions of the Church of Rome. The Bohemian national movement, as Dr. Gindely has remarked, acquired through him a somewhat Puritan character. When Budova presided over the Protestant meetings, he always called on all present to pray before he opened the proceedings. All then fell on their knees and sang a hymn. The signing of the "Letter of Majesty," and of the agreement that was drawn up simultaneously,[2] is principally due to Budova. Though the force of circumstances prevented these enactments from entering fully into practice, and the events of 1618 and 1620 swept away all religious liberty in Bohemia, they might, had time permitted, have established in Bohemia a just and fair system of religious toleration.

In the events which followed the memorable Defenes-

[1] Following the Bohemian writers, I thus describe jointly the Lutherans, Utraquists, and Bohemian Brethren, who were united in their opposition to Rome.
[2] See my *Bohemia, an Historical Sketch,* p. 299 *et seq.*

tration of Prague in 1618, Budova played a less prominent part. He was, however, chosen as one of the "directors,"[1] and was also a member of the deputation that welcomed King Frederick at the Bohemian frontier. The new king appointed Budova president of the Court of Appeal, and in consequence of his former relations with Turkey he was attached as special commissioner to the Turkish ambassador who appeared at the court of Prague. He was present at the banquet given to the Turkish embassy by Count Thurn, of which Slavata has left us so insidious, and probably mendacious, an account.[2] After the battle of the White Mountain, Budova accompanied his wife and other members of his family to the frontier, where they were in safety. He then returned to Prague, stating that he could not abandon the Bohemian crown that had been intrusted to his custody. When asked why he had not fled, he spoke the often-quoted words: "I am weary of my days. May God deign to receive my soul, so that I may not behold the disaster which, as I know, has overcome my country." Budova was one of the Bohemian leaders who were decapitated on June 21, 1621, and is mentioned in Skála's account of that tragic event.[3] He refused the assistance of both Capuchins and Jesuits, and as no member of the Unity was allowed to assist the dying brethren, he walked resolutely and alone to the scaffold.

Of several religious works of Budova that have been preserved, the already-mentioned *Anti-Alkoran* is most worthy of notice. In the preface Budova explains how the book came to be written. The firm and intense

---

[1] See Note 1, p. 200.   [2] See Chapter VI.
[3] See Chapter VI.

religious feeling of the man is noticeable in every word. "From my earliest youth," he says, "God influenced my parents to that purpose that they sent me out of Bohemia to distant countries that I might acquire learning, and this happened in 1565. After having viewed the most prominent Christian countries, and having spent some time studying at academies, and seen the courts and governments of the foremost potentates, kings, and princes, and also the Italian land and Rome, I by God's grace returned to Bohemia and to my dear family in 1577. Then, however, I became very desirous of visiting the Eastern countries—those that the Turk, that Gog and Magog, who is the chief enemy of Christendom, has taken from the Christians, and now rules—and of seeing what the manner of the infamous Turkish religion is, and how the work of God continues among those Christians who live under the Turkish yoke, as it were in a Babylonian captivity."

Budova then tells us how he became a member of the numerous embassy that accompanied the ambassador John of Zinzendorf to Constantinople. While most of his companions, after a short stay at Constantinople, continued their travels to "Jerusalem, Damascus, Babylon, Arabia, and Persia," Budova was detained there, for he had accepted the position of *hofmistr* (master of the ceremonies) to the ambassador. "I then," Budova writes, "decided to make inquiries as to what the religion, or rather irreligion, of the Turks really was, and, as it were, to outline and depict for others that Turkish Antichrist with his fables and other frauds. It was of great assistance to me that I had with me a copy of the *Alkoran* (Koran), which in Spain had been translated from the ancient Arabic, such as it was at the time of Mahomet, into the Latin speech. This book was then, at the time of Luther, about the year 1550, printed with a preface by Philip Melanchthon. I, possessing this work, often entered into discussions, not only with the Turks, but also with the renegades—that means those who have fallen from the Christian faith, and of such there are here not hundreds but thousands. The result was that they themselves were surprised, and had to laugh at those most foolish fables (of the Koran), which are sillier than anything that has been taught by any heathens since the beginning of the world. Then, overcome by their consciences, they arrived at this conclusion—that they did not believe in God and in eternal life, but that, in accordance with Epicurus and the Sadduceans, they considered every religion as a political institution, and favoured such religious doctrines as were convenient to their bodily welfare, and contributed to their glory and advantage in the world. And as at Constantinople I saw all this with my eyes, that 'Gog and Magog,' which in Bohemian can be described as the secret building, the extraordinary edifice composed of parts of the New and Old Testament, in which that Satan (*i.e.* the Sultan) endeavours to hide himself with his *Alkoran*—as I talked much on these subjects with Turks and renegades, that is, men who have abandoned the Christian faith, therefore am I better able to write on these subjects than those who only write what they have heard at second-hand." The *Anti-Alkoran* is divided into three parts. The first consists of copious extracts from the edition of the Koran mentioned in the preface; the second contains a refutation of the Mohammedan creed. The third part, scarcely connected with the others, consists of nine small treatises, which prove that the inclination to mysticism, that proved so harmful to Komenský and many brethren, existed in Budova's mind also, and that, like so many of his contemporaries, he was given to the study of astrology.

Budova's letters, some of which, addressed to Peter of Rosenberg and preserved in the archives of Wittingau (Třebon), have recently been published, bear witness to the fervent piety so characteristic of Budova. In a letter addressed to Lord Peter in 1611, Budova informs his correspondent of the state of public affairs in Bohemia; he adds: "The Poles have obtained a victory over the Muscovites, and the German Electors will meet shortly at Nuremberg. May God deign to grant that all these matters may, to His honour and glory, be settled in a manner conducive to the general welfare, and above all, to concord, love, and enduring peace; then may we in Bohemia also be able, after all these incessant tempests, whirlwinds, and storms of the last three years, to obtain rest, and, as it were, to recover a little. But God threatens us with the plague, perhaps wishing to rescue us from the evil things that are preparing and to render us more obedient to His will and counsel. I constantly commend your Grace to God's mercy. May God's love render your Grace and all those who through God's favour believe in the Lord Christ day by day more able to find and expect those eternal heavenly blessings to which with certain faith we look forward."

This short notice of Budova's literary work would be incomplete if I omitted to mention that many of the state papers published by the Provisional Government of 1618, and by the Government of King Frederick—

which both displayed a feverish but futile diplomatic activity—are the work of Wenceslas of Budova.

Before referring to Komenský, the last great Bohemian writer of the Unity, mention should be made of some fruits of the literary activity of the brethren which were the joint works of several members of the community. Of these, the most important is the translation of the Holy Scriptures known as the "Bible of Kralice." From the time of Hus, when the Bohemian people obtained free access to the Bible, parts of the Scriptures had been frequently translated into Bohemian, and Brother Blahoslav, as already mentioned, published the whole New Testament in the national language. Towards the end of the sixteenth century the authorities of the Unity decided on publishing a complete Bohemian version of the Bible. Several clergymen of the Unity took part in the labours necessary for this purpose, which began in 1577 and ended in 1593, when the complete version was printed and published at Kralice in Moravia. Other editions followed in 1596 and 1613. The New Testament was printed in these editions exactly according to Blahoslav's already existent translation. The translation of the Old Testament was the joint work of several divines. The Bible of Kralice endeared itself to the Bohemian Protestants in the course of a very few years. With Komenský's *Labyrinth of the World*, that will be mentioned presently, it was the only book that many Protestants whom the Austrian Government expelled from Bohemia after the battle of the White Mountain took into exile with them. This is referred to in the well-known song of the Bohemian exiles, in which they are made to say—

> "*Nothing have we taken with us,*
> *Everything is lost;*
> *We have but our Bible of Kralice,*
> *Our 'Labyrinth of the World.'*"

After the forcible re-establishment of the doctrine of Rome, it became a grave offence to be found in possession of a copy of the "Bible of Kralice." The Jesuits in particular were indefatigable in their endeavours to discover and destroy all copies of the book. The "Bible of Kralice" has recently been reprinted by the British Bible Society exactly from the edition of 1613.

Another interesting record of the Unity is the collection of reports of the proceedings at the general meetings of the community. It has already been mentioned that these meetings were very frequent. The numerous hymn-books ("Kancionaly," as they were called) of the brethren also deserve notice. They contained hymns by Brothers Lucas, Augusta, Blahoslav, and many others. The last Bohemian Kancional was published by Komenský in 1659, when the brethren had already long been expelled from their native land.

I have now to deal with KOMENSKÝ, who, under the Latinised name of Comenius, is widely known beyond the limits of Bohemia. The value of Komenský's writings has been judged very differently at different periods. His mystic, not to say superstitious and credulous, nature was particularly antipathetic to a French writer such as Bayle. The latter has, therefore, in his *Dictionnaire Historique et Critique* judged the whole work of Komenský very unfavourably, and this judgment has often been repeated. With time opinion changed. His educational works, though for a long time only those that are little more than school-books were well known, began again to attract attention. In the present century the first Bohemian edition of the *Didactica Magna* was rediscovered, and extracts were made from the almost inaccessible Amsterdam folio of 1657, in which alone some of his educational works are contained. The very great merits of Komenský as an instructor of the young are now recognised by most prominent teachers, who alone are competent to give an opinion on this point.

Recently public opinion has perhaps veered too much in the contrary direction. Not content with declaring, what is undeniable, that Komenský was a learned and original writer on educational matters, and the author of one of the most fascinating allegorical tales that have ever been written, great importance has been attributed to his writings on philosophy, or, as he would have called it, "Pansophy." No one can impartially claim for Komenský high rank as a philosopher, and it is certainly a mistake to speak of Komenský's system of philosophy. There is no philosophical system of Komenský in the sense that there exists a philosophical system of Spinoza. Komenský is not only, when writing on "pansophy," constantly carried away by mystic ideas—the idea of "light," which he interpreted in a mystic manner, seems ever to have pursued him—but his "pansophic" works constantly encroach on the domain of natural history. This is the more to be regretted, as Komenský's views on natural history were very often incorrect, and the fatal credulity which induced him to study the "prophecies" of Kotter, Ponatovská, and Drabik here also led him to accept as true the most absurd statements.

The life of Komenský is a very sad one, and his

patience, resignation, and unlimited trust in God must win for him the esteem of all sympathetic readers of his many works. An exile from his country early in life, only once the hope of a return to Bohemia appeared to him. It was when, after the victories of Gustavus Adolphus, his Saxon allies for a time expelled the Catholics from Bohemia. Komenský was then already celebrated as a writer on educational topics, and he would probably, had the task of reorganising the schools of Bohemia been confided to him, have rendered these schools models for all Europe. He indeed confidently expresses this idea in his writings. But Wallenstein soon drove the Saxons out of Bohemia, and it is in any case doubtful whether the Lutheran Saxons would have intrusted Komenský with the mission which he so ardently desired. Fate willed it that he was only able to make isolated attempts at establishing his new system of education in various countries and without continuity. The circumstances of his life were also as unfavourable as possible to his career as a writer. Travelling from Moravia to Bohemia, thence to Poland, Germany, England, Sweden, Hungary, Holland, ever unable to obtain tranquillity, often in financial difficulties, twice deprived of his library by fire, forced to write schoolbooks when he was planning metaphysical works that he believed to be of the greatest value, he always undauntedly continued his vast literary undertakings. The critic who judges Komenský from a purely literary standpoint will probably give preference over all his other works to the thoughtful, pessimistic, yet sometimes playful, allegorical narrative which he has called the *Labyrinth of the World*. This opinion coincides with that of the people of Bohemia. Since they have been free to read the works of their ancient writers, no book is more constantly in their hands than the *Labyrinth*.

Before noticing a few of the many works of Komenský, I shall give a brief account of his adventurous life.[1] John Amos Komenský was born at Ungarisch Brod in Moravia, or, according to some authorities, in the small neighbouring town of Nivnice, in 1592. He received his first education at Ungarisch Brod, and after the early death of his parents visited the school of Stražnic, where Drabik—destined to have so fatal an influence on Komenský—was also then studying. Komenský's early impressions of the schools of the Unity were decidedly unfavourable. He complained that the masters made no attempt to attract the interest and attention of their pupils, overburdened their memories by insisting on unnecessary mechanical enumerations of words and facts, and stimulated the failing memory by the incessant and exaggerated application of corporal punishment. In the *Labyrinth*, written in Komenský's youth, he graphically describes his school experiences. It is probable that these experiences first suggested to him his vast plan of remodelling the then accepted system of education. From Stražnic Komenský proceeded to Prerau (Přerov),

---

[1] Those who wish to study the life of Komenský in greater detail should read Mr. Keatinge's biographical and historical introduction to his recently published English version of the *Didactica Magna*. The biography of Komenský is founded on the best German and Latin authorities. It is only occasionally that mistakes occur, as when it is stated (on page 1 of the introduction) that the Unity "took a position midway between the Utraquists and the Roman Catholics." The Utraquists were, on the contrary, nearest to Rome, and some of them were indeed prepared to accept all its teaching if the right to receive communion *sub utraque*, in the two kinds, were granted them. The Brethren were of all Bohemian reformers most antagonistic to the Church of Rome, and refused to recognise all institutions which, according to their views, had not existed in the primitive Church.

then one of the centres of the Unity. He here continued his studies in view of becoming a member of the clergy of the community. He seems when very young already to have resolved to adopt this career.

For the purpose of completing his studies Komenský was by the chiefs of the Unity sent to the University of Herborn in Nassau. That university, founded at the end of the sixteenth century by John the Elder, Count of Nassau, was then at the height of its fame. The religious teaching there was in accordance with the "Catechism of Heidelberg," that is to say, mainly founded on Calvin's views. The Unity was more in sympathy with these views than with the teaching of the Utraquist University of Prague. The brethren, therefore, often sent their promising youths to Herborn, though the regulation that the students dined at three different tables, where different meals were served according to the payment made by each student, offended their democratic views. At Herborn Komenský became acquainted with Altsted (or Altstedius), who, though still a young man, was already celebrated as a writer on educational subjects. His theories had a considerable influence on Komenský. From Herborn Komenský proceeded to Heidelberg, where he also pursued his studies for some time. Before returning to his country he made a somewhat extensive journey through Germany and the Netherlands. Writing forty years later, he tells us that at this time (in 1613) he first visited Amsterdam, "the pearl of towns, the ornament of the Netherlands, the delight of Europe."

In 1614 Komenský returned to Moravia, and was ordained a minister of the Unity in 1616, as soon as he had attained the necessary age. He was first sent to the small town of Fulneck in Moravia, where he married and spent the happiest and almost the only tranquil years of his life. It was not his destiny to continue long undisturbed in the pursuit of his religious duties, and of the studies to which he was already devoted. The events of the Bohemian war cast their shadow even over the peaceful community of Fulneck. Rumours of the events of the war between Bohemia and Austria occasionally reached the brethren. As Komenský wrote: "Lightning shines before it strikes, and by its light we could see the glooming, gathering clouds of persecution." After the battle of the White Mountain the brethren, as the most decided opponents of Rome, were naturally the first to suffer. Detachments of troops, generally Spaniards, who were chosen for this purpose because of their greater bigotry and ferocity, scoured Bohemia and Moravia in every direction, burning down the settlements of the brethren, and killing or driving from the country the members of the communities. In 1621 a Spanish detachment attacked Fulneck and burnt down the town, forcing the brethren to fly for their lives. The MSS. and library of Komenský were here for the first, but unhappily not for the last time burnt and destroyed. Komenský himself managed to escape and sought refuge in Bohemia at Brandeis-on-the-Adler, which has already been mentioned as one of the centres of the Unity. The little town then belonged to Charles, Lord of Žerotin.[1] Though during his whole life a devoted member of the Unity, Žerotin had remained faithful to the House of Austria during the war that had just ended, and had even been menaced by the Moravian nobles, who had adopted the cause of Frederick of the Palatinate. In

[1] See Chapter VI.

acknowledgment of his services, he was not by the Catholics included in the general decree of exile, and the Austrian authorities at first even overlooked the fact that many members of Žerotin's Church, among whom was Komenský, sought refuge at Brandeis. Komenský's intense literary activity, that had already begun at Fulneck, continued at Brandeis. There, besides minor works, the *Labyrinth of the World* was written, though the book was afterwards enlarged.

All Komenský's writings while at Brandeis bear witness of an intense mental depression. Not only did he feel deeply the ruin and dispersion of the religious community which he had just begun to serve, but he also about this time lost his young wife, probably during the flight from Fulneck to Brandeis. Writing of this period about ten years later Komenský says: "God willed it that, not only through the lamentable war, but also through the plague that spread throughout the country, great slaughter took place. I thus lost miserably my wife and my children, relations, connections, and kind benefactors. I suffered anxiety on anxiety that filled my heart. But what was harder to bear than all else was that God appeared to have abandoned our country and Church and left us orphans, for all the churches of Bohemia and Moravia were deprived of their faithful spiritual guides, many subjects lost their evangelic lords, these again lost their beloved subjects,[1] and the servants of God lost their churches."

The respite granted the brethren through the inter-

[1] Komenský alludes to the confiscation of the estates of the nobles who belonged to the Unity. The peasants on their estates were generally of their faith, and were treated more mildly than on other estates. Komenský therefore uses the word "subject" (*oddaný*) instead of "serf."

cession of Žerotin did not last long. Every year the persecution of all in Bohemia who were outside the pale of the Church of Rome became severer and their position more precarious. At a secret meeting of the brethren in 1625, at which Komenský was present, it was decided altogether to abandon Bohemia, and a discussion arose as to the country where the members of the Unity should seek refuge. It was finally decided that the brethren should separate, some proceeding to Poland, others to Hungary and Transylvania. Poland then had a large Protestant population, and this is still the case as regards the two other countries mentioned. Before finally leaving Bohemia, it was decided that messengers should be sent out in different directions to obtain information as to where the brethren could find quarters. Komenský, with two companions, started for Poland. In that country Count Raphael Lescynski, himself a member of the Unity, was known as a warm friend of the brethren.

During his journey Komenský first heard of the so-called prophecies of one Christopher Kotter. Characteristically enough Komenský immediately forgot all other preoccupations and obtained an interview with the "prophet." Henceforth his belief in Kotter was implicit, and he immediately decided on translating into Latin and into Bohemian the German prophecies, which are a tissue of absurdities.[1] The fact that a generally respected Protestant divine as Komenský had desired an interview with Kotter of course greatly increased the man's celebrity. Even the Elector of Brandenburg, and Frederick,

---

[1] See my *Bohemia, an Historical Sketch*, pp. 397 and 398. Want of space prevents my repeating the short account of Kotter's "prophecies" given there.

ex-king of Bohemia, requested that he should be presented to them. From Germany Komenský continued his journey to Poland, and having, as he tells us, received satisfactory assurances from Count Lescynski, he returned for the last time to Bohemia towards the end of the year 1626.

He here again fell under the influence of a visionist, in whom he thoroughly believed, and whose hallucinations he even many years afterwards considered worthy of being recorded in print. Julian Ponatovský, an impecunious Polish nobleman, had been received as a member of the Unity and appointed preacher at Mladá Boleslav. When the communities of the brethren were dispersed, Charles of Žerotin secured Ponatovský's safety by appointing him to the office of librarian at his castle at Naměst in Moravia. Christina, Ponatovský's daughter, appears to have been of a highly hysterical nature, which, added to the intense religious excitement of the times, induced her to deliver "prophecies," which were generally received with the greatest interest. The pathological side of the question need not be dealt with here. It is sufficient to state that Christina, who had recently been reading the Revelation of St. John, declared that she had heard the voice of the Lord, who had chosen her as intermediary for the purpose of informing the faithful of the approaching defeat of Rome.

It was the misfortune of Komenský to be brought accidentally into contact with the "prophetess." Christina had not joined her father in Moravia, but remained at Branna in Bohemia, not far from Třemešna, where Komenský was then staying. Christina suddenly became dangerously ill at Branna, and as the minister of the Unity who resided at Třemešna happened to be absent,

R

Komenský was sent to Branna in his stead. He has given a rather curious account of his visit to the prophetess. She appeared to be in a state of ecstasy, and constantly repeated the words "Bridegroom, bridegroom!" Somewhat later she began to communicate her prophecies to Komenský and the other persons present. She again prophesied that the Protestants would shortly obtain a complete victory over Austria and the Pope. To these prophecies also Komenský gave immediate implicit faith. Though he soon left Branna, he remained in communication with Christina. The latter soon recovered from her illness, but continued to prophesy; her prophecies, indeed, became even more definite. She now announced that, through the will of her heavenly bridegroom, Jesus, Papacy would be abolished; that the Turks would be converted to Christianity, and that Ferdinand II. and Wallenstein would perish by violent deaths. Wallenstein was then residing at Jičin in Bohemia, and Christina, accompanied by a female friend, proceeded there to acquaint him with her prophecies. The great general was not at home, but Countess Wallenstein, who saw Christina, was greatly embarrassed, and consulted some Jesuits on the subject of her visionary visitor. The Jesuits advised that Christina should immediately be sent to jail; but it was finally agreed merely to remind her of the decree that had already banished from Bohemia all members of the Unity. Wallenstein was, on his return home, informed of the visit of the prophetess. He smiled, and remarked that the Emperor indeed received messages from Rome, Constantinople, and Madrid, but that he had received one from heaven.

Christina returned to Branna, and as her father

had died meanwhile, she decided to join Komenský and his wife—he had remarried very shortly after the death of his first wife—and a party of other exiles, who were on the point of leaving Bohemia. They set out in January 1628, and on crossing the frontier of their country in the direction of Silesia, "they all knelt down and prayed, with cries and many tears, to God, entreating Him not to exclude them for ever from their native land, and not to allow the seed of His word to perish within them." In February Komenský arrived at Lissa, a small town in that part of Poland that is now known as the Prussian province of Posen. Ponatovská for some time continued a member of Komenský's household, and the controversy concerning the true inspiration of her prophecies raged for a considerable time. A joint meeting of doctors and ministers of the Unity did not settle the question, as the opinion of the doctors was in direct opposition to that of the ecclesiastics, of whom Komenský was one. The latter never wavered in his belief in Christina's prophecies.[1] He maintained that it could nowhere be proved that the Church had been deprived of the gift of prophecy. Before dismissing Christina Ponatovská it should be stated that some time after these events she married a young man employed at the printing-work of the Unity at Lissa, had two sons and three daughters, and in later years "disliked all reference to her prophecies."

It would, however, be doing Komenský bitter wrong if we supposed that he was, while at Lissa, exclusively occupied with the prophecies of Kotter and Ponatovská.

---

[1] As late as in 1657 Komenský, in his *Lux in Tenebris*, republished the prophecies of Kotter, Ponatovská, and Drabík. The last-named disreputable prophet will be mentioned later.

The period of his first residence at Lissa was, on the contrary, one of incessant and fruitful hard work. His duties as a preacher and schoolmaster were fulfilled with equally great conscientiousness, and, from the few sermons that have been preserved, it appears that in this respect also his ability was exceptional. It was also at this time that most of Komenský's educational works were written, though many were re-modelled later. It is therefore very difficult to fix the chronological order of Komenský's works, and even to decide whether the Bohemian or the Latin version of some of them is the original one. The beginning of the "pansophic" studies also dates from this time, and the *Physica*, Komenský's first philosophical work, was completed as early as in 1632.

Of external events there is at this period of Komenský's life little that requires mention. The monotonous life of the brethren was only occasionally interrupted by the echoes of the events of the Thirty Years' War. In 1631 the news of Gustavus Adolphus's great victory at Breitenfeld, and in the following year that of the occupation of Bohemia by the Saxons, reached Lissa. I have already noticed the brief and vain hopes that Komenský founded on these events.

It is worthy of notice that even in those troublous times Komenský's literary work soon became known. His "pansophic" studies, that appeal so little to modern readers, then attracted almost more attention than his really valuable educational works. Among those who appear to have taken an early interest in Komenský's "pansophy" was Samuel Hartlib, a learned Englishman, who was probably of German origin, "who resided in London, and took a keen interest in everything that savoured of intellectual progress."[1] Hartlib seems, indeed, first to have heard of Komenský as the author of the *Janua Linguarum*, an educational work that then, and even long after, enjoyed great celebrity; but he was principally interested in Komenský's philosophical studies. Hartlib entered into correspondence with him, requested information on the subject of "pansophy," and offered pecuniary assistance should Komenský wish to visit England.

The latter seems to have received these proposals favourably, and he forwarded to Hartlib a sketch describing all the pansophic works he intended to write. Many of these works perished afterwards when the town of Lissa was burnt down, and it is therefore a mere matter of conjecture how many of them already were in existence. It is, however, certain that Komenský at that time had already compiled a complete table of contents of his pansophic works under the name of *Synopsis Operis Consultatorii*.[2] Hartlib appears to have been delighted with Komenský's communication, and, contrary to the author's wishes, he published his pansophic sketch at Oxford in 1637.

Komenský does not seem to have resented this breach of faith. He had perhaps already made up his mind to visit England, where the publication of his work was likely to increase his fame. Disputes with other ministers of the Unity, who disapproved of Komenský's visionary opinions, had rendered residence at Lissa distasteful to him. The death of Count Lescynski in 1637 was also a reason

---

[1] Mr. Keatinge: *The Great Didactic*. Mr. Keatinge's preface contains much interesting information concerning Hartlib and his friends.

[2] This table of contents can be found in my *Bohemia, an Historical Sketch*, p. 403.

for leaving Lissa, though his son and successor, Count Bohnslav Lescynski,[1] continued to afford protection to the brethren even after he had adopted the Roman faith.

In the year 1647 Komenský started for England, and, after a very perilous journey, during which his vessel was once driven near to the Norwegian coast and he was once nearly shipwrecked, he arrived in London on September 21st of that year. The description of the perils of the sea, which Komenský introduced into the later editions of the *Labyrinth*, is founded on these personal experiences. Of the small coterie that welcomed Komenský in London, Mr. Keatinge gives the following interesting account. "Komenský," he writes, "was received with open arms by the little band, of which Hartlib was the centre. A man of great enthusiasm but less judgment, Hartlib knew everybody in England who was worth knowing. . . . At that time in easy circumstances, he was living in Duke's Place, Drury Lane, an address which, we may be sure, was the centre of Komenský's London experiences. Here would have met to discuss the intellectual and political problems of the day men like Theodore Haak, John Durie, John Beale, John Wilkins, John Pell, and Evelyn, who had just returned to London after a three months' journey through Europe. Milton was living in London, and must certainly have met and conversed with the illustrious stranger."

Komenský's impressions of England are contained in an interesting letter which, shortly after his arrival on the 18th (old style 8th) of October 1641, he addressed to

---

[1] Bohnslav Lescynski was the grandfather of Stanislas Lescynski, for some time King of Poland.

his friends at Lissa.[1] After describing his journey and the kind reception given to him by his English friends, Komenský writes: "What, after having now spent nearly a month here, I have been able to see, hear, and understand, I will briefly report, dealing first with public affairs and then with my own.

"This nook of the earth has much that differs from other countries, and is worthy of admiration. What interests me most are those matters which concern the glory of God and the flourishing state of the Church and the schools (both now and, it is to be hoped, yet more in the future).

"If I enumerate some points specially, I know it will not be displeasing to you and to the friends of God.

"I.[2] The ardour with which the people crowd to the churches is incredible. The town has 120 parish churches, and in all of them—of all those which I have visited, I state this as an ascertained fact—there is such a crowd that space is insufficient.

"II. Almost all bring a copy of the Bible with them. . . . Therefore the preacher, when reading his text, twice mentions book, chapter, and verse. If the text is short (for he often chooses a single line), he reads it twice over also.

"III. Of the youths and men, a large number copy out the sermons word by word with their pens. For here, thirty years ago (under King James), they discovered an art which now even the uneducated practise, that of 'tachygraphia,' which they call stenography. . . .

"IV. After the sermons, most fathers of families repeat

[1] Published in Mr. Patera's *Korrespondence Komenského*.

[2] I have retained Komenský's plan of dividing his letter into numbered paragraphs, but want of space has obliged me to abridge the letter considerably, and I have omitted altogether one or two paragraphs of little interest.

the sermon at home with the members of their household. Sometimes two or three families meet for this purpose.

"Of books on all subjects in, their own language they have an enormous number, so that I doubt whether any country is equal to them, particularly as regards books on theology. There are truly not more bookstalls at Frankfurt at the time of the fair than there are here every day. Verulamius's (Bacon's) work *De Scientiarum Augmentis* has also recently appeared in English.

"VI. Their thirst for the word of God is so great, that many of the nobles, citizens also and matrons, study Greek and Hebrew to be able more safely and more sweetly to drink from the very spring of life. Do not think that only one or two do this; there are many, and day by day this holy contagion spreads farther.

"VII. Some select men designated by Parliament are now working that they may have the text of the Bible as accurate as possible, corresponding in everything with the sources, and furnished with very short marginal notes. Here, however, political considerations have somewhat interfered, for they have fixed them a term of a few months only; but I hope the time will be prolonged.

"VIII. They are vehemently debating on the reform of the schools of the whole kingdom in a manner similar to that to which, as you know, my wishes tend, that is, that all young people should be instructed, none neglected, and that their instruction should be such that it lay down the foundations of Christianity more deeply and more solidly in the tender minds, thus afterwards rendering greater the efficacy of religious ministration.

"IX. They are endeavouring to found a special illustrious school—whether in London or elsewhere has not yet been settled—for young men of noble birth, separated from all mixture with plebeians.

"X. An instruction for parents as to the provident care of their children in infancy and their wise preparation for further culture in accordance with my *Instruction*[1] . . . had been prepared here before I arrived." . . .

Paragraphs XI. and XII. have little interest, but the last part of the letter, which deals with the political situation of England, and reflects, no doubt, the opinions of Komenský's English friends, is worth quoting. Paragraph XIII. begins thus: "The questions concerning episcopal rank give much trouble here; some wish to preserve it in its entire former dignity, others to abolish entirely both the name and the office; others again wish to retain the episcopal name and office, but to suppress the worldly pomp, the too great luxury and the uncalled-for interference in temporal matters, which are too often the results of the episcopal system. The larger part of the nobles, however, and almost all the people, desire the complete suppression (of the episcopal rank); so hated has the whole order of bishops become because of the abuse of their office, and because of their endeavours to rule men's consciences and oppose the liberty of the people. Even our own Bishop of Lincoln (of bishops the most learned, the most cultivated, and politically the most sagacious), who was three years ago deprived of his office by the Archbishop, imprisoned, but then liberated by Parliament, is beginning to be badly spoken of, and there are some who predict evil for him. They say he will not only be deprived of his office together with the other bishops, but also that he will again be im-

[1] See later, p. 286.

prisoned. For new plots against the Parliament have been discovered, some secret, some almost open. But I hope and believe in better things for the good bishop. When, the other day, he invited me as well as Duræus (Durie) and Hartlib to dine and discuss with him, he spoke most reservedly on all these matters. He only remarked that he did not know whether he and his colleagues should be reckoned among the dead or among the living. Should things take a more peaceful turn, he promised great aid to us and to ours. . . .

"XIV. Archbishop Laud is detained in prison, with no hope of liberation. For while Parliament is prorogued, commissioners have been appointed who will inquire into his acts and be informed of the various grievances against him, which Parliament had not time to hear. This has been done. They also say that such matters have been produced that there is no hope for his life.

"XV. The decision of the Parliament, published before its prorogation, which decreed the removal from all churches of such 'articles of ceremony' as altars, crosses, &c., which had been introduced by the Archbishop, has within the last days been carried out almost everywhere, In one of the churches here in London there was a window, the religious and very artistic painting of which, they say, cost £4000, that is 16,000 imperials. The ambassador of the Spanish king who resides here offered to pay the whole of this sum if he could have the window intact. But the somewhat exaggerated zeal of the people despised the proffered money and broke the window, considering that it was wrong to obtain gain by means of idolatrous objects."

Komenský's visit to England was, like so many of his

undertakings, a complete failure. He seems indeed to have realised this soon, and to have acquired in a short time a considerable insight into the state of affairs in England. Komenský's plan of founding a "Christian Academy of Pansophy" was at best absurd, but it was doubly so at a moment when England was drifting rapidly towards civil war. Quite at first, however, Komenský appears to have believed in the feasibility of his favourite plan, and he even meditated whether "the Savoy in London, Winchester, outside of London, or Chelsea, very near the capital, would be the best site for the academy." The question naturally arises, What was the object of the academy that Komenský, Hartlib, and other enthusiasts planned? Mr. Keatinge suggests that the academy had no further purpose than "to organise a collection of laboratories for physical research." This, though undoubtedly part of the plan, was certainly not the whole plan. The academy, according to Komenský, was to be composed of the wisest men of all countries, who, among many other things, were to elaborate a universal language. They were to meet in England "because of the heroic deeds of the Englishman Drake, who by five times circumnavigating the world furnished, as it were, a prelude to the future holy unity of all nations." Komenský's plans are so obviously utopian that it is scarcely necessary to mention that they came to nothing. An universal language will never be accepted, and universal peace, or the "holy unity of all nations," as Komenský termed it — though the events of the last few months prove that that ideal still has believers — was certainly impossible in Komenský's time, and probably will continue an impossibility.

Though long convinced that his fantastic plans found

little favour in England, Komenský yet remained in London up to June 1642. He here wrote, for the benefit of Hartlib and his other English friends, his *Via Lucis*, in which millennarian views are very noticeable.

Soon after his arrival in London, Komenský had received a letter from Louis de Geers, a rich Dutch merchant, who had important business connections with Sweden. He had already entered into correspondence before, and the letter of De Geers was forwarded to Komenský from Lissa. De Geers in his letter suggested that Komenský should proceed to Sweden for the purpose of reorganising the schools of that country according to his new educational theories. It is a proof how soon he had lost his hope in English aid for his pansophic plans that in November 1641 Komenský already conditionally accepted the offer of De Geers. The latter had really thought of Komenský only as a man who was already an authority on matters of education; but Komenský himself, sanguine as ever, saw in a visit to Sweden an opportunity of expounding his pansophic views to the Chancellor Oxenstiern, and also—a more sensible object—of enlisting the sympathies of the Swedish statesman for the Bohemian exiles.

In June 1642 Komenský left England, and first proceeded to Holland. It is a proof of the great celebrity that he had already attained that he here received yet another invitation. While travelling in Holland, Komenský met Richard Charles Winthrop, formerly Governor of Massachusetts, who suggested to him that he should proceed to America and become rector of Harvard College, that had been founded six years before. Komenský, who was bound by his agreement with the Swedish Government, in the name of which De Geers had negotiated with him, declined the offer. In September 1642 Komenský arrived in Sweden, had an interview with De Geers, and afterwards at Stockholm met the Chancellor Oxenstiern. Komenský has left a detailed and very interesting account of the latter interview, from which want of space unfortunately prevents my quoting. Komenský, of course, laid great stress on his visionary views and on his "pansophic" — philosophical one can hardly call them—writings. The great Chancellor, on the other hand, warmly praised Komenský's educational works, and suggested, as De Geers had already done, that he should write a series of Latin schoolbooks for the use of the Swedish schools. With characteristic tact, Oxenstiern remarked that if he facilitated the study of the Latin language, Komenský would prepare the way to further more profound studies. As Komenský refused to remain in Sweden, it was decided that he should settle at Elbing, in Prussia, not very far from Sweden.

Komenský spent six years (1642–1648) at Elbing, occupied partly with the preparation of the schoolbooks he had been commissioned to write, partly with his favourite "pansophic" studies. His life here, as almost everywhere, was a troubled one. The agents of the Swedish Government urged him, in a manner that was not always delicate, to proceed with the task he had accepted and not to waste his time on works of a different nature. On the other hand, Hartlib, with the characteristic inability of a rich man to understand that others have to work for their living, bitterly reproached Komenský with having abandoned the sublime works that had been planned in London for the purpose of writing school-books.

In 1648, on the death of Bishop Justinus, the members of the Unity assembled at Lissa chose Komenský as one of their bishops. He outlived all his colleagues, and eventually became the last bishop of the Bohemian Brethren. On receipt of the news of his election, Komenský started for Lissa, but not until he had forwarded to Sweden some of the school-books which he had been commissioned to write. The year 1648 brought a great blow to the members of the Unity and to the Bohemian Protestants generally. The Treaty of Westphalia was signed in that year, and no stipulations in favour of the Bohemian exiles were contained in it. At the risk of prolonging the war, the Austrian Government maintained its principle that no one who did not profess the creed of Rome should be allowed to reside in Bohemia or Moravia; to Silesia slight concessions were granted. All the hopes of the exiles that they might once be able to return to their beloved Bohemia were now destroyed for ever. Oxenstiern had to the last defended the cause of the exiles, and did not deserve the severe reproaches that Komenský addressed to him.

All hopes of worldly aid having vanished, Komenský relied more than ever on the intervention of God, and on the visions and prophecies which announced that such an intervention would shortly take place. "If there is no aid from man," he wrote to Oxenstiern, "there will be from God, whose aid is wont to commence when that of men ceases." Komenský's relations with Kotter and Ponatovská prove sufficiently that it was not now that mysticism and credulity first obscured his generally clear brain; but it is evident that Komenský never quite recovered from the blow inflicted by the

Treaty of Westphalia, which to his generally optimistic nature appeared unexpected. His reliance even on the prophecies of an impudent liar and humbug such as Drabik injured his reputation in the learned world, and threw obloquy even on his masterly, wise, and perfectly sane educational works.

Ever restless, Komenský was not prevented, even by the responsibilities of his new dignity, from undertaking new wanderings. It has already been mentioned that when the members of the Unity were expelled from Bohemia many brethren sought refuge in Hungary. They now complained that for many years they had not seen their brother Komenský, who had meanwhile acquired such celebrity. Komenský was already meditating a visit to Hungary when he received a letter from George Rakoczy, prince of Transylvania, inviting him to visit his domains, and to introduce there the educational reforms which had rendered him celebrated. Rakoczy then ruled not only over Transylvania, but also over a considerable part of Northern Hungary, including the towns of Tokay and Saros Patak; the latter of these towns was indeed a frequent residence of the Transylvanian princes. Having obtained the consent of the other seniors or bishops, Komenský in 1650 again set out on his travels. On his journey he passed through Puchö, a small town in Northern Hungary, and assisted at a meeting of the members of the Unity which took place there. Among those present was Nicholas Drabik, a former school-fellow of Komenský, who proposed to accompany him on his farther journey. Drabik had already some years previously forwarded some "prophecies" to Komenský, and the latter now fell entirely under his influence.

It is with pity and shame that I refer to Drabik's prophecies in connection with so great and good a man as Komenský; their value was about the same as that of the political predictions of a third-rate writer of leading articles; the style is a vile imitation of that of the Revelation of St. John. The leading idea is the destruction of the House of Austria, which is described as the *bestia* of the Apocalypse. The nations that were to effect this downfall varied in the predictions according to the political situation of the day. Turkey was then almost always at war with the House of Habsburg, and therefore always figured among these nations. At this moment Drabik announced that he had just had a vision informing him that enemies coming from four directions were surrounding "the beast." They were the princes of the House of Rakoczy, "the dearest instruments of God," from the east; the Greeks and Servians from the south; the Poles, Lithuanians, Russians, Tartars, and Turks from the north; the Swiss from the west! The Hungarian crown was assured to Sigismund Rakoczy, at whose expense Drabik was then living. Komenský, who had received former "prophecies," ventured to remark that in them the crown of Hungary had been assured to Sigismund's father, Prince George Rakoczy (who had died in 1648). Drabik then "burst out into tears," and thus pacified the kind-hearted Komenský. It may incidentally be remarked, that when Prince Sigismund died in 1652, Drabik again calmly transferred his prophecy, this time to that prince's brother and successor, George II. of Transylvania. While Kotter may have believed in his visions, and physical circumstances probably explain those of Ponatovská, Drabik was simply an impostor, who managed not only to live at free quarters, but also to obtain considerable sums of money as a remuneration for alleged negotiations with Turkey. It was indeed through him that Komenský, who was integrity personified, was at Saros Patak accused of indelicacy in financial matters and of greediness for money. These accusations were afterwards echoed by the divines with whom Komenský was engaged in controversies during the last years of his life, and they also found their way into Bayle's *Dictionnaire Historique et Critique.*

It must be sufficient to note the enormous influence Drabik acquired over Komenský; to account for it is impossible, unless we assume that much suffering and disappointment had weakened his intellect. This is, however, disproved by the fact that the educational works which Komenský continued to write nearly to the end of his life show little trace of waning mental power. It must be taken into account, also, that visions and prophecies found very general belief in those days. Mr. Keatinge, in his interesting book to which I have already referred, mentions several instances of learned Englishmen who had read the prophecies of Drabik (or Drabicius, as he was called in England), and fully believed in them. Bayle also writes that when, in 1683, the news that the Turks were besieging Vienna reached Paris, the name of the prophet Drabik was in every mouth. Drabik at last came to an evil end. A few months (fortunately) after Komenský's death, Drabik was arrested as a swindler and conspirator. He confessed his impostures and was executed, though he had accepted the creed of Rome in the hope of saving his life.

Komenský's activity as a teacher while at Saros Patak was indefatigable. He attempted to improve and reorganise the "gymnasium" of the town, and also wrote several new educational works during his stay in Hungary. He encountered, however, many obstacles; the local teachers were opposed to him, and reproached him with his intimacy with Drabik; linguistic difficulties also arose. If Komenský yet remained four years in Hungary, it was mainly for political purposes. He still hoped to contribute to the formation of a Protestant League which would drive the Austrians out of Bohemia, and thus enable the brethren to return to their beloved country. Komenský now hoped for aid from England, since Cromwell was famed all over the Continent as the protector of persecuted Protestants. After the death of Sigismund Rakoczy, Komenský actually succeeded in inducing his brother and successor, George II., to endeavour to negotiate an alliance with England and Sweden against Austria. When the Transylvanian embassy started for London, it was instructed to pass by Lissa to consult with Komenský, who had already returned to Poland. His knowledge of English affairs would, it was thought, prove useful, and it is probable that the state paper which the ambassadors presented to Cromwell was from the pen of Komenský. Komenský, indeed, always seems to have continued to communicate with his English friends. As late as in 1658, Cromwell and Thurloe, no doubt through the intermediation of Hartlib, suggested that the Bohemian Brethren, together with the Vaudois or Waldenses, whom the Duke of Savoy was then persecuting, should be established in Ireland. Lands formerly belonging to Roman Catholics were to have been given to them, and it was thought that the Protestant element in Ireland would thus be strengthened. Komenský, perhaps injudiciously, declined the proposal.

He stated, either in consequence of his own conviction or because of his belief in the wretched Drabik's prophecies, that the brethren would shortly return to their own country, and therefore could not travel to distant lands.

In 1654 Komenský returned to Lissa, but his stay there was now short and troubled. War between Sweden and Poland broke out in the following year, and the victorious Swedes occupied Lissa in August 1655. The only policy for the homeless community of the brethren evidently was to remain neutral in these alien quarrels. Unfortunately, Komenský employed his ever-ready pen in composing a panegyric on Charles Gustavus, the victorious Swedish king. In the following year the town of Lissa was retaken by the Polish army, pillaged, and burnt down. Komenský's library and his MS. were again destroyed. The brethren, perhaps not without reason, accused Komenský of having, through his injudicious writings, caused the downfall of the community of Lissa, to which the Poles had never been hostile before.

Komenský, now sixty-five years old, was again homeless, and he was at first uncertain where he should seek refuge. He proceeded to Hamburg, but there received an invitation to Amsterdam from Lawrence De Geers, the son of his old patron Louis De Geers. Komenský started for Amsterdam, and here spent the latest years of his life. His literary activity continued to the last. He published at Amsterdam the only complete edition of his educational works, and even wrote new "pansophic" books. Differing on this point from his father, Lawrence De Geers took great interest in these studies, and even in the writings of the "prophets," in whom Komenský obstinately continued to believe. De Geers was foolish enough to invite Drabik to Amsterdam, and it was through his financial aid that Komenský was enabled to publish in 1657 his *Lux in Tenebris*, a book in which all the prophecies of Kotter, Ponatovská, and Drabik were again brought before the public.

The mystic and now openly professed chiliastic views of Komenský involved him during the last years of his life in numerous theological controversies. Detailed accounts of them have recently been published in Bohemian, perhaps rather because everything concerned with Komenský is valued by his countrymen than because these controversies now have much interest. Among Komenský's theological antagonists were Nicholas Arnold, Daniel Zwicker, and Samuel Des Marets, a professor at Gröningen. The last-named attacked the aged bishop of the Unity with great violence, calling him "a fanatic, a visionary, and an enthusiast in folio." He also accused him of obtaining large sums from the De Geers family by means of "pansophic hope and chiliastic smoke." A polemical essay directed against Descartes also belongs to Komenský's last years. These years were very melancholy, though the old man, characteristically enough, found great relief in the society of an aged French prophetess and visionist named Antoinette Bourgignon. His old comrades died off one by one. Of the bishops of the community, Gertichius died in 1667, and Figulus (Komenský's son-in-law) in January 1670. In the same year, on November 15th, Komenský, the last bishop of the Bohemian Brethren, ended his long and troubled life.

It would require a book larger than the whole of this

volume to give even a slight account of the 142 works[1] of Komenský. Such a book would hardly have much general interest. The enormous total includes prayer-books, lists of regulations for the Unity, mere school-books, sermons, works on natural history that long since have become valueless, and so on. These lists, however, which include only books that are still in existence, do not comprise the entire fruits of the literary activity of Komenský. Several "pansophic" works that are enumerated in a table of contents, to which I have already referred, are no longer in existence, and were probably destroyed when the town of Lissa was burnt down.

While at Fulneck, Komenský was already busy writing works on grammar as well as a Bohemian translation of the Psalms. The melancholy events of the year 1621, when he lost his wife and his home at Fulneck and began his many wanderings, inspired him to write several religious books, all bearing witness to the deep depression of the author. Such works are the *Help for the Soul*, *The Impregnable Castle, which is the Name of the Lord*, *The Dismal Complaint of a Christian*, *The Centre of Security*, and others. All these writings are in Bohemian, as also is the far better known *Labyrinth*, which Komenský wrote at Brandeis-on-the-Adler shortly after his arrival there, and dedicated to his patron, Lord Charles of Zerotin. The *Labyrinth of the World*, perhaps one of the best allegorical narratives that has ever been written, professes the same pessimism, combined with a fervent belief in the revelations of the Christian faith,

---

[1] According to Dr. Kvacsala's calculation. Dr. Zoubek only enumerates 137 books. The difference is caused by the uncertainty whether certain re-written books, sometimes republished in a different name, should be counted twice. Mr. Keatinge's book contains a list of 127 books of Komenský.

which can be found in the other works also which I have just mentioned. The *Labyrinth* from its first appearance obtained an immense popularity with the Bohemian people,[1] to which I have already referred. Since the Bohemians have again been able to read freely the records of their ancient literature, the *Labyrinth* has regained its former popularity, as is proved by the numerous recently published editions.

The *Labyrinth of the World*, written in Komenský's youth, is, from a literary point of view, undoubtedly his greatest achievement. Rarely perhaps has the vanity of all worldly matters, the hopelessness of men's struggles, the inevitable disappointment which is the result of even the most successful ambition, been more clearly expounded than in this small and unknown work. Were we not constantly reminded that we are reading the book of a devout Christian and member of the Unity, we should fancy that we were reading the work of a forerunner of Schopenhauer. Komenský's *Labyrinth*, in fact, reeks with pessimism, though his admirable religious faith and piety enabled him to give a supernatural and consolatory ending to his book. Happiness, unattainable here, is to be found elsewhere.

The little book is well worth being translated into English, and I hope some day to attempt that task. It will here only be possible to give an outline of the tale and a few quotations. Komenský tells us of the adventures of a young man who, "when arrived at that age when the human mind begins to understand the difference between good and evil, sees how various are men's stations and ranks, their vocations, and the works and undertakings which occupy them." He then meditates

[1] See p. 248.

as to "what group of men he should join, and with what subjects he should occupy his life." The youth then starts on his wanderings, having accepted "Impudence" and "Falsehood" as his guides. They conduct him to the summit of a high tower. He now beholds a city which appeared to him "beautiful, splendid, and broad, with countless streets, squares, houses, smaller and larger buildings, all swarming with people." The six principal streets, his companions tell him, are inhabited respectively by married people, tradesmen, scholars, priests, rulers, and soldiers. To the west of the city he is shown the "Castle of Fortune." In the middle of the city is a vast square, in the centre of which is the residence of the "Queen of Wisdom." The pilgrim is then shown two gates: the first, that of life, through which all must pass; the second, that of separation. Before entering this gate, all must draw lots and accept a career in the world in accordance with the lot they have drawn. They arrive at the gates of separation, and then the pilgrim, or rather Komenský, tells us: "We went downward by a dark winding staircase, and before the door there was a wide hall full of young people, and on the right side there sat a fierce-looking old man, holding in his hand a large copper jar. And I saw that all those who came from the gate of life stepped up to him, and each one put his hand into the jar and drew from it a scrap of paper on which something was written. Then each of them went down one of the streets, some running and shouting from joy, while others crept along slowly, looked around them, groaned and lamented.

"I also then came nearer, looked at some of the scraps of paper, and noticed that one contained the word 'Rule!' another 'Serve!' another 'Command!'

another 'Write!' another 'Plough!' another 'Learn!' another 'Dig!' another 'Judge!' yet another 'Fight!' and so forth. Impudence said to me: 'Here vocations and work are distributed, and according to this distribution every one has to fulfil his task in the world. He who distributes the lots is called Fate, and from him in this fashion every one who enters the world must receive his instructions.'

"Then Falsehood nudged me at my other side, thus giving me notice that I also should stretch out my hand. I begged not to be obliged to take any one lot directly without first examining it, nor to intrust myself to blind fortune. But I was told that without the permission of the Lord Regent Fate this could not be. Then stepping up to him, I modestly brought forward my request, saying that I had arrived with the intention of seeing everything for myself, and only then choosing what pleased me.

"He answered: 'My son, you see that others do not this, but what is given or offered them they take. However, as you desire this, it is well!' Then he wrote on a scrap of paper, 'Speculare,' that is to say, 'Look round you or inquire,' gave it to me and left me."

The pilgrim and his two companions now enter the city, and proceed first to the street of the married people. Here Komenský gives us what, for one who was married three times, and is not known to have been unhappy in marriage, seems an intensely gloomy and pessimistic view of married life. He dilates on the uncertainty of choice in marriage, on the trouble caused by children, on the disappointment felt by the childless, on all that is unlovely in love. The pilgrim then proceeds to the street of the tradesmen, and the many troubles, anxieties, and disappointments to which commerce is exposed are

THE "LABYRINTH OF THE WORLD" 281

eloquently described. Komenský, in the later editions of the *Labyrinth*, here inserted a curious passage referring to his own sea-voyage, from which I can only quote a few lines. "The wind," he writes, "had meanwhile increased so rapidly that we were tossed about in a manner that horrified our hearts; the sea rolled round us in every direction with such gigantic waves that our course was, as it were, up high hills and down deep valleys, once upward and then again downward; sometimes we were shot upwards to such heights that it seemed as if we were to reach the moon, then again we descended as into a precipice. . . . This continued day and night, and any one can imagine what anguish and fear we felt. Then I said to myself, 'Surely these men (the sailors) must be more pious than all other men, they who never for an hour are sure of their lives;' but looking at them, I observed that they were all without exception eating gluttonously, as in a tavern, drinking, playing, laughing, talking in an obscene manner, in fact, committing every sort of evil deed and licentiousness."

The pilgrim next visits the scholars or learned men. Komenský, here quite in his element, passes judgment on many *savants* of his time, and gives his opinion on astronomy, history, natural history, poetry, and philosophy as they appeared to him in the writings of his contemporaries. His erudition, judged, of course, by the standard of his time, does not appear profound, but he sometimes, in few words, describes epigrammatically currents of thought that had importance in his day.

The chapters which deal with the priesthood are closely connected with those that tell us of the pilgrim's visit to the men of learning. As Komenský had, when describing the former, laid stress on the many follies of philosophers and the vanity of human learning, he now deals severely with the professed teachers of religious truth, noting their obstinacy, their want of erudition, their constant reciprocal animosities.

The pilgrim and his companions now proceed to the street of the rulers. Here, in accordance with the pessimistic note which characterises the book, we are told that all earthly authority is evil, but that if it did not exist, the condition of the world would be yet worse. We here find interesting allusions to contemporary events, the sudden appearance and downfall of King Frederick of Bohemia and the executions at Prague in 1621. Komenský lays stress on the uncertainty of royal power. He writes: "Then the royal throne (that of Ferdinand of Austria is meant) suddenly shook, broke into bits, and fell to the ground. Then I heard noise among the people, and looking round, I saw that they were leading in another prince and seating him on the throne, while they joyously exclaimed that things would now be different from what they were. They flatter the new prince, strengthening the throne for him to sit on, and protesting how great a man he is. I, thinking it right to act for the advantage of the general welfare, also contributed a nail or two to strengthen the throne; for this some praised me, while others looked at me with disapproval. But meanwhile the other prince recovered himself, and he and his men attacked us with cudgels, thrashing the whole crowd till they fled, and many even lost their necks." Komenský here alludes to some service which he had rendered to the government of King Frederick, of which nothing is otherwise known. He no doubt sympathised with that government and was on terms of acquaintance with administrators of the Utraquist Consistory of Prague. One of the administrators, Cyrillus, who assisted the president, Dicastus, at the coronation of King Frederick, was the father of Komenský's second wife, whom he married about the time when he wrote the *Labyrinth*.

After the rulers, the pilgrim visits the soldiers. Komenský here gives a very lifelike description of the brutal ways of the soldiery at the time of the Thirty Years' War. His battle-picture is also striking. " Then suddenly," he writes, "the drums beat, the trumpet resounds, noisy cries arise. Then, behold, all rise up, seize daggers, cutlasses, bayonets, or whatever they have, and strike unmercifully at one another till blood spirts out. They hack and hew at one another worse than the most savage animals. Then in every direction the cries increased; one could hear the tramping of horses, the clashing of armour, the clattering of swords, the growl of the artillery, the whistle of shots and bullets round our ears, the sound of trumpets, the crash of drums, the cries of those who urged on the soldiers, the shouting of the victors, the shrieking of the wounded and dying; a fearful leaden hailstorm could be seen, dreadful fiery thunder and lightning could be heard; once this, then that man's arm, head, leg, flew away; there one fell over another; everything swam in blood! 'Almighty God!' said I, 'what is happening? Must the whole world perish?'"

The pilgrim now tells his companions that he has everywhere found but vanity. They answer him by informing him that those who have laboured hard eventually find their way to the castle of Fortune, where happiness, honour, and pleasure await them. The pilgrim is now conducted to this castle, but here also finds nothing that attracts him. He reflects on the many cares that are the consequence of riches, the misery that ever threatens libertines, gamblers, and gluttons, the vanity of glory and of ancient lineage. The pilgrim's guides, uncertain what to do with him, now lead him to the castle of the goddess of Worldly Wisdom. They bring him before the goddess and thus accuse him: "Most serene queen of the world," they say, "most brilliant ray of God's light, magnificent Wisdom! The young man whom we bring before you has had the fortune to receive from Fate (the regent of your Majesty) the permission to view all the ranks and conditions in this kingdom of the world. . . . But he always complains to us of everything; everything displeases him; he is always striving for something that is unattainable. Therefore we cannot satisfy his wild cravings nor understand them, and we bring him before your serene grace, and leave it to your prudence to decide what is to be done with him."

The queen receives the pilgrim graciously and invites him to remain at her court. Shortly afterwards Solomon appears at the queen's court with the intention of wedding her. He is accompanied by a large crowd of courtiers, among whom are Socrates, Plato, Epictetus, Seneca, many Christians and Jews. In their presence the queen receives numerous deputations, all bringing petitions, beggars, philosophers, who are represented by Theophrastus and Aristotle, judges, lawyers, and others. At last the queen receives a deputation of women. They state that it would be fair that they and men should alternately have dominion. Some even say that they alone should rule, as their bodies are more agile and their minds quicker than those of men. As men for so many years have ruled women, it is, they say, time that women should take superior rank. A few years ago, they add, a noble example of this was given in the kingdom of England under the reign of Queen Elizabeth, for she decreed that all men should give their right hand to women, a worthy custom that still endured.

Solomon, who had hitherto listened attentively to the petitions and to the queen's answers, now suddenly exclaims, "Vanity of vanities, and everything is vanity." He then tears away the mask which the queen wore, and she appears as a hideous hag. Yet shortly afterwards Solomon is, by means of flattery, again won over to her side and conducted to the street of married people, where he is unable to resist the female attractions that offer themselves to him. Fearful calamities are the consequence of Solomon's weakness, and the pilgrim despairingly exclaims, "Oh, that I had never been born, never passed through the gate of life! for after having surveyed all the vanities of the world, nothing but darkness and horror are my part. O God, God! if there is a God, have mercy on wretched me!" The pilgrim, whom his companions have meanwhile abandoned, now hears a voice from on high which exclaims, "Return from where you came into the house of your heart, and then close the doors." The voice is that of Christ, who appears to the pilgrim and instructs him in true religion; the teaching, needless to say, is strictly in accordance with the doctrine of the Unity. The pilgrim is then received into heaven, and the last chapter consists in a prayer to Christ, ending with the Latin words, *Gloria in excelsis Deo et in terra pax hominibus bonæ voluntatis.*

It is impossible to render justice to the *Labyrinth* in a few pages, and no book lends itself less to quotation. Komenský, who is generally diffuse and addicted to repetition, has here given us an enormous amount of thought and experience in a very small volume.

The great educational works of Komenský, on which his principal claim to posthumous fame is founded, but which do not perhaps require lengthy mention in a work that deals mainly with literature, were principally written during the author's first prolonged stay at Lissa. Though the order in which Komenský's educational works were written cannot always be ascertained with certainty, there is little doubt that one of the earliest was the *Informatorium Školy Mateřské* (=instruction for mother-schools).[1] It first appeared in Bohemian in 1628. The little book deals with the earliest instruction which a child receives from its mother. It soon obtained great popularity, and was speedily translated into German, Latin, and English. Anticipating Rousseau, Komenský lays great stress on the duty of mothers to nurse their children. The *Instruction for Mother-Schools* is still much read in Bohemia, and some of the regulations contained in it have been adopted for the modern "Kindergarten." Many other educational works of Komenský appeared in rapid succession during his stay at Lissa. The most valuable of them is the *Didactica Magna*, which, like the *Informatorium*, was originally written and first published in Bohemian. Komenský here establishes four degrees of education : the mother-school, the vernacular school, the Latin school or gymnasium, and the academy or university. The earliest education in Germany and

[1] The book has recently again been translated into English (probably from the German version) by Mr. W. Monroe, under the name of the *School of Infancy*. The book contains a "bibliography of Comenian literature," from which one would fancy that Bohemian works were purposely excluded, if two books written in that language, published respectively at Omaha and Racine, U.S., did not figure in the list.

Austria is, except in the case of the Kindergarten, still left to the mother's own discretion; but it is interesting to note that the three other divisions of educational establishments suggested by Komenský are almost exactly in accordance with the present system of education in these countries.

It is beyond the purpose of this book to give a detailed account of Komenský's educational theories. I must refer those who are interested in the subject to Mr. Keatinge's excellent introduction to his recently published English version of the *Didactica Magna*, which I have already mentioned. The writer here gives us a concise but very clear sketch of these theories.

One of the best known, probably formerly the best known, work of Komenský is also of an educational character. I am referring to the celebrated *Janua Linguarum Reserata*, which was first published in 1631. The book was an attempt—somewhat anticipating Ollendorf's method—of facilitating the study of Latin, and in the enlarged editions that of other languages as well.[1] The book immediately obtained an enormous success, and was constantly republished even up to the beginning of the present century. Philology and the science of languages generally have made such gigantic progress since Komenský's time that the modern reader has the impression that the book was immensely overrated. Komenský's peculiar system of introducing as many different words as possible, and of avoiding as far as possible the repetition of a word that had already

---

[1] The first edition of the book was Latin and Bohemian. Anglo-Latin versions are numerous, the last having been published at Oxford in 1800. There are also French, Greek, Polish, Dutch, Swedish, and Hungarian editions of the *Janua*, as well as some that, besides the Latin version, are printed in several modern languages.

been used, give the book an appearance of artificiality and constraint. The real leading idea of Komenský's *Janua* is an attempt simultaneously to teach a language and to enlarge as far as possible the extent of the pupil's ideas. I have elsewhere translated a portion of the curious chapter *De Statu Regio*. I shall here quote the first introductory chapter, which gives some idea of Komenský's method. It is written in the form of a dialogue between the reader and the author. The latter begins thus:—"Welcome, friendly reader! If you ask me what it is to be learned, receive this answer: It means to know the differences between things, and to be able to name and designate all things by their right names."

The pupil answers, "Nothing more than this?"

"No, certainly nothing beyond this. He who has learned the nomenclature of all things of Nature and Art has laid the foundation of all erudition."

"But that must surely be very difficult."

"It certainly is so if you attempt it unwillingly, and if you allow your prejudiced imagination to frighten you. Besides, if there is any difficulty, it will be at the beginning. Do not the shapes and characters of letters also appear to children who first see them singular, wonderful, and monstrous? But when they have taken some trouble and pains, they understand that they (the letters) are but a play and a recreation. The same applies to all things; they appear superficially more difficult than they are. But if you not only begin a work but also persevere, there is nothing that will not yield and submit itself to your intellect. Who wishes to do so can understand everything.[1] Therefore, who-

[1] In the Latin version of the *Janua* this reads as follows:—"Qui cupit capit omnia," a rather contestable statement, that is very characteristic of Komenský.

ever you are, I order you to hope; I forbid you to despair. See this small work (the *Janua*). Here—I say this without boasting—I shall place the whole world before your eyes and show you the Latin, French, Spanish, Italian, and German languages[1] as in a summary or handbook. Therefore strive to obtain instruction. Open this book, peruse it, and learn it by heart. Having done so, you will, with the help of God, find that you understand all arts and letters."

Many other educational works of Komenský could be enumerated; such are *The Violet Bed of Christian Youth*, *The Garden of Letters and of Wisdom*, &c. Komenský worked with particular energy at these works when he, about the year 1632, hoped, as already mentioned, to be able to return to Bohemia and reorganise the schools there. A similar motive induced him to write the curious work entitled *Haggæus Redivivus*, which, in spite of its Latin title, was written in Bohemian, and which has quite recently been published for the first time. In this book Komenský endeavoured to instruct the brethren as to the manner in which they should reorganise their ecclesiastical institution after their return to Bohemia, for which Komenský still hoped.

Komenský, probably soon after his arrival at Lissa, began his philosophical, or rather "pansophic" studies; for philosophy was to him still the handmaiden of theology, then already a rather belated standpoint. It has already been mentioned that at Lissa he composed a general plan and a table of contents of his future pansophic works, to which he gave the name of *Synopsis*

---

[1] I quote from the Elzevir edition of 1611, edited by Duez, which is written in the languages mentioned above. The passage, of course, varied in each edition according to the languages in which it was published.

Operis Consultatorii.[1] Some of these works, such as the *Panegersia* and *Panaugia,* were afterwards published at Amsterdam; others were destroyed by the fire at Lissa. The first complete philosophical work of Komenský, the *Physica,* was published during his stay at Lissa. The work has now no interest, and is, indeed, a token of Komenský's superficiality and credulity as regards matters of natural history. Statements concerning this subject are by Komenský constantly proved by texts from the Bible in a manner irritating to the modern reader.

One of the early "pansophic" works also is the *Via Lucis,* written principally during Komenský's stay in London. The pansophic plans, such as the foundation of a universal language and a universal academy, the mystic use of the word light, occur in this as in all the pansophic works. A short account of the *Via Lucis* will be my only attempt to elucidate the mysteries of "pansophy." Arid and unattractive as the subject must necessarily appear to the modern intellect, no account that altogether ignored "pansophy" could claim to give a truthful representation of Komenský.

The writer begins his book by naming, in his mystical manner, the three "books" (that is to say, three systems of educating humanity) which God has established; they are instruction by means of the world, by means of man, and by means of universal "light" (or enlightenment). Education by means of the world has failed, as worldly wisdom, atheism, and epicureanism, introduced by Satan, have crazed men's minds. Instruction from man by means of laws and punishment, and the endeavours of philosophers and founders of sects, has also resulted in failure; all attempts to amend humanity by human

[1] See note 2, p. 261.

means have had no result, for they were isolated and relied on violent means. There remains a third "school," the only successful one, which instructs by means of the "universal light." This light, or rather enlightenment, consists in the complete collection of God's revelations to man by means of Scripture, which through God's power will become intelligible to all. There is no doubt that this "universal light" will one day appear to the whole world. Komenský quotes the Revelation of St. John in support of this statement. He then proceeds to define this light, which is "a brightness that flows on things, discloses and discovers them, and through the influence of which spectators realise shapes, positions, movements, the distances of things, and their reciprocal relations." Light is threefold—eternal, exterior, and interior light. Besides the eternal divine light, there is the exterior light proceeding from the sun and the stars.[1] The interior light illuminates the mind, will, and heart of man. The interior light passes through seven gradations, the last of which, immediately preceding the end of the world and to be expected shortly, is "panharmony." The state of "panharmony" will be shortly attained, and we must prepare for it. This should be done mainly by the foundation of a universal academy, a universal language, and universal schools. When all this has been done, the whole world will be "one race, one people, one house, one school of God. The heathens will be converted. The Jews will perceive that they are still in darkness. All lands will become subject to God and Christ. In accordance with the

[1] Though nothing would have appeared more revolting to the pious Komenský, his ideas here somewhat recall the twofold sun of the Emperor Julian.

Revelations and the Acts of the Apostles, Satan will be taken prisoner and shown in triumph. The whole world will have peace; (there will be) one truth, one heart, one path. Thus will Christ's prophecy of 'one shepherd, one flock' be fulfilled. This will be the true Golden Age. It will be the Sabbath of the Church, the seventh period of the world, preceding the octave that will resound in happy eternity."[1]

The last years of Komenský were principally occupied in collecting, and sometimes re-writing, his works. The enormous collection of educational books was during Komenský's stay at Amsterdam republished in Latin in a gigantic folio volume under the name of *Opera Didactica*. The collection included books such as the *Didactica Magna*, the *Janua*, and the *Schola Materni Gremii* (information for mother-schools) that had long before been published in the Bohemian language.[2]

[1] I have written with more detail on Komenský's "pansophy" in my *Bohemia, an Historical Research*. Further study of Komenský's works on pansophy has not given me a higher opinion of their value.

[2] It may interest some readers to know the complete table of contents of the enormous volume, which is divided into four parts:—

PART I.

1. De primis occasionibus . . . relatio. 2. Didactica Magna. 3. Schola materni gremii. 4. Scholæ vernaculæ delineatio. 5. Janua Latinæ linguæ, primum edita. 6. Vestibulum. 7. Proplasma templi Latinatis. 8. De sermonis Lat. studio dissertatio. 9. Prodromus pansophiæ. 10. Variorum de eo censuræ. 11. Pansophicorum conatuum dilucidatio.

PART II.

1. De novis . . . occasionibus. 2. Methodus linguarum novissima. 3. L. L. vestibulum. 4. L. L. Janua nova. 5. Lexicon Januale Latino-Germanicum. 6. Grammatica Latino-vernacula. 7. De atrio relatio. 8. Quædam de his doctorum judiciis, novæque disquisitiones.

PART III.

1. De vocatione in Hungariam relatio. 2. Scholæ pansophicæ delineatio. 3. De Pans. studii obicibus. 4. De ingeniorum cultura. 5. De libris.

Other late pansophic works of Komenský were the *Lux in Tenebris*, consisting mainly of a collection of prophecies which have already been mentioned, and the *Unum Necessarium*, dedicated to Prince Rupert, and published in 1668.

The writers of the Unity are, during the last century, so infinitely superior to all others, that little space remains to mention theologians who belonged to other communities. The early writers of the Utraquist Church were mentioned in the last chapter, and I have in this chapter again referred to Archbishop Rokycan. The numerous later polemical writings of the Utraquists are infinitely inferior to the best works of the members of the Unity, which of course are the only ones to which I have made reference.

Of Roman Catholic theologians in Bohemia also scant mention at this period is required. In most countries the salutary deliberations of the Council of Trent, which so entirely reorganised and reformed the Catholic Church, were followed by the appearance of numerous brilliant Catholic theologians, who, both in their sermons and their writings, energetically defended the dogmas of their Church. Such was not the case in Bohemia. It was the sword, not the pen, that was destined to reconquer that country for the Church of Rome. Of

6. De schola Triclassi. 7. Erudit schol. pars I. Vestibulum. 8. Erudit schol. pars II. Janua. 9. Erudit schol. pars III. Atrium. 10. Fortius redivivus. 11. Præcepta morum. 12. Leges bene ordinatæ scholæ. 13. Schola Ludus. 14. Laborum schol. coronis.

PART IV.

1. Vita gyrus. 2. Vestibuli auctuarium. 3. Pro Latinate Januæ apologia. 4. Ventilabrum sapientiæ. 5. E. labyrinthis scholasticis exitus. 6. Latium redivivum. 7. Typographæum vivum. 8. Paradisus ecclesiæ reductus. 9. Traditio lampadis. 10. Paralipomena didactica.

Catholic writers we may mention Paul Židek, a Jew by birth; Henry Institoris, who was intrusted by Pope Alexander VI. with the task of recovering Bohemia for the Church of Rome, and wrote polemical works against Chelčicky and the brethren; and the barefooted monk, John of Vodnan, a voluminous writer, who has already been mentioned as an antagonist of Chelčicky. The works of Vodnan are an extraordinary tissue of absurdities written with an almost inconceivable degree of self-confidence. He maintains theories such as that of the immaculate conception of the Virgin (then by no means a dogma of the Roman Church), by arguments and in a tone that are equally unworthy of the dignity of the subject. His books teem with the most absurdly superstitious anecdotes. The Pope, he tells us, is always accompanied by two special angels, one who advises him on all occasions, and one who informs him of all occurrences. A more dignified defender of the Church of Rome was the Jesuit Wenceslas Sturm (born 1533, died 1601), who has left a considerable number of theological works, mostly of a polemical character.

CHAPTER VI

BOHEMIAN HISTORIANS OF THE SIXTEENTH AND SEVENTEENTH CENTURY

THE period subsequent to the Hussite wars was very favourable to the development of the Bohemian language, and especially to that of historical studies. The stirring events of the times directed general interest to the great political and religious struggle; for these words are nearly synonymous when we deal with the century that preceded the battle of the White Mountain (1620), with which the aspirations of the Bohemians for ecclesiastical as well as for political independence ended for a time. The constant references to the Divinity, the prayers and hymns which are inserted in historical works of a mainly secular character, prove that in Bohemia political and religious controversies were at that period even more closely connected than in other countries.

Other causes also contributed to the increase of intellectual activity which we find in Bohemia at the beginning of the sixteenth century. I have already referred to the "humanist" movement, which, in consequence of the religious isolation of Bohemia, reached that country late, but for a time had the greatest influence on the intellectual development of the land. I have also already alluded to the foundation and beginnings of the community of the Bohemian Brethren, which greatly influenced the literary as well as the political condition of Bohemia. The brethren from the first attached great importance to the study of history, and they had established archives at Senftenberg, and afterwards at Leitomischl. A school of writers on history sprung up among them whose works—judging by the scanty remains that have reached us—possessed both great value and great beauty of style. The greater part of these works has been lost long ago. The brethren who constituted the most advanced fraction of the party which desired Church reform were naturally most hated and dreaded by the Jesuits, to whom the return of Bohemia to the Roman Church must principally be attributed. The writings of the brethren were thus specially marked out for destruction. Among the historical works that are probably irretrievably lost is that which was, according to all accounts, the most valuable, Blahoslav's *History of the Unity*. Yet even the existent works of members of the brotherhood, such as Bilek, Blahoslav, Březan, Zerotin, to speak of historians only, sufficiently vouch for the high degree of culture which the brethren had attained. They attached great importance to the grammar of their language, and many of their works were, as already recorded, models of Bohemian style.

The political condition of the country also then favoured the development of the national language, which was during this period—and during this period only—almost exclusively used by historians. During the reigns of the kings of the House of Luxemburg the Bohemian language had to a great extent lost ground. King John was known to dislike the Bohemian language, and though this dislike was by no means shared by his son Charles, yet even the foundation of the University of Prague (though that university afterwards became a national one) was not at first favourable to the development of the Bohemian language. It was at first principally frequented by foreigners, and German and Latin were almost exclusively used there.

Of the contemporary chroniclers of the Hussite war many still wrote in Latin. Yet the Hussite movement undoubtedly favoured the development of the Bohemian language, if it was only by the isolation from the rest of the Western world which the religious separation produced. A great impetus was also given to the cultivation of the national language by the circumstance that a few years before the beginning of the sixteenth century (in 1495) the Bohemian law courts decided to carry on their proceedings in the national language. The law courts of Silesia and Moravia had already previously substituted Bohemian for the Latin language, which they had previously used. Of yet greater importance was the fact that Bohemian at this period became the language exclusively used at the "diets" or meetings of the three "Estates" of Bohemia. In the minds of many Bohemians the preservation of the national language was closely connected with the conservation of their political and ecclesiastical independence. As late as in 1615, only five years before the final collapse of Bohemia, the Diet decided that all those who became naturalised Bohemians should be bound to instruct and educate their children in the language of the country. It may be noticed that this fervent devotion to the national language, which has often astonished foreigners, is a marked feature also in the revival of Bohemian literature and in the present nationalist movement.

Among the most recent writers on Bohemian history

it has become the fashion to depreciate the social and intellectual condition of Bohemia in the years that preceded the battle of the White Mountain; they perhaps endeavour thus to attenuate the sentimental feeling of regret for the great defeat which a few Bohemians still cherish. That the political results of the battle of the White Mountain, which consisted in the establishment of an absolute but orderly government, were advantageous to Bohemia, and, indeed, saved the country from anarchy, is certain. Yet it is no less certain that nobles and citizens, such as Peter of Rosenberg, Charles of Žerotin, Budovec of Budova (mentioned in the last chapter), Harant of Polžic, Bartoš Pisář, Sixt of Ottersdorf, Skála ze Zhoře (who all belong to the sixteenth or the beginning of the seventeenth century), were intellectually vastly superior to the men of similar rank and position who lived a century later, after many years of absolutist government.

It is noteworthy that among the historians of the period with which I am dealing, the majority are men who themselves played a part in the political life of their time. The Bohemians of this period were—partly, though by no means exclusively, through the influence of "humanism,"—penetrated with a blind, almost superstitious, love of learning for its own sake. They seem always to have aspired to the "tall mountain citied to the top, crowded with culture." This, indeed, applies not only to the humanists, literary men, or translators of classical works, but also to many of the practical and matter-of-fact politicians of the time. Witness Peter of Rosenberg, who died deploring "that he had not sufficiently cultivated the study of literature;" or Harant of Polžic, whose constant show of classical erudition is striking, if sometimes tedious, and who, even when in immediate peril of life, could not refrain from a classical allusion.

The two earliest historians who belong to this period both sprang from the class or "estate," as it was called, of the citizens; they both held important municipal offices at Prague, and they have both described short but momentous episodes in Bohemian history, in which they had played a conspicuous part.

BARTOŠ PISÁŘ (Bartholomew the writer), author of the *Chronicles of Prague*,[1] may be considered one of the most valuable Bohemian historians. Bartholomew obtained the by-name by which he is known because he had, though a linen-draper by trade, frequently sought employment of a literary character. We are, indeed, told that he neglected his business for his literary pursuits, and that whilst his wife was selling linen in the market-place, Bartholomew spent a large part of his time in transcribing ancient manuscripts. He held a municipal appointment at Prague for some time, and documents are still existent which were copied out by Bartholomew.

It is certainly a proof of the extension of education and of the intellectual activity of the time, that Bartoš, a tradesman, should have undertaken, and successfully undertaken, to write an important historical work. Bartholomew's chronicle deals indeed with a very limited subject, the troubles which, during the years 1524 to 1537, occurred in Prague; they were caused by the rivalry of two ambitious upstarts, John Pasěk and John Hlavsa. During the weak reign of King Louis these men both strove to obtain supreme authority in the city of Prague, which thus became the scene of great

[1] Edited and published by Dr. Erben in 1851.

tumults and disturbances. Though dealing with an apparently unimportant subject, Bartholomew's book is of the greatest interest in giving a striking picture of the town-life of Bohemia in the sixteenth century. Religious controversy was the one engrossing interest among the citizens, and the "Catilinarian individuals" (as a recent Bohemian writer has called them), who contested for the government of Prague, used religion as a pretext for their ambitious endeavours. The rivals, indeed, both belonged to the so-called Utraquist Church, which prided itself in being directly based on the teaching of Hus. This Church was the Established Church of Bohemia, from the time of the Council of Basel and the signing of the so-called "compacts" (1436), to the battle of the White Mountain (1620).

Very characteristic of Bartholomew's manner are his accounts of the disturbances of Prague, which formed the original motive for his book. It is very evident to a student of Bohemian history that in this portion of Bartholomew's work light and shade are very unequally divided; there was really very little to choose between the two demagogues, Pasěk and Hlavsa, whose rivalry caused the disturbances at Prague. But Bartholomew's style is here often quaint and picturesque ; and I think I could give no better specimen of it than by translating his portraits of the rival Cleons of Prague. Bartholomew writes: "Concerning those two persons, John Hlavsa and Master John Pasěk, they both appeared as two brilliant lights, not only in Prague, but also within the 'estate' of the townsmen generally ; for God had granted to both of them an enlightened intellect, and eloquence greater than is usual among men; yet they differed greatly with regard to their character. Though in his manner Pašek appeared inclined to kindliness, yet the immense and inexorable malice of Cain ruled him, while on the contrary Hlavsa was guided by his peaceful and yielding nature.

"Pašek was born at Old Knin, of poor parents; his mother had been a huckstress; as to his father, I have been unable to ascertain anything certain. Therefore, to avoid erring against truth, it is often fitter to give room in my book only to the statements of men who are trustworthy and sensible, rather than believe the assertions of certain people. Pašek then was a poor school-servant, and later on a schoolmaster. Afterwards he proceeded to the University of Prague, where he became a bachelor and master of arts. Then, ever rising in the world, he was chosen by the citizens of the old town of Prague as their chief town-clerk. . . . He was afterwards chosen as alderman, and by his practice in the law courts also gained large possessions, and his general fortune in the world ever increased; for God is able to raise a needy school-servant to high rank, as is said in God's Scripture in the Psalms. And now, besides the coat-of-arms which he had already received, a title, as a further honour, was bestowed on him. He thus acquired the right of calling himself John Pašek of Vrat, obtaining thus a name that well befitted his individuality, for it is true that he overturned and overthrew much.[1] He then became excessively cruel, immoderately severe, and tormented the people intolerably and unjustly. . . . Indeed, he once said openly to some people (for he was unable to conceal his revengefulness, in which few were

---

[1] It is impossible to translate this pun. Bartholomew plays on the similarity of the name "Vrat" to the words *zvratiti* and *převratiti* (to overturn and to overthrow).

equal to him), 'Do not quarrel and dispute much in words with your enemy, but wait till he is crossing a bridge; then draw away his feet from under him so that he may fall in.' This also he said boastingly: 'I am unable to be so good a Christian as that I could forgive my enemies what they have done against me.'"

Of Hlavsa Bartholomew writes: "John Hlavsa was born in the town of Stříbro (Mies), of honest and orderly parents, who belonged to the estate of the townsmen. He also, having previously been a needy scholar, afterwards became a schoolmaster. Then, after he married, he rose in the world, and during the reign of King Vladislav obtained a coat-of-arms with the title of 'Liboslav.' Having an enlightened intellect and great talents, he was elected an alderman, and soon obtained the highest rank in that court. How much good he did for the king and the estate of the townsmen, that is known to many in Bohemia and elsewhere; but as to the merits of the other (Pasěk) there is silence. Thence, in consequence of the king's taking away his appointments from the one (Hlavsa) and giving them to the other (Pasěk), great hatred and jealousy sprung up between them and spread widely; for it is the result of vain worldly vanity that every one desires honours for himself and not for others. And yet we must truthfully admit (let who will be angry with me) that through these discords much benefit and profit was obtained, rather from the deeds of the one who had not obtained the degree of master[1] (Hlavsa) than from those of the other, as I have already stated. In consequence of the differences between these two parties arose, one called that

---

[1] It is impossible to paraphrase in fewer than eight words the Bohemian word *nemistrovaný*.

of Pašek and the other that of Hlavsa, and this extended to many. Many also took part in these dissensions, and were enraged against one another; the consequence was a lamentable persecution of one party by the other."

Bartholomew, like most Bohemian historians of his time, lays no claim to impartiality, and he attacks the Utraquists of the moderate faction almost more ferociously than the partisans of Rome. Bartholomew was certainly "a good hater," and his portrait of Archbishop Rokycan is distinctly unfair. He indeed gives a totally incorrect account of the negotiations of the Bohemian Utraquists with the Eastern Church,[1] for the purpose of discrediting Rokycan by insinuating that he had been treated with contempt by the dignitaries of the Greek Church. Bartholomew, as already noticed, often extends his narrative beyond its immediate subject, and he has the taste for theological controversy which was innate in almost all Bohemians at that time. The last part of Bartholomew's book deals with the election of Ferdinand I. as King of Bohemia in 1526; it has considerable historical value, and has been largely used by the writers who have reconstructed Bohemian history in the present century. Bartholomew died in 1535, it is not certain at what age.

The political career of the next historian with whom I shall deal, SIXT OF OTTERSDORF (born about the year 1500), was similar to that of Bartoš the Writer; but Sixt appears to have taken a more prominent part in the events which he related, and, differing herein from Bartoš, he is by no means chary of references to his own person. Like Bartholomew, Sixt belonged to the estate

[1] See my *Bohemia, an Historical Sketch*, pp. 231, 232.

of the citizens. His talents and learning—we are told that he studied for some time in foreign lands for the purpose of acquiring a thorough knowledge of the Greek language—raised him to a prominent position among the citizens of Prague. As early as in 1537 we hear of him as town-clerk of the old city of Prague, and he was chancellor of the town in the momentous year 1546. His political career as well as his writings prove him to have been a zealous partisan of the ancient privileges of the Bohemian "Estates." Ferdinand I. of Habsburg had in 1526 succeeded the weak sovereigns of the Jagellonic dynasty as ruler of Bohemia. His constant though often occult purpose was to strengthen the royal prerogative and to limit the power of the Bohemian Diet or Parliament. It seemed indeed at one time probable that Ferdinand I. would accomplish this task, which his grandson finally successfully achieved after the battle of the White Mountain. In this struggle between the king and the "Estates" Sixt took an active part, and an episode of this struggle (which lasted intermittently from 1526 to 1620) is the subject of his memorable work, entitled the *History of the Troubled Years in Bohemia, 1546 and 1547.*

To no literature is the sentence "Habent sua fata libelli" more truly applicable than to that of Bohemia. While the writings of Bartoš and Sixt, and indeed those of the other historians also with whom I shall deal in this chapter, remained almost unnoticed up to the beginning of the present century, HAJEK OF LIBOČAN'S *Bohemian Chronicles* were widely known and circulated from the moment that the book appeared. Hajek's work was dedicated to Ferdinand I., and produced under the auspices of that sovereign, who, indeed, appointed officials for the purpose of examining the contents of the book before its appearance.

When, after the battle of the White Mountain, all independent works of an historical character were suppressed and many were completely destroyed, Hajek's chronicle became, and continued for nearly two centuries, the one source of information to which the few writers on Bohemian history went. Many of the foolish, displeasing, and untruthful tales referring to his country, which a Bohemian so often finds in the writings of foreign lands, can be traced to Hajek. It is in his work that we find that account of Zižka's death which has been so often repeated, though it is as entirely contrary to all we know of that great warrior as it is to the reports of the contemporary chroniclers. Hajek tells us that Zižka, when dying, ordered that his body be flayed and then thrown to the wild beasts, and that his skin should be used as a drum.[1] This and so many other foolish tales have greatly contributed to the totally false interpretation of ancient Bohemian history that is current up to the present day.

The *Hussitenkrieg* of Theobaldus, and Lenfant in his *Histoire des Guerres Hussites* (George Sand's authority for her *Jean Zyska* and her *Comtesse de Rudolstadt*), both borrow extensively from Hajek. As the works of Theobaldus and Lenfant were recognised authorities on Bohemian history up to the end of the eighteenth century, Hajek's tales have been repeated by many writers (for instance, Carlyle), who had probably never heard of his name.

Since the beginning of the present century it has become possible to study freely the documents that refer

[1] See Chapter IV.

to the ancient history of Bohemia. The result has been that the glory of the "Bohemian Livy," as Hajek was formerly called, has been completely obscured. It has been proved that Hajek's work is totally untrustworthy, and that he not only copied from earlier writers without any attempt at criticism, but that he was often intentionally mendacious, and for party purposes distorted his account of historical events. The great Bohemian historian Palacký's judgment on Hajek has often been quoted. Palacký wrote : " Hajek is the most narrow-minded slyboots, the most naïve humbug, and the apparently most innocent calumniator whom I have met in the course of my historical studies."

It is hardly necessary to mention that at a period when the rule "Scribitur ad narrandum, non ad probandum," was ignored by all Bohemian historians, Hajek's work shows traces of party spirit almost on every page. The author, who was a Romanist priest, writes as a strong Catholic, and as a strong partisan of the Bohemian aristocracy. Among the adherents of Rome, who were then few in number in Bohemia, and who were Hajek's principal protectors, were found several of the greatest Bohemian nobles. These Catholic lords were always the most decided enemies of the Bohemian cities, while the Utraquist and Protestant nobles—though their caste pride may have been as great—regarded the townsmen as valuable allies in their struggle against the sovereign, while the democratic character of the community of the "Bohemian brethren" naturally also influenced the nobles who belonged to it.

In his preface already Hajek enters into the question of the rank and precedence among the Bohemian estates, of course in a sense favourable to his patrons. He writes: "Some have, for the purpose of disparaging the estate of the nobles and that of the knights, dared to maintain that the estate of the townsmen is the first, and dates from the foundation of Prague. The estate of the nobles, they say, sprung up afterwards, when they (the nobles) acted as officials, and other men were intrusted to their rule; then, they say, many years later the estate of the knights was created, when the king allowed them (the knights) to bear a device on their shield because of certain deeds and brave exploits. But both these statements are untrue." Hajek here writes in contradiction to a Utraquist historian, Martin Kuthen, who had stated that the origin of the Bohemian estates was that mentioned above. Kuthen's work, which has little value and requires no further notice, was then very much read, and it has even been said that Hajek was instructed to write his work as a refutation of that of Kuthen.

Of Hajek's chronicle, which (as was customary in those days) begins with the deluge, and which ends with the coronation of his patron Ferdinand I., the earliest part is by far the most attractive. Dealing with an almost entirely mythical period, and one in which it was nearly impossible to introduce political and ecclesiastical controversies (though even here Hajek occasionally does so), the author is at his best. He borrows largely from Cosmas and from Dalimil, whose influence even on Hajek's manner of writing can be traced in the early part of his book. Hajek's style, indeed, always varies greatly according to the authorities which he is using. His account of the foundation of Prague is very curious.

But even in Hajek's accounts of semi-mythical occurrences the insincerity and dishonesty that characterise him are often apparent. Cosmas and Dalimil related the legends and traditions of their land just as they had reached them from the earliest available oral or written depositions. Hajek, on the contrary, always assumes the part of a conscientious and systematic historian. He indeed mentions Tacitus, Ptolemy, Strabo, Orosius, and a limited number of mediæval writers among the authorities whom, according to his statement, he had consulted. Hajek's object was to join together various, often contradictory, tales, and to give them the shape of a chronologically consistent record of the lives of the Premyslide princes. Was it for this purpose necessary to alter traditional dates? That appeared to Hajek a matter of no great importance!

Writing as a fervent partisan of Rome, Hajek of course judges Hus and Jerome of Prague severely. Of the latter he tells us: "In 1400 there arrived in Prague, coming from England, a young man who had gone there for the purposes of study, Jerome by name, a citizen of the new town of Prague, the son of one Albert (Vojtěch). . . . This Jerome had brought books with him from England, into which he had copied out some of the writings of 'John the Englishman,' whom they call Wycliffe. This man had by his teaching corrupted first a town in England called 'Oksa' or 'Oksonia,' and afterwards the whole English kingdom." Of Hus, Hajek tells us that he was originally a good and pious man, but that he came under the influence of two Englishmen, "Jacob the Bachelor" and "Conrad of Kandelburgk" (=Canterbury). These men used to visit (according to Hajek!) the young masters of the university, spreading Wycliffe's teaching and perverting many from the true faith. At last "Master John of

Husinec, Master Jerome of Prague, Jacob of England, and Conrad of 'Kandelburgk' were like one man." This account of the origin of the Hussite movement—totally incorrect, as so many of Hajek's statements—yet proves that the writer was indeed the "narrow-minded slyboots" Palacký has called him. By greatly exaggerating the English influence on the foundation of Hussitism, and stigmatising it as a foreign movement, Hajek, as he well knew, greatly injured the Hussites; for the intense national feeling that has always animated the Bohemians has produced among them an often exaggerated distrust of foreign interference.

With all its faults, Hajek's work will always find readers. His style, though varying according to the authorities which he is using, is generally animated, a priceless merit in his pedantic age. An interest also is connected with Hajek's chronicles which the author could not have foreseen, and would not have desired. Hajek's work, sanctioned by the Roman Church, and therefore accessible to the people, continued to be read when every other book on the early history of Bohemia disappeared. It is thus to a large extent through Hajek's chronicles that the Bohemians preserved some recollection of their former greatness. A copy of Hajek's chronicles went down from generation to generation among the Bohemian peasantry, and was cherished as an heirloom. As a lover would rather that evil be spoken of his love than that her name remain unmentioned, thus the Bohemians welcomed eagerly even hostile accounts of the deeds of Zižka, Prokop, and the other leaders under whose guidance Bohemia had once defied all Europe.

Of Hajek's life little is known, and that little is by no

means to his credit. The year of his birth is uncertain, but we know that when very young he left the Utraquist Church, in which he was born, became a Roman Catholic, and took orders in that Church. We read of him as preaching in the Church of St. Thomas at Prague in 1524, and by the aid of some Catholic nobles he obtained in 1527 the deanery of Karlstein. Later he obtained other ecclesiastical dignities. Of all these honours he was subsequently deprived in consequence of an accusation of having embezzled money belonging to the Church. It has been suggested, though on insufficient evidence, that Hajek wrote his chronicles for the purpose of regaining the lost favour of his patrons. In 1544 Hajek, perhaps as a reward for his book that had appeared in 1541, obtained the provostship of Stará Boleslav (Alt Bunzlau), but of this dignity he was again deprived in 1549 because of various offences against canon law. Hajek died in 1553.

Several minor historians belong to this period. I have already mentioned Martin Kuthen. The *History of the Emperor Charles IV., King of Bohemia*, by Prokop Lupáč (published in 1584), also deserves special notice. The book is of interest to English readers, as the author has inserted in it a considerable portion of a ballad describing the death of King John at the battle of Crécy, which was probably written shortly after that event.

The most prominent historians of this period were probably the members of the community of the "Bohemian Brethren." This is, however, unfortunately little more than a conjecture. The works of the brethren were specially singled out for destruction during the Catholic reaction. Mere fragments remain, and even with regard to these doubts as to their authorship often exist. The writings of Professor Goll, who has with admirable skill and ability reconstructed the early history of the brotherhood, also throw incidentally much light on the literary activity of the brethren. The greatest historian among them was probably Brother Blahoslav, whose *Historie Bratrska* (" History of the Brotherhood ") was greatly admired; the book is known to us only by quotations in some contemporary works which have been preserved. As already mentioned, Blahoslav devoted much time to the study of the grammar of the Bohemian language, and he was celebrated for the beauty of his style. It is, therefore, probable that in the *History of the Brotherhood* we have lost not only a valuable historical document, but also a masterpiece of Bohemian prose-writing. With the exception of a short Latin treatise on the history of the brotherhood, the writings of Blahoslav that have been preserved are not of a historical character; I have therefore referred to him more fully in the last chapter.

In connection with Blahoslav I shall mention a work that was formerly often attributed to him; this is the *Captivity of John Augusta*. Recent research has proved that this book was really written by the young clergyman JOHN BILEK, Augusta's companion during his captivity. It is, however, probable that the first part of the work was revised by Blahoslav. The book deals with the imprisonment of John Augusta, bishop of the Bohemian Brethren, who was accused of having participated in the negotiations with the German Protestant princes, into which some Bohemians had entered in 1546 and 1547.[1]

Bilek, Augusta's companion in captivity, has with touching simplicity described his sufferings, the treachery

[1] See page 229.

of Schönaich, town-captain of Leitomischl, the tortures which Bilek and Augusta underwent, their long imprisonment in the castle of Pürglitz (or Křivoklat), their attempts to communicate from their prison with their brethren who were at large, the relief of their sufferings through the intercession of Philipina Welser, wife of the Archduke Ferdinand, and their final liberation. The book, written in a truly saintly spirit, never reveals the slightest animosity against the officials who were treating Augusta and his companion so cruelly. When narrating the tortures that were inflicted on Augusta for the purpose of forcing him to admit the complicity of the Brotherhood in the supposed conspiracy, Bilek simply writes: "The officials then ordered that he (Augusta) should again be put on the rack, because of the questions mentioned before; but it did not last long, as he had become quite silent and swooned away. I think, had they but continued a little longer, he would have died during the torture."

Bilek's simple account of the daily routine and the little incidents of prison life, often recalling Silvio Pellico, is both interesting and touching. I will give one quotation referring to the attempt of the prisoners to establish communications with their friends outside the prison. Bilek writes: "After they (the prisoners) had been in prison some time, a year and a half and ten weeks, in the year 1550, God our Lord wrought a great miracle; He opened to them in their solitude and concealment a secret and concealed path, by means of which their friends could visit them, receive news of them, and also convey news to them. And this happened thus. Among the warders who guarded them, and who had received rigid instructions how they were to guard them, was a servant who knew them slightly, and knew also what sort of men they were; for he had formerly been an artisan at Leitomischl. He knew that they were enduring all this suffering, not because of any crime, but for the sake of the religion; and he felt a certain compassion for them. This man risked all, and permitted that they should receive from the brethren and from their friends everything they required; and he also undertook to forward secretly their friends' communications to them, and their own to their friends. He began doing this in 1550, before the Vigil of St. Paul's Confession, and continued doing so up to the year 1553. He conveyed to them the letters and communications of their brethren and dear friends, and he supplied them with ink, paper, and everything that is required for writing. A few books also he brought them and other things which they required, money and tapers; and they accepted these things with no slight fear, principally with regard to the servant; for he might have forfeited his life had it been discovered that he had given us these things. As regards themselves, they had commended their souls to God and His grace, whatever might befall them; they knew that they were acting rightly, and had therefore little fear for their own persons; rather did they rejoice that God had granted these things to them, and they accepted them with gratitude and thanksgiving, and praised their Lord God for this." The fact that so large a part of the historical as well as of the theological writings of the brethren has been destroyed enhances the value of Bilek's book. The passages quoted above give a true insight into the inner life of the Brotherhood; they give evidence of their invincible courage and absolute reliance on God, which gave them great strength, as well as of their exaggerated subserviency to even unjust temporal authorities, which sometimes made them poor politicians.

Of Bilek little is known but what he himself tells us in his book. He was a clergyman of the Brotherhood, and acted for a considerable time as secretary to Augusta, the head of the community. He died at Napajedl in Moravia in 1581, at the age of sixty-five. As already mentioned, his book was formerly attributed to Blahoslav, and only recent researches have awarded the authorship to Bilek.[1]

Very noteworthy among the historians of the Brotherhood is WENCESLAS BŘEZAN. To him Palacký's remark, that the Bohemians cared more for their history than for the biographies of their historians, is particularly applicable. Neither the year of the birth nor that of the death of Březan can be accurately ascertained; it has been conjectured that he was born about the year 1560, and died about the year 1619. Peter Vok, Lord of Rosenberg, the greatest of the Bohemian nobles, and a strenuous friend and protector of the Brotherhood, appointed Březan "archivarian, librarian, and historiographer of the House of Rosenberg." Most of his works deal with the annals of that great House, which for centuries figured so prominently in Bohemian history.

The writings of Březan, like those of so many other Bohemian writers, have been only partially preserved. Besides minor works referring to the annals and the genealogy of noble Bohemian families, Březan wrote a large *History of the House of Rosenberg*, which is said to

---

[1] *The Life* (or rather *Captivity*) *of John Augusta* was edited and published by Franta-Sumavsky in 1837. The work has recently been translated into German by Dean Joseph Müller of Herrenhut.

have consisted of five volumes. Of this work only portions, containing the biographies of William of Rosenberg and of his brother, Lord Peter, the last of the Rosenbergs, have reached us. From recent researches it, however, appears probable that the German *Rosenbergische Chronica* of Heerman, a monk of the monastery of Wittingau (Třeboň), is an abridged translation of the lost parts of Březan's book. In any case, the parts of Březan's work that have been preserved in Bohemian are sufficient to prove that the work was far more than a mere family record, and that it is of great value for the social as well as for the political history of Bohemia.

The two biographies convey a vivid impression of the court life (for it can hardly be otherwise described) of the great Bohemian nobles during the period that preceded the battle of the White Mountain. It is true that the position of the Lords of Rosenberg, the first of the Bohemian nobles, was a somewhat exceptional one. This appears very clearly from the letters, published by Březan, which were interchanged between the members of the imperial family and the Lords of Rosenberg. Of the two biographies, that of William of Rosenberg, the less interesting of the two brothers, is the more valuable one. William held several important appointments under the Imperial Government, and Březan gives a very clear outline of his official career. Very interesting are Březan's notes, which refer to the proposed election of Lord William to the Polish throne. He tells us that "the Lord of Rosenberg had then many adherents among the Polish nobles, more indeed than the House of Austria; and I do not say this to harm or disparage that illustrious House." Březan further tells us that "the Poles, after they had thus been mocked (by the flight of their king, Henry of Valois), searched for a new king. Some favoured the House of Habsburg, others desired Lord William as king, particularly as he was a descendant of the ancient family of the Orsinis, as by his ancestry, several centuries back, he was a Bohemian, and therefore belonged to a cognate country; also because he was a sensible, learned, temperate, Catholic noble." The election of Stephen Bathory to the Polish throne (1576) destroyed William of Rosenberg's hopes.

Březan's biography of Lord Peter of Rosenberg is a very disappointing book, if we consider that he was dealing with an intensely interesting subject. The semi-independent position of the great Bohemian nobles, who lived principally on their vast estates, surrounded by dependents and servants, free from the control of a court, and to a great extent even from the criticism of their equals, in some cases greatly developed their individuality. To no one does this apply to a greater extent than to Lord Peter of Rosenberg. The heir of the great family that had supplied so many leaders to the Romanist Church, Peter joined the community of the Bohemian Brethren, it is said through the influence of his wife, who belonged to that Church. Whether there is any connection between this change of creed and the scandalous stories which Catholic writers (whose works alone were known in Bohemia during two centuries) have circulated I do not wish to determine. They tell us that Lord Peter established a "harem" at his castle of Wittingau, to which the fairest women from all parts of Europe were conveyed. This is obviously an absurd exaggeration, though it is probable that Lord Peter had in his youth led an immoral life. With regard to the accusations of intemperance and of cruelty to his servants, it is probable that Peter of Rosenberg was in such matters neither better nor worse than the other great Bohemian nobles of his time.

Where he indeed differed from many of them was in his taste for literature and art. The Rosenbergs had at all times taken much interest in the archives of their family, and indeed preserved them so carefully that most of these documents are even now in a state of perfect preservation. Palacký, who examined them in the present century, witnesses to this, as well as to their great importance for the history of Bohemia, in which the Lords of Rosenberg played so large a part. Peter showed the same interest in the family archives as his predecessors. When selling one of his castles to the Emperor Rudolph II., he stipulated that he should retain possession of one thousand documents which he considered of historical value. In printed works also Lord Peter's interest was great. As early as in 1573, twenty years before he acceded to the family estates, Peter had collected 243 printed volumes. Březan, who had charge of Lord Peter's library, and was authorised to enlarge it, tells us that it was from this modest beginning that the far-famed Rosenberg library sprang. Many books were inherited from Lord William, and many purchased from monasteries and elsewhere. The library at last became a very extensive one. The Rosenberg library, in consequence of the events of the Thirty Years' War, eventually found its way to Stockholm, where Březan's catalogue of the library is also still preserved. Peter of Rosenberg is notable also as a patron of literature, and, among others, the poet Lomnický[1] enjoyed his protection for many years. Lomnický showed his gratitude by writing on

[1] See Chapter V.

the death of Peter of Rosenberg perhaps his one touching and heartfelt poem. That Peter was, like his brother, interested in alchemy, hardly requires mention, for almost all the great Bohemian nobles then followed the example of Rudolph, their sovereign, who delighted in the study of alchemy.

Peter's interest in music was also very great. Even before inheriting Wittingau from his brother William, he had established a small orchestra at Běychin, and he afterwards devoted much time and expense to the improvement and aggrandisement of the magnificent orchestra which Lord William had founded at Wittingau. Březan, in his biographies of both brothers, gives an interesting account of the cultivation of music in Bohemia in the sixteenth and the beginning of the seventeenth century. Lord Peter also undoubtedly showed a considerable amount of interest in other arts. In Březan's biography, written in chronological order, we read under " December 19, 1598.—The Lord of Hradec sent our sovereign lord (Lord Peter) eighteen pretty painted figures, very poetical, and representing Venus."

In Bohemian politics Peter of Rosenberg played a very important part, and his change of creed appeared as an event of the greatest importance on the ever-varying stage of Bohemian political life. Peter of Rosenberg was on terms of intimacy with Christian of Anhalt, perhaps the greatest statesman of the seventeenth century. He acted as Anhalt's representative in Bohemia, and was no doubt initiated into his far-reaching plans. Anhalt, as recent research has sufficiently proved, intended to use the dissensions between Rudolph and his brother Matthew for the purpose of totally destroying the power of the House of Habsburg. On these and similar subjects of the greatest interest Březan has little or no information to give, and his biography, as already stated, is disappointing.

The book, written in chronological order, contains accounts of Lord Peter's travels, but here, too, a mere outline of the occurrences is given. When mentioning Peter's journey to England, Březan merely tells us (under February 1563) that "after Lord Peter had been received in England with Christian kindness by her royal majesty Queen Elizabeth, and had then been kindly and graciously dismissed, her majesty was graciously pleased to grant him a royal decree addressed to all her officials and to those of all the towns." Březan then gives the full wording of this passport, if we may thus call it, in which Lord Peter is described as "one of the chamberlains of our good brother the King of the Romans."

Březan devotes much space to detailed accounts of the domestic arrangements at the castle of Wittingau, and his book is a treasury for those who would study the social condition of Bohemia at this period. Březan's style has little grace, partly no doubt in consequence of the chronological form which he has given to his book. The following portrait of Lord Peter of Rosenberg is a characteristic specimen of Březan's style: "Lord Peter's motto was 'In silentio et in spe.' It should be mentioned that this lord, for the purpose of living wisely, prudently, and in a way that beseems a Christian, and also that he might constantly remember death, always had a death's head placed on a board over the table in his apartment. He even founded an association, the device of which was a golden death's-head of the value of eight ducats. This badge he himself usually wore round his neck. It had on one side the inscription, 'Memento mori,' and on the other, 'Cogita æternitatem.' And this order he distributed among his friends, both lords and ladies, and he ordered me to keep a special register, where the names of these persons were entered."

"He was a nobleman of well-shaped figure, and more refined than his brother William. His features were charming, his manners dignified and truly princely, his speech was sensible, he was compassionate and affable, and though he was sometimes angry, whenever he had scolded or cursed some one he always afterwards excused himself with mild words. He was a gay and jocose nobleman, though in his old age he gave himself up entirely to piety, read religious books with pleasure, and listened eagerly to the word of God. He was keen for all novelties, a lover of all sciences and arts, and he spent large sums on them. He had a special fancy and predilection for building, and in this resembled his brother William. He was in the habit of standing oftener than sitting, and of walking constantly, and so quickly that it was difficult even for young men to keep up with him. By a bequest in his will he provided for the maids of the woman-apartments, and freed them (from bondage), ordering that each should receive a sum of gold as a present; and as trustees for this bequest he appointed Albert Pauzar of Michnic and Volesná, Henry Caslav of Podol, and Frederick Frokštejn of Naceslavic, his servants and courtiers."

"He was a very valorous nobleman, courageous and even somewhat venturesome; for he boldly approached wild beasts, bears, wolves, horses, and dogs without feeling any fear. And, on the whole, I do not know that anything was wanting in this heroic personage, except that which he himself deplored on his death-bed, that he had not sufficiently cultivated the study of literature."

Peter of Rosenberg died in 1611, only a few years before the momentous events which so completely changed the destinies of his country.

It is a natural and easy transition from Peter of Rosenberg to another great Bohemian nobleman, Charles of Žerotin, who indeed was often politically associated with Rosenberg, particularly during the contest between King Rudolph II. and his brother Matthew, which occurred in the early years of the seventeenth century. Žerotin was, it is true, a maker rather than a writer of history. On two occasions, in 1608 when Rudolph was contending with his treacherous younger brother Matthew, and in 1619, when Frederick of the Palatinate attempted to oust the house of Habsburg from the Bohemian throne, Žerotin's attitude to a great extent decided the fate of his country. Žerotin's numerous writings may also be considered materials for history rather than historical works. Yet no outline of Bohemian literature would be complete were the name of Žerotin omitted.

CHARLES OF ŽEROTIN was born in 1564 at Brandeis, on the Adler, one of the Bohemian estates of his powerful family. Like many Bohemian noblemen of this period, Charles spent a considerable part of his youth in foreign countries, both as a student and as a soldier. At Genoa he fell under the influence of the Calvinist divine Theodore de Beza, but he never (as has been stated) abandoned for Calvinism the Church of the Bohemian Brethren, to which his family had belonged from the time that the Brotherhood had been founded. His writings as well as his political career prove that he was a faithful adherent of that community, of which he was one of the most illustrious members.

In the year 1591 he took service under Henry IV. of

X

France, whom all Protestants then recognised as their leader. Žerotin's correspondence, which is very extensive, is particularly interesting when he refers to this period of his life.[1] He appears to have felt very little sympathy for the French prince, to have distrusted him, and almost to have foreseen his conversion to the Church of Rome. Žerotin, whose motives were always disinterested and elevated though often unpractical, could not have felt much sympathy for an "opportunist."

Žerotin's later life was spent almost entirely in Bohemia and Moravia, the countries where his ancestral estates were situated. He favoured the cause of the Archduke Matthew against King Rudolph in 1609, and in 1618 was one of the few Protestant noblemen who remained faithful to the House of Habsburg. As reward for his fidelity, he was allowed to remain in his country after the battle of the White Mountain, when most Protestants had already been expelled. He was even able to afford aid and shelter to many other members of the Brotherhood. Among these was Komenský. He sought refuge at Brandeis, and wrote there his *Labyrinth of the World*, which was dedicated to Žerotin.

The increasing persecution of all who did not belong to the Church of Rome finally induced Žerotin to leave Bohemia and Moravia and to retire to Breslau. It was here that he spent the last years of his life, and he left his extensive library to that city. Žerotin was, however, still permitted to visit occasionally his extensive estates. During one of these visits he died at Prerov in Moravia in 1636. His body was interred at Brandeis on the Adler, his ancestral home.

---

[1] Professor Léger in his *Nouvelles Etudes Slaves* has translated into French some of Žerotin's letters which refer to his French campaign.

CHARLES OF ŽEROTIN

Žerotin has left voluminous writings. His correspondence, to which I have already alluded, was very extensive. Continued, as it was, during the whole of his life, it is, of course, of the greatest value for the history of his time. Žerotin has also left several volumes of memoirs, referring principally to the doings of the Diet of Moravia during the period that he presided over that assembly. He also wrote a very curious work entitled *Obrana* or *Apology*, addressed to George, Lord of Hodic. It appears that Hodic had blamed Žerotin publicly for having temporarily retired from political life. This work, written in a pure but eloquent manner, showing traces of profound study of the classical writers, is a recognised masterpiece of Bohemian prose. The original great reluctance of the members of the Brotherhood to enter the stormy arena of political life had indeed decreased since many nobles and other influential persons had joined their Church, but traces of this feeling appear in Žerotin's work. He writes: " You were pleased, my Lord of Hodic, to remark of me at the meeting of the Estates that 'I act wrongly in stifling the gifts which God has given to me.' By these words —few and quickly spoken, yet containing much meaning—you were pleased to attack me sharply and to deal me a severe blow; for what else is stifling God's gift but refusing to remain in that state in which God has placed us? And what, again, is not remaining in the state in which God has placed us but not being as I should be? What conclusion then can be drawn other than that if I am not as I should be, then—though I declare that I am a lover of my country, her true son, an own limb of her body, sharing her wounds—in fact, her twin-brother, who was born with her and will die with her—my pride is idle and my word worthless if my acts are not in accordance with my sentiments. Idle indeed would it be if I could bring nothing forward and give no proof that I am what I say that I am. Then indeed your argument would be powerful and your words conform to truth and justice, and I myself should then agree with them. For it is my firm conviction that no man is good but he who by his deeds proves that he is good.

"But I—deign to excuse me—have given no cause for your judgment on me. That my manner is somewhat different from what it was some time ago, and that I do not labour so assiduously for the welfare of my country as I did some time back, that is no proof that I have lost and abandoned all my innate love and affection for it. As the sun does not cease to be the sun when for a moment it sets in the midst of clouds, and as a fire does not lose its heat if it does not immediately pierce through cold tiles, and as a field also must not be considered barren when for a time it lies fallow, and so to speak rests; so I also ought not and should not be declared wanting in the love and care for my country which it is my duty to have, because I do not try my skill on every course (=take part in every political contest).

"For as prudent sailors are carried, when the sea is calm, here and there and catch the wind in their sails, and then, when a storm arises, and for a time drives them from their straight course, they yet remain out at sea and guard themselves as best they can with the compass till a more favourable wind guides them to their destined port; thus I also avoid the present evil times and their difficulties, and conceal myself from the storm as under a roof till more convenient times arise."

Žerotin has here in beautiful words expressed thoughts that almost condemn him as a statesman. It is true that shortly after the publication of the *Obrana* he appeared more prominently on the political scene than at any other time during the struggle between King Rudolph and his brother Matthew; but during the far more momentous struggle of the last years of Bohemian independence (1618-1620) Žerotin as far as was possible chose the part of the prudent mariner, but the port which he finally reached was exile!

Before mentioning the latest historians of this period, I must notice a considerable number of accounts of travels, books which are closely connected with history. The Bohemians were great travellers in those days, and a considerable number of them have recorded their journeys and adventures. I have already referred to John of Lobkovic when dealing with his more celebrated brother Bohnslav,[1] and the travels of Zerotin and Rosenberg have also been already mentioned. Of other records of travel, it will be sufficient to mention those of Prefat, Vratislav, and Harant of Polžic. Ulrick Prefat of Vlkanov, a citizen of Prague, undertook in 1546 a journey to Venice and Palestine, of which he has left us an interesting account. His descriptions of the Holy Land are, however, inferior to those of Harant, written somewhat later. VENCESLAS VRATISLAV of Mitrovic, born (1576) of a Roman Catholic family, was educated by the Jesuits, and had from his earliest youth a strong desire to visit distant lands. When not yet eighteen years of age he obtained permission to join the staff of Baron Krekvic, whom the Emperor Rudolph was sending as ambassador to Constantinople. He has left us a record

[1] See Chapter V.

of his journey and imprisonment;[1] for the Turks of that period had little regard for international law and diplomatic privileges. Vratislav's book has a certain youthful grace and simplicity, and he was by no means devoid of the gift of observation.

Vratislav, on his return to Bohemia, published in 1599 the description of his travels and adventures. He afterwards, not unnaturally, took part in several campaigns against his old enemies, the Turks. Educated by the Jesuits and a staunch Romanist, he was, of course, on the side of the Archduke Ferdinand during the Bohemian troubles of 1618 to 1620.

Far more interesting as an author, and far more representative of his time than the two last-named writers, is CHRISTOPHER HARANT, Lord of Polžic and Bezdruzic. It is therefore perhaps not amiss to study his work and his life somewhat more in detail. Harant was born in 1564, of an ancient knightly family of Bohemia. He received the thorough education and literary training which was then customary with many of the Bohemian noble families. Harant, we are told, possessed a thorough knowledge of Greek, Latin, German, Italian, Spanish, as well as, of course, his own language. It has even been said that it was out of patriotism that he published his celebrated book of travels in Bohemian instead of in German, though that would, of course, have secured for the book far more numerous readers. Harant's classical erudition was considered extensive even at that period, when in Bohemia the almost superstitious veneration for the great writers of Rome and Greece was at its height. Harant's own list of his authorities includes

[1] This work has been translated into English by the late Rev. A. H. Wratislaw.

almost all known writers, both Greek and Latin, from Homer and Herodotus to Statius and Claudianus. Later Latin writers, such as Gregory of Tours and Orosius, are also quoted by Harant; his vast erudition included even Byzantine writers such as Suidas, Zonaras, and Chalkokondylas. More recent works, such as the writings of Guicciardini, were also well known to Harant; he quotes even from such (now) little known works as the French histories of Du Tillet and Bernard de Girard, and the *Res Burgundicæ* and *Res Austriacæ* of Pontus Heuterus. Harant's education was completed at the court of the Archduke Ferdinand at Innsbruck. When referring to his passage through Innsbruck on his way to Venice, Harant gives an interesting account of his stay at the archducal court. The years 1591 to 1597 were spent by Harant in the service of the Emperor Rudolph, who, in his capacity of King of Bohemia, had demanded aid from that country in his wars against the Turks. Harant appears greatly to have distinguished himself in these campaigns, and we are told that Rudolph, in consideration of his services, granted him an annuity chargeable on the Bohemian revenue. Harant's campaigns in Hungary (a large part of which country was then under Turkish rule) may have suggested to him the idea of visiting countries yet farther east. He tells us in his preface to his book of travels that he wished "to see those countries which were the scene of the holiest, wisest, and most celebrated events mentioned in the Old and in the New Testament . . . those lands which were once an earthly paradise. These lands," he continues, "I purposed to visit with special ardour and with great danger for my life, and I set out with God's help." A family bereavement—Harant's first wife died in 1597—probably confirmed him in his decision, and he started from Pilsen in April 1598 on his long and perilous journey, accompanied by his friend Herman Čérnin, Lord of Chudenic, and only one servant.

Harant's account of this journey, published as *Christopher Harant's Journey to Venice, and thence to the Holy Land and to Egypt*,[1] has assured to the author a not inconsiderable place in the annals of Bohemian literature. Harant undoubtedly possessed the gift of observation to an unusual extent, and his descriptions of the scenery he viewed and the men he met are often very vivid. Though the book is generally written in a grave and somewhat pedantic manner, yet some passages show that Harant was by no means devoid of humour. The work has, however, the fault of being somewhat long-winded, and Harant is too fond of lengthy historical digressions, introduced for the purpose of exhibiting his learning. This is particularly true of the part of the book which deals with Harant's visit to Egypt. He here introduces a lengthy treatise on the early dynasties of Egyptian rulers, which is, of course, valueless from the point of view of modern research. Harant was very fond, almost too fond, of quoting; yet his quotations, chosen from many writers in various languages, are often quaint and amusing, and remind the reader of Montaigne. On the whole, Harant's work is one of those ancient Bohemian books that can still be read with amusement as well as interest.

From Pilsen, Harant and his companions travelled through Tyrol to Venice, where they stayed some time. The indefatigable Harant studied not only the monuments, but also the constitution of Venice, which he

---

[1] Edited and published by Dr. Erben in 1854 and 1855.

greatly admired. The Venetian constitution in many ways resembled that which Harant and his party wished to establish in Bohemia, and he gives a full account of it, "as an example for us and for our benefit," as he writes. Harant and his friend were obliged to remain some time in Venice before they found other pilgrims to the Holy Land, with whom they jointly chartered a ship to Jaffa. Among these new companions was "Lambert the Dutchman," who appears to have been a constant cause alternately of indignation and of amusement to the other travellers. On leaving Venice the pilgrims sailed along the coast of Dalmatia, and by way of the Ionian Islands, Candia, and Cyprus, finally reached the harbour of Jaffa. From here they proceeded to Jerusalem. Harant thus describes their arrival there :—

"When we had arrived within four Bohemian miles of Jerusalem, we noticed everywhere the industry of the Jews and former inhabitants of the land; for they had laid out all those hills in vineyards, gardens, and fields, though they are now deserted and overgrown with thorns, yet the traces of the former divisions of the fields by means of low wells and small steps still remain; we can thus know how full of cities this land was; and on this short journey we remarked the astonishing laziness of the present inhabitants, of whom the country now feeds about ten to a thousand formerly. Yet the northern side of the hill has remained tolerably fertile in vineyards, olives, figs, pomegranates, and other fruits.

"When we were about two miles from Jerusalem the dragoman [1] from that town came out on purpose to meet us; for our dragoman from Rama had hurried on, leav-

---

[1] It is not easy to recognise this word in Harant's self-coined translation or rather adaptation, *trucelman*.

ing us behind, and had informed the guardian of the monastery (of St. Salvador) and the other dragoman of our arrival.

"With the guardian the *vicarius* of the monastery also appeared, and when they came near us they greeted us in Italian and asked us many questions; for instance, from where we came, how we had fared on our journey, and what had happened during our travels in our own country and the lands through which we had passed. And thus continuing our conversation we arrived at the gates of the city of Jerusalem about vesper-time. Our whole journey from Venice to Jerusalem had lasted forty-four days; we had then travelled 458 Bohemian miles from Venice and 582 from Bohemia, both by land and by sea."

Harant and his companions spent a fortnight at Jerusalem as guests of the monks of the Monastery of St. Salvador, and he gives a detailed account of their visits to the historical spots in the city and neighbourhood. Harant's description of his visit to the Chapel of the Holy Sepulchre is interesting. He writes: "When we approached these Turks (there were eight altogether, some of whom sat on stone benches covered with carpets, which since ancient times have been placed beside the gates of the church), one of them came forward with the keys and opened the locked gates of the church; then they immediately let us into the church one by one, counting us till they had got us all in line, then they hastily closed the gates and sealed them; there are two gates, one next to the other, made of fine marble, on which costly figures are carved. That gate which opens on the right into the church is walled up, but the other one opens by halves, and in the lower half there is a gap or window through which one can see into the court, and from the court into the church. And having entered the church, we next arrived before the chapel or cell in which is the grave of our Lord, and then we all immediately knelt down piously. But Master Antonio Donato (one of Harant's fellow-travellers) fell to the ground heavily as soon as he entered the chapel, just as if he had fainted, and we, seeing this, were greatly frightened, for we knew of no other cause of his fall except his great religious ardour; but he soon recovered, and, after he had recited some prayers, he rose together with us. The guardian then put on his vestments ... and first led us to a cupboard in the wall, similar to a blind window. There we saw a portion of a pillar of stone similar to marble; to this column the holy body of Christ was bound while he allowed himself to be scourged and cruelly flogged in the house of Pilate. This portion of the column is three spans in length, and the breadth is somewhat greater; it stands behind a very thick iron trellis fastened to the wall. There is a small window opposite, which opens with a lock, and before the pillar there always hangs a lamp, which continually glistens and burns. At this spot we began to sing the hymn—

> '*Eia Fratres Charissimi Christe*
> *Christi mortis mysteria*
> *Canamus*,' &c."

Of all other memorable sites in Jerusalem itself, as well as of those at Bethlehem, Jericho, and elsewhere, Harant gives equally detailed and accurate accounts; his book is indeed still of value for the topography of Palestine. Harant also gives a very curious description of the city of Jerusalem as he himself saw it. He writes: "In the town of Jerusalem there are some streets that are vaulted over, and in some of these shopkeepers, Christians, Jews, and Turks, in others tradesmen such as shoemakers and weavers, and yet in others cooks have vaulted stalls, just like the booths in the old town of Prague. . . . The houses in the town are mostly tolerably solid; the greater part are without roof, and have only terraces; others have vaulted roofs. A third part of the houses in the town are deserted and in ruins. There are many open spaces, and they occupy a third part of the city. Of wood there is very little in the buildings, indeed there is less in the whole town than in some houses at Prague; the town is therefore very safe from fires. Its size is about that of Kuttenberg (Kutná Hora) here in the Bohemian land."

Harant's account of the different Christian communities, the members of which then visited Palestine, and who had religious foundations there, are still of the greatest interest. He enumerates, "besides the Latin, that is to say, Roman Catholic Christians, many other sects, Christians belonging to various nationalities, such as Greeks, Armenians, Georgians, Syrians, Nestorians, Jacobites, Abyssinians, Maronites, and others." In the Greeks, Harant, as a lover of classical antiquity, naturally took far greater interest than in the adherents of the other churches which he enumerates. Harant's chapter on the Greeks is written with interesting and very evident enthusiasm. "The Greek nation," he tells us, "was in former days far superior to all others in matters of government and politics. Among them first arose lawgivers, from whom others took and acquired the true rules of government. Among them (the Greeks) were wise men, 'sapientes Græciæ,' famous all over the world, and the most learned of men in all sciences; they first of all discovered botany and medical science; they divided time by months and years. Arithmetic, geometry, physics, ethics, and other kinds of philosophy they improved and advanced; they then faithfully and carefully preserved all these things, so that they were called the mother and origin of all literary and other free arts; and thus they were superior to all other nations.

"Besides this, for many centuries they knew neither kingly nor monarchical rule; they governed themselves according to their own constitutions, some in a democratic, others in an aristocratic manner (what the latter was I have explained in my description of Venice); therefore all the neighbouring kings in every direction were their mortal enemies, whom they had to encounter in many great wars."

From Palestine the travellers proceeded to Egypt, embarking at Gaza for Damietta, then the principal seaport of Egypt. The sea-voyage was tedious and unpleasant. Harant (from whose mind Bohemia was hardly ever absent) described the passengers who embarked with him and his companions as a "Senftenberg rabble."[1]

After a short stay in Egypt, Harant and his companions returned to Venice, and thence to their own country. In 1608 he published, on the request of his friends, the graphic description of his travels, which fortunately has been preserved. Harant appears to have enjoyed great favour with King Rudolph, who raised him

[1] A proverbial expression. Senftenberg is a small town in North-Eastern Bohemia. I don't know how its inhabitants acquired this invidious distinction.

to the rank of a noble. Harant had hitherto belonged to the "estate" of the knights. Somewhat later, Harant, who had been brought up as a Romanist, joined the Utraquist or Calixtine Church, probably mainly from political motives. Harant was a zealous partisan of the ancient Bohemian constitution and of the national language. The Jesuits, then the most prominent leaders of the Roman party in Bohemia, well knew that it would only be possible to destroy the old Church of Hus and to re-establish Romanism if the ancient constitution were suppressed, and the Bohemian language and literature also, as far as possible, destroyed.

In the stirring events of the last years of Bohemian independence (1618–1620) Harant played a very prominent part. He commanded the artillery of the Bohemian army which, under Count Thurn, invaded Austria and besieged Vienna in 1619; it is stated that he ordered his gunners to point their cannon against the windows of the palace (Burg) in Vienna in which the Emperor Ferdinand had taken refuge. This probably caused Harant to be singled out as one of those Bohemian nobles to whom the severest punishment was awarded, and in fact sealed his fate. During the short reign of King Frederick, Harant held high office, and when the battle of the White Mountain ended that prince's short reign, he sought refuge in his castle of Pecka. He was there taken prisoner by the Austrian troops in March 1621. It is characteristic of the man that on the day when the troops arrived he should, when, on his leaving his castle for an early walk, a gust of wind blew off his hat, have remarked: "If I were a Roman, I should immediately turn back and not stir a step from the house to-day." Harant was one of the Bohemian leaders who

SKÁLA ZE ZHOŘE

were decapitated on June 21, 1621. I have quoted[1] Skála ze Zhoře's account of his last moments.

Of the latest historians of this period, PAUL SKÁLA ZE ZHOŘE is certainly the most important. Palacký has called him "not only the most voluminous, but also the most valuable historian of Bohemia;" he might perhaps have been considered the foremost historian of his country before the present century, since which time that rank belongs uncontestedly to Palacký himself. I cannot formulate my opinion of Skála more accurately than I did some years ago, when I wrote: "Skála's description of the turbulent scenes on the Hradčin on the day of the defenestration, and the truly pathetic account of the last hours and execution of the Bohemian leaders in 1621, are masterpieces of historical writing. I may confidently say that they would do credit to the literature of a larger and better known country than Bohemia."

Paul Skála ze Zhoře, born in 1583, belonged, like Bartoš and Sixt, to the "estate" of the citizens or townsmen. He was educated at the then very celebrated Protestant university of Wittenberg, and his life and writings both prove that he was a staunch adherent of the Protestant faith. He was for some time employed in the municipal offices of the town of Saaz (or Žatec), and he held a Government appointment at Prague during the Provisional Government of 1618 and the short reign of Frederick of the Palatinate. He was an eye-witness of some of the events of that memorable period. He left Bohemia after the battle of the White Mountain and the flight of King Frederick, at whose court he remained during the first years of his exile. He afterwards settled

[1] See pp. 343 and 344.

at Freiberg in Saxony, not very far from the frontier of Bohemia, to which country many of the exiles still hoped once more to return.

It was here that Skála undertook his great historical works. He first wrote a *Chronology of the Church.* This book is a mere compilation of dates, including some that are of a very fantastic character. Skála counts 1656 years from the creation of the world to the deluge, and 1717 thence to the foundation of the first Chaldæan monarchy. This book seems only to have been intended to be a preparation for his great historical work, the *Historie Cirkevni* ("History of the Church"), a book which, in spite of its title, deals as much with political as with ecclesiastical matters. This colossal work is preserved in MS. in ten enormous volumes (the largest contains 1700 pages, the others but little fewer) in the library of Count Waldstein at Dux. The part of the book that refers to the Bohemian events of the years 1602 to 1623 has been edited and published by Dr. Tieftrunk in two large volumes. It is, of course, the most interesting part of the enormous work, as Skála here writes as a contemporary, and sometimes as an eye-witness.

Skála of course writes as a staunch Protestant and an enemy of the absolutist party. No Bohemian historian of this period, as I have already remarked, was without a strong political and theological bias; yet Skála tells us at the beginning of his account of the Bohemian movement of 1618: "I have not the intention, either here or in any part of my narrative, of writing anything whatever under the inspiration of partiality or of good-will or ill-will towards this party or that. Neither will I personally endorse the praise or blame which others have expressed. I only state those various facts which I have found in other authors' writings (printed or in manuscript) which are conform to truth. Judgment I leave to prudent, truth-loving men, who have a more profound knowledge of these events than I, in my exile, have been able to obtain." These statements, written to prove Skála's impartiality, are not entirely correct, or at least apply only to the years after 1620, when Skála, an exile from Bohemia, had to rely on the authority of others. Of previous events he frequently writes as an eye-witness. Thus, when referring to the removal of the altars and paintings from the cathedral-church of St. Vitus at Prague in 1619, Skála writes: "Though I and other officials were working in the neighbouring state offices between one and two o'clock, we heard nothing of what was happening in the royal church (St. Vitus); only next morning, when I entered the church, I saw that the pictures had been removed."

Skála gives a very able account of the ancient Bohemian constitution, of which he writes as a fervent admirer. He then states what in his opinion was the cause of the destruction of that constitution. "The Bohemian nation," he writes, "has indeed this peculiarity, that it can endure neither complete tyranny nor complete liberty unfettered by law. And as the Bohemians defended their ancient liberties with such true zeal, they might have been happier than other nations had they but at home maintained sincere concord among themselves. I doubt that any one would have been able to overcome them by force of arms if they had been bound together by the bond of patriotic mutual confidence; but in consequence of religious differences, great

Y

discord reigned among them, and therefore mutual distrust. One section, which conformed to the Church of Rome, assumed the name of Catholics or communicants in one kind. The other section, which loved to worship and serve God according to the definitions and rules of the Holy Scripture, and not according to the fancies of men, are called communicants under both kinds (Utraquists), or Evangelicals or Hussites, from the name of their teacher, that true martyr for Christ, John Hus, or 'of Husinec,' who in his time re-established pure doctrine in the Bohemian land, and from the darkness of Papacy raised it to light. . . . Many years ago regulations, which the Bohemians obtained by the bravery with which they defended God's truth, stipulated that nobody who did not receive the flesh and blood of our Lord Christ in both kinds should occupy the offices of the state and of the towns. . . . Thus almost all men acknowledged the salutary doctrine that man is redeemed by his faith in Christ and through His holy merit, and that he thus obtains eternal salvation."

But afterwards Skála says : "The Jesuits endeavoured, with all their might, to disseminate among imprudent young men, whose confidence they obtained by flattery, not only the teaching of the Roman school, but also hatred against the National Church and contempt for the glorious rights, regulations, and constitutions of the land ; and thus they strove to form them according to their own will; but yet more they approached with flattery the highest officials and judges of the land also, as well as some of the greatest lords ; and then, when they had inspired them with their own Jesuitical spirit, then, as if they had been soulless bodies, possessing neither reason nor common-sense, they ruled them according to their own will ... and they thus obtained that all real strength and ruling power was concentrated in them (*i.e.* the Jesuits), though the name and appearance of power and political importance was retained by the officials. Then only the Roman religion, which had almost died out in Bohemia, seemed suddenly to bloom again and to recover its power. On the other hand, the respect for the royal majesty constantly decreased; the kingdom, hitherto peaceful, became turbulent and seditious; the estates not only differed among themselves, but were also irritated against the king their lord, when under cover, and in the name of the royal majesty, evil and turbulent men artfully carried out their knavish plans and endeavours; in fact, every sort of licentiousness appeared openly and without restraint among the people."

But of greater interest than any other part of Skála's book are the pages that deal with the closing days of Bohemian independence. In writing of the tragedy that opened with the defenestration in 1618, and ended with the executions at Prague in June 1621, Skála is always graphic and often pathetic.

I shall quote a short portion of Skála's account of the events that mark the beginning and the close of the Bohemian movement.

In his account of the defenestration Skála writes: "... Then Joaquin, Count Schlick, ardently and with tears in his eyes, for he was a true and zealous follower of the religion, addressed the assembly and violently attacked Martinic and Slavata.[1] He reminded them of the wrongs which they had inflicted both on Utraquists individually and on the whole Evangelical Church, and

[1] See p. 345.

of how they had dealt with them according to the suggestions of those malicious teachers of theirs, the members of the sect of the Jesuits. He said that they had unlawfully attempted to deprive the Protestants of their offices, and that they had given proof of this when they deprived that noble Bohemian hero, Count Thurn, of his office as burgrave of the Karlstein, which office the Lord of Smečno (Martinic) had usurped; he had done this contrary to the constitution of the land. For who had ever heard that in Bohemia officials could be dismissed and offices redistributed without the consent of the Diet and a vote of the three Estates? 'But you,' he said, 'worthless disciples of the Jesuits, you with your followers and little secretaries,[1] you have dared to take it on yourselves to do this, not knowing how otherwise to harm us and to disparage our party. But you shall learn that we are not old women'—and here he snapped his fingers at them—'and that we shall not allow you to deceive us. For we consider you as of rank equal to our own, but we recognise his Majesty as our most gracious lord, and being now well satisfied with him, we shall undertake nothing against his Majesty. As long as old men, honest and wise, governed this kingdom, everything went well in it; but since you, disciples of the Jesuits, have pushed yourselves forward, the contrary has been the case. You will not be able to take from us the privileges which God has given us and our gracious sovereign has confirmed; we will not till we are conquered consent to this.'"

The indignation of Count Schlick and his intense excitement, which render his speech at times incoherent, appear very clearly from Skála's account. The various

[1] In Bohemian *sekretaričky*.

THE DEFENESTRATION

opinions of the nobles assembled in council are very clearly and minutely set forth.

I have only space for the final passage: "Then while he (Kinsky) still wished to continue his speech, Count Thurn quickly approached Slavata and seized him by the hand, while Ulrick Kinsky seized Martinic — but many nobles did not yet know what would be done with them, whether they would be thrown into a dungeon or merely put under arrest; then they (Thurn and Kinsky) led them right through the crowd of nobles; and only then did every one know that they would be thrown from the windows. They also now understood that the Estates were not jesting with them, though in consequence of their haughtiness and obstinacy they had as yet spoken to no one; they now began to entreat that their lives be spared; wringing their hands and invoking the name of God, they strove to keep their feet on the ground and begged for mercy.

"The Lord of Smečno mournfully entreated that he might be granted a confessor; he received the short answer that he should commend his soul to God. Slavata did not ask for a confessor, but prayed to the Lord to be with him.

"But no mercy was granted them, and first the Lord of Smečno was dragged to that window near which the secretaries generally worked, for Kinsky was quicker and had more aid than Count Thurn, who had first seized Slavata. Then they were both thrown, dressed in their cloaks and with their rapiers and decorations, just as they had been found in the Chancellor's office, one after the other head foremost out of the westward window into the moat beneath the palace, which by a wall is separated from the other deeper moat. They loudly screamed,

'Ach, ach, ouvé,' and attempted to hold on to the window-frame, but were at last obliged to let go, as they were struck on the hands. They were thus punished for having been unworthy of their offices and positions, which they had not sufficiently valued, and had indeed used to the detriment of His Imperial Majesty and to the ruin of their country; and this, said the Estates in their larger apology, was done according to ancient precedents in the Bohemian kingdom and in the city of Prague, and following the example of that which was done to Jezebel, the tormentor of the Israelite people, and also that of the Romans and other celebrated nations, who were in the habit of throwing from rocks and other elevated places those who disturbed the peace of the commonwealth."

As already stated, the part of Skála's enormous work which is of general interest ends with the execution of the Bohemian leaders, which took place at Prague on June 21, 1621. Skála had fled from his country immediately after the battle of the White Mountain, and thus undoubtedly escaped sharing the fate of those whose last moments he has so graphically described. He had therefore to rely on the information from Bohemia that reached him in his exile at Freiberg. He tells us, however, that he has "given word by word the narrative of three clergymen who were with the prisoners to the end and prepared them for the violent and, in the eyes of the world, dishonourable death that awaited them." Here also I can only give a short extract from Skála's very lengthy account. He writes: "Then the imperial executioners appeared before the lords, saying that the hour of death had come, that they should be ready, and that each one whose name was called should come out (of the prison). Immediately afterwards the judges entered the prison and called out the name of Count Schlick. With them arrived four German priests, and when they had descended the steps, two Jesuits stood there, one of whom was called Sudetius. He said to the Count, 'Domine Comes recordare adhuc.' But the Count answered sharply, 'Jam me facias missum.'

"After him they called out the name of Venceslas of Budova. He took no clergyman with him.

"Meanwhile Harant of Polžic sent for John the clergyman, asking him to come, as it would soon be his turn. . . . Then Lord Harant said, sighing, 'O my dear God, through how many lands have I travelled, how many dangers have I encountered, for how many days have I not seen bread; once I have been buried in the sands. From all these perils God has rescued me, and now I must die guiltless in my own dear land. Forgive my enemies, O my dear Lord.' Then they called out his name, and he started for that mournful stage and slaughterhouse of Antichrist.[1]

"But this is worthy of notice, that when one of these holy men and martyrs for God's cause was called forth, then to our great astonishment a leave-taking occurred in a pleasant manner, which rejoiced our hearts, just as if they were preparing to go to a banquet or some pastime. 'Now, my dear friends, may our Lord God bless you, may He grant you the consolations of the Holy Ghost, patience and courage, so that you may be able to prove, now also in the moment of your death, that you have heartily and bravely defended the honour of God. I go before you that I may first see the glory of God, the glory of our beloved Redeemer, but I await you directly after me; already in this hour earthly grief

[1] The Altstädter Ring, where the executions took place.

vanishes, and a new heart-felt and eternal gladness begins.' The other prisoners who remained behind answered, 'May our Lord God bless you on your way for the sake of the guiltless death of Christ; may He send His holy angels to meet your soul. You go before us to the glory of heaven. We also will follow you, and we are certain because of Him in whom we have believed, Jesus Christ, that we shall all meet again to-day and rejoice for ever with our beloved Redeemer, the angels, and the chosen of God.' . . . But let us return to the account of the last journey and the words of the dying. When leaving the prison-room Harant said, 'In thee, my God, I have believed since my youth; do not let me be disgraced for all ages.' Meanwhile, John the clergyman was saying prayers till they reached the place of execution, then Harant said, lifting his eyes heavenwards, 'Into your hands, Lord Jesus Christ, I commend my soul.' He then took off his cloak, and then again prayed, 'In you, O God, I have believed since my youth, and therefore I now and ever believe and feel certain that, in memory of the shameful death of your Son and my Redeemer, Jesus Christ, you will deign to recompense me for this temporary disgrace by perpetual glory; and therefore, O God, I commend my soul into Thy hands, for Thou hast redeemed it. True God! Lord Jesus Christ! Son of the living God! Receive my soul; I commend it to you, O Lord Jesus Christ.' And then he was beheaded, and exchanged this wretched earthly life for a glorious and heavenly one.

"And the executioner, who was himself a Utraquist, was careful not to interrupt their prayers; and he always waited till each of them had finished his devotions."

Of the last years of Skála we have little knowledge; the last documents referring to him mention him as still living at Freiburg, and date from the year 1640. It is probable that he died shortly after that time.

WILLIAM Count SLAVATA (born 1572, died 1652), a contemporary of Skála, was also a very voluminous writer. His life belongs to the political history of Bohemia, and I shall here only allude briefly to it, because of its close connection with the writings which Slavata has left.

Slavata's father belonged to the community of the Bohemian Brethren, and he was himself educated in the doctrines of that Church. He afterwards proceeded to Italy for the purpose of study. He there joined the Roman Church, which obtained in him a most able and enthusiastic adherent. With the proverbial zeal of a convert, he, almost alone among the Bohemian nobles, refused to affix his signature to the celebrated "letter of majesty," by which King Rudolph, in 1609, granted, in agreement with the Estates, considerable rights and privileges to the Protestants. When the weak and sickly King Matthew, during the last years of his life, fell more and more under the influence of his heir, Archduke Ferdinand of Styria, Slavata rapidly obtained high office. He held the office of Lord Chief-Justice at the beginning of the Bohemian troubles in 1618. On the memorable day of the defenestration, Slavata was thrown from the windows of the Hradčin together with his colleague, the burgrave of the Karlstein, Martinic, Lord of Smečno.

After the re-establishment of the Habsburg dynasty in Bohemia, Slavata was rewarded for his fidelity by the victors. He held various important offices of state under the Emperors Ferdinand II. and Ferdinand III., and was one of the most trusted councillors of both these sovereigns. His literary work is an incidental and accidental episode in his momentous career.

When accompanying the Emperor Ferdinand II. to Regensburg in 1636, a pamphlet written by his old antagonist, Count Thurn, came into Slavata's hands. It dealt with the recent assassination of Wallenstein,[1] but Thurn's pamphlet went far beyond the immediate subject, and, in fact, contained a defence of the author's political career. Slavata immediately resolved on refuting this work, written by the originator of the defenestration. Though sixteen years had passed since that event, and both Bohemian Protestantism and Bohemian independence had been totally suppressed, the memory of his ignominious exit from the windows of the Hradčin still rankled in Slavata's mind. It should also be mentioned that several of his friends, his old companion Martinic in particular, had previously urged him to write memoirs of his time; he had, however, always declined to do so because of the stress of public business.

Slavata's work, intended merely as a refutation of the statements of Thurn (whose pamphlet he has in its entirety incorporated into his book), became a historical work consisting of two volumes of considerable size.[2] The book, entitled *Paměty* or memoirs, deals only with the events of the years 1618 and 1619. Founded, as it undoubtedly is, on notes taken by Slavata at the time of the stirring events which he relates, it has the greatest historical value. Slavata was in correspondence

---

[1] It has often been asserted that Slavata, who was a personal enemy of Wallenstein, was the cause of the estrangement between him and the emperor, and indirectly of Wallenstein's murder.

[2] This portion of Slavata's works has been edited and published by the late Dr. Jirecek.

with most of the leaders of the "Catholic reformation," as the suppression of Protestantism in Bohemia was officially designated. He has also transcribed many of the state documents which in his official capacity were accessible to him. His book is therefore valuable as a "Quellenwerk," and the historians who have in the present century rewritten the history of Bohemia have availed themselves largely of these memoirs. The whole system of the "Catholic reformation" appears very clearly in Slavata's book. It should be stated—though I run the risk of transgressing on the domain of history —that in the question which immediately caused the Bohemian movement the Protestants had the law on their side. The defenestration, in fact, only precipitated a conflict that was in any case inevitable. The only alternative would have been peaceful submission to the Church of Rome, such as Ferdinand had obtained in his hereditary lands, Styria and Carinthia,

It was, of course, Slavata's task to prove that the Protestants had been the aggressors, and he devotes much ingenuity and more sophistry to that task. I have before stated that in my opinion extensive quotations are an absolute necessity when writing of a literature such as that of Bohemia, where it may be assumed as a certainty that almost all the works mentioned are entirely unknown to the reader. This is, however, particularly difficult in the case of Slavata, whose writings are distinctly and constantly controversial, and whose style is entirely devoid of grace. I shall, as characteristic of Slavata, translate a portion of his account of the banquet which the officials of King Frederick gave to the Turkish ambassador on his arival at Prague. Slavata is as long-winded as most of his contemporaries, and even a very condensed extract of his account may, I fear, appear lengthy.

Slavata writes: "Some of the officers of the so-called King Frederick, Bohemians of the Utraquist Church, gave in the evening a banquet to the Turkish ambassador, and among them was Henry Matthew, Count Thurn. The envoys of the Prince of Transylvania were also present, and of others Bohuchval of Berka, master of the ceremonies; Venceslas William of Ruppa, high chancellor; Venceslas of Budova, president of the court of appeal; Peter Miller, vice-chancellor of the Bohemian kingdom. At this banquet various speeches were made. There was one present who has reported that he heard with his own ears these words that were spoken there.

"The Turkish ambassador, holding a glass of wine in his hand, drank it off to the health of Berka, begging him to consider him as his son, for both alive and dead, he said, he would be an obedient son to him. Berka gave as answer that he did not consider himself as being worthy that the ambassador and envoy of the great and powerful Turkish emperor should accept him as his father, he would rather wish to be his (the ambassador's) willing servant and menial.[1] The Turkish ambassador accepted this, and answered further, saying that he was a Turk by birth and would die as such; he, however, firmly and certainly thought that those who believed in Christ will be redeemed, even though they differed in opinion among themselves. Of the Emperor Ferdinand, however, he did not believe that he would be redeemed, for he had been the cause that the blood of many innocent people had been shed

[1] Slavata uses the German word *Knecht*.

and of their destruction. He therefore thought that the devil would fry him on a spit in hell. Berka then said that he hoped the Lord God would bless his beloved lord for this pledge; no toast had ever yet pleased him so much as this one, and his only wish was that that should happen to the Emperor Ferdinand, the greatest enemy of the Bohemians, which the Turkish ambassador had said; and he added, 'Amen! Amen! Amen!'

"The same Turkish envoy then exhorted the Bohemian nobles that they should never submit to the Emperor Ferdinand; if they were not sufficiently strong, his emperor would send 60,000 men to their aid. . . . Berka further said that he knew for a certainty that the Emperor Ferdinand would willingly give 50,000 ducats so that he might obtain his head; but that his friends would give the troops 200,000 ducats that they might fight Ferdinand till he was totally defeated and driven to despair. To this the Turkish ambassador answered that he would act wisely and justly in doing so, for Ferdinand had not held his word and promise, just as his predecessors of the House of Austria, Rudolph and Matthew, had not kept their promises to his Majesty, the Ottoman emperor.

"Berka then declared that the House of Austria had always been the ruin of Bohemia, because by its false Spanish practices it had sold the kingdom, his beloved fatherland, into perpetual servitude and made slaves and serfs of the Bohemians. Therefore the kind Lord God would not allow this any longer, nor permit that such tyranny and cruelty should be practised against them; but He in His great mercy had opened their eyes, and they had therefore taken up arms against

Ferdinand and began war against the House of Austria. And rather than succumb to Spanish tyranny they would a thousand times rather submit to the rule and government of the Turkish emperor, their powerful lord. . . . Venceslas of Budova, then president of the court of appeal, who was attached to the Turkish ambassador as special commissioner, declared that the lords and other members of the Estates of Bohemia belonging to the Utraquist creed had arrived at this resolution and decision, that they would rather be cut to pieces together with their wives and children than submit to the rule and domination of Ferdinand, or of any other member of the House of Austria. . . . Peter Miller, then vice-chancellor of the Bohemian kingdom, said to Budova: 'My kind lord father, we Bohemians have resolved, rather than that the Emperor Ferdinand should be our king—and supposing that the Turkish emperor is not able to help us sufficiently—we will seek refuge with the devil in hell and supplicate him to help us.'

"At last Count Thurn spoke, saying that the Lord God was his witness how truly he regretted with his whole heart that the Emperor Ferdinand should have been spoken of in such a manner; but that Ferdinand had been misled by listening to the counsels of the Jesuits; neither he nor the other Bohemians were responsible for his fall; rather should he attribute it to himself. Then Thurn ordered three small glasses of wine and one larger glass that was empty, and said, addressing the Turkish ambassador: 'I drink these three glasses with you, one to the health of his Majesty the Emperor (of Turkey), one to the health of our own most gracious King, and one to that of the Prince of Transylvania.' And raising the three glasses he poured their contents into the large empty glass, and then continued: 'As with wine mixed out of three glasses it cannot be known what wine was in the first, what in the second, and what in the third glass, and only one sort of wine appears in this full glass, thus I begin to drink this glass full of wine in the name of the most Holy Trinity, consisting of three persons, but one Divinity, in the hope that these three potentates to whose health I am drinking will be of one accord, of one heart, and of one will; so that they may triumph over and defeat all their enemies.' Then he emptied the full glass of wine. The Turkish ambassador answered that he had great pleasure in emptying his glass to this toast.

"From this account and information we can understand to what evil, heresy especially that of Calvin, leads people; yet Count Thurn in his pamphlet attempts to prove that the Bohemians and he, their leader, were not rebels. I do not endeavour to exaggerate the shameless rebellion of the Bohemians of those days; for every one who has read these lines must shudder at the speeches that were made at Count Thurn's banquet. Nothing more shameless or wicked can be imagined; nor is it true that his Majesty Ferdinand II. had not kept his word and promises."

As Slavata and all his friends were then in exile, it is not very clear to whom this highly-coloured and obviously exaggerated account of Count Thurn's banquet should be attributed. It is possible that some traitor may have been present who was Slavata's authority. It is, however, far more probable that the account is founded on the report of some servant who waited at table. In consequence of the habit of drinking freely at banquets, which was then very prevalent in Bohemia, much political information could be obtained by listening to the conversation at the dinner-table. The Protestants frequently accused the Catholics of employing servants as spies on such occasions.[1] Whatever Slavata's authority may be, the passage describing the Bohemian leaders as cringing in a servile fashion before the representative of the enemy of Christianity, while displaying blind and brutal hatred of the House of Habsburg, is a masterpiece of skilful animosity.

The composition of these memoirs seems to have inspired Slavata with a taste for historical studies. In the last years of his life he wrote a vast history of all the lands ruled by the House of Habsburg, from the reign of Ferdinand I. to Slavata's own time. This book, entitled *Historické Spisování* ("Historical Works"), consists of fourteen volumes, and the earlier memoirs were incorporated with it, forming (of course not in chronological order) volumes i. and ii. The work includes a lengthy treatise on the long-disputed question whether the Bohemian kingdom was an elective or a hereditary one, a question which the battle of the White Mountain settled "by blood and iron." Slavata here displays a considerable amount of erudition, though the arguments founded on his accounts of the reigns of the almost entirely mythical early Přemyslide princes are, of course, valueless. Generally speaking, Slavata's record of earlier events, based principally on such doubtful authorities as Æneas Sylvius and Hajek, do not possess the historical value which undoubtedly belongs to his personal recollections.

---

[1] Readers of Schiller's *Wallenstein* will remember the scene at the banquet at Pilsen (*Die Piccolomini*, act iv. scene 5), when the servants are listening to the conversation of the generals.

HABERNFELD AND STRANSKÝ

Though written in Latin, Andreas ab Habernfeld's *Bellum Bohemicum* and Paulus Stransky's *Respublica Bojema* should at least be mentioned, as they belong to this period. Habernfeld, who himself took part in the last war waged by Bohemia as an independent country, and was present at the battle of the White Mountain, has left us a clear though prejudiced account of the events of the years 1618 to 1620. Paulus Stransky, one of the many Bohemian Protestants who ended their lives as exiles, has given a short but lucid account of the ancient Bohemian constitution, and in the same volume a short history of his country.

CHAPTER VII

THE REVIVAL OF BOHEMIAN LITERATURE

THE misery and degradation of Bohemia that were the result of the battle of the White Mountain are beyond all description. Perhaps no country has, in comparatively modern times, suffered as Bohemia did at that period. Gindely, than whom no historian is less given to exaggeration, has written: "The misery under which the land (Bohemia) groaned can, as regards its extent and its depth, be compared only to that which, at the time of the migration of nations (*Völkerwanderung*), was inflicted on the inhabitants of Gaul and Northern Italy by their Frank and Lombard conquerors." From the battle of the White Mountain, Bohemian literature becomes, and continues for many years, an almost complete blank.

It was at this time that the great destruction of Bohemian books, so frequently alluded to in these pages, began, though it continued far into the eighteenth century. Catholic priests, generally Jesuits, accompanied by soldiers, visited the houses of the Bohemians; even the cottages of the peasants were not exempt. As these priests were generally unacquainted with the Bohemian language, it was thought best to destroy all books written in that language. The famous, or rather infamous, destroyer of Bohemian books, the Jesuit Konias, continued his bonfires—he boasted of having burnt 60,000 Bohemian volumes—up to the year 1760. It is, of course, only possible to attempt conjectures as to the value of the lost works, but Bohemian writers agree in thinking that many had considerable historical merit. Second, of course, to non-Roman theological writings, the book-destroyers relentlessly pursued all works of a historical character which might suggest to the Bohemian people the contrast between their glorious past and their present servile and miserable condition. It may be mentioned as a proof of this, that even the historical work of Pope Pius II. (Æneas Sylvius) which deals with Bohemia was ordered to be destroyed.

The numerous emigrants from Bohemia continued indeed for some time, as already mentioned, to write in the national language, and only the death of Komenský marks the cessation of such writing. In Bohemia itself, from the fatal year 1620 to the end of the eighteenth century, no book appeared in the native language that is worthy of general notice. Jungmann,[1] in his patriotic endeavour to conceal the complete cessation of Bohemian literature, enumerates many writers of prayer-books, collections of sermons, and calendars published at this period. Whatever historical and philological value such writings may have, they do not belong to literature.

The nobles and the educated classes in Bohemia at this period wrote—as far as they wrote at all—in German or in Latin. It is curious to note that Bohemian continued to be spoken long after it had ceased to be written among all classes of the population. When, in 1697, Peter the Great visited Prague, he was able to converse with the nobles in his own language, so similar to that of Bohemia. This would have been impossible a

[1] See later.

century later, and even at the present day more German than Bohemian is spoken in the salons of the Bohemian nobility at Prague.

Of the scanty German and Latin works written in Bohemia during the seventeenth and eighteenth century, a few are noticeable as having, though indirectly, contributed to preserve the ancient national memories which are so inseparably connected with the national language. The earliest of these writers is the learned Jesuit BALBIN or Balbinus, who was born in 1621, a year after the catastrophe of the White Mountain, and died at Prague in 1688. His very numerous works, all written in Latin, deal principally with the history of his country. Balbin's writings are, of course, in absolute accordance with the doctrine of Rome, and, besides, teem with legends of saints, pedigrees of the newly-established nobility of Bohemia, and other matters that should have insured him the favour of the ruling powers. Still Balbin found many difficulties in his path when he attempted to publish his works. It is hardly doing injustice to the Government officials if we suppose that these difficulties were raised, firstly, because it was considered desirable that the history of Bohemia should be altogether buried in oblivion; secondly, because Balbin's writings give evidence of a degree of fairness which necessarily displeased them. Balbin's fairness has already been alluded to when referring to the biography of Milič, which is contained in his *Miscellanea*. Balbin's judgment of Komenský also shows a degree of tolerance very unusual at that time. He writes in his *Bohemia Docta*: "He (Komenský) published very many works, but nothing whatever that was directly aimed at the Catholic Church. Reading his works, it has always seemed to me that he wrote with so much reflection that he did not wish to award superiority to any one religion, nor to condemn any."

Of Balbin's many works we may mention the *Miscellanea*, a vast compilation into which he admitted writings of earlier authors; the *Epitome Rerum Bohemicarum*, his most valuable work; the *Bohemia Docta*; and a curious work in defence of the Bohemian language entitled *Disertatio Apologetica Linguæ Slovenicæ*. The difficulties which Balbin encountered when he attempted to publish his works have already been alluded to. Great objections were raised, in particular, against the *Epitome Rerum Bohemicarum*; but after long negotiations, influential friends of Balbin induced the Emperor Leopold I. in 1677 to give his consent to the publication of the book. The *Disertatio Apologetica*, on the other hand, was totally condemned by the Austrian authorities, and was, indeed, only published a century after the author's death.

Another Catholic priest whose historical labours were valuable for his country was Tomas Pešina, who was ennobled and granted the title of Cechorod (born 1629, died 1680). The Latin works of Pešina, who was a friend of Balbin, treat principally of Moravia, and are still of interest. To the eighteenth century belong the German works of Joseph Bienenberg, which deal with the archæology of Bohemia. In 1778 Bienenberg published his *Alterthümer in Königreiche Böhmen*, and two years later his *History of the Town of Königgrätz*. The latter work has a far wider interest than its name suggests. Bienenberg gives many interesting details concerning Zižka's wars, and he prints the celebrated "Articles of war" of the great Bohemian general.

The fact that these and other writers who sympathised

with the Bohemian people yet wrote in foreign languages, proves how deep the national language had sunk. Become little more than an idiom used by the peasantry in some parts of Bohemia, it was no longer available for literature of a more elevated character.

Within the second half of the eighteenth century a change took place. The Emperor Joseph II. was indeed a determined enemy of the Bohemian national aspirations, and his regulations, as well as those of the Empress Maria Teresa, excluded the Bohemian language from even the humblest schools to a greater extent than any of their predecessors had attempted to do. On the other hand, the enlightened mind of the Emperor Joseph disapproved of the exaggerated system of restriction and coercion which during the reigns of his predecessors had been enforced on all the lands of the Habsburg empire, though it weighed with exceptional heaviness on Bohemia. During his reign a newspaper written in the national language was allowed to appear at Prague, a permission that even since his reign has several times been refused by Austrian Governments. It was also a result of the comparative freedom granted by Joseph that there began to appear new editions of ancient Bohemian works, and translations of foreign works into Bohemian, which contributed greatly to regain for Bohemian the character of a written language. These workers live in the grateful memory of their countrymen, but it seems unnecessary to enumerate them in a book written for non-Bohemian readers. It will be seen, however, that in the nineteenth century also even the most prominent writers considered this editing and translating as an important duty towards their country. During the reign of Joseph II. the Bohemian Society of Sciences was established. The publications of the society at first appeared in German only—they are now printed both in German and in Bohemian—and German only was used in its deliberations. Still, the historical studies which the society published reminded the Bohemians of their glorious past, and revived the feeling of pride in their country, which had greatly decreased. It was at the end of the eighteenth century also that a professorship of the Bohemian language was established at the University of Vienna, and somewhat later at that of Prague.

Before referring to the group of men who in the early years of the present century successfully effected the revival of the Bohemian language and literature, we must notice a writer who, though an enthusiastic student of the Bohemian language, did not believe that that language would continue, or perhaps rather again become, one of the languages of Europe that possess an independent literature. I refer to Joseph Dobrovský. Born in 1753, his earliest years coincide with the time when the decadence of the Bohemian language was most marked. His books, mostly written in German or Latin, give evidence of a knowledge of the science of languages that was very unusual at that period. The early education of Dobrovský, "the patriarch of Slavic philology," as he was called in later years, was entirely German. It was only when studying at the "Gymnasium," first of Deutsch Brod, then of Klattau in Bohemia, that he acquired some knowledge of the Bohemian language. An indefatigable worker, he soon devoted his entire energies to the study of the historical development of the Bohemian language and of its connection with the languages of other Slav countries. When very young Dobrovský became a member of the Society of Jesus, and after the suppression of that order lived for a few years as a tutor in families of the Bohemian nobility. During the later years of his life he, though he had been ordained as a priest, led the life of an independent scholar, living either at Prague or in the country residences of the Bohemian nobles, where he was always a welcome guest. Palacký quotes his own remark as to the uniformity of his life : " What interest," he said, " can the rather monotonous life of a private person have ? One works, that is, one writes ; has one's writing printed ; then rests, and then begins another work of a similar character."

Dobrovský was entirely devoid of the enthusiasm for the national language that animated Jungmann, Kollar, Šafařik, Palacký, and the minor writers of the first half of the present century. He was, on the other hand, a philologist of the highest rank. Not only the Bohemians, but all Slav races, are indebted to him for his studies on Slav philology, a subject which at that period, when even in Russia the national language had to a great extent given way to Latin, French, and German, was absolutely uncultivated. Of his works we may mention the (German) " Detailed Grammar of the Bohemian Language " (*Ausführliches Lehrgebände der Bohemischen Sprache*). This work has become the model of all Bohemian grammars that were published subsequently, as well as of those of other Slav nationalities which have recently attained to the dignity of possessing written languages. The book was first published in 1809, and again in an enlarged form in 1818. Dobrovský's " History of the Bohemian Language and its Older Literature " (*Geschichte der Bohmischen Sprache und aeltern Literatur*) first appeared in 1792, but subsequently so completely rewritten, that when it was republished in 1818 it appeared almost a new work. The book has become somewhat antiquated and incomplete, as so many Bohemian books have been rediscovered since it appeared, but it still has considerable value. While these and other works of Dobrovský were written in German, he employed the Latin language for his *Institutiones Linguæ Slavicæ Veteris*. In this, his most important work, Dobrovský, as in his grammar, paved the way for later workers. The *Institutiones* have been the foundation of the work of the many important Slav philologists of the present century.

It has already been mentioned that Dobrovský had no enthusiasm for the Bohemian language, to the development of which he so largely contributed. His early recollections carried him back to the time when it was little more than an idiom used by the peasantry in the outlying country districts of Bohemia. When, in the present century, the movement in favour of the national language acquired greater strength, Dobrovský never sympathised with it. When the publication of the *Časopis Musea Královstvi Českého* ("Journal of the Museum of the Kingdom of Bohemia") in Bohemian, as well as in German, was first discussed, Dobrovský expressed the wish that the new journal should appear in German only. It must, in justice to Dobrovský, be added that in the last years of his life he wrote a few Bohemian essays for the journal. They are, indeed, with a collection of letters, the only writings in the national language which he has left. Dobrovský's critical nature and his thorough philological training induced him to deny from the time of its discovery the genuineness of the "MS. of Grüneberg,"[1] an opinion

[1] See Chapter I.

that is now shared by almost all Bohemian scholars. Dobrovský expressed himself strongly on the subject. He wrote: "It (*i.e.* the MS.) is a knavery which they (the "discoverers") committed from hatred of the Germans, and from exaggerated patriotism, for the purpose of deceiving themselves and others."

Dobrovský died in 1829, at a time when the question whether the Bohemian language should live or not was already decided in the affirmative sense. He had during the last years of his life become very unpopular among the Bohemian patriots, but events have proved that his critical faculties sometimes guided him better than enthusiasm did others. As a philologist of the Slav languages Dobrovský was in advance of his time. Etymological monstrosities, such as Kollar sometimes committed in his *Staroitalia Slavjanska*, would have been impossible to Dobrovský.

Very different from the calm scholarly nature of Dobrovský was the temperament of the four enthusiastic patriots to whom, with, of course, the co-operation of minor writers, the revival of Bohemian literature is due. I refer to Jungmann, Kollar, Safařik, and Palacký.

JOSEPH JUNGMANN was born in 1773 at Hudlice, a small village near Beroun in Bohemia. As Hudlice was even then a thoroughly Bohemian village, Jungmann first acquired his native language; but when sent to school at Beroun—where, as indeed everywhere in Bohemia at that time, the teaching was entirely German—he almost forgot Bohemian, and soon found it far easier to express himself in German. When on a visit to his native village an old relation playfully accused him of "stammering" whenever he spoke Bohemian. This remark, as Jungmann has himself told us, made a great impression on the mind of the young student. "From that moment," he afterwards wrote, "I became a true Bohemian, at least to my best knowledge and will." Jungmann's life was by no means eventful, and requires little notice. He, soon after finishing his studies, became professor at the gymnasium of Leitmeritz, from which he was afterwards transferred to Prague. Here he spent the greatest part of his life, and died in 1847, a year before revolutionary events obliged so many Bohemian patriots to emerge from their seclusion and become popular leaders.

I have already alluded to the great activity the Bohemian writers of this period displayed as editors of the works of their ancient literature, as well as translators from the works of more advanced foreign literatures. The two tasks were closely connected, as the writers could only render in Bohemian the classical works of other countries by availing themselves of the rich verbal treasury which is contained in the works of their own ancient authors. Jungmann himself at the beginning of his life became known as a translator, and, in contradiction with his later vocation, oftenest attempted translations of poetical works. It may interest English readers to know that many of Jungmann's translations are from the English. Of all his translations, that of Milton's *Paradise Lost*, written in five-footed trochees, obtained greatest celebrity. It is really a wonderful achievement, if we consider that it was written in 1811, when the Bohemian language was only just awakening from its winter-sleep of nearly two hundred years. Jungmann also translated Gray's *Elegy in a Churchyard*, Goethe's *Herman und Dorothea*, and poems by Schiller and Bürger. From the French Jungmann translated Chateaubriand's *Atala*. It is stated that Jungmann planned a great original poem in the national language, but if this is true the plan was never carried out. In later years Jungmann devoted whatever leisure his official duties left him to studies of a scientific, and particularly of a philological character.

Great as were his merits as a translator, the last-named works constitute his principal claim to the gratitude of his countrymen. The earlier of the great works of Jungmann is his *History of Bohemian Literature.* Jungmann did not follow Dobrovský's example, but wrote in Bohemian. The book was first published in 1825, and a second enlarged edition appeared in 1849, after the author's death. The book is scarcely what in the present day would be called the history of a literature; perhaps such a task was impossible at the time Jungmann wrote. Jungmann's history contains an enumeration of all writers, great or small, of whom writings in the Bohemian language have been preserved. Jungmann's intense patriotism induced him to attempt to prove that at almost all periods works on almost all subjects written in Bohemian had existed. Every translator of even the most valueless work, every preacher who had caused even the most worthless Bohemian sermon to be printed, therefore finds a place in this book. Yet this very minuteness and absence of criticism which we find in the book render it very valuable as a collection of materials; and even now, seventy years after its first appearance, it is indispensable to all students of Bohemian literature. The introductions to each of the "odděleni" (divisions) contain a valuable historical and etymological account of the development of the Bohemian language and literature in each of the periods into which Jungmann has divided his history.

Jungmann also wrote numerous literary articles for

the Bohemian newspapers and reviews, which gradually sprung up in spite of the constant opposition of the Austrian Government. These articles contributed greatly to the success of the Bohemian movement. As I have noted elsewhere, that movement was, at its beginning, necessarily a purely literary one. No political paper that was not directly or indirectly under the control of the Government, then entirely German in its views, was allowed to exist.

The second great work of Jungmann that ranks with his history of Bohemiam literature is his vast dictionary of the Bohemian and German languages, published in five large volumes between 1835 and 1839. Jungmann's preparatory studies, both for this work and for the History, however, began as early as the year 1800. The work is a monument of indomitable energy and application. A work such as that of Jungmann would, if undertaken by a whole academy, have been most meritorious; but Jungmann worked almost alone, aided only in the merely mechanical part of his task by a few students of the University of Prague. His difficulties cannot be compared with those which the compiler of a dictionary of a more developed language encounters. A large part of ancient Bohemian literature, that within the last fifty years has been carefully edited and published, could then only be found in MSS. that were often difficult of access. Jungmann's work contains words that he only found once or twice in his sources; it was his desire to include all, for he laboured not only for the then scanty readers who wished to study the works of ancient Bohemian literature, but also for the modern Bohemian writers, whose vocabulary he endeavoured to enlarge.

Even now, when Bohemian literature has obtained an almost miraculous development, Jungmann's dictionary has not been superseded; and the same, as regards completeness at least, can be said of his *History of Bohemian Literature*.

The originators of the Bohemian revival, drawn together by a common passionate love for the national language, were mostly on terms of intimacy, and their correspondence, very voluminous, as was formerly the custom, gives a very clear insight into the views of the writers, and the disheartening circumstances under which they pursued their work. Of Jungmann's letters, the most interesting are those addressed to Kollar, who will be mentioned presently, and to Anthony Marek, an intimate friend of Jungmann, who was one of the minor Bohemian writers of this period. The degree of intimacy which existed among the small band of patriots is well described in one of Jungmann's letters to Kollar, written in February 1821: "I am writing to-day," he says, "to our dear Šafařik also, and to Palacký. You three form indeed my most beloved Trinity." The general impression of Jungmann's letters is distinctly a depressing one. The writer refers constantly to the incessant, often very puerile, vexations which he encountered from the Austrian authorities. Jungmann complains incessantly of the "censors," and we shall find the same complaints later when dealing with Palacký. Every book published in Austria had at that period to be previously submitted to the "censure-office" for inspection. There were two "censors" to each book, one of whom had to guard against anything contrary to the views of the Austrian Government being printed, while the other suppressed everything contrary to the teaching of the Church of Rome. Kollar had sent some sonnets, that were afterwards printed in his *Daughter of Slava*, to Jungmann for the purpose of submitting them to the censors. Jungmann writes in answer: "The poems confided to me I should be glad to get published, but the censure suppresses everything.... Those beautiful (O most beautiful) parts of your poem which refer to Sláva I cannot even present to the censors without much danger to the good cause" (*i.e.* the revival of the Bohemian language). "The other part also it will hardly be possible to publish. The other day Ziegler[1] complained that the censor had struck out thirty sheets from his writings, even love-songs set to music. We must touch neither Eros nor politics; such are the orders and commands of the censure."

Jungmann's letters to Marek, written in a very familiar manner, also give an interesting insight into the lives and thoughts of the little group of Bohemian literary men; they show their intense devotion to the national language, their firm belief in the solidarity of the Slavic races, which was intensified by the Russian victories over Napoleon, their heartfelt delight when one of the then almost Germanised Bohemian nobles appeared to be favourable to the national cause, their dissatisfaction with the Government of Vienna, which always regarded them with suspicion. To the last-named subject Jungmann refers in some of his earliest letters to Marek. Writing on May 29, 1809, he says: "On me truly falls every burden of human life. On one hand the malice of neighbours, magistrates, school directors, vintagers

---

[1] A minor Bohemian writer of the period. Though Ziegler was a professor of theology, love is the subject of some of his songs.

and ploughers,[1] soldiers (who give it me well[2]), and other ruffians oppress me; on the other hand, I have little hope of obtaining my object (which, between us, is to obtain the professorship of physics at the University of Prague), because of the fearful number of competitors, and also because of the injustice of the Austrian Government, which recently transferred to Prague three professors from Vienna, as if we Bohemians were all donkeys." ... The passage of the Russian army through Bohemia naturally greatly interested the Slavic enthusiasts. On September 24, 1813, Jungmann writes to Marek: "The Russian troops march through here (Leitmeritz) constantly. To-day 120,000 (?) are expected, whose passage will cost the town 9000 florins. I diligently *govorju* [Russian for talking] with them, and find that there are among them very good-natured men, and that that which is—principally by Germans—said of their stealing and robbing is not their fault, but that of the badly organised commissariat. ... On the whole, they are not worse than our own soldiers. It will not be to the disadvantage of the Bohemians that they should become better acquainted with the Russians. They will at least know that there are more Slavs in the world than they fancied." On May 4, 1814, Jungmann writes to Marek: "The Germans and half-Germans here" (at Leitmeritz) "are very angry with the newspapers, because they always—so they say—mention the Russians as if they were everything. This war has been advantageous to the Slav world, and has contributed in no slight degree to its advancement. Not in

---

[1] A proverbial Bohemian expression signifying "one and all."
[2] In Bohemian, "Mi hodně mnoho dávaji." The Bohemian colloquialism can here be literally translated by an English colloquial expression.

vain has Europe learned to know the Slavs and they Europe. I think the Slav languages will become better known than they are now. It is already certain, now that the Muses are establishing their realm in the North. I must endeavour to obtain a few Russian books. . . . Perhaps Count Waldstein [1] will be favourable to the Bohemians, as he knows Slavic languages. God be praised there is another nobleman who is not a German!"

When more peaceful times began, Jungmann's correspondence deals mainly with literary matters, but he continues to uphold the principle of solidarity or mutual intercourse (*vzdjemnost Slovanská*) between the Slavs. On January 3, 1827, Jungmann writes to Marek: "Of what else should I write but of the subject which we both carry in our hearts—Slavic literature. Yes, Slavic literature, I say, for I may at least name in writing to my friend what in print we can scarcely mention. So low have we fallen through the misdeeds of our countrymen,[2] that we scarcely dare openly to profess that we are Slavs. . . . They treat even the word 'Slav' with great suspicion at the censure-office, and Palacký has made it a rule to mention the Slavs as little as possible in the journal of the Museum. . . . How little they love us can be seen by the fact that the censors at Vienna only gave permission to print an ancient Bohemian chronicle on condition that it should be printed in Latin characters and published at a high price, that it may

---

[1] A Bohemian nobleman who owned estates near Leitmeritz.

[2] This alludes to the now uncontested fact that countrymen and literary rivals of Jungmann had denounced Jungmann's writings to the Austrian Government, attributing to them a political tendency, from which in reality they were absolutely free.

come into the hands of but few, and of none that are 'unholy' (*i.e.* whom the Government distrusts).[1] ... We have pleasanter news from the East. According to a letter of Šafařik, the treaty of Akjerman between Russia and Turkey guarantees freedom to the Servian nationality; so a new epoch for that nation and its literature may begin. At four Russian universities—Petersburg, Moscow, Kazan, and Charkov—professorships of general Slavic literature will be founded, and one at Warsaw is also in contemplation. There, then, the Bohemian language will be heard and its best works published. The Englishman Povring,[2] is translating Servian songs into English, and, stimulated by Šafařik, he will also translate the MS. of Königinhof. In England very many are learning Slavic languages, particularly Russian. Whenever a learned Englishman acquires a taste for one Slavic dialect, he wishes to learn a second," &c.[3] As a last quotation from Jungmann's letters, I shall give a short extract from one written in 1837, which is curious as referring to Count Kolovrat, one of the founders of the Bohemian Museum, who was then one of the principal members of the Austrian cabinet. It proves that Jungmann was by no means hostile to the Austrian Government, except when that Government treated its

[1] The few Bohemian books that appeared in the eighteenth, and even at he beginning of the nineteenth century, were printed in German (Gothic) characters, and it was hoped that the Latin characters would be unintelligible to many people of the lower classes, from whom the censors wished to withhold the chronicle.

[2] Thus written by Jungmann. The person referred to is Sir John Bowring.

[3] Writing for English readers, it is scarcely necessary to mention that there was not in the year 1827 a wide-spread enthusiasm in England for learning Slavic languages. Jungmann, sanguine, like all the Bohemian patriots of his time, generalised on the strength of some statements of English philologists whom he may have met at Prague.

Slav subjects unjustly. Jungmann writes: "Gay,[1] the Croatian, is at Karlsbad. The Hungarians wished to imprison him because he published some national songs; now to their great grief he has received permission from Vienna to establish a printing-press. Our Kolovrat obtained this favour for him, though the Hungarian Chancellor opposed it. This minister (Kolovrat) has acted like a true Slav. Thanks and glory to him!"

Closely connected with Jungmann is his friend Kollar, whose name has already been mentioned frequently in this chapter. He was the greatest poet of the early Bohemian revival, though living Bohemian poets have undoubtedly surpassed him. JOHN KOLLAR (1793-1852) was born at Mošovec, in the Slav district of Northern Hungary. His parents were Protestants, and it was decided that he should become a minister of that Church. In 1815 he proceeded to the then famous University of Jena in Germany, for the purpose of finishing his theological studies. The University of Jena was then one of the centres of the movement in favour of the unity of the German race, which has since been effected by "blood and iron." It does not seem improbable that the contact with the German patriots laid the germ of Kollar's passionate devotion to the idea of the unity of the Slav nations; though of course it was of a literary, not a political union of these nations—that are separated from each other by millions of aliens—that Kollar dreamt. It is, however, anticipating the future if we assume that these ideas ex-

---

[1] In Croatia, early in the present century, a national movement sprung up similar to that of Bohemia, but its results were smaller and less enduring. Gay, the leader of this movement, was persecuted by the Hungarians, just as the Bohemians were by the German officials.

clusively, or even principally, occupied young Kollar while at Jena. An event during his stay at Jena influenced his whole life, and became the origin of the only one of his works that will live. He became passionately attached to Mina (or Wilhelmina) Schmidt, the daughter of a Protestant clergyman who lived in a village near Jena. How the German country girl was by Kollar transformed into the *Daughter of Sláva* is one of the curiosities of literature. Kollar's suit for Mina Schmidt was for the present unsuccessful. Frau Schmidt declared that she would never allow her daughter to live in a "savage country," as she termed Hungary; and it was to that country that Kollar's ecclesiastical career obliged him to return. Kollar afterwards became minister to the Protestant Church at Pest, and continued there up to the year 1849. He corresponded with Mina for some time after his departure from Jena, but news—incorrect, as it afterwards turned out—was brought from Germany announcing Mina's death. The news proved untrue, and fifteen years after Kollar's departure from Jena, and some years after he had raised Mina to the Slav heaven, she became his wife. Kollar's life, like that of all the Bohemian patriots, was a very laborious and painful one. His letters contain constant complaints of the incessant persecutions on the part of the Hungarian Government which his Slav sympathies brought on him. A plot on the part of Hungarians to murder Kollar was even discovered. Kollar several times appealed, and appealed successfully, to the Emperor Francis I. for protection. Kollar's ideas of Slavic solidarity also resulted mainly in disappointment. The separation of the Slavs on the whole continued as before, and even Kollar's own language, the Bohemian, was abandoned by Kollar's own countrymen. The Slavs of Northern Hungary, identical in race with the Bohemians and Moravians, had always used the Bohemian language. Šafařik, as well as Kollar himself, both born in the Slavic districts of Hungary, wrote in Bohemian. In the present century only the Slavs of Northern Hungary adopted as a written language a dialect that slightly differs from Bohemian. The result of this injudicious step, which Kollar from the first strongly blamed, has been the almost complete absorption by the Magyars of the isolated Slavs of Northern Hungary.

During the Hungarian revolution Kollar left Pest. Like most Slavs, his sympathies were rather with the Austrians than with the Hungarians, who had, indeed, constantly persecuted him. He spent some time travelling in Germany and Italy. One of the results of his visit to the last-named country was that deplorable work, *Staroitalia Slavjanská* ("Slavic Ancient Italy"). In recognition of his faithfulness to the Austrian Government, Kollar, immediately after the suppression of the Hungarian revolution in 1849, was awarded the professorship of Slavic archæology at the University of Vienna. He did not live long to enjoy the comparative prosperity of which he was now assured. He died at Vienna on January 24, 1852, leaving his wife and children in a state of great destitution.

Kollar's *Slávy Deera* ("Daughter of Sláva") perhaps contributed more than any other work to the revival of Bohemian literature. Its first appearance was received with great enthusiasm, which continued for many years. Some of the Bohemian patriots boasted that they knew the whole enormous collection of sonnets by heart. The book, at first a small collection of sonnets, gradually grew to one of the largest books consisting entirely of sonnets which exists. The first collection was published in 1821, and consisted principally of reminiscences of Mina and of Jena, though Kollar's enthusiasm for the Slav race also already finds expression here. It was impossible that so fervent a Slav should love a German girl, but Kollar discovered that the family of Schmidt had come to Thuringia from Lusatia, which was formerly a Slav country, and where, indeed, a Slav dialect lingers to the present day. Mina thus being a Slav, it was possible to celebrate her as the "Daughter of Sláva," a goddess who personifies the Slavic race. Kollar firmly maintained that such a goddess had existed in the heathen mythology of the Slavs, but recent and more critical writers have expressed doubts on the subject. At any rate, Kollar gave the name of the *Daughter of Sláva* to the second and enlarged edition of his sonnets, which appeared in 1824. While the first collection had consisted mainly of love songs, the national Slav motive now becomes equally prominent. Kollar was greatly struck by the fact that large parts of Northern Germany, including the country near Jena, where Kollar had first loved and written, were formerly inhabited by Slavs. Constant warfare with the Germans, which began at the time of Charles the Great, has indeed long since destroyed all trace of these Slavs, but Kollar's imagination recalled them to life. Though very little is known of the Slav inhabitants of Northern Germany, there is no doubt that Kollar has greatly idealised them. The edition of the *Daughter of Sláva* published in 1824 consisted of three cantos. The poet, accompanied by Milek (the Slavic god of love), who has descended from heaven to bring him news of Mina, visits the countries that are

THE "DAUGHTER OF SLÁVA"

watered by the Saale, the Elbe, and the Danube, and the three rivers give their names to the three cantos. Kollar and his companion everywhere search and find traces of the former Slav inhabitants of the countries which they visit. The edition of 1824 first contained the "foresong" (*předzpěv*), or introduction, written in distichs, in which Kollar bewails the fate of the early inhabitants of Northern Germany. These verses rank among the finest in the whole range of modern Slav poetry. In 1832 Kollar published a third, again enlarged, collection of his sonnets. The second canto was considerably added to, and now entitled *The Elbe, the Rhine, and the Vltava*.[1] Two new cantos were added under the names of *Lethe* and *Acheron*. Kollar chose those names to give unity to his poem, as the former cantos had also been named after rivers. But the two new cantos are really a Slavic *Paradiso* and *Inferno* modelled on Dante. Kollar has here glorified and stigmatised those whom he considered prominent friends or enemies of the Slav race. It must be confessed that large portions of these cantos consist in a mere enumeration of names, often of persons who have long sunk into oblivion. Thus we find in hell a Miss Pardoe, who wrote a long-forgotten book of travels in Hungary, in which she, it appears, adopted the Hungarian standpoint, always hostile to the Slavs. Kollar, in his new peregrinations, is no longer accompanied by Milek, but by the "Daughter of Sláva," the glorified Mina Schmidt. The last sonnet of the poem, which I shall translate, contains an appeal of the "Daughter of Sláva" to all her countrymen, exhorting them to concord.

Though no subject could then be more original than the glorification of the then little-known Slav races,

[1] In German "Moldau."

Kollar's poem yet contains many reminiscences of other writings. It has already been stated that the leading idea of the two last cantos is borrowed from Dante. The pilgrim in the earlier cantos sometimes recalls *Childe Harold.* Mina, or the "Daughter of Sláva," is sometimes modelled on Beatrice, sometimes on Laura. Kollar indeed never made a secret of the fact that he had studied the poetry of Western Europe. Such study was indeed a necessity at a time when, with the exception of the songs of the people, the Slavs possessed no poetry. Bohemian critics agree in asserting that the first canto of the *Slávy Deera*, written under the influence of a passionate love for Mina, is infinitely the best. The introduction to the poem has also been justly admired. It is interesting also as containing a general exposition of the author's views and dreams concerning the past and future of the Slavic race. Want of space will oblige me to quote only a portion of the "fore-song." Kollar, viewing the former homes of his race, exclaims: "Here before my tearful eyes lies the land, Once the cradle, now the tomb, of my nation. Stop! it is holy ground on which you tread. Son of the Tatra (Carpathian mountains), raise your head towards heaven, Or rather guide your steps towards that oak-tree Which yet defies destructive Time. But worse than Time is man, who has placed his iron sceptre on thy neck, O Sláva; Worse than wild war, more fearful than thunder, than fire, Is the man who, blinded by hate, rages against his own race.[1] O ancient times that surround me as with night! O land that art a record of all glory and all shame! From the

---

[1] Kollar refers to those who, though of Slav origin, identified themselves with the Germans.

treacherous Elbe to the perfidious plains near the Vistula, From the Danube to the devouring waves of the Baltic, In all these lands the harmonious language of the brave Slavs once resounded. Succumbing to hatred, it now has perished. And who has committed this offence that cries to heaven for vengeance? Who has in one nation dishonoured humanity in its entirety? Blush, envious Germany, the neighbour of Sláva! It is thy hands that once committed this guilty deed. No enemy has spilt so much blood—and ink, As did the German to destroy the Slavs. He who is worthy of liberty respects the liberty of all. He who forges irons to enslave others is himself a slave. Be it that he fetters the language or the hands of others, It is the same; he proves himself unable to respect the rights of others. . . ." Kollar then proceeds to give the idealised account of the ancient Slav inhabitants of Germany, to which I have already referred. He attributes to them a very advanced degree of culture, and describes them as instructing Europe in seamanship, agriculture, and mining. Enumerating the Slav tribes, he writes: " Whither have you vanished, dear Slav nations, Nations that once drank the waters of Pomerania and the Saale, Peaceful tribes of the Sorbs, descendants of the Obotrites? And you tribes of the Ukres and Wiltes, whither have you gone? I look far to the right, I glance to the left, But in vain does my eyes seek Sláva in Slavic land. Tell us, O tree, growing as a temple, under which sacrifices were once offered to the ancient gods, Where are the nations, the princes, the towns, Who first spread civilisation in these northern lands?"

Writing as a poet, not as a politician, Kollar believed the Germanisation of these ancient Slav lands to be far less complete than it actually is. He writes: "As two rivers, though their waters have joined in one channel, yet differ in colour during a long part of their course, thus these two nations (the Germans and Slavs), though intermingled by the force of fierce war, yet still differ visibly in their manner of life. But the degenerate sons of Sláva often insult their mother, while they kiss the rod of their hateful stepmother (Germany). They are neither Slavs nor Germans in their ways. Hybrids, they belong half to one race, half to the other. Thus has the race of Osman settled down in the Hellenic lands. Its horse-tails are prominent on the summit of Olympus. Thus, too, did the avaricious Europeans ruin the two Indian worlds, giving the people indeed education, but robbing them of their virtue, their land, their colour, and their language. Nationality and honour with us, too, have disappeared; Nature alone has remained unchanged. Woods, rivers, towns, and villages would not abandon their Slav names.[1] The sound still remains, but the Slavic spirit has fled. . . ." The introduction ends thus: " It is shameful when in misery to moan over our fate; he who by his deeds appeases the wrath of Heaven acts better. Not from a tearful eye, but from a diligent hand fresh hope will blossom. Thus even evil may yet be changed to good. A crooked path may indeed lead men astray, but not humanity at large. The confusion of individuals may yet serve to the advantage of the community. Time changes everything, even past times. The errors of centuries may yet be repaired by time."

The fame of Kollar's introduction is so great that I

---

[1] This is still perfectly true. In Mecklenburg and some parts of Prussia the names of many towns and villages are obviously of Slav origin, as are the family names of some of the oldest families which are derived from localities.

THE "DAUGHTER OF SLÁVA"

have translated a considerable part of it, and I am therefore yet more limited in my quotations from the sonnets themselves. Those of the first canto, where the love-motive is still strong and enters into a quaint rivalry with the author's Slav enthusiasm, are the earliest and most valuable fruits of Kollar's muse. Čelakovský [1] was undoubtedly right in stating that the poetic genius of Kollar left him with his younger years. In the twelfth sonnet of the first book Kollar describes his hesitation between the two subjects that inspired him. There is an easily noticeable echo of Anacreon in the song. The poet writes:—

"*I wished to sing of the thrones of the Bohemian kings, of the arrival of the brothers, of Vlasta and Libussa,[2] of Attila, the scourge of God, and how he taught his Huns to use the crossbow.*

"*I wished to sing of the golden Carpathians, the wines of Tokay, the splendour of the moon; but when I touched the strings of my lyre, 'Mina,' and again 'Mina,' alone resounded in my ears.*

"*In simple style I wished to write of fables, flowers, kingdoms, but my pen, self-willed, traces other characters than those that I intended.*

"*My speech also does not obey my will, and what when in company my heart carefully conceals my rash tongue reveals.*"

The singular mixture of love and national enthusiasm already noted appears quaintly—it would be severe to say grotesquely—in another sonnet of the first book. Kollar writes:—

"*Once when a heavy sleep closed her weary little eyelids, I for half an hour practised kissing her as a true Slav should.*

"*My kisses were not such as Roman, Greek, or German describes—sensual buffooneries. They were pure, proper kisses, such as the customs of our Russian brothers allow.*

[1] See later.   [2] References to ancient Bohemian legends.

"*Thus then did I kiss my love: from the forehead downward to the chin, then in the shape of a cross from one little ear to the other.*

"*On this voyage twice I reached the little rose-garden of her lips, through which my soul enters into hers.*"

Of the sonnets of the second canto I shall quote one in which Kollar's enthusiasm for "Slavia," the Slav world, which he distinguishes from the goddess "Sláva," appears most clearly. He writes:—

"*Slavia, Slavia! Thou name of sweet sound but of bitter memory; hundred times divided and destroyed, but yet more honoured than ever.*

"*From the Ural Mountains to the summit of the Carpathians, from the deserts near the equator to the lands of the setting sun, thy kingdom extends.*

"*Much hast thou suffered, but ever hast thou survived the evil deeds of thy enemies, the evil ingratitude also of thy sons.*

"*While others have built on soft ground, thou hast established thy throne on the ruins of many centuries.*"

One of the sonnets of the third book contains a curious prophecy of the future greatness of the Slav race. Kollar writes:—

"*What will become of us Slavs a century hence? what of all Europe? Slavic manners, as the floods of a deluge, will extend their strength in every direction.*

"*That language, which the Germans falsely believed to be but a dialect fit for slaves, will be heard even under the ceilings of palaces and in the mouths of our very enemies.*

"*By means of the Slav language science will be developed. Our dress, the customs, the songs of our people will be the fashion on the Seine and on the Elbe.*

"*Oh! had it but been granted to me to be born at that time when the Slavs will rule, or might I at least then rise again from my tomb!*"

THE "DAUGHTER OF SLÁVA"

The recent development of the Slav races is so little known in England, that these lines will probably appear to many readers far more absurd than they really are. Professor Léger, who has devoted his life to the study of Slavic history and literature, and is wondrously in touch with the national feeling, writes of the sonnet which I have just quoted: "These lines were written about the year 1830. Is it necessary to state to how great an extent the predictions have been fulfilled? The Slav language, then considered a jargon of peasants, is now the recognised language of the courts of St. Petersburg, Belgrade, Sophia, and Cettigne, of the parliaments and representative bodies of Prague, Brünn, and Agram, of the universities of Russia, Bohemia, Poland, and Illyria. . . . Russian is ardently studied at Berlin, Paris, Vienna, and Budapest. Muscovite novels invade the libraries of Paris."[1]

The two last cantos of Kollar's great poem have little literary merit, and their always rather local interest has, as I have already mentioned, decreased with the lapse of time. I shall, however, translate the last sonnet of the fifth canto, which forms the conclusion of the whole work. Mina, in heaven, addresses thus the Slavs who are still on earth:—

"Oh you, brothers and sweet sisters who yet live iu the world, grant me willingly your ear that I may briefly instruct you.

"Beware of that smooth path which the devil has interwoven with nets that he may entangle the souls of traitors in his deceitful snares.

---

[1] This was written some years ago, when the enthusiasm for the works of Tolstoy, Dostoievsky, Tourguenev, Goncharov, and others was at its height in Paris.

"*Come here and find* (*in heaven and hell*) *an example in the good and a warning in the evil. Learn above all to love your country.*

"*May these words resound from your summits, O Carpathians, to the Černa Hora* (*Montenegro*), *from the Giant Mountains to the Ural:* '*Hell for traitors, heaven for faithful Slavs!*'"

Kollar's merit as a writer depends mainly on the "Daughter of Sláva," though he was a copious writer of prose as well as poetry. A small German pamphlet by Kollar entitled, *Ueber die literarische Wechselseitigkeit zwischen den verschiedenen Stämmen und Mundarten der Slavischen Nation* ("On the Literary Solidarity of the various Branches of the Slav Nation"), which appeared in 1837, caused great sensation, and for a time acquired even political importance. In Bohemian Kollar wrote, besides his *Slávy Deera*, an account of his travels in Germany and Italy and several archæological works. Of these, the *Staroitalia Slavjanská* ("Slavic Ancient Italy"), written in the last year of Kollar's life, and dedicated to the Emperor Francis Joseph, is the largest. The author endeavoured, on the slightest evidence and by means of the most fantastical suppositions, to prove that a large part of the population of Italy—particularly in the north—is of Slav origin. Kollar is here constantly carried away by his exuberant imagination, and the book has no scientific value. It is, indeed, scarcely an exaggeration to call it a tissue of absurdities. Kollar's recently published correspondence with Jungmann, Šafařik, Palacký, and others has great interest.

While Kollar devoted to the revival of the Bohemian language and literature his enthusiastic eloquence and poetic talents, Šafařik employed for the same purpose his vast erudition and unusual ability as a philologist. His works deal principally with the early origins of the Slav language and race, and of the early literature of Bohemia. The latter works were very valuable at a time when the Bohemian language was again acquiring the dignity of a written language. Like Jungmann, Šafařik also endeavoured to forward the advancement of his language by means of translations from more cultivated languages, and in his youth he also wrote poetry. But it is on his philological and archæological works on the Slav race that his fame is principally founded. Equal to Dobrovský, and perhaps superior to Jungmann in erudition, some of his writings on these subjects are still standard works.

PAUL JOSEPH ŠAFAŘIK (1795–1861), like Kollar, was a native of the Slav district of Northern Hungary. As the son of a Protestant clergyman he received his first education in his own country, and from his early youth gave proof of his enthusiasm for the Slavic race, which inspired him during his whole life. In 1815 he visited the then far-famed University of Jena in Germany, and on his return to Hungary accepted a situation as private tutor at Pressburg. He here became acquainted with Palacký, and the friendship that sprang up between them continued during the whole of their lives. In 1819 Šafařik was appointed director of the gymnasium at Nový Sad (Neusatz), in Southern Hungary. His life here was embittered by constant persecution on the part of the Hungarian authorities, whose aversion to the Slav aspirations was as great as that of the German officials in Austria.

Šafařik's writings had meanwhile attracted attention at Prague, and some of the Bohemian patriots, though by no means opulent, subscribed a sufficient sum to enable him to proceed to Prague. His life here also was a wretched one. He was in constant financial distress. While occupied with learned works of the highest importance, he was obliged to gain his living by writing in popular journals, and he had at one time even to accept the humiliating and invidious office of a "censor." Writing on Slav subjects is not at the present day a very lucrative occupation. It was yet less so at the time of Šafařik, when interest in these matters was still more limited. Šafařik's health began to fail in consequence of constant anxiety, but he continued his studies on the history and language of his country and race undauntedly. A speaker at the meeting of Bohemian scholars that in 1895 celebrated the centenary of Šafařik's birth, rightly described him as a "martyr of science." While the Austrian Government continued to regard Šafařik's researches with indifference, the attention of the Prussian authorities was attracted to his profound knowledge of Slavic philology and archæology, sciences that were then in their infancy. Šafařik was offered a professorship both by the University of Breslau and that of Berlin, but the Austrian Government, not wishing that he should expatriate himself, now appointed him professor of Slavic philology at the University of Prague. He, however, gave up this appointment a year later, when he became librarian of that university. In 1848 Šafařik made a brief appearance in the political arena. He was a member of the Slav congress that met at Prague in that year, and a speech in favour of the solidarity of the Slav nations which he delivered there caused great sensation. The failure of the congress and the German reaction,[1] which lasted

[1] See my article on the "Bohemian Question," *Nineteenth Century*, December 1898.

from 1849 to 1859, were deeply felt by Šafařik. He now confined his studies to the remote antiquity of the Slav race. Every allusion to Bohemian history of later times again became inadmissible during these years. Šafařik, whose health had long been failing, died on June 2nd, 1861. Some time before his death his mental faculties had been affected.

I shall only mention a few of the most important of Šafařik's numerous writings. His many Bohemian essays on Slavic philology and archæology—mostly published in the Journal of the Bohemian Museum—have indeed inestimable value for those who devote themselves to these studies, but little interest for others. Šafařik's first work was a small collection of Bohemian songs, written when he was only nineteen years of age, and entitled *Tatranská Músa s lyrou Slovanskou* ("The Carpathian Muse with Slavic Lyre"). Early works also were several translations, of which that of the *Clouds* of Aristophanes and that of Schiller's *Maria Stuart* are the most important. A work which had already occupied Šafařik at Jena, but which he only completed during his stay at Neusatz, was his German *Geschichte der Slavischen Sprache und Literatur* ("History of the Slavic Language and Literature"). Neusatz or Nový Sad, a town in the south of Hungary, close to the frontier of Croatia, and not far from that of the present kingdom of Servia, was situated very favourably for the purpose of studying the various Slav languages. In his book Šafařik, contrary to the now generally accepted method of dividing the Slavs into three branches, distinguishes two classes of Slav nations only, and divides his book into two parts in accordance with this system. The first part deals with the Old Slavic language, the Russian, Servian

Croatian languages, and some minor dialects. The second part contains the history of the Polish and Bohemian literatures, and notes on the now nearly extinct dialects of the Slavs of Northern Germany. The book became antiquated even during Šafařik's lifetime, and he planned a new revised and enlarged edition, which was to have been published in Bohemian. Failing health and other occupations prevented Šafařik from carrying out this work. Even in its first state the book, which was only reprinted after Šafařik's death, long remained the standard authority on the little-known subject of which it treats. It is only since Mr. Pypin and Mr. Spasovič published in 1865 their (Russian) *History of the Slav Literatures* that Šafařik's work can be considered as superseded. Another fruit of Šafařik's residence in the South Slav countries was his *Serbische Lesekörner*, an historical and critical analysis of the then little-known Servian language. This book also was written in German.

During his stay at Prague, Šafařik produced his most important work, which rendered him famous in all Slav countries. I refer to the *Starožitnosti Slovanské* ("Slavic Antiquity"), which was published in 1837. The book—written in Bohemian—is an attempt to record the history and culture of the Slavs in the earliest times. The subject, still very obscure, was then entirely unexplored. Šafařik intended the work to consist of two parts, but only the first, which is purely historical, was completed. Of the second part, only some essays on the ancient ethnography and archæology of the Slavs were published. The historical work, which Šafařik again divided into two parts, deals, in the first, with the history of the Slav race from the time of Herodotus to the fall of the West Roman empire. The second part continues

that history to the time when most Slavs were converted
to Christianity—that is to say, speaking roughly, to about
the year 1000. Šafařik's work entirely revolutionised
the then current ideas on the origin of the Slavs and
their early history. The more recent writers who, particularly in Russia, have studied these subjects, acknowledge that Šafařik's great work has been the foundation
of their researches. One of his minor works requires
notice, as it is connected with the much discussed
question of the antiquity of the MSS. of Königinhof
and Grüneberg. In 1840 Šafařik published jointly with
Palacký a German work entitled *Die ältesten Denkmäler
der Böhmischen Sprache*. In this book the two authors
maintain the ancient origin, not only of the MS. of
Königinhof, but also of that of Grüneberg, in which
scarcely any Bohemian scholar now believes. Of course
the question had not then—more than fifty years ago—
been so thoroughly thrashed out as is now the case.
Šafařik was an indefatigable worker. Besides his many
published works, a large number of MSS. in his handwriting dealing with Slavic research were found. They
prove that, had circumstances been more favourable,
and had his health not failed him, he might have produced yet more works on the subjects to the study of
which he devoted his life.

The works of Jungmann, Kollar, and Šafařik will always
be highly valued by Bohemians, and indeed by all Slavs.
But the career of Palacký, the greatest of the Bohemian
leaders, whom I mention last, has a far wider interest,
as have also the contents of his greatest work. Dealing
mainly with Bohemian history, it incidentally throws a
great deal of light on many questions connected with
the general history of Europe up to the year 1526. It

is much to be regretted that English historians have as yet availed themselves so little of Palacký's monumental *History of Bohemia*.[1]

FRANCIS PALACKÝ was born in 1798 at Hodslavice in Moravia, not far from Přerov or Prerau, an old centre of the Unity. The traditions of the Brethren never quite died out in this part of Moravia. Palacký's forefathers had belonged to the Unity, and the family, during the many years of persecution, continued secretly to worship according to its teaching. When the Emperor Joseph II., who, as regards religious toleration, was far in advance of his age, issued a decree authorising Protestant religious services according to the Augsburg and Helvetic Confessions, Palacký's parents declared their adherence to the former creed. It may be mentioned that the Bohemian Brethren have only during the present reign again been recognised as a religious community. The traces of the traditions of the Brethren are very noticeable in Palacký's works, particularly in his masterly account of the career of Hus.

After obtaining the rudiments of education in local schools, Palacký in 1812 proceeded to the Protestant lyceum at Pressburg in Hungary. Here already Palacký gave proof of his studious nature, and his predilection for historical research was already evident. Gifted with the Slav facility for acquiring languages, Palacký at Pressburg obtained a thorough knowledge of the English language. We are told that Bolingbroke's *Letters on the Study and Use of History*, Blair's

---

[1] I have dwelt with more detail on this subject in a (Bohemian) essay on " Some references to Palacký in the Works of English Writers," which appeared in the *Pamatnik Palackého* (Palacký Memorial), published in 1898 on the occasion of the centenary of Palacký's birth.

Lectures on Rhetoric and Belles Lettres,[1] and the historical works of Robertson and Gibbon were among Palacký's favourite books. Other historical works that he read with great interest were Karamsin's *History of Russia* and Johannes Müller's *History of the Swiss Confederation*. After finishing his studies at Pressburg, Palacký continued to live there for some time, and was engaged as tutor by several noble families. It was during his stay at Pressburg that his life-long friendship with Kollar, that has already been mentioned, began. It was, indeed, probably mainly through Kollar's influence that he decided to devote his life to the study of Bohemian history and literature; he had previously thought of becoming a minister of the Protestant Church.

Pressburg, and Hungary generally, was not then a desirable residence for one who intended to devote himself to Slavic studies, which the Hungarian Government regarded with marked displeasure. Palacký, therefore, travelled to Prague, where he had the good fortune to obtain the protection of Dobrovský, who from their earliest acquaintance had realised the exceptional talent of the young Moravian. Through Dobrovský's influence Palacký obtained from Francis Count Sternberg the appointment of archivist to the family of which Count Francis was the head. This appointment left Palacký sufficient leisure to pursue his historical studies, and the small salary attached to it was very welcome to Palacký. He had, indeed, while a tutor, laid by a little money, but that could

[1] Professor Kalousek, in the interesting essay on the "Leading Idea of Palacký's Historical Work," which he contributed to the Palacký Memorial, has noted that the principles according to which Palacký's *History of Bohemia* is written are in complete accordance with the rules established by Blair in his thirty-fifth and thirty-sixth lecture, *On Historical Writing*.

not last long, and his literary work was not likely to afford him much pecuniary gain. One advantage which Palacký obtained by his appointment as archivist to Count Sternberg will surprise English readers, but his Bohemian biographers lay great stress on it. Palacký's post secured him against all molestation on the part of the police. The Austrian police authorities in the earlier part of the present century were empowered to expel from any town "strangers of no profession," and they were particularly likely to do so in the case of a man known to be favourable to the Bohemian national movement.

In other ways, also, the modest appointment was a turning-point in Palacký's career. Through the favour of Francis Count Sternberg, and of his brother, Count Kaspar, president of the Bohemian Museum—which the two brothers had, jointly with Count Kolovrat, founded in 1818—Palacký became acquainted with many of the Bohemian nobles. He succeeded in obtaining from many of them the then quite exceptional permission to study the archives contained in their castles. Had it not been for the researches which he was allowed to make in these archives—particularly in those of Prince Schwarzenberg at Trěbon or Wittingau—Palacký would have been unable to write his *History of Bohemia*. The impulse to write the work, indeed, also came from the Bohemian nobles. The Diet in 1829 conferred on him the title of "Historian of the Estates of Bohemia;" but their legislative authority was very limited, and ten years passed before the title conferred on Palacký was confirmed by the authorities of Vienna.

It was on the suggestion of Palacký that it was decided that the newly-founded society of the Bohemian Museum should publish an annual journal, which was to contain principally studies on the history, ethnography, literature, and mythology of Bohemia. After some discussion as to whether the new journal should appear in Bohemian or in German—even so learned a Slavist as Dobrovský declared that it was impossible to publish a scientific periodical in the national language—it was decided to publish it in both languages. The *Journal of the Museum of the Bohemian Kingdom* (" Casopis Musea Království Ceskeho ") first appeared in 1827, and Palacký was its first editor. The German edition, which, though the great Goethe wrote in its favour, found few readers, was discontinued in 1831. The version which appeared in the national language, on the other hand, has been continued up to the present day. It is invaluable to those who endeavour to study the history and literature of Bohemia, and I have used its volumes extensively while writing this book. Mr. Morfill, one of the few English writers on Slavic subjects who writes with thorough knowledge and insight,[1] has truly described the volumes of the journal of the Bohemian Museum as a " mine of Slavonic lore."

Palacký's time up to 1837 was fully occupied with the duties connected with the editing of the new journal, with the composition of minor historical writings, and with his studies in the Bohemian archives. He soon, however, found that the preparations for his great history of Bohemia, which the Estates urged him to write, would necessitate study in foreign archives also. Palacký, therefore, visited Munich and Dresden, and in 1837 undertook a more extensive journey to Italy,

---

[1] Since the above was written, Mr. Morfill has published an admirable " Grammar of the Bohemian Language," the first ever written in English. I can strongly recommend it to readers who wish to acquire the Bohemian language.

where he spent considerable time in studying the valuable documents contained in the archives of Venice and Rome. In the latter town he found some difficulty in obtaining access to the library and archives of the Vatican. Count Rudolph Lützow, then Austrian ambassador at Rome, who was himself a Bohemian, and to whom Palacký had been recommended, succeeded, however, in obtaining for him permission to examine at least some of the MSS. which he wished to see. Palacký has himself left us an interesting account[1] of the difficulties he encountered on the part of Monsignor Marini, prefect of the Vatican archives. They were caused, it was stated, principally by alleged indiscretions committed by Ranke, who some time previously had been allowed to study the archives of the Vatican.

After Palacký's return to Bohemia, the task of continuing his great historical work absorbed him so completely that he ceased to edit the Journal. His quiet and studious life was, like that of other Bohemian scholars, interrupted by the revolutionary events of the year 1848. The movement in favour of the revival of Bohemian nationality had hitherto been an entirely literary one, and the Bohemians very naturally chose their most prominent writers as their political leaders. As Bohemia, with many other non-German parts of Austria, then formed part of the Germanic Confederation, prominent Bohemians, and among them Palacký, were invited to take part in the proceedings of the German National Assembly that met at Frankfort in 1848. Palacký's reply, which caused great sensation at the time, is still worth quoting, as it became the watchword of the Bohemian patriots. He wrote: "I am not a German, but a

---

[1] In his (German) work, *Zur Böhmischen Geschichtschreibung.*

Bohemian. Whatever talent I possess is at the service of my own country. My nation is certainly a small one, but it has always maintained its historical individuality. The rulers of Bohemia have often been on terms of intimacy with the German princes, but the Bohemian people has never considered itself as German." It is a proof of the rapidity with which Palacký acquired consideration, that one of the short-lived Austrian cabinets of 1848 (that of Pillersdorf), wishing to obtain the support of the Bohemian nation, offered him the post of Minister of Public Instruction. Though his national theories prevented Palacký from taking part in the deliberations of the German National Assembly, he was a member of the Slav Congress at Prague and of the Austrian Parliament which in 1848 and 1849 met first at Vienna, then at Kremsier.

The short period of liberal government in Austria ended with the year 1849. Palacký suffered, like all the Bohemian patriots, from the German and absolutist rule, which was re-established in Bohemia in a more aggravated manner than before.[1] A paper to which Palacký contributed was suppressed because of an article from his pen which had caused sensation, and the military authorities deliberated whether the writer should be tried by court-martial.

In 1861, when a new attempt to establish constitutional government in Austria was made, Palacký was made a life-member of the Upper Chamber of the Parliament of Vienna. He only spoke there twice, in August and September of the year that he had been named. The question of an agreement with Hungary was then

[1] For further particulars I must again refer my readers to my article on "The Bohemian Question," published in the *Nineteenth Century*, December 1898.

under discussion. Hungary claimed almost complete independence, and Palacký rightly maintained that the establishing new small states was contrary to the tendency to union that then prevailed in Europe. Palacký advised the Hungarians, as well as the Bohemians, to make considerable concessions to the Central Government of Vienna. He seems already to have foreseen, what actually occurred six years later, that Hungary would be granted almost complete independence, and Bohemia considered a mere Austrian province.

Though Palacký, always favourable to the preservation of the Austrian empire, was prepared to concede to the Central Government in Vienna far more extensive powers than the Hungarians were, he yet claimed for Bohemia and the Parliament of Prague a very extensive autonomy, on lines similar, though not identical, with those of the ancient Bohemian constitution, which perished on the day of the battle of the White Mountain. When Palacký found that the Parliament of Vienna was discussing matters that he considered beyond its competency, and encroaching on the rights of the Bohemian representative body, he left Vienna on September 30, 1861, and never again took his seat in the Austrian Upper House. Of the Bohemian Parliament Palacký was a member from the time that it first met in 1861. He attended its meetings whenever the National or Bohemian party took part in its deliberations, which they, from political reasons, often refused to do. From 1861 to his death in 1876, Palacký was the recognised leader of the National party in Bohemia. A detailed account of his life during that time would be a record of the political struggles of Bohemia during those years, and would be out of place here. The admiration and veneration of the Bohemians for the "Otec Vlasti" (Father of the Country), as he was called, increased with his increasing years. On April 23, 1876, the completion of Palacký's great historical work was celebrated by a banquet at Prague, at which the historian was present. He seems to have felt the presentiment of approaching death, and indeed described the speech which he delivered as his testament. The speech is so characteristic of Palacký that I shall quote a few words from it. "Our nation," he said, "is in great danger, surrounded, as it is, by enemies in every direction; but I do not despair; I hope that it will be able to vanquish them, if it has but the will to do so. It is not enough to say 'I will;' every one must co-operate, must work, must make what sacrifices he can for the common welfare, particularly for the preservation of our nationality. The Bohemian nation has a brilliant past record. The time of Hus was a glorious time. The Bohemian people then surpassed in intellectual culture all other nations of Europe. . . . It is now necessary that we should educate ourselves and work in accordance with the demands of culture and intellect. This is the only testament that, speaking almost as a dying man, I wish to leave to my people." Palacký's presentiment proved but too true. He died, after a very short illness, on May 26, 1876. His funeral was the occasion of general national mourning in Bohemia.

Though, as already mentioned, the study of history from his early youth appealed particularly to Palacký, it was by a work of a very different character that he first became known to the small group of men who in the earlier half of the present century were interested in Bohemian literature. While still studying at Pressburg, Palacký published a translation of some of the poems of Ossian, which was enthusiastically welcomed by his friends.

It was at Prague only that he decided on writing his *History of Bohemia*, which made him the foremost man of his nation, and which he has himself described as "especially the work of my whole life." Palacký's preliminary labours in the archives of his own country and then in those of Germany and Italy have already been noticed. Of the immense difficulties which Palacký's historical work encountered he has himself given an interesting account. All printed writings were then in Austria and Bohemia under the control of the "censure-office," to which I have already referred. The Government, there is no doubt, was in principle opposed to the publication of a history of Bohemia founded on the best available documents, that is to say, of a work really deserving the name of a history. They were too ignorant to know to how great an extent such a work would contradict the short accounts of the past of Bohemia—written with a strongly Romanist and anti-Bohemian tendency, and founded on Hajek's chronicle—that were then in general use; but they somehow felt that this would be the case. "The Austrian Government was convinced," Palacký writes, "that its past conduct as regards Bohemia would not obtain praise from the tribunal of history. What occurred during the Thirty Years' War and since that period in the interior of Bohemia is still one of history's secrets; it makes the few who have attempted slightly to lift the veil under which these events are hidden shudder."

In 1836 the first volume of Palacký's *History of Bohemia* appeared. It was published in German, as were all the volumes that were issued up to the year 1848. Henceforth the book appeared simultaneously in German and Bohemian. When Palacký, towards the end of his life, re-wrote his great work, the earlier parts also appeared in Bohemian. The first volume, dealing with a period when the history of Bohemia is more than half mythical, was treated very leniently by the censors, who considered the fables of Přemysl and Libussa very harmless. In the Austria of the earlier part of this century the words "Securus licet Æneam Rutulumque committas . . ." were as true as in the Rome of the emperors.

Difficulties, however, began when Palacký had reached the period of Hus. The masterly account of the life and death of the great Bohemian, no doubt the most brilliant part of Palacký's work, greatly displeased the censors to whom it was submitted. The ecclesiastical censor suggested a very plain course, namely, that Palacký's work should be entirely suppressed. Prince Metternich, who was consulted, proposed that Palacký should omit all "objectionable reasoning," but should be allowed to state facts.

The correspondence between Palacký and the censors —published by the former after the suppression of that detestable institution—is irresistibly comic. The censors had not only, as is generally supposed, the power of striking out passages in an author's work that displeased them, they were also entitled to insert passages in a book that were often in direct contradiction with the writer's views. Palacký's description of the corruption of the Roman clergy in the fifteenth century was suppressed, and he was ordered to attribute the rise of the Hussite movement to the "stubbornness, inflexible obstinacy, and dogmaticalness" of Hus. Palacký patiently consented, but he ventured to remonstrate when objections were raised against his account of the courageous demeanour of Hus when before the Council. He was instructed to state that Hus had "appeared irresolute" when brought before his judges. Palacký remarked that this statement would be in contradiction with the passage quoted above which he had been ordered to insert. The ignorance of the censor is proved by the fact that when Palacký quoted Poggio Bracciolini's account of the death of Jerome of Prague, he was unaware of the existence of the well-known Italian humanist, and requested to be informed who he was. He also expressed doubts as to the authenticity of the letter to Lionardo Aretino in which that account is contained, though it had then already been frequently printed, and is quoted by numerous Protestant and Catholic writers, including Pope Pius II. Palacký lived to see the abolition of censure, and to republish in their original form the volumes of his History that he had been obliged to submit to it.

Political events and the ever-increasing mass of materials, which of course proportionately increased Palacký's labours, delayed the progress of the History, and it was only in 1867 that the second part of the fifth volume, which reaches to the accession of the House of Hapsburg to the Bohemian throne in 1526, was published. Bohemian historians generally end their work with the battle of the White Mountain in 1620, and this was no doubt Palacký's intention. His remark, quoted above, proves that he never intended to write the history of Bohemia during and after the Thirty Years' War. In 1861 he had, however, already formed the decision to end his narrative with the year 1526, and he informed the Estates of Bohemia—who contributed to the expenses of the publication—of that intention.

During the last nine years of his life Palacký employed whatever spare time his political engagements left him in re-writing parts of his History in accordance with fresh materials, in completing the Bohemian version of parts that had at first appeared in German only, and in eliminating the passages that the censors had obliged him to insert. This new revised edition was, as already mentioned, completed only in the year of the author's death.

Palacký's *History of Bohemia* is now recognised as one of the great historical works of the nineteenth century. Though less known in England than on the Continent, it has there also obtained the praises of historians, such as Bishop Creighton and the late Mr. Wratislaw. It is not easy to define the circumstances that rendered the publication of Palacký's monumental work a political event in Bohemia, contributing greatly to the revival of national feeling. The record of a glorious past came as a revelation to the Bohemians, whom the German inhabitants of Austria were, in consequence of their long supremacy, in the habit of treating with contempt. It fortified the patriots in their belief that their nation and its language would not perish. It is this conviction which alone explains the intense veneration for Palacký which all Bohemians felt, many of whom had neither the money to buy nor the time to read his great historical work. The recently published centenary memorial of Palacký contains many striking instances of the devotion with which Bohemians of all classes regarded the historian of their country. I may be permitted to quote one anecdote from the Memorial. A young tailor's apprentice from Moravia, named Breynek, during a visit to

Prague, met Palacký in the street. Innumerable photographs of the great historian had rendered Breynek familiar with his features. He walked up to him, stating that he was a Moravian and a countryman. Palacký conversed affably with him for several minutes and then gave him his hand. This meeting became the principal event of Breynek's life. Every date was designated as having happened "before I met Palacký" or "after I met Palacký." He only regretted that he had been too shy " to kiss the hand that had written the history of his country." Palacký's History, as already noted, was published simultaneously in German and in Bohemian; the earliest volumes indeed at first appeared in the former language only. The book is therefore not so inaccessible as the works of the earlier Bohemian historians, from which I have given copious quotations. An English translation of Palacký's history of Bohemia is, however, still a desideratum.

With the exception of a short German biography of Dobrovský, most of Palacký's minor works are connected with his great History; some are the results of studies preparatory to the great work; others contain documentary evidence in support of statements made in the book; in others again, Palacký enters into controversies with some of the critics of his work. I shall mention some of the most important of these works. In the year 1829 the Bohemian Society of Sciences offered a prize for the best essay on the early historians of Bohemia. Palacký won this prize with his first historical work, entitled *Würdigung der alten Böhmischen Geschichtschreiber*. The book was written in German, and was first published in the Journal of the Bohemian Museum, that then appeared in German as well as in Bohemian. In 1830 it was republished separately in an enlarged form. The book gives short and concise sketches of the lives of the Bohemian historians from Cosmas to Hajek. It is still of value, and indispensable to all who study the works of these historians. Like this book, closely connected with Palacký's principal work, is a short historical sketch entitled *Die Vorläufer des Hussitanthums* ("The Precursors of Hussitism"). The fate of this little book is rather curious. In 1842 Palacký read a paper on "The Precursors of Hus" before the Bohemian Society of Sciences. Wishing to publish its contents, he, as in duty bound, submitted the MS. to the censure-office. The officials there, however, entirely declined to give their consent to the publication of the book. A copy of the MS. came into the hands of Dr. Jordan of Leipzig, who in 1846 published it there under his own name. This was done with the consent of Palacký, who was more desirous that the fruits of his research should become public than that he should obtain personal recognition. The book has since been reprinted under the name of the real author, and still has great value. I have availed myself of its contents when writing of the precursors of Hus in chapter ii. of this book.

It is not surprising, if we consider the previous general ignorance on the subject of Bohemian history, that from the moment his book began to appear Palacký became the object of violent attacks. The first attacks proceeded from German writers, but after the publication of the volume that deals with Hus, other Catholic writers also joined in these attacks. The treatment which the Slavs of Northern Germany, and sometimes those of Bohemia also have endured on the part of the Germans, could only be defended by describing these tribes as brutal, savage, and cruel barbarians. Palacký has certainly proved that these descriptions, founded on vague statements of German monks or on the mendacious Hajek, are at least grossly exaggerated. Palacký's impartial account of the career of Hus, who had in Austria previously been described in accordance with the words of the censor, which I have quoted, displeased the more prejudiced Roman Catholics. Professor Höfler, who was both a fanatical Teuton and a bigoted Roman Catholic, was the most persistent opponent of Palacký. Palacký replied to his criticism in his *Geschichte des Hussitanthums und Professor Höfler*, which appeared in 1868. Mainly polemical also was Palacký's small work, *Zur Böhmischen Geschichtschreibung*, published in 1871. In this book the author defends his historical work against the attacks of Professor Höfler and other German critics. He gives here also an account of his old controversies with the censure-office, from which I have quoted.

Several collections of documents are also due to the diligence of Palacký. In 1860 he published a collection of—mostly Latin—documents referring to the reign of King George of Poděbrad. A similar but far more interesting collection of Latin and Bohemian documents was published in 1869. I have in chapter iii. frequently quoted this collection, on which, indeed, my account of the career of Hus is principally based. The Latin documents are printed in that language only, but Palacký has given a Latin translation of those that were written in Bohemian. An additional collection of documents, published in 1873, refers to the period of the Hussite wars. In the last years of his life Palacký published in three volumes s election of the most important historical, political, and literary essays which he had written in Bohemian. This is by no means a complete list of Palacký's works. In the "question of the MS." he, as already mentioned, figured as a defender of the authenticity of these documents.

It is to the four writers whom I have now successively referred to that the revival of the Bohemian language and of Bohemian literature is principally due. They were the centre of a group of writers who, if less talented, were no less patriotic and enthusiastic. The isolated position in which they were at first placed, surrounded by Germans or Germanised Bohemians, and living under an absolute Government, that always treated them with suspicion and often with positive enmity, caused these men to draw closely together; many of them were indeed on terms of intimate friendship. The vast amount of correspondence that passed between them, to which I have already referred, is now gradually being published. It is characteristic of these writers that they rarely limited their labours to one subject, but generally wrote both in poetry and in prose, and on the most varied subjects. Their patriotic motive was the wish to prove that the new, or rather revived, literature possessed works on all subjects and in every literary form. That this sometimes led to superficiality and mediocrity cannot be denied.

WENCESLAS HANKA (1791–1861) has already been mentioned in these pages as the discoverer of the MS. of Königinhof, and it is as such that he is principally known. He is, however, the author of a collection of Bohemian songs that soon became very popular, and of several works on Bohemian grammar and etymology. He also published numerous translations from the German and from the Slav languages, and edited Hus's

Deerka and *Dalimil's Chronicle*, which were then almost unknown.

A better poet than Hanka was his contemporary Ladislav Čelakovský. The best of his many poetical works are two collections of national songs entitled respectively *Echoes of Russian Song* and *Echoes of Bohemian Song*. These books, contrary to what the title would lead one to infer, are mainly original, though Čelakovský has made thorough use of his knowledge of the legends and traditions of the Slav peasantry. Another collection of poetry is entitled *The Hundred-Leaved Rose*. As in Kollar's *Daughter of Sláva*, the love motive struggles with the patriotic motive for supremacy in this poem—not perhaps to its advantage. We possess prose works also of Čelakovský dealing with the Bohemian language. That subject was ever before the minds of the Bohemian writers of the earlier half of this century, of whom Čelakovský is one of the most correct.

It is beyond the purpose of this book to give a complete list of the modern "minor poets" of Bohemia. I may mention as among the best, Macha, who imitated Byron, Jungmann's friend Marek, Halek, Koubek, and Rubes. The last-named is the author of a song entitled *Ja jsem Čech a kdo je vic?* ("I am a Bohemian, and who is more?"), which is still very popular in Bohemia. The drama has only been greatly cultivated in Bohemia within the last twenty years, particularly since the establishment of the large Bohemian theatre at Prague. At present Bohemia possesses a considerable number of dramatic authors. Of older dramatists we must first mention Joseph Tyl (1808–1856), the author of very numerous dramatic works. In one of these Tyl introduced a song beginning with the words *Kde ie domov muj?* ("Where is my home?"). This song rapidly became very popular, and can now almost be considered as the national air of Bohemia. Wenceslas Klicpera (1792-1859) wrote over fifty comedies and tragedies, and contributed, though none of his plays are above mediocrity, largely to the development of the Bohemian stage, which possessed no ancient dramatic works. Count Zdenko Kolovrat (1836-1892) wrote several clever comedies. Of Bohemian novelists I may mention Pfleger-Moravsky, also known as a writer of tragedies, Benes Třebezky, a fruitful writer of historical novels, and Mrs. Božena Němcova. The novels of Mrs. Němcova, dealing principally with the simple life of Bohemian villagers, have obtained a well-deserved celebrity. Mrs. Němcova's masterpiece, the *Babička* ("Grandmother"), has been translated into English, French, Russian, German, and many other languages.

Of writers on scientific subjects, one of the earliest is JOHN PRESL (born in 1791). Presl was professor of natural history at the University of Prague, and the first modern Bohemian writings on this subject are his work. The patriots, as already mentioned, wished to prove that all subjects could be treated in the national language. Presl is the originator of the present system of Bohemian phraseology, used for the subject on which he wrote, and he has thus deserved the gratitude of the Bohemian people. It is of him and Marek that the story is told that, when they were visiting Jungmann to discuss the future of the Bohemian literature, the latter remarked to his visitors, "It needs only that the ceiling of this room should fall in and there would be an end of Bohemian literature!"

Great also are the merits for the Bohemian cause of

Charles Jaromir Erben; born in 1811, he died in 1870 as archivist of the city of Prague. Like those of so many Bohemian writers of his time, Erben's works deal with many subjects. He published several collections of Bohemian popular poetry and several interesting works on the folklore of the country. Very great are the merits of Erben as an editor of the works of the ancient writers of his country. We have to thank him for a new edition of selected works of Hus. The works of Hus, particularly the Bohemian ones, had hitherto been almost inaccessible. He also edited Stitný's books of *General Christian Matters*, Harant of Polzic's Travels, the Chronicle of Bartos, and other minor works. These editions have valuable notes and biographies of the writers. I have frequently availed myself of the valuable information contained in Erben's editions of ancient Bohemian authors. More limited was the range of the studies of Joseph Jireček (1825-1888). His works mostly deal with Slavic, specially Bohemian literature. Jireček's *Rukovet* or *Handbook of the History of Bohemian Literature*, is perhaps the best book on its subject. The portion that deals with the writers of the Unity, founded principally on sources that were not known before, is most valuable. Jireček played a considerable part in Bohemian and Austrian politics, and was for a short time member of the Austrian cabinet as Minister of Public Instruction.

The last twenty years have contributed immensely to the development of the Bohemian language and literature. Numerous now living Bohemian writers have added greatly to the fame of their land. Continuing in the footsteps of their forerunners, they have brought the Bohemian language to a degree of purity and polish

JAROSLAV VRCHLICKÝ

that it never possessed before. The critics of the future will perhaps call the last quarter of the nineteenth century the "golden age" of Bohemian literature. The foundation of the Bohemian university at Prague, of the new national theatre also at Prague, and of a third learned society which was richly endowed by the patriotic architect Hlavka, have greatly contributed to the revival of Bohemian literature.

Within the last few years Bohemian poetry has been largely cultivated. Emil Frida, who writes under the name of JAROSLAV VRCHLICKÝ (born 1853), is undoubtedly the greatest living Bohemian poet. Of his many works, his *Rok v Jihu* ("A Year in the South") and his *Ponti k Eldoradu* ("Pilgrimages to Eldorado") may be mentioned. Vrchlický is also a fruitful dramatist; of his many dramas the *Brothers* and *Drahomira*, both founded on events in Bohemian history, deserve mention. A very accomplished linguist, Vrchlický has also published numerous Bohemian translations from the works of foreign, particularly Italian poets. His latest work on this field are his *Moderni Basnici Anglicti* ("Modern English Poets"), a series of translations from English writers, which begins with Thomson's *Rule Britannia* and ends with Macaulay's *Lays of Ancient Rome*. Perhaps the best translations in this volume are those of some of Lord Byron's poems, which have always appealed greatly to the Bohemians. Many poems of Byron have also been translated by Mr. J. V. Sládek (born 1845), for many years editor of the Bohemian review entitled *Lumir*. Mr. Sládek has also translated the poems of Burns and Coleridge, some of Shakespeare's plays, and some of the Polish works of Mickiewicz into Bohemian. Of Bohemian poets of the present day, Svatopluk Cěch (born 1846)—whom most

Bohemian critics place next to Vrchlický—Julius Zeyer, and Adolphus Heyduk should be mentioned. Svatopluk Cěch (born 1846) is also a very successful prose writer; he has published several collections of short stories under the name of *Arabesky*. A very talented Bohemian novelist of the present day is Jacob Arbes (born 1840). His *Romanetta* (short novels) would well deserve to be translated into English. Eliška (Eliza) Krasnohorská (born 1847), Karolina Světla (born 1830), and Jaroslav Vlcěk are also popular novelists.

Bohemian literature has at most periods been rich in historians, and at the present day many writers are successfully following in the footsteps of Palacký. The lately-deceased Dr. Anton Gindely, whom Palacký himself considered as his successor, dealt principally with the period of the Thirty Years' War and the events in Bohemia at the beginning of the seventeenth century which led to it. Of living historians, Professor Wenceslas Tomek (born 1818) should be mentioned first. Of his many historical works, his *Dějepis Města Prahy* ("History of the Town of Prague") is the most valuable. Professor Tomek has also written a short "History of Bohemia" in German. Next to Professor Tomek we should mention Professor Josef Kalousek (born 1838), who is the author of the valuable work entitled *České Statní Pravo*. In this book Dr. Kalousek gives a detailed account of the ancient Bohemian constitution, as it existed in the days of independence; Professor Goll (born 1846), who has devoted his attention principally to the history of the Bohemian Brethren, but has also recently published a valuable work on the early relations between Prussia and Bohemia. The historical works of Professors Karl Tieftrunk (born 1829) and Anton Rezek (born 1853) mainly deal with the period of Bohemian history that begins with the accession of the house of Habsburg (1526) and ends with the battle of the White Mountain (1620). Professor Tieftrunk has also published a short history of Bohemian literature.

The study of philology has recently been greatly developed in Bohemia. One of the greatest living Bohemian philologists is Professor Gebauer, to whose writings it is principally due that the genuineness of the MSS. of Grüneberg and Königinhof is now generally considered doubtful. Professor Gebauer has now begun the publication of a *Historical Grammar of the Bohemian Language* on a very large scale. Only Part I. and Part III. (consisting of two volumes) have as yet appeared. Of the many younger philologists, Dr. Flajšhans should be mentioned. He has for some time been occupied in publishing a history of Bohemian literature in short parts. It is to be regretted that the publication does not proceed more rapidly. Very valuable for Bohemian philology and early literature are the labours of Mr. Adolphus Patera, head-librarian of the Bohemian Museum at Prague. For many years Mr. Patera has employed his annual holidays in searching for early Bohemian MSS., many of which, though forgotten, still exist in the libraries of the towns and monasteries of Bohemia and Moravia. Mr. Patera has been indefatigable in deciphering these very ancient MSS., and has published the results of his study in the *Časopis Musea Královstoi Českého*. The very interesting but long-neglected study of Bohemian folk-lore has greatly progressed through the labours of Dr. Zibrt. He has published many of the results of his researches in the periodical *Česky Lid* ("The Bohemian People") of which he is editor. To render his studies accessible to a larger number of readers, Dr. Zibrt very wisely publishes a French edition of his periodical. Very valuable are the philological studies of Professor Mourek, who is also the author of excellent Bohemian-English and Anglo-Bohemian dictionaries.

BIBLIOGRAPHY

NOT unnecessarily to extend this list, I here enumerate only a few books dealing either with Bohemian literature as a whole, or with considerable portions of it. Bohemian books have increased rapidly within the last few years. The works which owe their origin alone to the "question of the MSS." are very numerous. I have therefore left unmentioned many valuable monographs which are indispensable to those who wish to acquire a more thorough knowledge of Bohemián literature than I have been able to give in this book. Literature and history are very closely connected in Bohemia, and many of the modern historians of Bohemia, particularly Palacký, Tieftrunk, Goll, Gindely, and Kalousek, throw a great deal of light also on the literature of Bohemia; some foreign historical works on that country, particularly Mr. Ernest Denis's brilliant *Fin de l'Indépendance Bohême*, also give much attention to the literature of the country. Much valuable information on Bohemian literature is also contained in the numerous editions of ancient Bohemian writings—frequently mentioned in my book—that have appeared at the end of the last and during the whole of the present century. Most of them contain valuable commentaries and biographies. Besides the Journal of the Bohemian Museum, the yearly publications of the Bohemian Society of Sciences incidentally devote their attention to the literature of the country. Periodicals such as the Světozor, Lumir, Osvěta, and others contain many interesting articles on Bohemian literature.

ČASOPIS MUSEA KRÁLOVSTVI ČESKÉHO. Journal of the Museum of the Bohemian Kingdom. Published annually since 1827.

DOBROVSKÝ (Joseph). Geschichte der Böhmischen Sprache und Literatur. Prag, 1818.

FLAJŠHANS (Dr. Václav). Pisemnictvi Ceské (Bohemian Literature). Only part of this illustrated work has as yet appeared.

JERÁBEK (Dr. F. V.). Stara Doba romantického básnictoí (The Ancient Period of Romantic Poetry). Prague, 1883.

JIREČEK (Joseph). Rukovět k dějinam literatury ceské do Konce XVIII. Věku (Handbook of the History of Bohemian Literature up to the End of the Eighteenth Century). Prague, 1875 and 1876.

JUNGMANN (Joseph). Historie Literatury Ceské (History of Bohemian Literature). Second enlarged edition. Prague, 1849.

LÉGER (Professor Louis). Le Monde Slave [1 vol.], Etudes Slaves [3 vols.], Russes et Slaves [2 vols.]. Professor Leger has devoted thirty years to the study of the Slav race. All the books mentioned contain valuable essays on Bohemian literature.

LÜTZOW (Francis, Count). Ancient Bohemian Poetry (New Review, Feb. 1897).

MORFILL (W. R., M.A.). Slavonic Literature. Contains in a few pages a concise and interesting account of the literature of Bohemia.

MURKO (Dr. Matthias). Anfänge der böhmischen Romantik. A very interesting work. Murko, however, attempts to prove too much when he maintains that the Bohemian patriots mainly imitated the Germans in their desire for unity.

PALACKÝ (Franz). Würdigung der alten bömischen Geschichtschreiber. New edition. Prague, 1869.

PALACKÝ (Franz). Die Vorläufer des Hussitenthums. New edition. Prague, 1869.

PYPIN (A. N.) und SPASOVIČ (V. D.). Geschichte der Slavischen Literaturen. Written in Russian. Translated into German by Traugott Pech. A French translation by Ernest Denis remained uncompleted. Nearly a whole volume is devoted to the history of Bohemian literature.

ŠAFAŘIK (Paul Joseph). Geschichte der Slavischen Sprache und Literatur. New edition. Prague, 1869.

TALVIJ (Mrs. Robinson). Historical View of the Slavic Language in its Various Dialects. This is not an original work, but an extract from Šafařik's book, which has just been mentioned. Palacký and Šafařik himself pointed this out many years ago.

BIBLIOGRAPHY

TIEFTRUNK (Karel). Historie Literatury České (History of Bohemian Literature). Second edition. Prague, 1880.

VLČEK (Jaroslav). Dějiny Literatury České (History of Bohemian Literature). Like Dr. Flajšhans's book, this History is also still incomplete, and appears in short parts at considerable intervals.

WRATISLAW (Rev. A. H.). The Native Literature of Bohemia in the Fourteenth Century.

With the exception of Messrs. Pypin and Spasovič's work, I have quoted the titles of these books in the language in which they were published, adding an English translation of the titles of books written in Bohemian.

INDEX

ALBERT of Uničov, Archbishop of Prague, 104
Alexander V., decree against heresy, 99
Alexander V. recognised as Pope, 98
Alexander VI. appoints Cardinal of Monreale to see of Olmütz, 177
Alexandreis—
  Account of, 18
  Account of festivities when Alexander entered Babylon, 23
  Extract from battle-piece, 22
Amos, Brother, theological treatises, 228
Andrew of Duba, author of early legal work, 51
Arbes, Jacob, *Romanetta*, 408
Arnold, Nicholas, antagonist of Komenský, 276
Augusta, Bishop—
  Hymns, 231
  Sketch of career, 228
  Summary, 230
Austi, John of, Hus retires to his castle, 107

BALBIN (Balbinus)—
  Account of Nilič of Kremsier, 59
  Miscellanea and other works, 356
Bartoš Pisař, *Chronicles of Prague*, 299
Bayle, judgment of Komenský, 249, 273
Bechin, Wenceslas of, lays articles from Wycliffe's writings before assembly at Prague, 91

Benedict XIII., 95
Beneš of Weitmil, Canon, incorporates Charles IV.'s notes in his chronicle, 49, 50
"Bible of Kralice," 248
Bienenberg, Joseph, *Alterthümer in Königreiche Böhmen* and *History of the Town of Königgrätz*, 357
Bilek, account of Bishop Augusta's prison life, 229, 311
  Quotation from, 312
Blahoslav—
  Account of *Summary*, 230
  Filipika, 233
  Grammatika Česká, 239
  History of the Unity lost, 296, 311
  Knowledge of writings of Humanists, 174
  Replika proti Misomusům, extract from, 237
  Sketch of career, 232
  Visits Sigismund Gelenius, 185
Bohemia—
  Březan's account of social condition of, 319
  Chivalrous poetry, 17
  Clergy, 58
  Greek and Latin ritual in, 13
  Humanist movement in, 174
  Intellectual activity at beginning of sixteenth century, 295
  Invaded by troops of Margrave of Meissen, 90
  Prosperous during reign of Charles IV., 57
  Religious sects in, 143, 152

Bohemian books burnt, 354
Bohemian Brethren ("Unity")—
  Conferences of two parties, 216
  Cromwell's suggestion for, 274
  Decide to abandon Bohemia, 256
  Discord among, 215
  Effect on Bohemian literature, 201, 296
  "First persecution," 205
  Foundation of, 174
  Historians of, 310
  Historical archives, 296
  Institutions modelled on Waldenses', 219
  Luther's teaching affecting, 221
Bohemian language and literature, development of, 174, 295, 354, 403, 406
Bohemian lyric poems, 25
Bohemian writings, character of early, 8
Borč directs Hanka's attention to manuscript, 2
Bořivoj, Prince, concession of, 45
Brand, Erasmus and Sebastian, 189
Březan, Wenceslas, *History of House of Rosenberg*, 314
Březnov, Laurence of, 50; *Chronicon*, record of Hussite wars, 147
"Brothers of Chilčic," 157; join community of Kunwald, 205
Brünn, account of St. Catherine's martyrdom in Church of St. Jacob, 10
Budovec, Wenceslas, of Budova—
  Anti-Alkoran, 243, 244
  Letters, 247
  Sketch of, 242
  State papers, 247
  Views of, 192

CALIXTINES (Utraquists), party of Hussites, 143
"Canon of Vyšehrad," chronicle of, 46

Cantio Zavisonis, extract from, 28
Cato, adaptation from Latin, 41
Čech appears in Bohemia, 32
Čech, Svatopluk, short stories of, 408
Čechs, account of their establishment in Bohemia, 44
Čelakovský, Ladislav, collections of national songs, 404
Charles IV.—
  As Bohemian historian, 48
  Establishes Slavonic monks at Prague, 13
  Invites Conrad Waldhauser to Bohemia, 58
Chatillon, Philip Gaultier (Walter) de, Latin poem of, 18
Chelčicky, Peter, 153
  Character of writings, 157
  Influence on "Bohemian Brethren," 171
  Net of Faith, 153, 155; summary of, 160 *seqq.*
  Opinion of towns, 215
  Originator of "Unity," 202
  Postilla, 159
  Reply to Nicholas, 148, 158
  Reply to Rokycan, quoted, 155, 170
  Socialism, 153
Chlum, John of, accompanies Hus to Constance, 110
Chronicle of Dalimil. See *Dalimil's Chronicle*
Chronicle of Troy, 56; first Bohemian work printed, 57
Chronicon Boemorum—
  Continuations of, 46
  Described, 44
  Early prose Latin work, 42
  Numerous MSS. of, 46
  Quoted in *Dalimil's Chronicle*, 31
Cimburg, Ctibor, of Tovačov, *Book of Law*, 172
Colloredo, Count, owner of estate of Grüneberg, 6

INDEX

Colonna, Cardinal, rejects appeal of Hus, 103
Comenius. See Komenský
Constance, Council of, 108
Cosmas, "the father of Bohemian history," 42
   Chronicon Boemorum. See that title
   On "Gospodi pomiluj ny," 8
   Sketch of his life, 42
   Tales of Crocus, Libussa, Premysl, and "war of the maidens," 45
Cromwell's suggestion for Bohemian Brethren, 274
Curtius, Quintus, *Alexandreis* based on work of, 18

Dalimil's Chronicle, account of, 29
   Preface quoted, 31
De Ecclesia, summary of, 119. (*See* also under Hus.)
De Geers, Lawrence, invites Komenský to Amsterdam, 275
De Geers, Louis, correspondence with Komenský, 268
Des Marets, Samuel, antagonist of Komenský, 276
Dietmar, Bishop of Prague, "Gospodi pomiluj ny" sung at his installation, 8
Dobrovský, Joseph, "patriarch of Slavic philology," 359
   Detailed Grammar of Bohemian Language, 360
   History of Bohemian Language and its Older Literature, 360
   Obtains appointment of archivist for Palacký, 389
   Opinion of "MS. of Grüneberg," 361
Drabik, influence over Komenský, 252, 271
   Prophecies, 272
Duba, Wenceslas of, accompanies Hus to Constance, 110

EASTERN and Roman ritual, rivalry between, 13, 14
Erasmus of Rotterdam, and apology of "Unity," 220
Erben, Charles Jaromir, as editor and poet, 406
   Edited and published books *Of General Christian Matters*, 65
Ernest of Pardubic, Archbishop of Prague, 36, 60
Ernest of Prague, Archbishop, enactment against avarice of clergy, 93

FLAJŠHANS, Dr., history of Bohemian literature, 409
Flaška, Smil—
   Advice of a Father to his Son, 36
   Groom and the Scholar, 40
   New Council, account of, 38
   Sketch of career, 36
Francis, Provost of Prague, chronicle of, 48
Frederick II., Emperor, circular to princes, 139

GEBAUER, Professor, writings on philology, 409
Gelenius, Gregory, 175; translations of classical works into Bohemian, 184
Gelenius, Sigismund, sketch of, 185
George, King of Bohemia, 204
Germany, war between Charles V. and Protestants, 229
Gindely, Dr. Anton—
   Historical works, 408
   Opinion of Jaffet's list of ordinations, 241
Glagolitic alphabet employed, 13
Goethe, adaptation of *Kytice*, 2
Goll, Professor—
   History of Bohemian Brethren, 408
   Investigations on Bohemia and Greek Church, 137

Goll, Professor—
  On authorship of "Gospodi pomiluj ny," 8
  On torture inflicted on Gregory, 206
  Researches into life of Chelčicky, 156
Gregory, Brother, founder of "Unity," 203; St. Kunwald, 205
  Controversy with Lucas of Prague, 217
  Followers, 205, 207
  Letters to Rokycan, extract from *Fourth*, 208
  Tortured (?), 206
Gregory XII. recognised as Pope by Prague University, 95

HABERNFELD, Andreas ab, *Bellum Bohemicum*, 353
Halek, minor poet, 404
Hanka, Venceslas—
  And falsification of manuscripts, 8
  Collection of Bohemian songs, 403
  Discoverer of MS. of Königinhof, 2, 403
  Publishes *Tkadleček the Weaver*, 51
Harant, Christopher, of Polžic—
  Classical erudition, 298
  Journey to Venice, Holy Land, and Egypt, 328; extract from, 329, 333
  Sketch of career, 326 *seqq.*
  Views of, 192
Harasser, Walter, and articles from Wycliffe's writings, 91
Hartlib, Samuel, interested in Komenský's "Pansophy," 260, 269
Hattala, Professor, edition of *Reči Besedni*, 73, 75
Hayek, semi-mythical tales, 32
Henry of Baltenhagen recognises Gregory XII. as Pope, 95
Henry of Carinthia, 29
Heyduk, Adolphus, 408
Hilferding on Bohemians and Greek Church, 137
Hlavsa, John, Bartoš's account of, 302

Hodic, George, Lord of, and Charles of Žerotin, 323
Höfler, Professor, criticism of Palacký, 402
Horaždovic, Minorite monastery of, 242
Hradil discovers MS. of *Grammatika Ceskd*, 239
Hübner, John, makes selections from Wycliffe's writings, 91
Humanist movement, growth of, and development of Bohemian language, 174
Hus, John—
  Affection for national language, 122
  Attends Council of Constance— forebodings, 109
  Character, 140
  Dcerka, 127
  De Ecclesia, 111, 113; summary of, 119
  Expositions (*Výklad*), 123 *seqq.*
  Influence of Wycliffe on, 137
  Latin and Bohemian letters, 131 *seqq.*
  Letter to Richard Wyche, 131
  O Savtokupectví, treatise on simony, 127
  On indulgences, 105, 129
  Postilla, 130
  Relations with Archbishop Zbynek, 93, 94, 98
  Summary of career, 87 *seqq.*
  Works, Bohemian and Latin, 57, 107, 117
Huska, Martin ("Loquis"), sketch of, 153
Hussite movement and development of Bohemian language, 297
Hussite wars, 143 *seqq.*
  War songs, 9

INNOCENT IV. deposes Emperor Frederick II., 139
Institoris, Henry, works against "Unity," 294

INDEX

JACOBELLUS of Mies—
  Articles of Prague, 146
  Maintained necessity of communion in two kinds, 112, 145
Jaffet, Brother, writings of, 241
Jagič, Professor, on influence of Chelčicky's works, 153
Janov, Matthew of—
  Precursor of Hus, 79
  Recantation, 81
  Sketch of, 80
  Theological works, 81, 82, 83
  Writings influenced by schism, 80, 84
Jarlock, Abbot of Muhlhausen, chronicle of, 47
Jerome of Prague—
  Connection with Hus, 141
  Letter to Lord Lacek of Kravář, 142
Jireček, Dr.—
  Biography of Lucas of Prague, 222
  Handbook of History of Bohemian Literature, 406
John, King, dislike to Bohemian language, 296
John of Luxemburg, cosmopolitanism of, 29
John XXII.—
  And Hus, 102
  Crusade against King Ladislas of Naples, 105
  Deposed, 113
Joseph II. excluded Bohemian language from schools, 358
"Joys of St. Mary," legend of, 16
Judas, Legend of, 10
Jungmann, Joseph—
  History of Bohemian literature, 143, 364
  Letters to Marek, 367
  Sketch of life, 362
  Translations from English, 363
Justinus, Bishop, Komenský succeeds, 270

KALOUSEK, Josef—
  České Statni Pravo, 408
  Investigations on Bohemia and Greek Church, 137
  Kbel, John, lays articles from Wycliffe's writings before Assembly at Prague, 91
Keatinge—
  Account of Komenský's reception in London, 262
  On prophecies of Drabik, 273
Klicpera, Wenceslas, plays of, 405
Kniha starého pána z Rozmberka, oldest prose work in Bohemia, 51
Kollar, John—
  Correspondence with Jungmann, Safařik, and Palacký, 382
  Daughter of Sláva, 372; "foresong" quoted, 376; sonnets quoted, 379
  Sketch of career, 371
Kolovrat, Count, one of founders of Bohemian Museum, 370
Kolovrat, Count, comedies, 405
Kolovrat-Liebsteinsky, Francis Count, manuscript of Grüneberg sent to, 6
Komenský, 249—
  "Christian Academy of Pansophy," plan of founding, 267, 290
  Didactica Magna, 250, 287
  Educational works, 251, 260, 286, 289
  Impressions of England, 262
  Janua Linguarum, 261; account of, 287
  Labyrinth of the World, 251, 262; summary of, 277 seqq.
  Last Bishop of Bohemian Brethren, 270, 276
  Lux in Tenebris, 276, 293
  Pansophic works, 261, 269, 289, 293
  Physica, 260
  Sketch of life, 250, 252 seqq.
  Via Lucis, 268, 290

Konáč, Nicolas (Finitor), *The Book of Lamentation and Complaint of Justice*, 189
Konias burns Bohemian books, 354
Königinhof, discovery of manuscript at, 2
Kotter, Christopher, Komenský's belief in, 256
Koubek, minor poet, 404
Kovár, John, declared he found manuscript of Grüneberg, 6
Kralové Dvur, Königinhoff, 2
Krasnohorská, Eliška, novelist, 408
Krasonický, works of, 227
Križ founds Bethlehem Chapel, Prague, 88
Krok, adventures of, 32
Kuthen, Martin, Utraquist historian, 307
Kutna Hora (Kuttenberg), decrees of, 97, 98

LACENBOK, Henry of, accompanies Hus to Constance, 110
Ladislas, King of Naples, incurs enmity of Pope John XXIII., 105
Ladislaus Posthumus, King, hostile to Utraquist creed, 202
Latin used by writers, 42
Laurin, epic poem, 25
Lažan, Henry of, Lord, adherent of Hus, 107
Lechler, Dr.—
  On Hus's letter to Archbishop Zbynek, 94
  On works of Janov, 83
  Opinion of lectures of John Hus, 88
Legends. (*See* names of various saints.)
Léger, Professor—
  On Slav language, 381
  Translates account of Zižka's campaigns, 172
Lenfant, *Histoire des Guerres Hussites*, 305

Lescynski, Bohuslav, protects Bohemian Brethren, 262
Lescynski, Count Raphael, member of "Unity," 256
"Letter of Majesty" granted to Protestants, 243
Libočan, Hajek of, *Bohemian Chronicles*, 304
  Account of Zižka's death, 305
  Date of commencement, 35
  Judgment of Hus and Jerome of Prague, 308
Libussa, adventures of, 32
Lissa occupied by Swedes, 275
Lobkovic, Bohuslav of, "ultramontane" Bohemian humanist—
  Influence on Bohemian literature, 180
  Letter to John of Domoslav, 178
  Relations with Victorin Cornelius ze Všehrd, 176
  Sketch of career, 176
  Works in Latin, 179
Lobkovic, John of, *True Bohemian Mentor*, written in Bohemian, quoted, 181
Lobkovic, Nicholas of, influence over Wenceslas, 97
Lomnický, Simon, of Budeč, "founder of Bohemian song," 191
  Advice to a Young Landowner, 192
  Ballad on executions at Prague quoted, 199
  Cupid's Arrow, 194
  Dirge on Peter of Rosenberg, 318; quotations from, 196, 197
  Smaller poems, 195
Loserth, Professor, on Wycliffe's influence on Hus's writings, 138
Lucas of Prague—
  Appeal to Erasmus, 220
  Controversies, 217, 224
  Mission to Waldenses, 219
  Relations with Luther, 221, 222
  The Bark, 219, 223

INDEX 421

Lucas of Prague—
  Witnesses death of Savonarola, 220, 227
  Works, 222
Lupáč, Prokop, *History of Emperor Charles IV., King of Bohemia*, 310
Luther, Martin, and Lucas of Prague, 221
Lützow, Count Rudolph, obtains permission for Palacký to examine MSS. at Rome, 392

MACHA, imitated Byron, 404
Manuscript of Grüneberg, 5—
  A falsification, 6
  "Judgment of Libussa," 7
  Sent to Francis, Count Kolovrat-Liebsteinsky, 6
  "The Decree of Domestic Law," 7
Manuscript of Königinhof—
  Ballads in, 4
  Discovered in tower of church, 2
  Genuineness, 3, 5
  Locutions traced to Moravian dialect, 4
  "The Cuckoo," translation of, 5
  Translations, 2
Manuscript of Königgrätz, 3, 9
  Legend of St. Prokop in, 12
Manuscript of St. Vitus, 3, 9
Manuscripts of beginning of present century, 7
Marek, Jungmann's friend, 404
Maria Teresa, Empress, excluded Bohemian language from schools, 358
Marsiglio of Padua, *Defensor Fidei*, 139
Michael of Deutschbrod (de Causis)—
  Complaint against Hus, 106
  Draws up accusation of Hus, 111
Milheim, John of, founds Bethlehem Chapel, Prague, 88
Milič of Kremsier, sketch of, 59; sermons in Bohemian, 60

Mladenović, Peter of—
  Account of Hus's journey, imprisonment and death, 116, 145
  On accusation of Hus, 112
  Record of Hus's journey, trial and death, 110
"Monk of Sazava," chronicle of, 47
Morfill, on Journal of Bohemian Museum, 391
Mourek, Bohemian - English and Anglo - Bohemian dictionaries, 410
Mühlberg, Protestants defeated at, 229

NASSAU University, 253
Neander studies works of Janov, 82
Nemcova, Mrs. Božena, *Babička* (Grandmother), 405
New Council, beast-epic, 35; account of, 38
Novikov, Eugene, on Bohemians and Greek Church, 137

Ottokar and Zavis, 35
Ottokar II., account of reign of, 33
Oxenstiern, Chancellor, Komenský's interview with, 269

PALACKÝ, Francis—
  Defends Ottokar II., 33
  Edits Journal of Bohemian Museum, 391
  Examines early Bohemian histories, 46
  Examines Rosenberg archives, 317
  History of Bohemia, 390, 396; censors and, 397
  Investigations on Greek Church and Bohemia, 137
  Latin and Bohemian documents, 402
  Minor works, 400
  Opinion of Manuscript of Königinhof, 2

Palacký, Francis—
  Opinion of Skála ze Zhoře, 335
  Opinion of Štitný, 74
  Reply to Höfler's criticisms, 402
  Reply to invitation to German National Assembly, Frankfort, 392
  Sketch of career, 388 *seqq.*
  Speech at banquet quoted, 395
Paleč, Stephen—
  Abandons Hus, 106
  Banished by Wenceslas, 108
  Draws up accusation of Hus, 111
Pardubic, William of, 36
Pasek, John, Bartoš's account of, 301
Patera, Adolphus, searches for early Bohemian MSS., 409
Payne, Peter, English Hussite, adversary of John of Přibram, 144
  Sketch of, 146
Pelhrimov, Nicholas of ("Biskupec"), work of, 148
Pešina, Tomas, Latin works treating of Moravia, 357
Peter the Great conversing with nobles at Prague, 355
Pfauser mediates between Maximilian and Blahoslav, 233.
Pfleger-Moravsky, novelist, 405
"Pickharts" or "Beghards," 205
Pisecký (Wenceslas Illadič)—
  Greek studies, 184, 186
  Sketch of career, 185
Ponatovská, Christina—
  Influence on Komenský, 79
  "Prophecies" of, 227
Ponatovská, Julian, 257
Prague—
  Account of foundation of, 45
  Wycliffe's works burned at, 101
Prague University—
  Articles from Wycliffe's works condemned by, 91, 106
  Change in organisation, 97
  Divisions, 91, 97

Prague University—
  Recognises Gregory XII. as Pope, 95
  Wycliffe's writings discussed at, 91
Prague University and development of Bohemian language, 297
Precursors of Hus, 57
Prefat, Ulrick, of Vlkanov, descriptions of Holy Land, 325
Premysl, adventures of, 32
Presl, John, account of, 405
Pribik. (*See* Pulkava.)
Přibram, John of, champion of moderate Utraquists, 144
  Works, 144
Prokop of Neuhaus (Jindřichuv Hradec), theological writer of "Unity," 215, 217
  Works in Bohemian, 218
Pulkava, account of his Bohemian chronicle, 49
Pypin and Spasovič, *History of Slav Literatures*, 386

QUEEN KUNEGUND, 28
Queen Sophia—
  Friendly to Hus, 98, 136
  Letter to Pope protesting against severity to Hus, 103
"Question of the Manuscripts," 1

RAKOCZY, George, Prince of Transylvania, invites Komenský to visit him, 271
Ranke studies archives of Vatican, 392
Rezek, Anton, historical works, 408
Rokycan, Archbishop, leader of advanced Calixtine party, 148
  Originator of "Unity," 202
  Postilla, 147
  Relations with Gregory, 204, 206
  Teaching of, 202
Romanist song, "Woe to you, Hus," 172

INDEX

Rosenberg Library, Stockholm, legend of St. Catherine discovered in, 10
Rosenberg, Lords of, Březan's history of, 314
Rosenberg, Peter of—
Important part in Bohemian politics, 318
Love of literature, 298
Rubes, popular song of, 404
Rudolph II. grants "Letter of Majesty" to Protestants, 243
Rukopis Kralodvorsky. (*See* Manuscript of Königinhof.)

ŠAFAŘIK, Paul Joseph—
Opinion of Manuscript of Königinhof, 2
Sketch of career, 383
Starožitnosti Slovanské (Slavic Antiquity), 386
Works on Slav language and race, 383, 382, 387
St. Anselm, legend of, 17
St. Bridget, visions of, and Štitný, 79
St. Catherine, account of her martyrdom, 10
St. Catherine, legends of, 10
St. Cyrillus as author of "Gospodi pomiluj ny," 8
St. Cyrillus introduces Greek ritual into Bohemia, 13
St. Dorothy, legend of, 11
St. George, legend of, 17
St. Methodius as author of "Gospodi pomiluj ny," 8
St. Methodius introduces Greek ritual into Bohemia, 13
St. Prokop, legend of, 12, 47
St. Venceslas, hymn to, 8
St. Vitus, legend of St. Dorothy in, 11
Satires on Trades, 41
Sazava, monastery on, 13
Severus, Provost of Mélnik, *Chronicon Boemorun* dedicated to, 44

Sigismund, King, conduct towards Hus, 109, 111
Sixt of Ottersdorf—
History of the Troubled Years in Bohemia, 304
Political career, 303
Skála ze Zhoře—
Account of executions of Prague, 342
Chronology of the Church, 336; extracts from, 337, 339, 341
Historie Cirkevni (History of the Church), 336
Sketch of career, 335
Sládek, J. V., translations of English poets, 407
Slavata, William Count—
Account of Count Thurn's banquet to Turkish embassy, 244, 348
Historické Spisovani (Historical Works), 352
Paměty, 346
Sketch of life, 345
Šlechta, John, "ze Všehrd"—
Microcosmus, 188
Sketch of, 187
Songs at Daybreak (Svitanicka), 25; translation of one, 26
Spencer, Henry, Bishop of Norwich, Flemish crusade opposed by Wycliffe, 106
Stanislaus of Znaym, abandons Hus, 106
Banished by Wenceslas, 108
"Staři Letopisove Češti," ancient Bohemian chroniclers, 171
Sternberg, Count Francis, protects Palacký, 390
Sternberg, Count Kaspar, President of Bohemian Museum, 390
Štitný, Thomas of—
Of General Christian Manners, contents of, 65 *seqq*.
Precursor of Hus, employs native language, 42, 57, 63, 74

Stitný, Thomas of—
  Reči Besední, "Learned Entertainments," 73 *seqq*
  Sketch of career, 63
Stransky, Paul—
  On Bohemians adhering to Greek Church, 137
  Respublica Bojema, 353
Sturm, Venceslas, theological works, 294
Světla, Karolina, novelist, 408
Swinburne, poem on St. Dorothy, 11
Sylvius, Æneas (Pius II.)—
  Account of visit to Tabor, 148
  Account of Žižka's death, 152
  Work on Bohemia destroyed, 355

TABOR City, Æneus Sylvius' account of visit to, 148
Taborites, advanced Hussites, 143
Tale of Alexander the Great, 56
Tandarius and Floribella, 25
"Tears of Mary Magdalene," legend of, 16
"Tears of St. Mary," legend of, 16
The Contest of the Body and the Soul, 17
The Death of King John, 35
The Garden of Roses, 25
The Painted Monks, written from Roman standpoint, 173
Theobaldus, *Hussitenkrieg,* 305
Theodoric, legends about, 25
Thurloe, suggestion for Bohemian Brethren, 274
Thurn, Count, pamphlet on assassination of Wallenstein, 346, 351
Tkadleček the Weaver, account of, 51
  Lament to Misfortune quoted, 53
  Misfortune's reply, extract from, 56
Tieftrunk, Karl, historical works, 408
Tiem, Venceslas, Dean of Passau, preaches crusade at Prague, 105
Tomek, Wenceslas—
  Historical works, 408

Tomek, Wenceslas—
  On letter of safe conduct given to Hus, 109
Travels of Sir John Mandeville, translated into Bohemian by Březov, 147
Treaty of Westphalia and Komenský, 271
Třebezky, Benes, historical novels, 405
Tristram similar to *Morte d'Arthur,* 25
Truhlář, Professor Joseph, collection of Latin letters of Bohuslav, 177
Truth, allegorical poem, 17
Tyl, Joseph, dramatic works, 404

ULRICK, Prince, description of his meeting Bozena, 32
"Unity." (*See* Bohemian Brethren.)
Urban, Pope, and Milič of Kremsier, 61
"Utraquist Church," 300
Utraquists (Calixtines) party of Hussites, 143

VELENOVIC, Nicholas, Hus defends, 94
Veleslavin, Adam Daniel, sketch of career and works, 189
Veleslavin, Adam Samuel, sketch of career, 190
Venceslas, Prince, descriptions of murder of, 32
Victorin Cornelius ze Všehrd—
  Relations with Bohuslav, 176
  Sketch of, 183
  Ten Books on the Rights of the Bohemian Land, 183
Vita Caroli translated into Bohemian, 49
Vlček, Jaroslav, novelist, 408
Vodnan, John of, works of, 294
Vratislav, Venceslas, of Mitrovic, account of travels and adventures, 326

INDEX

Vrchlický, Jaroslav (Emil Frida), dramas and other works, 407

Výklad na pravo zemske, early legal work, 51

WALDENSES' influence on Hussite movement, 166

Waldensian consecrating priest of "Unity," 207

Waldhauser, Conrad—
Latin *Postilla*, 159
Sketch of, 58
Works, 59

Wallenstein, Christina Ponatovská prophesies his death, 258

Weaver. (See *Tkadleček the Weaver*.)

Wenceslas IV.—
Attitude towards Popes, 95, 96, 98
Publishes "Decrees of Kutna Hora," 97
Struggle with Bohemian nobles, 36

White Mountain, battle of—
Misery of Bohemia after, 354
Political results of, 298

William of Zajic, 35

Winthrop, Richard Charles, suggestions to Komenský, 268

Wratislaw, Rev. A. H.—
Biography of John Hus, 86
On Hus's treatise on simony, 128
On resemblance between *Tristram* and *Morte d'Arthur*, 25
On works of Janov, 83

Wyche, Richard, letter to Hus, 102, 131; reply, 131

Wycliffe's—
Articles condemned, 113
Works burned at Prague, 101
Works quoted by Hus, 57
Writings discussed at Prague, 91

ZABIC, Zbyněk, of Hasenburg, Archbishop of Prague—
Excommunicates Hus and his adherents, 101
Recognises Alexander V. as Pope, 99
Sketch of, 92

Zavis of Falkenstein, 28

Zelená Hora. (*See* Manuscript of Grüneberg.)

Zerotin, Charles of, 254, 257
Obrana or *Apology*, extract from, 323
Sketch of career, 321

Žerotin, John of, pupil of Blahoslav, 232

Zeyer, Julius, 408

Zibrt, Dr., study of Bohemian folklore, 409

Žídek, Paul, 294

Zittau, Peter of, chronicle, 48.

Žižka, John, of Trocnov, leader of moderate Taborites, 144, 149
Accounts of his death, 152
Regulations of War, Letters, 149
Taborite war-song quoted, 151

Zwicker, Daniel, antagonist of Komenský, 276

Printed by BALLANTYNE, HANSON & Co.
Edinburgh & London

Literatures of the World

A SERIES OF SHORT HISTORIES
BY EMINENT WRITERS

EDITED BY

EDMUND GOSSE

Each Volume Large Crown 8vo, price 6s.

"Mr. Gosse's introduction to this new series, the list of his collaborators, his own wide knowledge and delicate taste, all assure us that whatever high hopes he may raise, we need have no fear of their ample fulfilment."—*The Saturday Review.*

A History of Japanese Literature.

By WILLIAM GEORGE ASTON, C.M.G., D.LIT., late Japanese Secretary to H.M. Legation, Tokio.

"Mr. Aston has made a very valuable and acceptable contribution to the series. He approaches his difficult task in a sober but not unsympathetic spirit, and he has unquestionably enabled the European reader for the first time to enjoy a comprehensive survey of the vast and ancient field of Japanese literature, of which we have had hitherto only furtive and partial glimpses. He has clothed the dry bones of his subject with the flesh and blood of living reality, and we can follow with unflagging interest the whole process of evolution down to the most recent developments of the Japanese mind."—*The Times.*

"Justice has been done for the first time to the neglected, or rather never comprehended, subject of the prose and verse of Japan. This is what Mr. Aston has effected, in a volume of unique erudition, wide research, clear discrimination, and excellent design; while, by such an achievement, he has wrought a memorable service not only to those interested in Japan and Japanese studies, but to the world of letters at large, in the midst of which he now gives to her literature an intelligible, established, and a very honourable place. The literature of Japan will assuredly owe to Mr. Aston its first formal and adequate introduction to the good opinion and respectful attention of the West."—Sir EDWIN ARNOLD in *Literature.*

A History of Spanish Literature.

By J. FITZMAURICE-KELLY, Corresponding Member of the Spanish Academy.

"This is an excellent handbook. It is comprehensive, clear, concise; the judgments are judicial, impartial; the style is good, lucid, and interesting. It is work well done by one who has a thorough grip of his subject."—*The Academy.*

Literatures of the World

A History of Italian Literature.
By RICHARD GARNETT, C.B., LL.D., Keeper of Printed Books in the British Museum.

"Dr. Garnett is lucid in arrangement, agreeable and correct. He has done a real service to both English and Italian literatures."—*Literature.*

A History of Modern English Literature.
By EDMUND GOSSE, Hon. M.A. Trinity College, Cambridge.

"We know of no volume better fitted to give a general conception of our literature than this."—*The Spectator.*

"A really useful account of the whole process of evolution in English letters. . . . Full of insight and serenity of judgment."—*The Athenæum.*

A History of French Literature.
By EDWARD DOWDEN, D.C.L., LL.D., Professor of English Literature in the University of Dublin.

"Certainly the best history of French literature in the English language."—*The Athenæum.*

"This is a history of literature as histories of literature should be written. The more closely one looks into this book, the more clearly is it seen how much thought, how much mental selection, as well as how much reading, have gone to the making of these picturesque portraits of writers."—*The Saturday Review.*

A History of Ancient Greek Literature.
By GILBERT MURRAY, M.A., Professor of Greek in the University of Glasgow.

"A sketch to which the much-abused word 'brilliant' may be justly applied."—*The Times.*

"The book is brilliant and stimulating, while its freshness of treatment and recognition of the latest German research amply justify its existence. Professor Murray has made these old Greek bones live."—*The Athenæum.*

www.ingramcontent.com/pod-product-compliance
Lightning Source LLC
Chambersburg PA
CBHW051723300426
44115CB00007B/439